AF847773

Management for Professionals

The Springer series "Management for Professionals" comprises high-level business and management books for executives, MBA students, and practice-oriented business researchers. The topics cover all themes relevant to businesses and the business ecosystem. The authors are experienced business professionals and renowned professors who combine scientific backgrounds, best practices, and entrepreneurial vision to provide powerful insights into achieving business excellence.

The Series is SCOPUS-indexed.

Nirma Sadamali Jayawardena ·
Sara Quach · Park Thaichon ·
Abhishek Behl
Editors

Digital Advertising and Consumer Behavior

Springer

Editors
Nirma Sadamali Jayawardena
Assistant Professor at the Faculty of Management, Law, and Social Sciences
University of Bradford
Bradford, West Yorkshire, UK

Sara Quach
Associate Professor at the Department of Marketing
Griffith University
Gold Coast, QLD, Australia

Park Thaichon
Associate Professor at the School of Business
University of Southern Queensland
Toowoomba, QLD, Australia

Abhishek Behl
Associate Professor at Keele Business School
Keele University
Newcastle, UK

ISSN 2192-8096 ISSN 2192-810X (electronic)
Management for Professionals
ISBN 978-981-95-7808-5 ISBN 978-981-95-7809-2 (eBook)
https://doi.org/10.1007/978-981-95-7809-2

© The Editor(s) (if applicable) and The Author(s), under exclusive license to Springer Nature Singapore Pte Ltd. 2026

This work is subject to copyright. All rights are solely and exclusively licensed by the Publisher, whether the whole or part of the material is concerned, specifically the rights of translation, reprinting, reuse of illustrations, recitation, broadcasting, reproduction on microfilms or in any other physical way, and transmission or information storage and retrieval, electronic adaptation, computer software, or by similar or dissimilar methodology now known or hereafter developed.
The use of general descriptive names, registered names, trademarks, service marks, etc. in this publication does not imply, even in the absence of a specific statement, that such names are exempt from the relevant protective laws and regulations and therefore free for general use.
The publisher, the authors and the editors are safe to assume that the advice and information in this book are believed to be true and accurate at the date of publication. Neither the publisher nor the authors or the editors give a warranty, expressed or implied, with respect to the material contained herein or for any errors or omissions that may have been made. The publisher remains neutral with regard to jurisdictional claims in published maps and institutional affiliations.

This Springer imprint is published by the registered company Springer Nature Singapore Pte Ltd.
The registered company address is: 152 Beach Road, #21-01/04 Gateway East, Singapore 189721, Singapore

If disposing of this product, please recycle the paper.

Contents

Contributors

Vivek Aggarwal School of Business, Galgotias University, Greater Noida, India

Aishwaryaa Velayutham University of Madras, Chennai, India

Buvaneswari Pallikuppam Sachithanandan University of Madras, Chennai, India

Anurag Chaturvedi Birla Institute of Management Technology, Greater Noida, India

Hare Krishna Chaudhary Amity University, Noida, India

Umesha Dabare SLIIT Business School, Sri Lanka Institute of Information Technology, Malabe, Sri Lanka

Deepana Palanivel PSGR Krishnammal College for Women, Coimbatore, India

Keshav Prasad Gadtaula Tribhuvan University, Biratnagar, Nepal

Achyut Gyawali Tribhuvan University, Biratnagar, Nepal

Gyandeep Hazarika MICA: The Schoolof Ideas, Ahmedabad, India

Pratiksha Jha School of Business and Management, Christ University, Bengaluru, India

Jyotsna Puthalath Nadukkandi PSG College of Arts & Science, Coimbatore, India

Ujjwal Kalra School of Business and Management, Christ University, Bengaluru, India

Baljinder Kaur Chandigarh Business School of Administration, Landran, Punjab, India

Ajay Khatter Faculty of Higher Education, William Angliss Institute, Melbourne, VIC, Australia

Chathurini Kumarapperuma SLIIT Business School, Sri Lanka Institute of Information Technology (SLIIT), Malabe, Sri Lanka

Kaushal Kishore Mishra Chandigarh University, Mohali, India

Udgam Mishra Tribhuvan University, Biratnagar, Nepal

Uttam Mishra Purbanchal University, Biratnagar, Nepal

Zeeshan Majeed Nadroo Indian Institute of Management Visakhapatnam, Visakhapatnam, India;
School of Management, IILM University, Gurugram, India

Pawan Pant Chandigarh University, Mohali, India

Van Hau Pham School of Applied Business, Unitec Institute of Technology, Auckland, New Zealand

Rajakrithiga Ganesan University of Madras, Chennai, India

H. M. Udanee Sachithra Rathnayake Samarasinghe Beacon International College, Singapore, Singapore

Kumar Rohit Indian Institute of Management Visakhapatnam, Visakhapatnam, India

Jangyash Kumar Rout Assistant Professor (Contractual), Odisha State Open University (OSOU), Sambalpur, Odisha, India;
Research Scholar, KIIT School of Management, KIIT Deemed to be University, Bhubaneswar, Odisha, India

Parth Salunke FLAME School of Business, FLAME University, Pune, India

Shees Majid Shaikh Indian Institute of Management Visakhapatnam, Visakhapatnam, India

Animesh Kumar Sharma Amity University, Delhi, India;
Lovely Professional University, Phagwara, India

Swati Sharma Amity Institute of Travel and Tourism, Amity University, Noida, India

Malini Singh Amity University, Noida, India

Bhaskara Srinivas Chandigarh University, Mohali, India

Qazi Saima Syed Islamic University of Science and Technology, Awantipora, India

McIver Thomas Department of Information Technology, Otago Polytechnique, Dunedin, New Zealand

Akshita Tiwari Amity University, Noida, India

Uthamaramasamy Vani PSG College of Arts & Science, Coimbatore, India

Yashti Vyas Indian Institute of Management Visakhapatnam, Visakhapatnam, India

Ranitha Sachinthana Weerarathna SLIIT Business School, Sri Lanka Institute of Information Technology, Malabe, Sri Lanka

Mano Weligodapola International Business University (IBU), Toronto, Canada

Azmee Zaheer Chandigarh University, Mohali, India

Adil Zahoor Islamic University of Science and Technology, Awantipora, India

Introduction to the Concept of Social Proof in Social Media Marketing

Zeeshan Majeed Nadroo, Adil Zahoor, Kumar Rohit, Qazi Saima Syed, Yashti Vyas, and Shees Majid Shaikh

Abstract

The influence of social proof on consumer behavior has been significantly amplified in the digital age through the advent of social media and technological advancements. This chapter serves as the foundation for the rest of the book by shedding light on the historical perspective, empirical validation, and the evolution of social proof in the digital landscape. The study explores the rise of social media platforms and their role in social proof, with key sections discussing the shift from traditional advertising to peer-influenced marketing and how social proof is applied in modern marketing strategies. The chapter adopts a conceptual and narrative approach to explore the key mechanisms and applications of social proof in the digital age. It synthesizes existing literature and real-world practices to explain how social proof manifests through

Z. M. Nadroo (✉) · K. Rohit · Y. Vyas · S. M. Shaikh
Indian Institute of Management Visakhapatnam, Visakhapatnam, India
e-mail: zeeshanmajeed7@gmail.com

K. Rohit
e-mail: kumar.rohit22-02@iimv.ac.in

Y. Vyas
e-mail: yashti.vyas24-02@iimv.ac.in

S. M. Shaikh
e-mail: shees.shaikh23-01@iimv.ac.in

A. Zahoor · Q. S. Syed
Islamic University of Science and Technology, Awantipora, India
e-mail: adil.zahoor@iust.ac.in

Q. S. Syed
e-mail: qazi.saima@iust.ac.in

Z. M. Nadroo
School of Management, IILM University, Gurugram, India

© The Author(s), under exclusive license to Springer Nature Singapore Pte Ltd. 2026
N. S. Jayawardena et al. (eds.), *Digital Advertising and Consumer Behavior*,
Management for Professionals, https://doi.org/10.1007/978-981-95-7809-2_1

user-generated content (UGC), likes, comments, shares, reviews, ratings, and influencer marketing. The chapter focuses on the role of UGC in establishing social proof and its critical influence on consumer decision-making. It highlights how likes, comments, and shares act as indicators of popularity and discusses the importance of reviews and influencer marketing as modern expressions of social proof. Special attention is given to the psychological aspects, such as the bandwagon effect and parasocial interaction, which contribute to shaping consumer behavior. The chapter explores technological advancements enhancing social proof, including AI-driven personalization, social proof algorithms, and AR/VR-based immersive experiences. It also emphasizes the challenges and ethical concerns around fake reviews and misleading endorsements, calling for greater integrity in social proof practices.

1 Understanding Social Proof

Social proof "refers to the act of presenting individuals with responses of others in a given situation" (Hu et al., 2018, p. 1045). Individuals "view a behaviour as correct in a given situation to the degree to which one sees others performing it" (Cialdini, 1993, p. 95). To influence consumer behaviour, marketers have capitalized on the influence of social norms on individual decision-making by developing strategies that provide customers with information about the behaviour of social others. This information serves as social proof that the behaviour is appropriate. Therefore, social proof supplies information on behaviour prevalence in the environment to influence individual decisions and promote compliance. Social proof is particularly crucial in uncertain situations where information is scarce for making informed decisions or when processing the available information is complex. Under such conditions, social proof provides "an information processing advantage and a decisional shortcut" (Cialdini, 1988).

Historical Perspective

Social psychology has a long history of motivating researchers to understand the contextual forces that govern human behaviour. The underlying premise is rooted in the social influence theory, arguing that an individual's cognitions and behaviours are largely determined by the behaviour of 'significant others', i.e., observed social behaviour is a powerful driver of subsequent social behaviour (Milgram et al., 1969). As such, among the several social influences on individual decision-making, such as interpersonal relations, group dynamics, leader-member exchange, etc., researchers have significantly emphasized the impact of social norms as a predictive route to determining social behaviour (e.g., Berkowitz, 1972; Fishbein & Ajzen, 1975; McKirnan, 1980).

Social norms typically indicate an individual's perception of other people's behaviour in a similar situation. While examining the social sources of human motivation, researchers have attempted to delineate the distinctive impact of descriptive (what *is*) and injunctive (what *ought to be*) norms on decision-making (Cialdini et al., 1990). Injunctive norms indicate a socially approved course of behaviour. How a person ought to behave in a given situation reflects the morally approved mode of conduct. Thus, "injunctive norms specify what ought to be done" by enjoining the normative course "through the promise of social sanctions" (Cialdini et al., 1990).

Conversely, descriptive norms specify the observed behaviour of others, i.e., what people actually do rather than what they are supposed to do. They indicate what is considered a standard or typical mode of behaviour, whether or not it is morally approved. Guided by the notion that "if everyone is doing it, it must be a sensible thing to do", descriptive norms powerfully shape individual decisions and consumer choices (Melnyk et al., 2021) because they represent a salient source of normative influence (Stok & de Ridder, 2019). Social proof is a striking manifestation of descriptive norms, particularly in the contemporary marketplace.

Another thread of research that led to the emergence of social proof as a behaviour-influencing strategy dates back to the mid-twentieth century. During 1955–56, Solomon Asch conducted some of the most influential experiments to explain what he termed 'conformity'. Asch (1955, 1956) reported that group opinion overrides individual perceptual judgement. In a simple visual comparison task, individuals would abandon their perceptual judgement when confronted with a conflicting group perception of confederates, thereby acquiescing to the group norm to avoid jeopardizing social approval (Asch, 1955, 1956). These findings indicate that individuals tend to base their judgements on the collective opinion of significant others, soliciting social proof to affirm their behaviours.

Noelle-Neumann's (1974) spiral of silence theory also offers a theoretical perspective on understanding social proof. Although the theory primarily focuses on public opinion at the macro-social and political levels, its insights inform the micro-level individual decision-making and behaviour change. The theory argues that minority opinions fade away under the pressure of majority viewpoints. Driven by a fear of social isolation, people tend to refrain from sharing their opinions publicly if they fear their views are held by only a minority. As a result, the majority opinion dominates public discourse and gradually influences the perspectives of those in the minority (Noelle-Neumann, 1991). Eventually, the majority opinion operates as social proof for others seeking validation of their views and actions. The power of social proof in influencing behaviour is, however, dependent on the strength (e.g., the status of the source), immediacy (referent's proximity to the individual), and quantum (number of referents) of the social influence (Morgan & Laland, 2012; Nowak et al., 1990).

Cultural evolutionists have also studied an individual's propensity to disproportionately conform to the majority decision (Boyd & Richerson, 1985). The cultural transmission biases in individuals govern their choices of who and when to copy (Boyd & Richerson, 1985). Lately, advancements in medical technology have paved the way for cognitive neuroscience to initiate inquiry into the neural foundations of social learning (Morgan & Laland, 2012). In a nutshell, the role of social influences (social proof) on human behaviour has not been examined solely from the perspective of social psychology. Insights from neuroscience and cultural evolutionary biology have also contributed to shaping our understanding of decision-making in a social context.

Empirical Validation

Academic research has thoroughly explored the power of social proof as a potent force shaping human behaviour and consumer choices. Ranging from topics of scholarly interest like a scientist's engagement in science communication (Hu et al., 2018) to social issues like charitable donation (Pascual et al., 2021), food choices (Begho & Liu, 2024), and driving behaviour (Bowden-Green & Vafeas, 2024) to the business arena like impulse buying (Huang et al., 2025), social media shopping (Talib & Saat, 2017), and e-commerce onboarding (Roethke et al., 2020), the study of social proof has penetrated multiple domains of human interaction and decision-making contexts.

Researchers have found broadly encouraging evidence for social proof in driving human behaviour. For instance, information about peer engagement as a social proof enhances scientist's participation intention in science communication (Hu et al., 2018). Social proof increases the likelihood of an individual's contribution to charitable donation for cancer research (Pascual et al., 2021). It also drives people to choose healthy food, even overriding their low self-control (Salmon et al., 2015). Social proof induces impulse buying behaviour among customers (Huang et al., 2025), besides enhancing purchase intention, nurturing customer satisfaction and engagement (Dwivedi et al., 2023; Santos et al., 2022; Vandenbosch et al., 2022; Zheng et al., 2022). These findings reflect the power of social proof as a compliance strategy to shape consumer decision-making and choice behaviour.

Social Proof in the Digital Landscape

The advent of digital technology, social media, and e-commerce has recently expanded the horizons of obtaining information about the behaviour of others (e.g., through user-generated content such as comments, shares, reviews, likes, etc.) (Walther & Jang, 2012), opening research pathways to explore how social proof operates in a virtual space. Recent evidence indicates that various forms of social proof in a digital market space powerfully influence consumer behaviour. For example, online comments guide a consumer's media content evaluation (Neubaum & Krämer, 2017), and the number of likes and comments (quantity of social proof) positively influence impulse buying behaviour (Huang et al., 2025). Social proof also helps to increase user registrations on an e-commerce platform (Roethke et al., 2020).

Social proof communicated via online digital content helps cultivate consumer trust (Huang et al., 2025), diminishes scepticism (Schneider et al., 2020) and uncertainty associated with the online marketplace, and steers customer choice behaviour. The information asymmetry between the customer and the service provider and the absence of physical evidence develop uncertainty and a divide in trust on digital platforms. By offering external validation through expert endorsements, user testimonials, and crowd reflections, social proof overcomes these concerns, reinforces trust, and minimizes the consumer's risk of making a wrong judgment. As such, social proof as a persuasion strategy assumes greater valence in a characteristically uncertain digital market space.

2 Rise of Social Media Platforms and Social Proof

Social media encompasses mobile and web-based technologies that facilitate content creation and distribution across geographical, social, and demographic boundaries through collaborative public interaction (Pan et al., 2019). Over the last two decades, social media platforms have not only transformed how businesses engage with their audiences but have also become powerful vehicles of social proof—influencing consumer behavior through peer validation and social endorsement.

The widespread adoption of platforms such as Facebook, Instagram, Twitter, LinkedIn, and TikTok has enabled brands to leverage various forms of social proof, including customer reviews, testimonials, influencer endorsements, and community engagement. The rapid consumer integration of social media into daily life has been reflected in the growing number of users worldwide, with businesses increasingly utilizing these platforms to establish credibility and trust (Rodriguez et al., 2012). The integration of algorithm-driven social proof—such as engagement metrics (likes, shares, and comments) and personalized recommendations—has further strengthened social media's role in shaping consumer decision-making. The global social media advertising market is projected to reach 5,855.0 million users by 2029, emphasizing its increasing dominance in brand communication (Statista, 2024).

Digital and social media marketing have enabled businesses to achieve their marketing objectives at a lower cost while amplifying trust signals (Ajina, 2019). The proliferation of social media, coupled with increased internet accessibility and smartphone adoption, has fostered a digital landscape where billions of users actively participate in online interactions. These platforms allow businesses to deploy targeted advertisements that leverage social validation cues, such as the number of people who have purchased, reviewed, or engaged with a product. Consequently, social proof embedded in digital marketing strategies reduces perceived uncertainty and enhances consumer confidence in purchasing decisions (Saravanakumar & Lakshmi, 2012).

Consumers increasingly rely on peer recommendations and shared experiences to make informed choices about products and services, a behavior reinforced by the interactive nature of social media (Stephen, 2015). Companies respond by strategically embedding social proof in their marketing strategies, making platforms like Facebook and Twitter central to digital branding. For instance, Facebook hosts over 50 million registered businesses, while 88% of businesses use Twitter for marketing purposes (Lister, 2017).

The effectiveness of social proof in social media marketing is well-documented: businesses leverage user-generated content, influencer endorsements, and community-driven discussions to establish brand credibility (Buechel & Berger, 2018; Gkikas et al., 2022). Research confirms that social media significantly influences consumer decision-making, with peer-generated content perceived as more trustworthy than traditional advertisements (Sadovykh et al., 2015; Zhang et al., 2017). However, poor management of social media presence—such as negative reviews or lack of engagement—can undermine social proof and damage brand perception (Benthaus et al., 2016).

Social media facilitates real-time consumer engagement, allowing brands to amplify positive sentiment, gather market intelligence, and drive sales through word-of-mouth advocacy (Aswani et al., 2018; Izogo & Jayawardhena, 2018). Organizations leverage these digital spaces to cultivate a sense of community and credibility, thereby enhancing consumer trust and loyalty (Huang et al., 2019; Park et al., 2021). The overarching objective of social media marketing—branding, customer engagement, and stakeholder trust—is fundamentally rooted in establishing social proof (Kumar et al., 2021).

The Shift from Traditional Advertising to Peer-Influenced Marketing: Social Proof in Action

The marketing environment has undergone a seismic shift from traditional advertising to a peer-influenced model, reinforcing the power of social proof in shaping consumer perceptions. Traditional advertising—characterized by one-way brand messaging—is increasingly losing ground to social media-based marketing strategies that prioritize trust-building through peer validation.

A dominant manifestation of social proof in social media marketing is influencer marketing—where businesses collaborate with trusted digital personalities to shape audience perceptions and purchasing decisions (Leung et al., 2022). This shift underscores the importance of peer approval and recommendations, as consumers tend to trust influencers who exhibit authenticity and credibility over corporate messaging. The key characteristics of social proof-driven influencer marketing include: (1) Brand-Influencer Partnerships—Businesses select and incentivize influencers to promote their products. (2) Authenticity and Engagement—Unlike celebrity endorsements, influencers maintain long-term relationships with their followers, positioning themselves as credible sources of information (Lee & Eastin, 2020). (3) Community-Driven Trust—Consumers rely on influencers' experiences and peer recommendations to validate their purchasing choices, reinforcing social proof.

Social media's rapid expansion has amplified the impact of endorsements, making influencers pivotal in shaping consumer trust (Appel et al., 2020). The source-credibility model (Ohanian, 1990), widely applied to social media marketing, highlights that influencer credibility is derived from trustworthiness, attractiveness, and expertise—all of which contribute to social proof (Schouten et al., 2019). With the advent of Web 2.0 and Web 3.0, consumer-generated trust mechanisms—such as reviews, ratings, and influencer content—have become critical to digital marketing (Leung et al., 2022). A growing distrust of traditional advertising has further fueled the shift toward peer-influenced decision-making (Gerdeman, 2019). Empirical evidence suggests that influencer marketing generates higher ROI than traditional advertising, as consumers perceive peer endorsements as more authentic and persuasive (Ahmad, 2018).

The Role of User-Generated Content (UGC) in Establishing Social Proof

In the digital era, UGC serves as a cornerstone of social proof, reinforcing brand trust and credibility. UGC—spanning reviews, social media posts, testimonials, and consumer-shared experiences—acts as a virtual word-of-mouth mechanism, influencing consumer attitudes and purchase decisions (Müller & Christandl, 2019). Social proof theory suggests that when individuals observe others engaging with or endorsing a brand, they are more likely to perceive it as credible and valuable (Yang et al., 2021).

Brand-related UGC, particularly in the form of online reviews and peer recommendations, significantly impacts purchasing behavior (Marchand et al., 2016). The exponential growth of social media has empowered consumers to create and disseminate content, fostering a digital environment where peer endorsements and communal discussions shape trust (Sreejesh et al., 2020). Social media's interactive nature enhances social proof by allowing users to validate their decisions through peer engagement (Gao et al., 2021). The presence of UGC, particularly positive product experiences and testimonials, fosters brand trust and credibility (Sohn & Kim, 2020). Businesses increasingly leverage UGC as a core component of their content marketing strategies to strengthen social proof (Roma & Aloini, 2018). Moreover, research highlights that creator attributes—such as social recognition, engagement, and expertise—enhance the perceived value of UGC, further strengthening its role as a trust-building mechanism (Choi & Leon, 2020). Monitoring customer-generated UGC and actively engaging with it can yield substantial advantages over traditional marketing approaches, as consumers inherently trust peer recommendations over direct brand communications (Wang et al., 2021).

Role of Social Proof in Consumer Decision-Making

Social proof as a psychological phenomenon induces individuals to make decisions based on the actions and behaviors of others. People inherently seek societal validation, often perceiving a behavior as appropriate in a given context when they observe others engaging in it (Cialdini, 1993). This effect intensifies when individuals mimic the actions of their peers, reinforcing the behavior as acceptable and desirable (Cialdini et al., 1999).

In modern marketing practices, businesses widely apply social proof strategies to enhance product credibility, build brand awareness, and foster trust through various indicators, including user ratings, reviews, and registration data (Burtch et al., 2017). Positive user feedback, such as favorable reviews and ratings, instills confidence and prompts informed purchasing behavior. Consumers often rely on online reviews, ratings, and video demonstrations to assess product credibility and reliability, thereby enabling more confident and thoughtful buying choices (Huang et al., 2025). The quality of social proof is particularly crucial in aiding consumer decision-making. When consumers see that others have had positive experiences with a product or service, they are more likely to trust the brand and make a purchase. This is why reviews, testimonials, and ratings are so influential in e-commerce.

Businesses use social proof to leverage the tendency of consumers to follow the actions of others, especially in uncertain or ambiguous situations. Retailers frequently apply social proof strategies to alleviate consumer hesitation and strengthen the credibility of a product or brand through social indicators (Roethke et al., 2020). The link between social proof and consumer engagement is well-documented. By demonstrating the popularity and credibility of a product, social proof enhances consumer engagement, which, in turn, influences purchase intentions. As social proof increases, consumers perceive the product as more valuable, leading to higher purchase intentions (Bhattacharyya & Bose, 2020).

3 Mechanisms of Social Proof on Social Media

The proliferation of social media has significantly transformed how individuals and brands shape opinions and influence behaviors (Anjorin et al., 2024). The dynamic interaction between user actions, brand strategies, and platform algorithms shapes the nature of social proof such as reviews, ratings, and testimonials act as visible endorsements, providing insights into users' shared experiences. Furthermore, likes, comments, and shares attributed to these posts enhance their credibility, amplify their momentum and expand their reach (Dedeoglu, 2019).

Brands strategically leverage the cycle of consumer behavior by integrating user-generated content, like testimonials and reviews, into their marketing mix (Sykora et al., 2022). This approach fosters engagement, as advertisements and promotional posts encourage user interaction, creating a feedback loop where popular content is elevated by platform algorithms. This continuous visibility enhances credibility and amplifies the impact of the content.

In addition, influencer marketing has proven to be a large and growing part of this ecosystem. Influencers use their trustworthiness and relatability to authentically promote products, further reinforcing social proof as a key driver of consumer trust and engagement. These mechanisms create a robust system where social proof not only shapes perceptions but also actively transforms engagement patterns and drives meaningful consumer decision-making (Hermanus, 2022).

To explore the mechanisms underlying social proof's influence on consumer behavior, it is important to consider: the role of likes, comments, and shares as popularity indicators; the impact of reviews, ratings, and testimonials in shaping decisions; and the transformative power of influencer marketing. Together, these elements shape perceptions, drive engagement, and influence decision-making in today's digital landscape.

Likes, Comments, and Shares as Indicators of Popularity

Likes, comments, and shares on social media have become powerful forms of social proof, helping users evaluate content and their behavior. Social influence theory suggests that these interactions signal the importance and relevance of content (Fulk et al., 1990). Likes function as quick, symbolic endorsements, signalling that a post resonates with audience and prompting further interaction and engagement. As a result, a high number of likes becomes a form of social validation, prompting viewers to believe that the content deserves attention. In contrast, comments develops deeper engagement by facilitating discussions about the content and creating a sense of community (Hillman et al., 2023). Along with building credibility, comments also establishes trust with the user. It also adds another layer of social proof to the content, while also increasing its visibility to new audiences and serving as a form of trust-based recommendation.

In modern society, where social validation is increasingly prominent, these mechanisms have emerged due to the rise of digital interactions. Metrics like these are well-known in the industry and have been leveraged on platforms such as Facebook, Instagram, and TikTok, becoming key indicators for discovering engaging content (Nowland et al., 2018). For instance, Starbucks' annual #RedCupContest is a prime example of social proof in action. The holiday-themed cups inspired thousands of users to create and share creative photos, comment on, and share the content. The social proof generated by Starbucks through the contest reinforced the idea that everyone is participating and encouraging others to join in (Scholl, 2018). Similarly, Nike's 'You Can't Stop Us' campaign on TikTok relied heavily on social proof by capitalizing on massive engagement (Manorome et al., 2023). The campaign's widespread popularity, reflected in millions of likes and shares, made others more likely to view and share it. Through this campaign, Nike strategically positioned itself as a brand that advocates for perseverance and inclusivity, a message further reinforced by the collective support of its audience.

These indicators of popularity also influence user behavior through the bandwagon effect, where people are drawn to popular content, and fear of missing out (FOMO), compelling users to engage with trending posts (Kang & Ma, 2020). Social media algorithms amplify this loop by prioritizing high-engagement content, making likes, comments, and shares critical drivers of digital influence.

Role of Reviews and Ratings

Reviews and ratings are powerful social validation tools that have leveraged the power of social proof into consumer behavior. Such forms of peer-generated content reduce uncertainty and help in purchasing decisions, allowing the users to experience the experiences of other users (Sridhar & Srinivasan, 2012). For instance, reviews offer detailed feedback on products or services, enabling consumers to evaluate their strengths and weaknesses comprehensively. In contrast, ratings, often represented through a five-star system, provide a quick and quantifiable measure of satisfaction, facilitating expedited decision-making for consumers. From a psychological perspective, these tools leverage authority bias and peer validation, both of which are integral to the concept of social proof (Tennant et al., 2017). Consumers tend to trust the opinions of experts and are also influenced by the validation of their peers, other consumers who have made similar choices reinforcing the effect of both authority bias and peer validation. Tools like these are already used by platforms such as Amazon, Airbnb, and TripAdvisor to provide visibility and build trust via user-submitted content (Nasser, 2023). Customer reviews and ratings on platforms like Amazon significantly influence purchase decisions by providing a 5-star rating system that offers a quick assessment of a product's quality, alongside the detailed insights that only a review can provide. To further enhance the credibility of these reviews, Amazon incorporates verified purchase labels, which help increase trust in the feedback. Positive reviews can drive sales, while negative reviews may impart valuable lessons that brands might prefer potential buyers not to learn (He et al., 2020). Consequently, both types of reviews play a crucial role in shaping consumer perceptions and decisions.

Influencer Marketing as a Form of Social Proof

Influencer marketing has emerged as one of the fastest-growing forms of social proof, utilizing individuals with a significant following within a specific niche to influence consumer behavior (Sigurðardóttir, 2019). Influencers, whether individuals or entities, possess an authoritative presence and a follower base large enough to render their endorsements both authentic and credible (Audrezet et al., 2020). These influencers are perceived as authorities, and their followers view them

Table 1 Mechanisms of social proof on social media

Mechanism	Definition	Advantages	Challenges
Likes, Comments, Shares	Indicators of content popularity and engagement	—Easy and quick measure of popularity	—Susceptible to manipulation (e.g., fake likes)
		—Enhances visibility and reach	—May not directly translate to purchases
Reviews and Ratings	User-generated evaluations of products or services	—Builds trust through transparency	—Potential for fake or biased reviews
		—Influences purchase decisions	—Negative reviews can deter customers
Influencer Marketing	Endorsements by social media influencers	—Leverages trusted relationships	—High cost and potential loss of credibility
		—Drives engagement and conversions	—Mismatch between influencer and brand image

Source Authors Own Creation

as experts within their area of influence (Wiedmann & Von Mettenheim, 2021). Additionally, the relatability factor, often referred to as the 'people like me' effect, amplifies the impact of influencers, as consumers are more likely to trust those who share similar values or lifestyles (Hjortaas & Øverås, 2018). This dynamic is further reinforced by the halo effect, which suggests that the positive qualities associated with an influencer extend to the products they endorse (Janssen & Croes 2022). Thereby enhancing their appeal to potential customers.

Influencer marketing has proven effective through case studies such as Nike's collaboration with Colin Kaepernick, which not only strengthened brand identity but also generated large-scale consumer engagement (Leduc, 2022). Similarly, Glossier effectively used micro-influencers to foster authentic communities and engage with highly specific niche audiences. However, influencer marketing also presents challenges, including the prevalence of fake followers, trust issues, and the risk of over-commercialization. The rise of paid followers and influencers promoting products that don't align with their personal brand can undermine credibility (Hahl, 2023). Therefore, social proof on social media has different advantages and challenges (Table 1), as to maintain authenticity and ensure long-term success, brands must carefully navigate these risks, balancing engagement with strategic, genuine partnerships.

Social Proof and Bandwagon Effect

Social proof and the bandwagon effect are closely interwoven, as both stem from the innate human tendency to rely on collective behavior for decision-making. Social proof functions as a psychological mechanism where individuals perceive the actions of others as a validation of appropriate behavior, particularly in uncertain situations (Leibenstein, 1950; Oyedele & Goenner, 2021). Firms strategically employ social proof to drive consumer decisions by leveraging cues such as user reviews, best-seller tags, and influencer endorsements (Tsiotsou, 2016). The bandwagon effect amplifies this influence by triggering consumers to conform to perceived popular choices, reinforcing the appeal of widely accepted products or brands (Cho et al., 2020). Digital platforms further escalate this effect by showcasing real-time data on trending purchases, reviews, and recommendations, effectively shaping consumer perceptions of desirability (Jeong & Kwon, 2012).

The bandwagon effect encapsulates the tendency of individuals to adopt behaviors based on the majority's choices, reinforcing social proof as a critical determinant of consumer behavior (Jawad, 2022; Nadroo et al., 2024). As marketplaces transition to digital landscapes, the role of social proof becomes even more pronounced, driven by the proliferation of online influencers who signal product credibility through mass appeal (Zhang, 2024). Consumers, seeking reassurance in their purchase decisions, increasingly rely on online ratings, social media trends, and community-driven endorsements, reinforcing the bandwagon heuristic (Nadroo et al., 2024). This collective validation fosters a sense of trust and reduces perceived risk, illustrating how social proof is intrinsically linked to the psychological underpinnings of the bandwagon effect in contemporary consumer decision-making (Das et al., 2021; Lehr et al., 2021).

Social Proof and Parasocial Interaction

Social proof is further reinforced through parasocial interaction (psi), where consumers form perceived relationships with influencers and media figures, shaping their purchase intentions based on these virtual connections (Labrecque, 2014). In an era dominated by digital interactions, influencers act as trusted sources of product recommendations, fostering credibility through consistent engagement and perceived authenticity (Hu et al., 2020). This phenomenon is particularly potent in social commerce, where psi amplifies social proof by creating an illusion of interpersonal trust between consumers and influencers (Kim & Kang, 2018). Unlike traditional marketing strategies, where credibility stems from institutional authority, psi-driven social proof relies on the perceived relatability and expertise of digital personalities (Ladhari et al., 2020; Yuan et al., 2016; Yuksel & Labrecque, 2016). This alignment between influencers and audience expectations enhances consumer confidence, thereby increasing brand engagement and purchase likelihood (Yuan et al., 2023).

Consumers increasingly depend on influencers as a form of social proof, mirroring the tenets of the bandwagon effect by conforming to prevalent social norms and purchasing behaviors (Berger & Heath, 2007). This reliance stems from deep-seated psychological needs, including the desire for social recognition and belonging, further strengthening the persuasive power of psi in shaping consumer attitudes (Men & Tsai, 2013). Social media platforms facilitate this dynamic by fostering interactive dialogues between influencers and followers, transforming conventional marketing into personalized endorsements that drive purchasing decisions (Lee & Lee, 2017). As a result, psi not only enhances brand trust and perceived credibility but also acts as a key conduit for social proof, demonstrating how digital interactions shape modern consumer behavior in alignment with collective validation principles (Koay et al., 2024; Walter et al., 2024).

4 Technological Advancements Enhancing Social Proof

The concept of social proof has been a cornerstone in marketing for decades, rooted in the psychological principle that individuals often look to others' actions and opinions to inform their own decisions (Cialdini et al., 1999). In today's digital era, technological advancements have revolutionized how social proof is integrated into consumer experiences (Rachmad, 2024). The interplay of cutting-edge tools like artificial intelligence (AI), augmented reality (AR), and virtual reality (VR) has expanded the boundaries of social proof, transforming it from static cues to dynamic, immersive, and highly personalized experiences (Tyagi & Tyagi, 2024).

These advancements enhance the efficacy of social proof by leveraging real-time data, interactive interfaces, and immersive technologies. AI-driven algorithms, for example, enable businesses to refine their recommendations and content based on detailed consumer behavior insights, thereby creating highly personalized social proof cues (Vashishth et al., 2025). Meanwhile, AR and VR introduce new dimensions to social proof by allowing consumers to interact with products and services in virtual spaces, effectively blending social validation with experiential marketing (Hadi et al., 2024).

The psychological impact of these advancements is profound. Where traditional social proof primarily relied on static testimonials, star ratings, or sales data, modern technologies infuse it with dynamic, real-time interactions. This shift not only heightens consumer trust but also aligns with the emotional and rational dimensions of decision-making (Wang et al., 2024). For instance, an AI-powered recommendation system develops a sense of individual connection by tailoring content to user preferences, while AR/VR technologies offer visually rich, immersive environments where consumers can experience social proof in real time. To further explore this transformative progression, we have explored two key areas, i.e., AI-driven personalization and AR/VR interactive experience, which are redefining the role and impact of social proof in today's digital landscape.

AI-Driven Personalization and Social Proof Algorithms

Advancements in AI-enabled technologies have empowered businesses to excel in the digital marketplace by leveraging vast volumes of consumer data to deliver highly personalized experiences (Chintalapati & Pandey, 2022). These systems employ machine learning and predictive analytics to uncover patterns in consumer behavior, thereby enhancing the relevance and impact of social proof on digital platforms (Roethke et al., 2020). Innovative e-commerce companies, such as Amazon, leverage AI algorithms to generate product recommendations with labels like "Frequently Bought Together" or "Customers Also Buy," effectively encouraging impulse purchases and fostering trust through data-driven validation (Habil et al., 2023). Similarly, streaming services like Netflix and Spotify use AI to personalize content recommendations, curating lists such as "Top Picks for You" and "Trending in Your Area" based on collective user behavior, which makes these suggestions resonate with individual preferences (Boksjö & Petricioiu, 2022).

Additionally, AI-powered sentiment analysis tools aggregate and summarize customer reviews, identifying key themes that help users make data-driven decisions. Platforms like Airbnb and TripAdvisor use such tools to categorize reviews into themes like "cleanliness," "location," and "value for money," offering concise insights derived from collective feedback (Alantari et al., 2022). AI also enhances real-time decision-making through chatbots and virtual assistants, which deliver contextually relevant social proof during critical moments in the purchase journey. For example, a chatbot on an online fashion store may present reviews from users with similar preferences when a customer hesitates over a purchase, creating a persuasive nudge to buy (Kyrylenko, 2024). These integrations of AI not only streamline the consumer experience but also strengthen trust by presenting highly relevant, socially validated information.

Use of AR/VR for Interactive Social Proof Experiences

The integration of augmented reality (AR) and virtual reality (VR) technologies has elevated the role of social proof by offering immersive and interactive experiences that replicate real-world environments (Marr, 2021). These technologies empower consumers to see, engage with, and even "experience" products or services before making a purchase, while leveraging crowd validation to build trust and credibility (Ilsha et al., 2024). AR applications, such as IKEA Place and Sephora's Virtual Artist, allow users to visualize furniture in their homes or test makeup on their faces. By combining AR with user-generated content, these platforms further enhance social proof. For example, Sephora encourages users to share their AR-enhanced looks on social media, creating a feedback loop that fosters peer validation and influences potential buyers (Lele, 2021).VR takes this one step further by immersing users in realistic, three-dimensional environments where they can explore products and services. In the travel industry, VR allows users to virtually visit hotels, resorts, and destinations, helping them make informed choices before booking, like Marriott hotels has implemented VR as a "travel teleportation" tool, enabling potential guests to explore rooms, amenities, and destinations while incorporating virtual testimonials from previous travellers to enrich the experience (Ulusoy, 2024).

These technologies also integrate live reviews and ratings into AR/VR experiences, dynamically bringing social proof into the decision-making process. For example, a virtual car showroom might feature pop-ups with model reviews or a live counter showing the number of users currently considering a vehicle, amplifying the bandwagon effect and influencing purchasing decisions (Fan et al., 2022). Moreover, AR/VR platforms can showcase the "wisdom of the crowd" through features like virtual shopping events. In such events, users can see real-time interactions, such as the number of viewers or purchasers of a particular item, creating visual cues of popularity. These cues resonate with the principle of social validation and encourage collective acceptance, further influencing consumer behavior (Koutromanou et al., 2023). The most powerful aspect of AR/VR is their ability to harmonize emotional and rational elements in the decision-making process. While AI-driven personalization relies on logical, data-driven insights, AR and VR generate authentic, immersive experiences that evoke emotional responses. Together, these technologies form a synergy that reinforces trust in social proof (Table 2), blending logic with emotion to create compelling and impactful consumer experiences.

Table 2 Technological advancements enhancing social proof

Technological advancement	Key mechanism	Psychological impact on consumers
AI-driven personalization	AI algorithms analyze user data—preferences, behaviors, and past interactions—to deliver tailored recommendations and dynamic content	Develops personalized connections, enhances trust in recommendations, and drives purchase behavior
Social proof algorithms in e-commerce	Algorithms use social data to highlight popular products, driving community validation and reducing purchase uncertainty	Amplifies the bandwagon effect, encouraging users to follow trends and rely on collective approval
Augmented Reality (AR) for Product visualization	AR allows real-time product visualization with peer reviews, increasing confidence in decisions	Enhances trust by showing how others experience products in real-world contexts
Virtual Reality (VR) for Immersive shopping	VR offers immersive shopping with social proof indicators like reviews and social signals	Creates interactive spaces where peer behaviors build trust and purchasing intent
AI-powered recommendation engines	AI improves recommendations by learning from interactions and integrating social signals	Builds reliability by showing products endorsed by similar consumers
Interactive social proof via AR/VR integration	AR/VR enable product visualization alongside peer feedback to strengthen social proof	Interactive experiences with virtual testimonials increase trust and influence decisions

Source Authors Own Creation

5 The Challenges and Ethical Considerations of Fake Reviews and Misleading Endorsements

Even though the social proof plays a critical role in shaping consumer perceptions and driving purchase decisions (Kim et al., 2023). However, the increasing reliance on online reviews and influencer endorsements has given rise to unethical practices such as fake reviews and misleading endorsements (Poddar et al., 2019). These deceptive tactics not only distort consumer trust but also challenge the integrity of digital marketplaces.

One of the most prevalent forms of review manipulation involves businesses or sellers fabricating positive reviews to artificially enhance their brand image and boost sales (He et al., 2022). Fake reviews, often disguised as genuine consumer feedback, mislead potential buyers into believing that a product or service is more reliable or popular than it actually is (He et al., 2022; Song et al., 2023). Similarly, brands sometimes incentivize influencers to provide biased endorsements without proper disclosure, misleading consumers into perceiving paid promotions as authentic recommendations (Salminen et al., 2022). These deceptive strategies exploit the psychological power of social proof, where individuals tend to trust peer-generated content more than traditional advertising (Burtch et al., 2018).

The ethical implications of fake reviews and deceptive endorsements are significant. First, they violate consumer trust by presenting manipulated information that can lead to poor purchasing decisions and dissatisfaction (Lou et al., 2023; Song et al., 2023). Second, they undermine fair competition, as businesses that engage in these unethical practices gain an unfair advantage over competitors who rely on genuine consumer engagement (Jabeur et al., 2023; Song et al., 2023). Third, they erode the credibility of digital platforms, leading to increased skepticism among consumers and reducing the effectiveness of social proof as a trust-building mechanism (Dwivedi et al., 2020).

Regulatory bodies and online platforms have implemented measures to combat these unethical practices. For example, platforms like Amazon and Yelp employ algorithms and human moderators to detect and remove fake reviews, while the Federal Trade Commission (FTC) mandates clear disclosures for paid endorsements. Despite these efforts, businesses and influencers often find ways to circumvent detection, highlighting the ongoing challenge of ensuring transparency in digital marketing (Salminen et al., 2022).

To maintain the integrity of social proof, ethical marketing practices must be prioritized. Businesses should focus on fostering genuine consumer engagement, while influencers should uphold transparency by disclosing sponsored content. Platforms, regulators, and consumers must work together to recognize and counteract deceptive tactics, ensuring that social proof remains a credible and trustworthy force in marketing.

6 Conclusion

The chapter, explored the fundamental concept of social proof and its increasing relevance in the context of social media marketing. Social proof, as a powerful psychological principle, influences consumer behavior by leveraging the actions, experiences, and opinions of others to guide decision-making. The chapter explained how social proof manifests in various forms, such as user-generated content, online reviews, influencer endorsements, and ratings, all of which significantly shape consumer perceptions and behavior on digital platforms.

The rapid growth of social media and the proliferation of digital interactions have boosted the role of social proof in marketing strategies. As consumers increasingly rely on the experiences and opinions of others when making purchasing decisions, understanding the dynamics of social proof becomes crucial for brands looking to build trust, enhance engagement, and drive purchase intention. Moreover, we touched upon emerging trends such as AI-driven recommendations and the rise of immersive experiences, which further optimize the influence of social proof.

References

Alantari, H. J., Currim, I. S., DeSng, Y., & Singh, S. (2022). An empirical comparison of machine learning methods for text-based sentiment analysis of online consumer reviews. *International Journal of Research in Marketing, 39*(1), 1–19.

Anjorin, K. F., Raji, M. A., & Olodo, H. B. (2024). The influence of social media marketing on consumer behavior in the retail industry: A comprehensive review. *International Journal of Management & Entrepreneurship Research, 6*(5), 1547–1580.

Asch, S. E. (1956). Studies of independence and conformity: A minority of one against a unanimous majority. *Psychological Monographs: General and Applied, 70*(9), 1–70.

Asch, S. E. (1955). Opinions and social pressure. *Scientific American, 193*(5), 31–35.

Audrezet, A., De Kerviler, G., & Moulard, J. G. (2020). Authenticity under threat: When social media influencers need to go beyond self-presentation. *Journal of Business Research, 117*, 557–569.

Begho, T., & Liu, S. (2024). Does social proof and herd behaviour drive food choices of consumers? *British Food Journal, 126*(3), 1050–1064.

Ben Jabeur, S., Ballouk, H., Ben Arfi, W., & Sahut, J.-M. (2023). Artificial intelligence applications in fake review detection: Bibliometric analysis and future avenues for research. *Journal of Business Research, 158*, Article 113631. https://doi.org/10.1016/j.jbusres.2022.113631

Berger, J., & Heath, C. (2007). Where consumers diverge from others: Identity signaling and product domains. *Journal of Consumer Research, 34*(2), 121–134.

Berkowitz, L. (1972). Social norms, feelings, and other factors affecting helping and altruism. In L. Berkowitz (Ed.), *Advances in experimental social psychology, 6* (pp. 63–108). Academic Press.

Boksjö, N., & Petricioiu, N. (2022). What's in a name? How the vocabulary of personalized playlists affects user's expectation and satisfactions in music streaming services.

Bowden-Green, T., & Vafeas, M. (2024). Recognizing motivation in others: The effectiveness of using social proof to change driving behaviour. *Journal of Social Marketing, 14*(3/4), 382–397.

Boyd, R., & Richerson, P. J. (1985). *Culture and the evolutionary process*. University of Chicago Press.

Burtch, G., Hong, Y., Bapna, R., & Griskevicius, V. (2018). Stimulating online reviews by combining financial incentives and social norms. *Management Science, 64*(5), 2065–2082.
Chintalapati, S., & Pandey, S. K. (2022). Artificial intelligence in marketing: A systematic literature review. *International Journal of Market Research, 64*(1), 38–68.
Cho, E., Yu, U.-J., & Kim, J. (2020). Either Bandwagon effect or need for uniqueness? Motivational factors driving young adult consumers' luxury brand purchases: An abstract. *Developments in Marketing Science: Proceedings of the Academy of Marketing Science*, 233–234. https://doi.org/10.1007/978-3-030-39165-2_96
Cialdini, R. B. (1988). *Influence: Science and practice* (2nd ed.). Scott, Foresman.
Cialdini, R. B. (1993). *The psychology of persuasion*. New York.
Cialdini, R. B., Reno, R. R., & Kallgren, C. A. (1990). A Focus Theory of normative conduct: Recycling the concept of norms to reduce littering in public places. *Journal of Personality and Social Psychology, 58*(6), 1015–1026.
Cialdini, R. B., Wosinska, W., Barrett, D. W., Butner, J., & Gornik-Durose, M. (1999). Compliance with a request in two cultures: The differential influence of social proof and commitment/consistency on collectivists and individualists. *Personality and Social Psychology Bulletin, 25*(10), 1242–1253.
Das, M., Habib, M., Saha, V., & Jebarajakirthy, C. (2021). Bandwagon vs snob luxuries: Targeting consumers based on uniqueness dominance. *Journal of Retailing and Consumer Services, 61*. https://doi.org/10.1016/j.jretconser.2021.102582
Dedeoglu, B. B. (2019). Are information quality and source credibility really important for shared content on social media? The moderating role of gender. *International Journal of Contemporary Hospitality Management, 31*(1), 513–534.
Dwivedi, Y. K., Ismagilova, E., Rana, N. P., & Raman, R. (2023). Social media adoption, usage and impact in Business-to-Business (B2B) context: A state-of-the-art literature review. *Information Systems Frontiers, 25*, 971–933.
Fan, X., Jiang, X., & Deng, N. (2022). Immersive technology: A meta-analysis of augmented/virtual reality applications and their impact on tourism experience. *Tourism Management, 91*, Article 104534.
Fishbein, M., & Ajzen, I. (1975). *Belief, attitude, intention, and behavior*. Addison-Wesley.
Fulk, J., Schmitz, J., & Steinfield, C. W. (1990). A social influence model of technology use. *Organizations and Communication Technology, 117*(1), 140.
Habil, S., El-Deeb, S., & El-Bassiouny, N. (2023). AI-based recommendation systems: The ultimate solution for market prediction and targeting. *The Palgrave handbook of interactive marketing* (pp. 683–704). Springer International Publishing.
Hadi, R., Melumad, S., & Park, E. S. (2024). The Metaverse: A new digital frontier for consumer behavior. *Journal of Consumer Psychology, 34*(1), 142–166.
Hahl, S. (2023). *Perception of uncredibility in influencers' paid social media marketing collaborations* (Master's thesis).
Han, D. I. D., Bergs, Y., & Moorhouse, N. (2022). Virtual reality consumer experience escapes: Preparing for the metaverse. *Virtual Reality, 26*(4), 1443–1458.
He, J., Wang, X., Vandenbosch, M. B., & Nault, B. R. (2020). Revealed preference in online reviews: Purchase verification in the tablet market. *Decision Support Systems, 132*, Article 113281.
He, S., Hollenbeck, B., & Proserpio, D. (2022). The market for fake reviews. *Marketing Science, 41*(5), 468–493. https://doi.org/10.1287/mksc.2022.1353
Hermanus, T. W. (2022). *A strategic communication framework to manage the effect of user-generated content on consumer-based brand equity of major retailers in the Cape Metropole* (Doctoral dissertation, Cape Peninsula University of Technology).
Hillman, J. G., Fowlie, D. I., & MacDonald, T. K. (2023). Social verification theory: A new way to conceptualize validation, dissonance, and belonging. *Personality and Social Psychology Review, 27*(3), 309–331.

Hjortaas, A. E., & Øverås, R. D. (2018). *Increasing the effectiveness of influencer marketing: applying parasocial interaction and Cialdini's principles of persuasion* (Master's thesis, Handelshøyskolen BI).

Hu, L., Min, Q., Han, S., & Liu, Z. (2020). Understanding followers' stickiness to digital influencers: The effect of psychological responses. *International Journal of Information Management, 54*. https://doi.org/10.1016/j.ijinfomgt.2020.102169

Hu, S., Li, Z., Zhang, J., & Zhu, J. (2018). Engaging scientists in science communication: The effect of social proof and meaning. *Journal of Cleaner Production, 170*, 1044–1051.

Huang, W., Wang, X., Zhang, Q., Han, J., & Zhang, R. (2025). Beyond likes and comments: How social proof influences consumer impulse buying on short-form video platforms. *Journal of Retailing and Consumer Services, 84*.

Ilsha, M., Malviya, C., & Vidani, J. (2024). Evaluating the influence of social media advertising on e-commerce sales.

Jawad, M. (2022). The dynamic threshold model of bandwagon innovations: Role of organizational attention and legitimacy. *Organizational Psychology Review, 12*(2), 162–180. https://doi.org/10.1177/20413866211054201

Jeong, H. J., & Kwon, K.-N. (2012). The effectiveness of two online persuasion claims: Limited product availability and product popularity. *Journal of Promotion Management, 18*(1), 83–99. https://doi.org/10.1080/10496491.2012.646221

Janssen, L., Schouten, A. P., & Croes, E. A. (2022). Influencer advertising on Instagram: Product-influencer fit and number of followers affect advertising outcomes and influencer evaluations via credibility and identification. *International Journal of Advertising, 41*(1), 101–127.

Kang, I., & Ma, I. (2020). A study on bandwagon consumption behavior based on fear of missing out and product characteristics. *Sustainability, 12*(6), 2441.

Kim, J., & Kang, S. (2018). How social capital impacts the purchase intention of sustainable fashion products. *Journal of Business Research, November 2017*, 0–1. https://doi.org/10.1016/j.jbusres.2018.10.010

Kim, K. K., Kim, W. G., & Lee, M. (2023). Impact of dark patterns on consumers' perceived fairness and attitude: Moderating effects of types of dark patterns, social proof, and moral identity. *Tourism Management, 98*, Article 104763.

Koay, K. Y., Cheah, C. W., & Yap, J. Y. (2024). Self-influencer congruence, parasocial relationships, credibility, and purchase intentions: A sequential mediation model. *Journal of Relationship Marketing, 23*(1), 1–20. https://doi.org/10.1080/15332667.2023.2216373

Koutromanou, E., Sotirakou, C., & Mourlas, C. (2023). Examining visual impact: Predicting popularity and assessing social media visual strategies for NGOs. *Online Media and Global Communication, 2*(4), 594–620.

Kyrylenko, Y. (2024). Chatbots and virtual assistants vs. human agents in IT customer support.

Labrecque, L. I. (2014). Fostering consumer-brand relationships in social media environments: The role of parasocial interaction. *Journal of Interactive Marketing, 28*(2), 134–148. https://doi.org/10.1016/j.intmar.2013.12.003

Ladhari, R., Massa, E., & Skandrani, H. (2020). YouTube vloggers' popularity and influence: The roles of homophily, emotional attachment, and expertise. *Journal of Retailing and Consumer Services, 54*, Article 102027.

Leduc, J. (2022). *Kneeling for justice: A study on how the 30th anniversary of the Nike "Just Do It" Campaign starring colin kaepernick was portrayed by the media* (Doctoral dissertation, Université d'Ottawa/University of Ottawa).

Lee, S. A., & Lee, M. (2017). Effects of relationship types on customers' parasocial interactions: Promoting relationship marketing in social media. *Journal of Hospitality and Tourism Technology, 8*(1), 133–147. https://doi.org/10.1108/JHTT-09-2016-0053

Lehr, A., Büttgen, M., & Bartsch, S. (2021). Don't jump on the bandwagon: Negative effects of sharewashing. *Schmalenbach Journal of Business Research, 73*(1), 75–123. https://doi.org/10.1007/s41471-021-00109-5

Leibenstein, H. (1950). Bandwagon, snob, and Veblen effects in the theory of consumers' demand. *The Quarterly Journal of Economics, 64*(2), 183–207.

Lele, A. (2021). *Factors influencing consumer loyalty in augmented reality beauty apps: Sephora virtual artist empirical study* (Doctoral dissertation, Toronto Metropolitan University).
Lou, C., Kiew, S. T. J., Chen, T., Lee, T. Y. M., Ong, J. E. C., & Phua, Z. (2023). Authentically fake? How consumers respond to the influence of virtual influencers. *Journal of Advertising, 52*(4), 540–557. https://doi.org/10.1080/00913367.2022.2149641
Manorome, C., Brodmerkel, S., & Mitchell, M. (2023). *It definitely makes me feel better about working in advertising: Exploring practitioners' perspectives on brand activism* (Doctoral dissertation, Bond University).
Marr, B. (2021). *Extended reality in practice: 100+ amazing ways virtual, augmented and mixed reality are changing business and society*. John Wiley & Sons.
McKirnan, D. J. (1980). The Conceptualization of deviance: A conceptualization and initial test of a model of social norms. *European Journal of Social Psychology, 10*, 79–96.
Melnyk, V., Carrillat, F., & Melnyk, V. (2021). The influence of social norms on consumer behavior: A meta-analysis. *Journal of Marketing, 86*(3), 98–120.
Men, L. R., & Tsai, W. H. S. (2013). Beyond liking or following: Understanding public engagement on social networking sites in China. *Public Relations Review, 39*(1), 13–22. https://doi.org/10.1016/j.pubrev.2012.09.013
Milgram, S., Bickman, L., & Berkowitz, O. (1969). Note on the drawing power of crowds of different size. *Journal of Personality and Social Psychology, 13*, 79–80.
Morgan, T. J. H., & Laland, K. N. (2012). The biological bases of conformity. *Frontiers in Neuroscience, 6*, 87.
Nadroo, Z. M., Lim, W. M., & Naqshbandi, M. A. (2024). Domino effect of parasocial interaction: Of vicarious expression, electronic word-of-mouth, and bandwagon effect in online shopping. *Journal of Retailing and Consumer Services, 78*, Article 103746. https://doi.org/10.1016/j.jretconser.2024.103746
Nasser, L. (2023). *Credibility of electronic word of mouth in the social commerce context: The case of tripadvisor* (Doctoral dissertation, Université d'Ottawa/University of Ottawa).
Neubaum, G., & Krämer, N. C. (2017). Opinion climates in social media: Blending mass and interpersonal communication. *Human Communication Research, 43*(4), 464–476.
Noelle-Neumann, E. (1974). The spiral of silence: A theory of public opinion. *Journal of Communication, 24*(2), 43–51.
Noelle-Neumann, E. (1991). The theory of public opinion: The concept of the spiral of silence. *Annals of the International Communication Association, 14*(1), 256–287.
Nowak, A., Szamrej, J., & Latane, B. (1990). From private attitude to public opinion—A dynamic theory of social impact. *Psychological Review, 97*, 362–376.
Nowland, R., Necka, E. A., & Cacioppo, J. T. (2018). Loneliness and social internet use: Pathways to reconnection in a digital world? *Perspectives on Psychological Science, 13*(1), 70–87.
Oyedele, A., & Goenner, E. (2021). Propensity to use smartbands to engage with brands and the moderating role of the bandwagon effect on satisfaction. *Journal of Consumer Behaviour, 20*(3), 709–724.
Pascual, A., Salanova, T., Bouhassine, I., Denis-Remis, C., Priolo, D., Girandola, F., & Guéguen, N. (2021). Does "Chaining" always work towards compliance gaining? The case of the "But You Are Free" technique and social proof applied to charitable donation. *European Review of Applied Psychology, 71*(3), Article 100654.
Poddar, A., Banerjee, S., & Sridhar, K. (2019). False advertising or slander? Using location based tweets to assess online rating-reliability. *Journal of Business Research, 99*, 390–397. https://doi.org/10.1016/j.jbusres.2017.08.030
Rachmad, Y. E. (2024). *The future of influencer marketing: Evolution of consumer behavior in the digital world*. Sonpedia Publishing Indonesia.
Roethke, K., Klumpe, J., Adam, M., & Benlian, A. (2020). Social influence tactics in e-commerce onboarding: The role of social proof and reciprocity in affecting user registrations. *Decision Support Systems, 131*, Article 113268.

Salminen, J., Kandpal, C., Kamel, A. M., Jung, S. gyo, & Jansen, B. J. (2022). Creating and detecting fake reviews of online products. *Journal of Retailing and Consumer Services, 64*. https://doi.org/10.1016/j.jretconser.2021.102771

Salmon, S. J., De Vet, E., Adriaanse, M. A., Fennis, B. M., Veltkamp, M., & De Ridder, D. T. (2015). Social proof in the supermarket: Promoting healthy choices under low self-control conditions. *Food Quality and Preference, 45*, 113–120.

Santos, Z. R., Cheung, C. M., Coelho, P. S., & Rita, P. (2022). Consumer engagement in social media brand communities: A literature review. *International Journal of Information Management, 63*, Article 102457.

Schneider, D., Klumpe, J., Adam, M., & Benlian, A. (2020). Nudging users into digital service solutions. *Electronic Markets, 30*, 863–881.

Scholl, H. (2018). *Facebook Instagram stories marketing ads pictorial training guide*. Estalontech.

Sigurðardóttir, G. R. (2019). *Using social proof techniques and attributes of social media influencers to promote fresh fish products* (Doctoral dissertation).

Song, Y., Wang, L., Zhang, Z., & Hikkerova, L. (2023). *Do fake reviews promote consumers' purchase intention?* https://doi.org/10.1016/j.jbusres.2023.113971

Sridhar, S., & Srinivasan, R. (2012). Social influence effects in online product ratings. *Journal of Marketing, 76*(5), 70–88.

Stok, F. M., & de Ridder, D. T. D. (2019). The focus theory of normative conduct. In K. Sassenberg & M. Vliek (Eds.), *Social psychology in action* (pp. 96–110). Springer.

Sykora, M., Elayan, S., Hodgkinson, I. R., Jackson, T. W., & West, A. (2022). The power of emotions: Leveraging user generated content for customer experience management. *Journal of Business Research, 144*, 997–1006.

Talib, Y. Y. A., & Saat, R. M. (2017). Social proof in social media shopping: An experimental design research. In *SHS Web of Conferences, 34*. EDP Sciences.

Tennant, J. P., Dugan, J. M., Graziotin, D., Jacques, D. C., Waldner, F., Mietchen, D., & Colomb, J. et al. (2017). A multi-disciplinary perspective on emergent and future innovations in peer review. *F1000Research, 6*.

Tsiotsou, R. H. (2016). The social aspects of consumption as predictors of consumer loyalty: Online vs offline services. *Journal of Service Management, 27*(2), 91–116. https://doi.org/10.1108/JOSM-04-2015-0117

Tyagi, M., & Tyagi, S. (2024). Consumer experience and decision-making in the metaverse: Marketing 2.0 beyond traditional boundaries. In *Consumer experience and decision-making in the metaverse* (pp. 57–77). IGI Global.

Ulusoy, S. (2024). The use of augmented reality (ar) and virtual reality (vr) in tourism marketing. *Bulletin of Dulaty University, 14*(2), 212–225.

Vandenbosch, L., Fardouly, J., & Tiggemann, M. (2022). Social media and body image: Recent trends and future directions. *Current Opinion in Psychology, 45*, Article 101289.

Vashishth, T. K., Sharma, K. K., Kumar, B., Chaudhary, S., & Panwar, R. (2025). Enhancing customer experience through AI-enabled content personalization in E-commerce marketing. *Advances in Digital Marketing in the Era of Artificial Intelligence*, 7–32.

Walter, N., Föhl, U., Sander, F., & Nies, A. (2024). Act as you preach! Authentic brand purpose versus "woke washing's" impact on brand credibility: The moderating role of cause involvement and consumer skepticism. *Journal of Business Research, 184*, Article 114868.

Walther, J. B., & Jang, J. (2012). Communication processes in participatory websites. *Journal of Computer-Mediated Communication, 18*(1), 2–15.

Wang, R., Bush-Evans, R., Arden-Close, E., Bolat, E., McAlaney, J., Hodge, S., Thomas, S., & Phalp. K. (2023). Transparency in persuasive technology, immersive technology, and online marketing: Facilitating users' informed decision making and practical implications. *Computers in Human Behavior, 139*, 107545.

Wiedmann, K. P., & Von Mettenheim, W. (2021). Attractiveness, trustworthiness and expertise–social influencers' winning formula? *Journal of Product & Brand Management, 30*(5), 707–725.

Yuan, C. L., Kim, J., & Kim, S. J. (2016). Parasocial relationship effects on customer equity in the social media context. *Journal of Business Research, 69*(9), 3795–3803. https://doi.org/10.1016/j.jbusres.2015.12.071

Yuan, C., Wang, S., Liu, Y., & Ma, J. W. (2023). Factors influencing parasocial relationship in the virtual reality shopping environment: The moderating role of celebrity endorser dynamism. *Asia Pacific Journal of Marketing and Logistics, 35*(2), 398–413. https://doi.org/10.1108/APJML-06-2021-0402

Yuksel, M., & Labrecque, L. I. (2016). Digital buddies": Parasocial interactions in social media. *Journal of Research in Interactive Marketing, 10*(4), 305–320. https://doi.org/10.1108/JRIM-03-2016-0023

Zhang, H. (2024). Influencer-generated content on social media: How does influencers' self-disclosure affect followers' purchase intentions? *Asia Pacific Journal of Marketing and Logistics, 37*(2).

Zheng, R., Li, Z., & Na, S. (2022). How customer engagement in live-streaming affects purchase intention and customer acquisition: E-Tailer's perspective. *Journal of Retailing and Consumer Services, 68*, Article 103015.

Exploring the Role of Social Media-Based Marketing Strategy

Akshita Tiwari, Hare Krishna Chaudhary, and Malini Singh

Abstract

This chapter aims to explore the significant impact of social media on business practices, consumer engagement, and brand management. By examining how social media marketing has transformed traditional marketing methods, the chapter highlights the dynamic, interactive nature of social media and its influence on consumer behaviour and brand perception. The chapter begins by tracing the evolution of social media platforms and their increasing role in shaping the marketing landscape through theory synthesis method. It then shifts focus to the analysis of various social media-based marketing strategies, such as content marketing, influencer marketing, and targeted advertising. The chapter shows that social media marketing strategies, including content marketing, influencer marketing, and targeted advertising, have reshaped how businesses approach consumer engagement and brand management. However, the analysis also identifies several challenges within social media marketing. Ethical issues such as data privacy concerns, misinformation, and the impact of algorithmic biases present ongoing challenges for businesses and consumers alike. Maintaining transparency and integrity in social media marketing is essential to sustaining consumer trust. The findings of this chapter have several key implications for businesses and marketers. It emphasizes the importance of creativity, audience engagement, and timely execution in developing successful social media marketing campaigns. As the landscape continues to evolve, staying up-to-date with emerging trends and new platforms is essential for marketers

A. Tiwari · H. K. Chaudhary (✉) · M. Singh
Amity University, Noida, India
e-mail: hk2191chy@gmail.com

A. Tiwari
e-mail: atiwari11@amity.edu

M. Singh
e-mail: msingh22@amity.edu

© The Author(s), under exclusive license to Springer Nature Singapore Pte Ltd. 2026
N. S. Jayawardena et al. (eds.), *Digital Advertising and Consumer Behavior*,
Management for Professionals, https://doi.org/10.1007/978-981-95-7809-2_2

to remain competitive. The increasing role of artificial intelligence in personalizing marketing efforts also highlights the need for businesses to adopt innovative technologies to enhance consumer targeting and engagement.

1 Introduction

In today's world, driven by the digital revolution, the relationship between businesses and consumers has undergone a significant transformation, and this shift has radically altered marketing practices. The rise of the internet, rapid technological advancements, and the increasing penetration of digital devices into daily life have all disrupted the traditional frameworks of marketing. In this new reality, social media platforms have emerged as pivotal players in marketing, opening up unprecedented economic opportunities. Initially developed for social interaction and communication, social media channels have evolved into powerful marketing tools that enable businesses to establish their brands, foster customer loyalty, and drive growth (Kaplan & Haenlein, 2010). This digital transformation is reshaping how marketing is conducted. Traditional marketing methods, which relied on print media, television commercials, and radio advertising, are being replaced by more engaging and interactive approaches facilitated by social media. One of the main distinctions between old and new marketing strategies is the communication style. Traditional marketing was predominantly a one-way communication channel where businesses broadcast their messages to consumers with little to no feedback. In contrast, social media marketing facilitates an active two-way dialogue between businesses and consumers, allowing customers to influence brand narratives and perceptions (Mangold & Faulds, 2009). This shift has given consumers a more significant role in shaping the stories and identities of the brands they interact with.

In today's competitive market, it would be nearly impossible for businesses to thrive without utilizing social media as a marketing tool. Social media offers a novel approach by integrating real-time communication, personalization, and analytics into a single platform. With billions of users across Facebook, Instagram, Twitter, LinkedIn, and TikTok, social media presents businesses with vast, diverse audiences. This enables companies not only to retain existing customers but also to explore new markets and demographics. Brands now have the ability to build stronger, more personal relationships with their audiences, offering them exceptional experiences. Through various strategies, including content marketing, influencer partnerships, and targeted advertising, social media has revolutionized the ways businesses create and expand their brand presence. Furthermore, social media marketing provides businesses with valuable data that can guide decision-making. Through metrics like engagement rates, clicks, and demographic information, businesses can tailor their marketing campaigns to meet specific goals. Social media platforms allow companies to experiment with different types of content, refine messages, and instantly gauge consumer reactions. The seamless integration of social media with other marketing channels gives businesses control over and visibility into every aspect of their marketing efforts, making it one of the most dynamic and adaptable tools available in the marketing landscape.

However, as social media has become more integral to marketing, it has also introduced new challenges. This chapter seeks to explore the growing significance of social media in marketing, examining how it has evolved and how businesses can strategically leverage it. The objective is to provide a comprehensive understanding of how businesses can harness social media as a tool for marketing success. The chapter will begin by exploring the history and rise of social media platforms and their increasing use in business. It will also focus on the changing dynamics of marketing, particularly with the advent of new strategies such as content marketing, influencer marketing, and targeted advertising, which have reshaped both marketing practices and consumer behavior (Felix et al., 2017).

One of the key components of this chapter is a detailed examination of content marketing, where businesses create and distribute valuable, relevant content to attract and retain customers. This approach is crucial for building brand authority and long-term customer loyalty. Similarly, influencer marketing has emerged as a vital strategy, where companies collaborate with social media personalities to promote their products. Influencers often possess highly engaged followings, allowing businesses to target specific groups effectively and authentically. In addition, the chapter will explore targeted advertising, a strategy that uses user data to direct advertisements to precise audience segments based on their behavior, preferences, and demographics. This level of personalization helps businesses optimize their advertising budgets by ensuring that their messages reach the right consumers (Freberg et al., 2011).

The effectiveness of these strategies will be illustrated through industry examples and case studies, which will highlight how different tactics have been successfully executed to meet marketing goals. These case studies will emphasize the importance of creativity, audience engagement, and the timing of marketing campaigns, all of which are critical to achieving success in social media marketing (Tuten & Solomon, 2017). However, social media marketing is not without its challenges. The chapter will address key ethical concerns, such as data privacy, the spread of misinformation, and the risks of algorithmic biases. These issues highlight the need for businesses to uphold transparency and high ethical standards to maintain consumer trust and confidence in their marketing efforts (Huang & Rust, 2021).

In addition to these challenges, the chapter examined the changes occurring in social media marketing due to the emergence of new platforms, evolving user behaviors, and the increasing role of artificial intelligence (AI) in marketing. AI is playing a critical role in automating tasks, segmenting consumer groups, and enhancing personalized marketing strategies, which helps businesses improve the effectiveness of their campaigns. As consumer preferences shift towards engaging and meaningful content, marketers must quickly adapt to these trends to remain competitive. The objective of this chapter is to empower marketers and businesses with the tools and knowledge necessary to navigate the complexities of social media marketing in the digital age. By examining strategic approaches, case studies, and anticipating future trends, this chapter will provide a comprehensive analysis of how social media can be leveraged effectively in the modern marketing environment. The research gap identified in this chapter lies in the rapidly evolving nature of social media platforms, consumer behavior, and emerging technologies like AI, which necessitate ongoing adaptation and exploration in marketing practices.

2 Evolution of Social Media and Marketing

Historical Development of Social Media Platforms

Social media is constantly reshaping itself having started as simple social networks. The first social networking sites that gained great popularity were Friendster, 2002 and MySpace, 2003, during their heydays people could create profiles and post updates, but it was rare for people to remain active on such pages. This changed with the advent of Facebook in 2004, which was originally envisioned as a platform for college students, but quickly expanded its reach in a short time. Whereas previous social networks operated on users' pseudonyms, Facebook and its users utilized real names and uploaded pictures, which were more appealing to others than the outdated social networks (Kaplan & Haenlein, 2010).

A few years later, other content-based platforms came into the spotlight: video platforms include YouTube (2005) and photo sharing services include Instagram (2010) and even microblogging on Twitter (2006). These resources allowed users to do more than just post text. There were options to upload videos and pictures, and even voice communication was possible. The growth in social media was the consequence of the evolution of mobile devices; social media websites changed their structure to serve the lifestyle of the average user who is constantly on the go (Kietzmann et al., 2011).

The Evolution of Social Media from Social Interactions to Branding

Social media's function changed from a tool of interpersonal communication to a fully developed marketing tool as enterprises appreciated its ability to connect and engage with consumers. Marketers around the world took another leap in 2007 when Facebook introduced its ad system that permitted companies to target their advertising to specific user information like geography, interests and patterns of behavior (Leeflang et al., 2014). This was the first revolution in the evolution of social networks into effective marketing tools.

With the increasing number of companies in social networks the development of these platforms has acquired new dimensions. In 2016, Instagram rolled out the Instagram Stories feature, which provided brands the opportunity to engage their customers with content that is time-bound and drives engagement in more spontaneous and authentic ways. Sponsored content on YouTube also proved useful for brands in targeting niche audiences via influencers and content creators. Social media became an important element of the marketing mix that was able to engage the brand directly with the offered audience and interacted with them (Mangold & Faulds, 2009).

Notably, the incorporation of social commerce—the ability to buy things directly from the social network—has endorsed the use of social media in the purchase decisions of consumers. Now users can shop on apps without leaving them, something that blends social communication with eCommerce but which traditional marketing channels never achieved (Kaplan & Haenlein, 2010).

Emerging Role of Social Media Marketing in Changing Marketing Style

The role of social media in the development of marketing tendencies nowadays is not to be neglected. In 2023, a study revealed that there were about 4.8 billion social media users around the world, and consequently, such platforms have become vital sources of information for marketers wanting to target a broad and diverse audience (Statista, 2023). Apart from advertising, social media has an even bigger function in the modern world, namely, brand development, consumer relations and brand reputation. Businesses have found social media sites such as Instagram, TikTok, and Pinterest as effective marketing platforms in advertising their businesses by creating exciting ways to market their goods and services. Influencer marketing is among the best performing salt over other conventional marketing techniques. This target segmentation is key in reaching the most distinct consumers of Generation M which according to the Harvard Business Review constitute a third of the total population (Fuchs, 2015). Generation of Z has always relied on peer-to-peer marketing campaigns and repeats a mantra "Don't tell me how great your products are, show me." One of the most evident ways of showing a product is showcasing it in various platforms, short videos being the most effective. Over the years, short videos have expanded Montana's narrative with transformational connotations targeting the cultural appropriation perspective and the need for change.

Furthermore, the implementation of data-driven personalization has changed the status quo in the way businesses engage with consumers through social networks. Marketing and responsible tourism practices go hand in hand (Chaudhary et al., 2024, 2025; Chaudhary & Sharma, 2023; Divya Bose & Hare Krishna Chaudhary, 2023; Kumar & Chaudhary, 2023). This was allowed after the brands began practicing data analytical research, creating content, advertisements, and proposals for certain users based on their interests, the history of their activity, and their preferences. This kind of personalization improves the experience of the users as it helps consumers feel important and appreciated, thus promoting brand loyalty and satisfaction towards the given company (Kietzmann et al., 2011). It also appears that as social media advances, so too will its impact on marketing strategies. Marketers should track the latest trends and adjust their strategies according to consumers as well as utilize what is distinct about a particular social media platform for the purposes of the business.

3 Social Media Marketing Strategies

See Table 1.

4 Benefits of Social Media Marketing

The ability to connect with clients is arguably one of the most significant benefits of social media marketing. Intuitively, social networking sites allow businesses to have communications with their clients within the scope of time, thus fostering relationships. Customers can be active through likes, comments, direct messages and shares of their friends encouraging two-way communication that is rarely effective in traditional advertising. Real Time Response: Social media provides

Table 1 Social media marketing strategy (*Source* Authors own work)

Strategy	Description	Benefits	Examples
Content marketing	Creating and sharing valuable, relevant, and consistent content to attract and retain a target audience	Builds brand authority, fosters customer loyalty, educates audience, and drives organic traffic	Blog posts, infographics, videos, eBooks
Influencer marketing	Collaborating with influencers who have a strong following to promote products or services	Increased brand credibility, effective audience targeting, and authentic endorsements	Collaborations with Instagram influencers, YouTube reviews
Targeted advertising	Using social media algorithms to serve tailored ads to specific audience segments based on demographics, interests, and behaviors	Maximizes ROI by reaching the right audience, boosts conversions, and enhances personalization	Facebook Ads, LinkedIn Sponsored Content, Instagram Ads
Social commerce	Integrating shopping features directly into social platforms, allowing users to make purchases without leaving the platform	Simplifies purchase process, enhances user experience, and boosts sales directly from social media	Instagram Shopping, Facebook Marketplace, TikTok Shop

(continued)

Table 1 (continued)

Strategy	Description	Benefits	Examples
Engagement marketing	Encouraging interactions between brands and consumers through polls, comments, likes, and shares	Strengthens customer relationships, builds brand loyalty, and increases brand awareness	Running polls on Twitter, Facebook Q&A, Instagram Stories
User-generated content	Encouraging customers to create and share content related to the brand, such as reviews, photos, or videos	Increases authenticity, builds trust, and enhances social proof	Customer reviews, Instagram hashtag campaigns, testimonials
Live streaming	Using live video to engage with the audience in real-time, showcasing products or services	Provides real-time interaction, boosts engagement, and fosters trust through authentic communication	Facebook Live, Instagram Live, YouTube Live
Hashtag campaigns	Creating and promoting branded hashtags to encourage audience participation and boost visibility	Expands reach, builds community, and increases brand awareness	#JustDoIt (Nike), #ShareACoke (Coca-Cola)
Contests and giveaways	Running promotional contests or giveaways to increase brand awareness and engagement	Drives traffic, increases engagement, and enhances brand visibility	Instagram contests, Twitter giveaways, Facebook sweepstakes
Retargeting	Targeting ads to users who have previously interacted with the brand but did not make a purchase	Increases conversion rates by reminding potential customers of products they viewed	Facebook Retargeting Ads, Google Display Network

Source Developed by authors

an avenue for brands to get instant feedback on any product, service or campaign. For instance, companies are able to monitor customer response and adapt their plans using Twitter and Instagram which improves the overall customer experience (Hudson et al., 2016).

Ability to Engage with the Customers: Polls, quizzes and live streaming create a passive understanding among customers. Instagram stories and Facebook live showcase new products or host Q&A with the audiences i. Consumer Targeting: Social media is effective in building loyalty on its users. A simple reply to a customer/tweet or Facebook wall post can trigger emotions leading to customer loyalty. Wendy's brand personality is shaped by its successful engagement with its users through the witty use of its Twitter account. In the end, social networking sites offer brands the ability to establish a two-way interaction allowing themselves to feel valued thus increasing loyalty and customer retention.

Cost-Effectiveness Compared to Traditional Marketing

It is also worth noting that social media marketing has a much lower cost, making it absolutely realistic even for small enterprises. Placing advertising on TV, in print or billboards is often much more expensive than the few dollars spent on social media advertising. Such platforms allow pages to grow naturally or include paid constructs with reasonable limits.

Free Business Profiles: Creating profiles on websites of social networks such as Facebook, Instagram, and Twitter do not require to pay which encourages different business entities to create an account online without incurring expenses. This is quite essential especially for small businesses or new establishments that are in their first phases of business development.

Affordable Advertising: Advertising on social media platforms such as Facebook Ads and Instagram Ads allows focused advertising however at a lower cost compared to traditional media. Ads can be run for just a few dollars per day, with an emphasis on a specific audience. Therefore, reaching out to the company's audience becomes easier and less costly.

Higher ROI: Social media marketing usually enjoys a higher return on investment (ROI) than other traditional marketing methods as it has the capability to reach a certain target audience with more accuracy. With regards to campaign performance, marketers do not have to wait until the end of the campaign as they are able to analyse its performance through analytics and modify their campaign strategies through based on the results obtained.

The Ability to Engage a Global Market and Enhance Brand Recognition

Social media marketing provides one of the most powerful tools for engaging a wider audience across borders. As of 2023, there are more than 4.9 billion social media users and platforms such as Facebook, Instagram, TikTok and LinkedIn allow companies to market their products and services in diverse aquatic environments (Statista, 2023).

Global Reach: Other than the traditional media that is geographically limited, social media makes it easy for a business, brand or organization to penetrate and engage foreign markets. For example, e-commerce brands such as ASOS or Shein apply social media to capture and maintain customers across several countries with the aim of boosting their sales and recognition internationally (Kaplan & Haenlein, 2010).

Fostering Brand Recall: Brands are more visible on social media than on any other medium. With consistent posts, engrossing content, and engaging campaign activity, companies can potentially grow their audiences. Social media events such as the #IceBucketChallenge and the LeBron James and Nike 'Dream Crazy' campaign used the power of the social media network to promote and generate discussions globally.

Reaching Out: In as much as it global, social media allows branding companies to aim at precision through targeted ads. Many social networking sites like Facebook and Instagram come with advertising targeting tools enabling business to concentrate on specific characteristics such as age, gender, region, education, occupation, and even lifestyle. This enables businesses to focus their advertising strategies towards selected market segments and match their resources adequately.

5 Challenges and Ethical Considerations

One of the foremost issues that raises concern in social media marketing is the ethical use of consumer data. Social media sites gather huge amounts of user data, including demographics, interests, activities, places, and many more. Owing to such a fact, creating a targeted advertisement campaign becomes easier, although this raises a lot of issues in regard to the privacy of people. It is essential for marketers to make sure that they are not infringing the rights of the users about privacy concerns by using or exceeding the limits of data.

Informed Consent: It is crucial for brands to make the consumers aware of the data which is being collected and the purpose of its collection in the first place. It is necessary to provide focuses on what the consumers will be subjecting themselves upon and what the data collection is about by ethically (Martin & Murphy, 2017).

Data Security: Safeguarding end-user information from unauthorized access is extremely important to prevent exposure and abuse. Some responsibility measures such as correct methods of data segregation, and accumulation, and further de-identification of details should be respected in order to protect confidential data.

Minimal Data Collection: Marketers should emphasize data collection aimed at only what is presumed to be the objective. Accumulation of great amounts of data without appropriate justification represents a breach of fundamental ethical standards and could bring distrust (Belanger & Crossler, 2011).

Regulatory Considerations (GDPR, etc.): Governments have instituted several strict measures designed to protect the data belonging to consumers in a bid to protect their privacy. One such regulation is the General Data Protection Regulation (GDPR) which was created by the European Union and went into effect in 2018. In compliance with GDPR, enterprises have to follow stringent rules with regards to personal information collection, storage, and processing. Consent Requirements: Due to GDPR regulations, consent for the collection or processing of personal data should be purely voluntary and explicit. For marketers it means being very careful, so that users understand what is going to be done with their data and that such use is agreed upon. Right to Access and Deletion: It is often referred to as the "right to be forgotten" as people are often able to access their data and request its deletion. This adds extra level for social media marketers to ensure that they have the systems that would prevent non-compliance to requests of this nature. Data Breach Notifications: In this case, organizations are also obligated to inform users and relevant authorities of the breach within a period of 72 h of becoming aware of the breach. This reiterates the need to maintain high data security levels when engaging in social media marketing.

6 Emerging Trends in Social Media Marketing

Rise of New Platforms and Evolving User Behavior

The realm of social media marketing is witnessing new dynamics mainly caused by the entry imperatively new platforms and the evolution of user behavior patterns. Facebook and Instagram might still be loved by many, but there are new entrants in the mix like TikTok, Clubhouse, and BeReal who are gaining traction especially with the younger audience.

TikTok's Explosive Growth: Within the Tiktok application, the emphasis on short videos and the young user group that the platform has easily appealed to, around the world has positioned Tiktok, in no time, as among the fastest growing platforms in the world. With brands beginning to profit from seeing Tiktok content as engaging and able to attract younger audiences through creativity and humor. If their content is appealing to their audience, small content creators and brands can also find huge success through the content-based exploration and dissemination provided by TikTok's algorithm (Kaye et al., 2021).

Evolving User Behaviour: Although consumers are now increasing the number of hours spent on social media platforms, there has been a behavioural change. People do not like to watch well-edited ads anymore, instead they wish they could see something more real and down to earth. This is the reason for apps like BeReal's growing popularity that from the outset is based on users being able to post real moments as they unfold (Iglesias et al., 2020).

The Emergence of Auditory Social Networks: Platforms like Clubhouse, and many others, became very well-known during the COVID-19 period when people were quarantined. Such platforms let their users participate in live, audio only rooms, thus, offering companies a different and more casual approach to communicating with their audience. As such new platforms gain more and more traction, companies will have to re strategize their approach on marketing to fit the new and changing patterns of the audiences who use the platforms to maintain their relevance and enhance engagement on any given social media platform.

Use of AI in Customized Marketing

One of the most influential developments in social media marketing is the advent of AI and the ability for the brands to hyper personalize the experience. AI is used in understanding user information and how they behave so as to develop messages that can be delivered to specific individuals.

AI powered Hyper Personalization: Users of platforms also benefit from AI in terms of recommendation, Facebook and Instagram advised users to only show people and pages relating to their interests, and AI-assisted chatbots offered customer service and suggested products via AI interaction in real-time (Davenport et al., 2020).

AI Content: Thanks to the creation of AI analytical tools, companies can produce dynamic content that best resonates with different audiences. AI utilizes audience data in a number of ways such as recommending when to post, which format to use, be it a video or an image or text, and what type of message will be effective for which audience segment (Jarek & Mazurek, 2019).

AI tools are particularly important for SMO because they help create a structure around social media marketing campaigns which in turn results in more personalized interactions with the consumers and an improvement in the brands' marketing strategies.

7 Future Directions of Social Media Marketing

Future Trends of Social Media Marketing

As a result of technological advancements, changing consumer behavior, and the development of social networks, the environment of social media marketing will look completely different in a few years. The following are some prominent expectations for the future of social media marketing strategies:

Heavier Utilization of Augmented Reality (AR) and Virtual Reality (VR): AR and VR technologies will gradually become common factors in the marketing of social media platforms. Instagram and Snapchat have extended these features by incorporating AR where users get to experience the brand by applying various filters and lenses. In the future as the technology advances, marketers will offer the ability to engage in brand experiences such as trying on clothing virtually or taking a tour of a house virtually when selling real estate (Hilken et al., 2017).

Expansion of Social Commerce: Many social media platforms such as Instagram, Facebook and Tik Tok are anticipated to incorporate e-commerce in their platforms in a form of social commerce which allows consumers to make purchases in their social media platforms. Platforms such as Instagram Shopping, Facebook Marketplace, and Tik Tok's e-commerce features are merging social media with online retail shops. In the future, people will be able to shop directly in social apps which would mean that brands will have to enhance their profile for effective shopping (Zhou et al., 2021).

Evolution of Video Content: There is no doubt that video content, especially short video clips, will remain the most popular form of interaction on social media. TikTok and Instagram Reels have made this type of content popular, so it is something brands have to focus on. Furthermore, the trend of using live content for communication and interaction will also grow which will give brands the ability to conduct live events, launches, and Q&A sessions (Burgess & Green, 2018).

Emergence of Decentralized social media: Due to the increasing number of concerns for data and platform ownership and control, it can be expected that more and more decentralized social media will emerge. Many of these platforms are based on blockchain technology, which gives users more power over their data and interactions and allows them to compete with more established platforms such as Facebook or Instagram. In addition, it will be necessary for brands to find ways to communicate with their consumers on these decentralized platforms without losing transparency and trust (Nguyen et al., 2020).

8 Conclusion

Social media has undeniably transformed the marketing landscape, offering brands unparalleled opportunities for consumer engagement, real-time interactions, and innovative sales avenues through social commerce. As the digital environment evolves, platforms like TikTok, BeReal, and Clubhouse continue to shape new consumer behaviours, particularly among younger audiences such as Gen Z, while traditional platforms like Facebook, Instagram, and LinkedIn adapt by incorporating features like social commerce and augmented reality (AR). The increasing integration of artificial intelligence (AI) into social media marketing has streamlined processes such as ad targeting, automation, and sentiment analysis, resulting in enhanced marketing efficiency and improved ROI. Simultaneously, consumer expectations are shifting towards authenticity, transparency, and genuine engagement, putting pressure on brands to adopt ethical marketing practices. To maintain a competitive edge in this rapidly changing marketing environment, companies must remain agile, continually explore emerging platforms and technologies, and create engaging, personalized content that resonates with their target audience. Authenticity in brand messaging, strengthened by user-generated content and micro-influencer partnerships, will be crucial for fostering consumer trust and loyalty.

Theoretical Implications

This chapter underscores the shift from traditional one-way communication in marketing to a more interactive, two-way engagement, highlighting the need for marketers to adjust their strategies to reflect consumer preferences for engagement and transparency. It challenges conventional product-focused marketing theories, emphasizing the importance of authenticity and trust in building consumer relationships. The rise of AI and automation in marketing also calls for a re-evaluation of established marketing models, showing how personalized, data-driven approaches can enhance customer satisfaction and loyalty. Furthermore, the emergence of social commerce, blending content with direct purchasing options, signals a significant shift in e-commerce, requiring theories to adapt to this convergence of social interactions and transactions.

Managerial Implications

For managers, the key takeaway is the need for flexibility in navigating the ever-changing digital marketing environment. Brands should continuously experiment with new platforms like TikTok and BeReal while adopting AR, VR, and AI to create more engaging and innovative marketing campaigns. Content creation must focus on authenticity, with interactive formats such as live events, user-generated content, and behind-the-scenes insights building deeper connections with audiences. Managers must also adopt data-driven approaches to understand consumer behaviour, ensuring that personalization is balanced with a commitment to data privacy and transparency. Ethical marketing practices are essential for long-term brand loyalty, as consumers expect brands to be genuine, transparent, and responsible in how they engage with them.

Limitations

This chapter has several limitations, primarily due to the rapidly evolving nature of social media. New platforms and technologies emerge frequently, which means that marketing strategies discussed may need constant re-evaluation. While the case studies provide valuable insights, their applicability may vary across different industries and regions, so managers must tailor strategies to their specific context. Over-reliance on AI could also lead to a loss of the personal touch that consumers value, potentially diminishing the effectiveness of automated marketing strategies. Additionally, the ethical and regulatory challenges surrounding data privacy, misinformation, and algorithmic biases remain significant, and businesses must continue to adapt to these evolving challenges to maintain consumer trust.

References

Bakir, V., & McStay, A. (2018). Fake news and the economy of emotions. *Digital Journalism, 6*(2), 154–175.

Baltes, L. P. (2015). Content marketing—The fundamental tool of digital marketing. *Bulletin of the Transilvania University of Brasov, 8*(2), 111.

Belanger, F., & Crossler, R. E. (2011). Privacy in the digital age: A review of information privacy research in information systems. *MIS Quarterly, 35*(4), 1017–1041.

Brennen, J. S., Simon, F. M., Howard, P. N., & Nielsen, R. K. (2020). Types, sources, and claims of COVID-19 misinformation. *Reuters Institute, 7*(3), 1–13.

Brown, D., & Hayes, N. (2015). *Influencer marketing: Who really influences your customers?* Routledge.

Burgess, J., & Green, J. (2018). *YouTube: Online video and participatory culture.* John Wiley & Sons.

Chaffey, D., & Ellis-Chadwick, F. (2019). *Digital marketing: Strategy, implementation and practice.* Pearson Education.

Chaudhary, H. K., & Sharma, T. (2023). Efficient strategies for managing food waste in institutional catering: A comprehensive study. *PUSA Journal of Hospitality and Applied Sciences, 9*(2), 68–75.

Chaudhary, H. K., Singh, M., & Ghosh, P. (2024). Balancing act: Achieving carbon neutrality in star-rated hotels through net zero methodology and responsible tourism practices In *International Conference on Innovation and Regenerative Trends in Tourism and Hospitality Industry (IRTTHI 2024)* (pp. 337–360).

Chaudhary, H. K., Singh, M., & Ghosh, P. (2025). The impact of green technology on guest safety: the mediating roles of responsible tourism practices and guest satisfaction. *Journal of Hospitality and Tourism Insights, 8*(6).

Culnan, M. J., & Armstrong, P. K. (1999). Information privacy concerns, procedural fairness, and impersonal trust: An empirical investigation. *Organization Science, 10*(1), 104–115.

Davenport, T. H., Guha, A., Grewal, D., & Bressgott, T. (2020). How artificial intelligence will change the future of marketing. *Journal of the Academy of Marketing Science, 48*(1), 24–42.

De Veirman, M., Cauberghe, V., & Hudders, L. (2017). Marketing through Instagram influencers: The impact of number of followers and product divergence on brand attitude. *International Journal of Advertising, 36*(5), 798–828.

Divya Bose, & Hare Krishna Chaudhary. (2023). Challenges and opportunities in scaling millet-driven cloud kitchen businesses: A comprehensive study. *EPRA International Journal of Multidisciplinary Research (IJMR),* 155–164.

Felix, R., Rauschnabel, P. A., & Hinsch, C. (2017). Elements of strategic social media marketing: A holistic framework. *Journal of Business Research, 70,* 118–126.

Freberg, K., Graham, K., McGaughey, K., & Freberg, L. A. (2011). Who are the social media influencers? A study of public perceptions of personality. *Public Relations Review, 37*(1), 90–92.

Ghahremanlou, L., Ghasemian, S., & Alvari, H. (2019). Social listening and sentiment analysis using AI: Challenges and opportunities. *IEEE Transactions on Computational Social Systems, 6*(4), 642–653.

Glucksman, M. (2017). The rise of social media influencer marketing on lifestyle branding: A case study of Daniel Wellington. *Elon Journal of Undergraduate Research in Communications, 8*(2), 77–87.

Hilken, T., de Ruyter, K., Chylinski, M., Mahr, D., & Keeling, D. I. (2017). Augmenting the eye of the beholder: Exploring the strategic potential of augmented reality to enhance online service experiences. *Journal of the Academy of Marketing Science, 45*(6), 884–905.

Holliman, G., & Rowley, J. (2014). Business to business digital content marketing: Marketers' perceptions of best practice. *Journal of Research in Interactive Marketing, 8*(4), 269–293.

Huang, M. H., & Rust, R. T. (2020). Artificial intelligence in service. *Journal of Service Research, 21*(2), 155–172.
Huang, M. H., & Rust, R. T. (2021). Artificial intelligence in service. *Journal of Service Research, 24*(1), 30–41.
Hudson, S., Huang, L., Roth, M. S., & Madden, T. J. (2016). The influence of social media interactions on consumer–brand relationships: A three-country study of brand perceptions and marketing behaviors. *International Journal of Research in Marketing, 33*(1), 27–41.
Iglesias, O., Ind, N., & Schultz, M. (2020). Building brands together: Emergence and outcomes of co-creation. *California Management Review, 52*(1), 50–75.
Jarek, K., & Mazurek, G. (2019). Marketing automation and artificial intelligence: The future of marketing? *Entrepreneurial Business and Economics Review, 7*(3), 85–101.
Jefferson, S., & Tanton, S. (2015). *Valuable content marketing: How to make quality content your key to success*. Kogan Page Publishers.
Kaplan, A. M., & Haenlein, M. (2010). Users of the world, unite! The challenges and opportunities of social media. *Business Horizons, 53*(1), 59–68.
Kaye, D. B. V., Chen, X., & Zeng, J. (2021). The co-evolution of TikTok and Instagram: Authenticity, creativity, and algorithmic curation. *New Media & Society*. https://doi.org/10.1177/14614448211013938
Kietzmann, J. H., Hermkens, K., McCarthy, I. P., & Silvestre, B. S. (2011). Social media? Get serious! Understanding the functional building blocks of social media. *Business Horizons, 54*(3), 241–251.
Koblin, J. (2018). How Glossier thrives by building a cult following. *New York Times*. https://www.nytimes.com
Kumar, A., & Chaudhary, K. H. (2023). Empowering diversity: Role of artificial intelligence in promoting gender inclusion within the hotel industry. *Social, Economic and Gender Inclusiveness in Tourism and Hospitality Industry*, 2–11.
Leeflang, P. S., Verhoef, P. C., Dahlström, P., & Freundt, T. (2014). Challenges and solutions for marketing in a digital era. *European Management Journal, 32*(1), 1–12.
Luo, X., & Xu, M. (2021). How AI-Driven automation is transforming social media advertising. *Journal of Interactive Marketing, 56*, 23–36.
Mangold, W. G., & Faulds, D. J. (2009). Social media: The new hybrid element of the promotion mix. *Business Horizons, 52*(4), 357–365.
Martin, K. E., & Murphy, P. E. (2017). The role of data privacy in marketing. *Journal of the Academy of Marketing Science, 45*(2), 135–155.
Nguyen, B., Simkin, L., & Canhoto, A. I. (2020). Blockchain and the future of digital marketing. *Journal of Strategic Marketing, 28*(1), 1–14.
Noble, S. U. (2018). *Algorithms of oppression: How search engines reinforce racism*. NYU Press.
O'Neil, C. (2016). *Weapons of math destruction: How big data increases inequality and threatens democracy*. Crown.
Pera, R., Viglia, G., & Furlan, R. (2016). Who am I? How compelling self-storytelling builds digital personal reputation. *Journal of Interactive Marketing, 35*, 44–55.
Powers, T. (2018). The evolving nature of online targeted advertising: Past, present, and future. *Journal of Interactive Advertising, 18*(1), 1–6.
Pulizzi, J. (2012). The rise of storytelling as the new marketing. *Publishing Research Quarterly, 28*(2), 116–123.
Pulizzi, J. (2014). *Epic content marketing: How to tell a different story, break through the clutter, and win more customers by marketing less*. McGraw-Hill Education.
Schaefer, M. W. (2020). *Marketing rebellion: The most human company wins*. Schaefer Marketing Solutions.
Sharma, R. (2020). Authenticity in the age of social media. *Journal of Consumer Research, 46*(4), 673–675.
Sokol, M. (2018). Nike's bold gamble: The Colin Kaepernick "Dream Crazy" Campaign. *Forbes*. https://www.forbes.com
Spotify. (2022). *Spotify wrapped 2022: The year in listening*. https://newsroom.spotify.com

Statista. (2023). *Number of social media users worldwide from 2017 to 2027 (in billions)*. https://www.statista.com/statistics/278414/number-of-worldwide-social-network-users/

Tene, O., & Polonetsky, J. (2018). Big data for all: Privacy and user control in the age of analytics. *Northwestern Journal of Technology and Intellectual Property, 11*(5), 239–273.

Tuten, T. L., & Solomon, M. R. (2017). *Social media marketing*. Sage.

Verhoef, P. C., Kannan, P. K., & Inman, J. J. (2015). From multi-channel retailing to omnichannel retailing: Introduction to the special issue on multi-channel retailing. *Journal of Retailing, 91*(2), 174–181.

Voorveld, H. A. M., van Noort, G., Muntinga, D. G., & Bronner, F. (2018). Engagement with social media and social media advertising: The differentiating role of platform type. *Journal of Advertising, 47*(1), 38–54.

Zhou, L., Zhang, Y., & Zimmerman, J. (2021). Social commerce research: An integrated view. *Electronic Commerce Research and Applications, 48*, Article 101077.

Digital Influence: Leveraging Social Media to Drive Brand Awareness and Product Discovery

Deepana Palanivel, Jyotsna Puthalath Nadukkandi, and Uthamaramasamy Vani

Abstract

With the advent of the digital era, social media platforms have become a crucial aspect of consumer product discovery, evaluation, and purchase. This chapter explores the intricate role of social media in product discovery, examining the mechanisms, strategies, and impacts that make up this new process. Through a close analysis of the top influencer marketing strategies, user-generated content (UGC), and targeted advertising, the chapter highlights how brands leverage social media to engage and connect with potential buyers. Successful brand examples of Glossier, Gymshark, and Starbucks illustrate the actual application of these strategies, the effectiveness of which is illustrated by the capacity of social media to drive product discovery and activity. The chapter also discusses the psychological factors of consumer behavior, including the role of social proof and engaging content in influencing purchase decisions. It also addresses the problems and ethical issues of social media marketing, including algorithm changes, information overload, and data privacy. Continuing, the chapter discusses trends such as social commerce, augmented reality (AR), and live shopping, and how these will affect brands. By understanding the tactics and mechanisms of success on social media, brands can best leverage these sites to maximize visibility, engagement, and sales in a constantly evolving digital landscape.

D. Palanivel (✉)
PSGR Krishnammal College for Women, Coimbatore, India
e-mail: deepanapalanivel@gmail.com

J. P. Nadukkandi · U. Vani
PSG College of Arts and Science, Coimbatore, India
e-mail: vani@psgcas.ac.in

© The Author(s), under exclusive license to Springer Nature Singapore Pte Ltd. 2026

N. S. Jayawardena et al. (eds.), *Digital Advertising and Consumer Behavior*,
Management for Professionals, https://doi.org/10.1007/978-981-95-7809-2_3

1 Introduction

Social media sites in the present online era have become some of the strongest forces that significantly influence consumers' learning, evaluation, and purchasing of goods. With millions, if not billions, of users and several interactive methods at their reach, such platforms offer several channels through which brands can reach out to prospective consumers in new forms (Kaplan & Haenlein, 2010). The effortless integration of social media into everyday life has created a vibrant ecosystem where product discovery is not only made easy but also intensified through a number of innovative platforms.

Other than influencer marketing, social media websites use advanced algorithms to provide targeted advertising. These advertisements are tailored to suit the interests, actions, and demographics of unique user groups such that the right products are being offered to the right people at the right moment (Tuten & Solomon, 2020). Such targeted precision raises conversion rates and engagement, and as such, it is a solid technique for brands that want to promote their presence and sales. Moreover, social media sites offer room for user-generated content (UGC), where users post their reviews and experiences of a product. UGC serves as social proof and drives others' purchase decisions based on authentic and compelling testimonials (Chen et al., 2011). Brands also invite users to utilize particular hashtags or engage in campaigns that create UGC, subsequently increasing their reach and trustworthiness.

This chapter discusses the role of social media in product discovery by examining mechanisms, strategies, and effects on this phenomenon. It looks into how brands exploit various social media capabilities to talk to consumers, raise brand consciousness, and prompt purchases. Through an exploration of pivotal tactics like influencer marketing, user-generated content, and targeted ads, this chapter points out the way in which social media has redefined the dynamics of product discovery (Kotler et al., 2021). Case studies of brands like Glossier, Gymshark, and Starbucks also provide the real-life application and efficacy of social media tactics in boosting product discovery and consumer interaction. From these examples, readers learn about best practices and innovative methods that can be emulated to achieve similar success.

The chapter also delves into the psychological effects of consumer behavior, highlighting how social proof and compelling content drive buying decisions (Cialdini, 2001). In addition, it discusses the issues and ethical dilemmas of social media marketing, such as algorithm updates, content overload, and data privacy, to give a balanced view. Finally, new trends like social commerce, augmented reality (AR), and live shopping are analyzed in terms of their possible influence on brands. Deciphering the strategies that make social media successful, brands can maximize these platforms to increase visibility, engagement, and sales in a constantly changing digital environment. This analysis provides readers with the insight to deal with the intricacies of social media marketing and maximize its potential effectively.

2 The Evolution of Social Media as a Commerce Platform

Historical Context

Social media first began as a venue for interpersonal communication and exchange of personal information. Sites like Facebook, Twitter, and Instagram initially were created to establish social connections and communities (Kaplan & Haenlein, 2010). These sites, over time, developed by adding business features, ultimately becoming very effective tools for business and e-marketing.

Early Days: The Dawn of Social Media

During the beginning of social media, socialization on an individual level was the major emphasis. MySpace, Friendster, and eventually Facebook were built to create connections and interactions among people (Boyd & Ellison, 2007). People rushed to these websites to share updates about themselves, making small revelations about their day, their thoughts, and experiences with their group of friends and relatives. The updates in those early days were personal and casual, a means of staying in touch.

Sharing pictures was another central aspect of early social media. People posted pictures of vacations, family events, and everyday life, building virtual photo albums that their friends could see and comment on (Lenhart & Madden, 2007). Through visual storytelling, people were able to convey their experiences in a more interactive and immersive manner. Media like private messaging, public comments, and reaction buttons like "likes" further increased engagement to help solidify social connections and enhance a sense of belonging in online communities. Overall, the early history of social media was marked by a focus on personal relationships and personal expression (Ellison et al., 2007).

3 Business Integration: The Rise of Social Media for Businesses

As social media sites became more popular and grew in user numbers, companies saw a huge opportunity to use these sites for building brand awareness and engaging with customers. This has resulted in business features being incorporated into social media sites, turning them into a crucial tool for marketing, customer support, and commerce (Tuten & Solomon, 2020).

Facebook Pages was a revolutionary step in online marketing, granting companies their own platform to have an online presence and communicate face-to-face with their followers. In contrast to personal profiles, these pages were created keeping business in view and provided business-centric features like professional profiles, allowing brands to be represented as who they are using logos, cover photos, and descriptive service offerings, in a way acting like digital stores (Zarrella, 2009). They facilitated live customer interaction, with companies posting messages, advertising promotions, and responding to questions using comments or messages, which deepened relationships and increased satisfaction rates (Ashley & Tuten, 2015). Businesses were able to post varied content such as updates, photos, videos, and links, using a content-led approach to display products, provide insights, and keep audiences interested (Kietzmann et al., 2011).

Additionally, Facebook Pages gave brands rich insights into metrics like likes, reach, engagement, and demographics, which enabled companies to optimize marketing efforts and tailor content to what consumers wanted (Tuten & Solomon, 2020). Companies also gained from advertising features that enabled highly targeted campaigns, with audience segmentation used to target specific groups and enhance return on investment (Dwivedi et al., 2021). In addition, these pages enabled brands to promote events, creating buzz around new product releases, sales, or community causes, encouraging user engagement (Hanna et al., 2011). These features made Facebook Pages a critical tool for defining digital marketing strategies, allowing brands to build stronger consumer relationships and drive sales in a more digital world.

4 The Impact of Business Integration on Social Media

The integration of business operations within social media platforms transformed the way companies engage with customers and promote products. It allowed for increased reach, instant interaction, and personalized experiences, ultimately making social media a crucial component of modern business strategies (Tuten & Solomon, 2020). Companies that effectively utilized these features were able to establish strong online communities, foster brand loyalty, and generate revenue through targeted and interactive content. The evolution of business functions on social media marked a fundamental shift in corporate marketing and customer engagement strategies, paving the way for today's advanced digital advertising landscape (Kaplan & Haenlein, 2010).

5 E-Commerce Integration

The integration of e-commerce functionalities, such as shoppable posts and in-app purchases, has transformed social media into a fully functional commerce platform (Dwivedi et al., 2021). Users can now discover and purchase products without leaving the app, streamlining the shopping experience and increasing conversion rates.

Key Milestones

1. **Introduction of Business Pages**

The introduction of business pages on platforms like Facebook allowed brands to establish an online presence and engage directly with customers (Hanna et al., 2011). These pages served as platforms where businesses could post updates, promote offers, and communicate with their audience. Over time, business pages evolved to include features such as customer reviews, direct messaging, and analytics, further enhancing brand-consumer interactions (Ashley & Tuten, 2015).

2. **Instagram Shopping**

Instagram introduced shopping features that enable users to purchase products directly from the app. This development simplified product discovery and purchasing, allowing brands to visually present their products and offer a seamless shopping experience (Kietzmann et al., 2011). Shoppable posts and stories have made it easier for users to browse and buy products without leaving the platform, increasing the efficiency of social commerce (Tuten & Solomon, 2020).

3. **Influencer Marketing**

The rise of influencer marketing has significantly influenced product discovery. Social media influencers with large followings leverage their credibility to endorse products and create authentic content that resonates with their audience (Kaplan & Haenlein, 2010). This marketing strategy has become a fundamental aspect of social media-driven product discovery, as consumers tend to trust influencers' recommendations (Dwivedi et al., 2021).

6 Mechanisms of Product Discovery on Social Media

Influencer Marketing

Influencers are crucial when it comes to product discovery because they promote and recommend products in real life experiences to their followings (Zarrella, 2009). Influencer marketing has been categorized into two broad groups:

Micro-influencers: Such individuals have from 10,000 to 100,000 followers and in most cases maintain highly active fans. Micro-influencers generally specialize in subjects that are a little niche in nature and gain support from committed communities that truly appreciate their verdicts (Ashley & Tuten, 2015).

Macro-influencers: Having more than 100,000 followers, macro-influencers have a wider reach. Though they might have less engagement compared to micro-influencers, their visibility can play a crucial role in product discovery (Kaplan & Haenlein, 2010).

Brands engage with influencers through several strategies, such as sponsored posts, giveaways, and product reviews, to attain new consumers and capitalize on the credibility influencers have built among their audience (Dwivedi et al., 2021). For example, a beauty blogger may develop a makeup tutorial on a cosmetic brand's products and invite people to buy them. User-generated content (UGC) is very significant in the process of discovering products since customers offer personal stories and reviews that contribute to increased trust and social endorsement, which in turn stimulates other people to look into the product (Kietzmann et al., 2011). Hashtag campaigns also strengthen UGC as customers are motivated to use specific hashtags when posting the product.

This not only establishes a store of UGC that prospective customers can discover but also creates a feeling of community and participation, such as in sportswear brands' campaigns encouraging customers to share fitness photos (Tuten & Solomon, 2020). Social media reviews and testimonials on social media sites such as Facebook and Instagram are good indicators of product quality and functionality, giving future buyers confidence and strongly influencing their purchasing decisions (Ashley & Tuten, 2015). Social media's feature of targeted advertising enables brands to develop custom ads based on the behavior and interest of users, thus making the chances of product discovery high (Kaplan & Haenlein, 2010).

Behavioural targeting extends this method further by presenting targeted advertisements according to users' web activities, including the things they have liked or responded to in a similar way (Dwivedi et al., 2021). For instance, people who habitually view fashion-related content can be presented with ads regarding apparel brands of their interest. Geotargeting is a complement to behavioural targeting, and it involves sending ads to people according to their locations, hence more relevant ads that have chances of being discovered. The technique is particularly useful for local companies, including restaurants providing discounts to users within a defined area (Hanna et al., 2011). Combined, these strategies and tools enable brands to establish valuable connections with customers while enhancing product awareness and discovery in a digital age.

Case Study Model 1: Glossier—Creating a Community on Social Media

Glossier is a beauty company that has leveraged social media to create a strong community of active customers. Established in 2014, Glossier has rapidly become a significant force in the beauty industry by focusing on customer feedback and relatable content. The company's customer-centric approach is central to its success. Glossier actively listens to customers and integrates their feedback into product design, which not only aids in creating products that meet audience needs but also fosters community and trust. Regularly sharing user-generated content on its Instagram feed, the brand showcases real customers using its products, building authenticity and relevance. This strategic use of testimonials and user-generated content has been instrumental in cultivating a loyal and active customer base.

Glossier excels in visual storytelling, using high-quality images and videos to demonstrate products and capture audience attention. This is complemented by friendly captions and behind-the-scenes glimpses, which emotionally engage the audience. By revealing how products are developed and sharing real client stories, Glossier establishes a genuine and connective approach. This method boosts engagement and strengthens customer loyalty by creating personal connections with the brand. Additionally, Glossier collaborates with influencers to produce tutorials and product reviews, leveraging their large followings to reach new customers and validate product effectiveness. These partnerships result in authentic and appealing content for prospective customers. Sponsored posts and giveaways further enhance brand visibility, encouraging user interaction and exploring product lines. The synergy between influencer collaborations and promotional efforts has significantly expanded Glossier's customer base and facilitated product discovery.

The outcomes of Glossier's strategic use of social media are evident in its rapid growth in Instagram followership and engagement. This online success is supported by high customer loyalty and frequent repeat purchases, as satisfied customers continue to return. Moreover, Glossier has cultivated a vast network of brand influencers who voluntarily share their experiences with its products. These influencers and active customers contribute to increased brand awareness and credibility, creating a positive feedback loop that strengthens product discovery and fosters enduring brand loyalty.

Case Study Model 2: Gymshark—Using Influencer Marketing and User-Generated Content

Gymshark is a sportswear company that has effectively utilized social media, particularly Instagram, to cultivate a large and dedicated following. Since its launch in 2012, Gymshark has experienced exponential growth due to its innovative and strategic social media marketing approach. A significant contributor to the brand's success is its use of influencer marketing and user-generated content (UGC). By partnering with fitness influencers who align with the brand's values, Gymshark has been able to engage with a well-targeted audience of health-conscious individuals. These influencers, often with large and active followings, produce organic and shareable content that showcases Gymshark's products in real-world contexts. Typical tactics in these collaborations include sponsored material, exercise videos, and giveaways, which help increase product exposure and interaction.

In addition to influencer marketing, Gymshark encourages customers to share their fitness journeys and experiences through specific hashtags. This generates a wealth of user-generated content that the brand actively features on its official social media platforms. This approach not only fosters a sense of community but also creates social proof that resonates with potential buyers. Overall, Gymshark's ability to harness the power of social media has been instrumental in its rapid growth and enhanced brand visibility. By focusing on influencer collaborations and promoting a community-oriented strategy through UGC, the company has established itself as a leading fitness apparel brand.

Gymshark's key strategies include influencer partnerships, community engagement, and a diverse content mix. Through influencer partnerships, Gymshark collaborates with fitness influencers who embody the brand's ethos to showcase products to a highly engaged audience. These collaborations feature sponsored posts where influencers share personal experiences, workout videos highlighting Gymshark apparel, and giveaways that encourage participation. Such partnerships boost the brand's visibility while building trust and credibility among fitness enthusiasts, successfully reaching new customers and fostering community loyalty. Community engagement is another vital strategy, as Gymshark motivates customers to share their fitness journeys using branded hashtags. This creates a repository of motivational content that celebrates individual achievements while inspiring others to join the fitness movement. It builds a strong sense of belonging within the Gymshark community and enhances the brand's credibility through social proof, which appeals to prospective customers. The company also maintains a well-balanced content mix on social media, combining professional product shots, customer testimonials, and motivational posts. Professional images showcase the quality of Gymshark's apparel, while testimonials provide authentic experiences and motivational posts inspire fitness enthusiasts. This cohesive and relatable content strategy helps attract and retain a dedicated audience.

The outcomes of Gymshark's clever social media strategies are evident in its increased brand awareness and sales. The company has built a loyal customer base that actively engages with its content, often sharing their fitness experiences and showcasing Gymshark products. This interaction has fostered a strong sense of community and brand loyalty, with customers feeling deeply connected to the brand and its mission. As a result, Gymshark has emerged as one of the industry leaders in fitness apparel, driven by its successful social media efforts and dedicated customer base.

Case Study Model 3: Starbucks—Engaging Customers Through Interactive Campaigns

Starbucks, a global coffeehouse chain, has effectively used social media to engage customers and drive product discovery. The brand's innovative and interactive campaigns have garnered significant attention and engagement.

Starbucks successfully interacts with its customers by introducing seasonal promotions and challenges that invite users to get involved. A classic instance of this is the "Red Cup Contest," in which customers are encouraged to post pictures of their festive-themed Starbucks cups on social media. These promotions not only create buzz about the brand but also foster a feeling of community among customers. By being a part of these challenges, customers become closer to the brand and to each other, cultivating loyalty and enhancing customer experience overall. The generated content from the campaigns also provides social proof that drives new consumers in and gets brands noticed more.

Starbucks proactively urges customers to share their experiences through branded hashtags, producing a chain of user-generated content that focuses on the individual connections customers feel towards the brand. By engaging with these hashtags, Starbucks develops a sense of community and engagement between its customers. The brand also showcases this user-generated content on its official social media pages, which constructs authenticity and relatability. This approach not only increases the exposure of customer experiences but also provides a level of trust and credibility to the brand, as prospective customers view real-life instances of other people enjoying Starbucks products.

Starbucks actively engages with customer comments and feedback on social media, creating a perception of community and interaction with its fans. By responding to customer questions, accepting compliments, and fixing problems, Starbucks shows that it is dedicated to customer satisfaction. The brand also uses high levels of engagement on its posts as social proof, presenting the interaction and support of its customer base. This heavy engagement works to draw in more customers, as potential customers are driven by the resultant visibility of interest and validation of others. With these measures, Starbucks can successfully establish a loyal and engaged customer base around its brand.

The outcome states that Starbucks' social media efforts have led to strong levels of engagement and participation in interactive campaigns. These campaigns, for example, seasonal challenges and user-generated content efforts, have greatly enhanced both seasonal and new product visibility and discovery. Through the development of a high sense of community and customer interaction, Starbucks has enhanced customer loyalty and brand advocacy. The active engagement and positive word of mouth from customers not only improve the credibility of the brand but also bring in new customers, further establishing Starbucks as a popular and innovative brand in the market.

7 Influence of Social Media on Consumer Conduct

The rise of social media has reshaped the traditional consumer buying process by introducing real-time information and opinion reviews that influence every stage of buying. During the awareness phase, social media creates visibility for new products through organic posts, ads, and influencer mentions. Brands can reach vast audiences and spark interest in their offerings. For instance, a new fashion brand can leverage Instagram ads to display its latest collection to thousands of potential customers. In the consideration phase, consumers explore products by watching reviews, unboxing videos, and engaging with user-generated material, enabling them to make informed decisions. For example, a potential smartphone buyer might watch YouTube reviews and browse social media posts to gather relevant information before purchasing. The purchase stage has been streamlined with direct shopping functionalities on platforms like Facebook and Instagram, offering customers a seamless experience where they can view products, read reviews, and complete purchases within the app. This frictionless process increases the likelihood of completing transactions.

Social proof, a psychological phenomenon where people emulate others' actions, is greatly amplified on social media. Positive engagement, compliments, and influencer endorsements serve as social proof, encouraging others to purchase items. Customer reviews play a pivotal role in building trust and credibility, as high ratings and positive feedback significantly influence prospective buyers' decisions. Social media platforms, much like websites such as Amazon or Yelp, showcase customer feedback, and products with numerous favorable reviews on platforms like Facebook or Instagram are more likely to attract attention. Influencer endorsements further enhance product discovery, as fans view influencers' recommendations as credible. For example, when a popular beauty influencer promotes a skincare product, their followers are often motivated to consider and purchase it. Lastly, user engagement through likes, comments, and shares acts as another layer of social proof, indicating a product's value. Posts that generate substantial attention often prompt users to explore the product themselves, triggering a viral effect that amplifies interest and visibility.

8 Strategies for Effective Social Media Product Discovery

Content reigns supreme on social media, and brands should strive to create visually appealing, informative, and engaging content that resonates with their target audience. Visual content, including high-quality images, videos, and graphics, captures attention and effectively communicates the brand message. This is especially important on platforms like Instagram, where aesthetics play a crucial role in engagement. Brands can use a mix of professional product images, user-generated content, and behind-the-scenes visuals to craft an engaging visual narrative.

Storytelling also plays a key role in driving engagement and product discovery. Emotionally compelling stories help brands convey the value and unique attributes of their products in a way that resonates with customers. For instance, a fashion brand might share the story of its eco-friendly manufacturing process to connect with environmentally conscious consumers. Interactive content, such as quizzes, polls, and live Q&A sessions, boosts user engagement and participation. This type of content not only grabs attention but also provides valuable insights into customer preferences and behavior, which brands can use to refine their marketing strategies and improve product discovery.

Leveraging data analytics is essential for optimizing social media strategies. By analyzing engagement metrics, demographic data, and user activity, brands can fine-tune their content and targeting approaches. Sentiment analysis of customer comments and reviews offers insights into how customers perceive the brand and its products, enabling brands to tailor their content to meet customer needs. For example, if a beauty brand notices negative sentiment around a specific product, it can address the issue and make necessary improvements. A/B testing allows brands to experiment with different content formats and ad types to identify what resonates most with their audience. This method helps refine strategies and optimize engagement for instance, testing two versions of an ad to determine which one drives more clicks and conversions.

Monitoring performance metrics, such as engagement rate, click-through rate (CTR), and conversion rate, provides brands with a clear understanding of the effectiveness of their social media campaigns. By evaluating these key indicators, brands can identify what works and make informed decisions to enhance product discovery. Through a combination of engaging content and strategic analytics, brands can create impactful social media strategies that foster customer engagement and drive success.

9 Challenges and Ethical Considerations

Social media offers numerous opportunities for product discovery, but it also presents challenges such as algorithm changes, content saturation, and maintaining authenticity. Frequent algorithm updates on platforms can affect content visibility, requiring brands to continuously adjust their strategies. Staying informed about these changes and their impact on engagement is essential for maintaining consistent interactions. Brands must remain flexible and ready to adapt their content strategies as algorithms evolve. Content saturation is another challenge, as the vast amount of online content makes it difficult for brands to stand out. To differentiate themselves, brands need to create high-quality, unique content that resonates with their audience. Understanding their target audience thoroughly and crafting tailored content are critical to achieving this goal. Authenticity, especially in the era of sponsored posts and influencer collaborations, is also a significant challenge. Consumers value genuine content, and brands must strike a balance between promotional and authentic messaging. Being transparent about sponsored content and aligning it with the brand's values can help in maintaining authenticity.

Ethical considerations in social media marketing include transparency, data privacy, and responsible influencer partnerships. Transparency is vital, as brands and influencers must clearly disclose sponsored content to maintain audience trust. Practices such as using hashtags like #ad or #sponsored indicate that a post is part of a paid partnership, ensuring credibility. Data privacy is another crucial aspect, with brands needing to protect user data and comply with regulations like GDPR. Being transparent about data collection and usage, implementing robust security measures, and respecting user privacy help build trust with customers. Responsible influencer partnerships are equally important, requiring brands to collaborate with influencers who share their values and ethics. Such partnerships involve clear communication, fair compensation, and adherence to ethical guidelines. Ensuring that influencers provide honest reviews and disclose partnerships fosters trust and authenticity in the relationship. Together, these strategies can help brands navigate the challenges of social media marketing while staying true to their core values.

10 The Future of Social Media in Product Discovery

The landscape of social media is ever-evolving, with new trends and technologies shaping the future of product discovery. Social commerce is expected to grow with the integration of e-commerce features directly within social media platforms, making it easier for users to shop seamlessly. Social commerce allows users to browse, purchase, and share products without leaving the platform. For example, platforms like Instagram and Facebook have introduced in-app shopping features that enable users to buy products directly from the app. Augmented reality (AR) features, such as virtual try-ons, are enhancing the online shopping experience, allowing users to interact with products in a more immersive way. AR can bridge the gap between online and offline shopping by providing a realistic preview of how products will look and fit. For example, beauty brands like Sephora use AR technology to allow users to virtually try on makeup products before making a purchase. Live shopping, which involves live-streaming shopping events, is gaining popularity as it offers real-time product demonstrations and interactions with brand representatives. This allows users to ask questions, see products in action, and make purchases during the live stream, combining the convenience of online shopping with the interactive experience of in-store shopping.

Advances in AI and machine learning are enabling more personalized shopping experiences on social media. Brands can leverage user data to deliver tailored product recommendations and targeted advertisements. Personalization enhances product discovery by presenting users with relevant products based on their preferences and behaviours. For brands, staying ahead of these trends and continuously innovating their social media strategies is crucial to remaining competitive. Adaptability is essential, as brands need to be flexible and adapt to new features and trends. Brands should stay informed about the latest updates and be willing to experiment with new formats and technologies. Focusing on customer needs and preferences ensures that social media efforts resonate with the target audience. Brands should prioritize building relationships with their customers and creating content that adds value to their lives. Consumers are increasingly looking for brands that align with their values, including sustainability and social responsibility. Brands that demonstrate a commitment to ethical practices and social causes can build stronger connections with their audience and enhance product discovery.

11 Conclusion

Social media sites have revolutionized the product discovery and consumer interaction landscape. These sites offer immense opportunities for brands to engage with their target markets in creative ways. Influencer marketing has proven to be a potent weapon, enabling brands to tap into the credibility and reach of users who have established significant followings. Through collaborations with influencers, brands can introduce products in an organic way to fresh audiences and establish trust by way of content relatable to everyday people. User-generated content (UGC) has also become a staple of social media marketing. When customers provide their own personal experiences and reviews, it brings an element of authenticity and social proof that is extremely compelling. Brands that invite and feature UGC enjoy more engagement and a sense of belonging among their customers. Targeted social media advertising allows brands to reach precise groups of people with specific messages. By leveraging knowledge about user habits and interests, brands can offer extremely relevant advertising that will resonate better with targeted consumers. Such accuracy in targeting not only improves the performance of marketing campaigns but also maximizes ad spend. With social media continuously developing, brands must remain in front of trending concepts. Social commerce, in which e-commerce features are brought natively within social media apps, is developing exponentially. With this trend, customers can explore, review, and buy products smoothly within the app, enhancing the customer journey.

Augmented reality (AR) capabilities are also improving the experience of online shopping. AR enables customers to virtually try on merchandise, like clothes or cosmetics, offering a more interactive and engaging means of viewing products. Live shopping events are another phenomenon in the making, providing real time product demonstrations as well as enabling direct interaction between consumers and brands. To continue to thrive in this ever-changing digital world, brands need to keep a customer-focused mindset. This means listening intently to what customers have to say, constantly interacting with the community, and adjusting strategies according to changing consumer tastes. By keeping the needs and interests of their audience at the forefront, brands can establish long-term relationships and foster loyalty. In general, social media websites provide diverse and efficient means for product discovery, and by knowing and utilizing these processes, brands can greatly increase their visibility, interaction, and sales. In the future, with the ever-changing nature of the digital environment, being sensitive to upcoming trends and keeping customer centricity in mind will be increasingly important to success.

References

Ashley, C., & Tuten, T. (2015). Creative strategies in social media marketing: An exploratory study of branded social content and consumer engagement. *Psychology & Marketing, 32*(1), 15–27.

Boyd, D. M., & Ellison, N. B. (2007). Social network sites: Definition, history, and scholarship. *Journal of Computer-Mediated Communication, 13*(1), 210–230.

Chen, J., Fay, S., & Wang, Q. (2011). The role of marketing in social media: How brands influence consumer behavior. *Journal of Marketing Research, 48*(6), 1146–1162.

Cialdini, R. B. (2001). *Influence: Science and practice.* Allyn & Bacon.

Dwivedi, Y. K., Kapoor, K. K., & Chen, H. (2021). *Social media marketing and advertising.* Edward Elgar Publishing.

Ellison, N. B., Steinfield, C., & Lampe, C. (2007). The benefits of Facebook "friends:" Social capital and college students' use of online social network sites. *Journal of Computer-Mediated Communication, 12*(4), 1143–1168.

Hanna, R., Rohm, A., & Crittenden, V. L. (2011). We're all connected: The power of the social media ecosystem. *Business Horizons, 54*(3), 265–273.

Kaplan, A. M., & Haenlein, M. (2010). Users of the world, unite! The challenges and opportunities of social media. *Business Horizons, 53*(1), 59–68.

Kietzmann, J. H., Hermkens, K., McCarthy, I. P., & Silvestre, B. S. (2011). Social media? Get serious! Understanding the functional building blocks of social media. *Business Horizons, 54*(3), 241–251.

Kotler, P., Kartajayasss, H., & Setiawan, I. (2021). *Marketing 5.0: Technology for humanity.* Wiley.

Lenhart, A., & Madden, M. (2007). *Social networking websites and teens: An overview*. Pew Internet & American Life Project.
Tuten, T. L., & Solomon, M. R. (2020). *Social media marketing*. Sage.
Zarrella, D. (2009). *The social media marketing book*. O'Reilly Media.

The Influence of Social Proof and Fear of Missing Out in Social Media Towards Product Experience

Parth Salunke, Anurag Chaturvedi, and Gyandeep Hazarika

Abstract

This chapter sheds light through an organizing framework on how various FOMO and social proof factors influence consumers and their product experiences on social media platforms.Through a rigorous review of past academic studies and marketplace evidence, the chapter develops a conceptual framework. The chapter explains how the coexistence of FOMO and social proof brings forward the synergistic effect of advertising campaigns on consumers' minds on social media platforms. And finally, how it affects the product experiences of consumers at three levels: cognitive, affective, and behavioral. Thus, it offers an in-depth understanding of positive and negative experiences encountered by consumers when faced with the influence of FOMO and social proof, offering a comprehensive outlook in the context of social media platforms. The chapter additionally highlights how consumer involvement, socio-demographic features, and social media platforms and their usage intensity among consumers play a critical role in influencing product experiences when consumers encounter social proof and FOMO. Social proof and fear of missing out (FOMO) are two socio-psychological concepts vital in advertising campaigns to connect with consumers and influence their experiences. The chapters shed light on practical examples and offer valuable insights into how the co-existence of FOMO and social proof affects product experiences.

P. Salunke (✉)
FLAME School of Business, FLAME University, Pune, India
e-mail: Parthsalunkedr95@gmail.com; parth.salunke@flame.edu.in

A. Chaturvedi
Birla Institute of Management Technology, Greater Noida, India

G. Hazarika
MICA: The Schoolof Ideas, Ahmedabad, India

© The Author(s), under exclusive license to Springer Nature Singapore Pte Ltd. 2026
N. S. Jayawardena et al. (eds.), *Digital Advertising and Consumer Behavior*,
Management for Professionals, https://doi.org/10.1007/978-981-95-7809-2_4

1 Introduction

In the digital age, social media platforms such as Instagram, Facebook, and Snapchat influence, shape, and reshape consumer experiences and behavior as consumers incorporate these platforms into their everyday lifestyles (e.g., Salunke & Jain, 2022). These platforms encourage two-way interaction between a brand and consumer, which helps engage consumers, build relationships, and shape experiences (Baumol et al., 2016; Qin, 2020). Thereby, social media becomes a nucleus for brand-consumer interactions. It serves as an advertising channel and redefines how a brand's products are perceived through peer validation, user-generated content, and maybe influencer endorsements (Alves et al., 2016; Salunke et al., 2025). Thus, through such dynamic digital interaction between brands' products on social media and consumers, marketers leverage the two most potent socio-psychological constructs, social proof and fear of missing out (FOMO), to enhance the brand's visibility and awareness, engage consumers, and improve consumer experiences (Amblee & Bui, 2011; Bui et al., 2022). Primarily, social proof enunciates how consumers align their choices and behavior through external validations in uncertain or ambiguous situations. FOMO capitalizes on consumers' feelings of anxiety and apprehensions about potentially missing rewarding product experiences. Even an industry report denotes that 92% of consumers trust friends' recommendations, 72% trust other users' recommendations on social media, nearly 97% believe that online reviews help them purchase, and 56% of American social media users experience FOMO (Wisernotify, 2025). Thus, social proof and FOMO intersection enunciate how immediacy and peer activities' visibility collectively shape and influence consumer product experiences and behavior.

Both social proof and FOMO are essential concepts that tap into consumers' psychological and social triggers that influence consumer perceptions, attitudes, and behavior toward product experiences that need in-depth understanding. Consumers rely primarily on social proofs (external validation or socio-psychological phenomena that consumers confirm through the actions and behaviors of others). However, these social media platforms, along with social proof, also create FOMO by infusing anxiety among consumers that others are enjoying the products while they miss out on opportunities (Flecha Ortiz et al., 2024). For example, through social media, brands create FOMO among consumers by advertising limited offers, offering exclusive content for limited hours, and creating other anxieties through advertising. Consumers purchase such products sometimes without thorough evaluation (Good & Hyman, 2021; Flecha Ortiz et al.,2024). Thus, social proof and FOMO influence consumers and shape attitudes and behaviors toward product experiences. However, sometimes FOMO and social proof create a very high expectation for advertised products, amplifying the positive mindset for product experience among consumers (Hodkinson, 2019). This may not be true in all cases because if products do not live up to the expectation of hype created by FOMO and social proof, consumers may feel tricked, leading to negative emotions and product experience (Morsi et al., 2024).

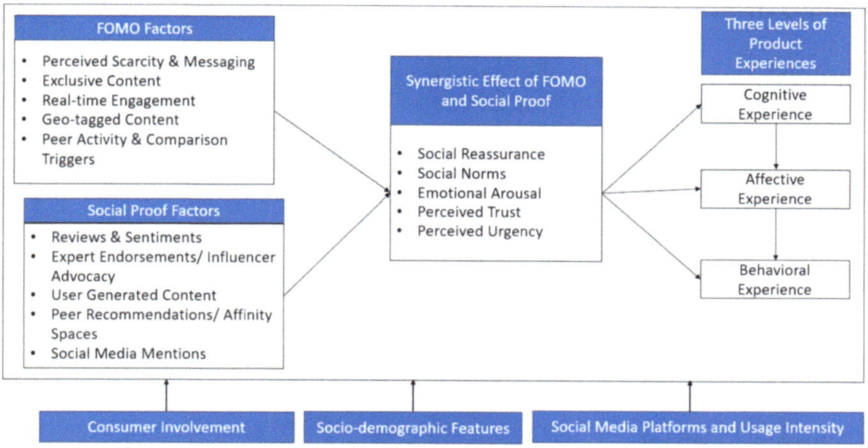

Fig. 1 Influence of FOMO and social proof on product experience

Several academic studies have considered the phenomena of FOMO and social proof in understanding how these concepts influence consumer behavior, and some have looked at experiences, but studies are in silos. Therefore, this chapter addresses the centrality of social proof and FOMO intersection in shaping consumer experiences through a conceptual organizing framework (*Fig. 1*), offering insights on leveraging these constructs in social media to benefit consumer product experiences. The framework presents how social proof and FOMO synergistically heighten the advertised product appeal through enhanced anticipation, urgency, reliability, trust, emotional engagement, etc. At the same time, the chapters elucidate an understanding of how various factors of FOMO and social proof contribute to creating product experiences through integrating research insights and industry examples, explaining the phenomena with practical implications. Figure 1 below highlights various FOMO and social proof factors and how they influence consumer product experiences.

2 FOMO: A Socio-Psychological Driver of Consumer Behaviour

Fear of Missing Out (FOMO) is becoming crucial in psychologically boosting consumer behavior (Hodkinson, 2019; Lu & Sinha, 2024; Meyer et al., 2024). FOMO usually happens when people fear missing out on expected opportunities, awareness, or goods. FOMO-driven marketing initiatives have become a common factor in today's consumer involvement (Sánchez-Fernández & Jiménez-Castillo, 2021; Lou & Yuan, 2019; Lu & Sinha, 2024). FOMO factors are explained briefly with real-time examples to showcase their influence in the subsection below.

Perceived Scarcity & Messaging

Perceived scarcity refers to the understanding that a product/service is in limited supply. This perception creates a sense of urgency and increases desirability, prompting customers to acquire the product for an enriching experience (Cengiz & Şenel, 2024). Marketing decision-makers often combine product shortages with priority messages to amplify these effects and trigger FOMO (Fear of Missing Out).

- *Example*: Airline booking websites usually have a pop-up, "*10 individuals are seeing this flight currently !*" or "*Prices may rise in the next 30 min!*". These strategies impact the customer's emotions to miss out on amazing deals.

Exclusive Content

Exclusive content is created specifically to target niche market consumer segments or to be accessible under certain conditions. Brands cultivate an understanding among consumers about the uniqueness of the content, thereby enhancing FOMO (Aitamurto et al., 2021; Good & Hyman, 2021; Lu & Sinha, 2024). Exclusive content often includes premium versions or early access to goods and services.

- *Example: Director's Cut Versions*: Films like *James Cameron's Avatar: Special Edition* offer fans additional footage, extended scenes, and character moments not available in the original release. Fans are drawn to social media content to experience a richer narrative, creating an exclusive allure.
- *Example:* Bollywood's *Dilwale Dulhania Le Jayenge (DDLJ)* celebrated its 25-year legacy by releasing rare behind-the-scenes footage and archival interviews. These were made available only on specific streaming platforms, compelling fans to subscribe to relive iconic moments, and they were promoted on social media.

Exclusive content also drives social currency, encouraging consumers to share their association with these privileged experiences on social media. This increases FOMO among those who lack access, enhancing the perceived value of the brand or product.

Real-Time Engagement

Real-time engagement involves immediate, dynamic interactions between brands and consumers. By creating time-sensitive opportunities such as live shopping events, flash sales, or limited-time polls, brands foster a sense of urgency that aligns perfectly with FOMO-driven behavior (Lu & Sinha, 2024; Vempati et al., 2023).

- *Example: Instagram Live Shopping*: Retail brands such as Myntra use Instagram's live shopping feature to showcase products in real-time, often accompanied by exclusive discounts available only during the live session. This immediacy encourages impulsive purchasing decisions.
- *Example: Nike's Online Drops*: Limited-edition sneakers from Nike are often released through surprise online drops announced only hours before. Consumers scramble to secure their pairs, driven by the fear of missing out on rare, high-demand items.

The temporary nature of real-time engagement leaves little room for prolonged decision-making, fostering impulsive purchases and heightened consumer excitement.

Geo-Tagged Content

Geo-tagged content targets consumers based on physical location, creating hyper-localized and highly relevant FOMO experiences. By offering deals and promotions tailored to a specific area, brands make their offerings uniquely personalized and time-sensitive (Dijck, 2011; Jiang et al., 2015; Meyer et al., 2024).

- *Example: Domino's Pizza*: Domino's leverages geo-tagging to send app notifications about exclusive deals at nearby outlets, such as "*Buy One, Get One Free—only at your nearest Domino's!*". This encourages consumers to act quickly to capitalize on the offer.
- *Example: Starbucks*: Starbucks uses geo-targeted push notifications to inform customers about location-specific promotions like "*Happy Hour: Buy One, Get One Free at Starbucks Downtown!*". Such notifications drive footfall and make the offers feel highly personalized. Another instance is that some social media platforms, such as Instagram, often play geographically based advertisements for restaurant promotions or other purposes.

Peer Activity & Comparison Triggers

Social comparison is a key factor in FOMO. Watching peers on social media share their purchases, experiences, or achievements often drives people to emulate those behaviors. Brands capitalize on this by encouraging users to showcase their interactions with products or services, thus creating a viral FOMO cycle (Jiang et al., 2015; Whalen et al., 2006; Yaputri et al., 2022).

- *Example: Zomato Gold Membership*: The Zomato Gold Membership includes benefits such as 2-for-1 deals at popular restaurants. When consumers share their dining experiences on social media, their friends may feel forced to subscribe so they don't miss out on similar benefits.

The FOMO Loop: Integration Across Factors

FOMO has become a significant part of modern marketing strategies, using psychological triggers to drive consumer behavior. By employing scarcity perceptions and messaging, exclusive content, real-time engagement, and geolocated content, brands can create engaging campaigns that improve purchase intent and effectively drive engagement (Cengiz & Şenel, 2024; Erlinda & Fatmawati, 2025; Vempati et al., 2023). For example, a consumer might.

- Receive a notification about a limited-time deal (Perceived Scarcity & Messaging).
- Tune into a live shopping event to access the offer (Real-time Engagement).
- See geo-tagged content about the deal being available at a nearby store (Geo-tagged Content).
- Notice their peers' sharing purchases or experiences with the product online (Peer Activity & Comparison Triggers).
- Feel compelled to act immediately, fearing they'll miss out on this exclusive opportunity (Exclusive Content).

However, ethical norms must guide these plans of action to confirm long-term trust and loyalty. Comprehending these principles ensures marketers fully utilize FOMO’s power and construct sustainable associations with their audiences. while driving business success (Cengiz & Şenel, 2024; Lu & Sinha, 2024).

3 Social Proof: Principle of Social Influence

The concept of social proof was discovered in psychology literature while investigating persuasion techniques (Cialdini and Cialdini, 2007). However, it played a massive role in the evolution of humans from the homosapiens. The individual’s life, when zoomed in, the actions and everyday lifestyles are influenced by culture and community (Kroever & C Kluckhohn, 1952). Social proof connects this wavelength of actions and everyday lifestyle practices (Sigurdsson et al., 2020). For example, the way I write a piece of art to describe what my mind possesses is a pattern that is followed every day. Tomorrow, my peers will observe this writing pattern with the right hand or from the left side to the right and subsequently follow the same. But if they asked, where did I learn this pattern, and why did I only follow it? The answer to this question is that I immersed myself in the process of Social Proof (Van Maanen & Van Der Vecht, 2014). Social proof is where I have mimicked the actions as appropriate actions and, like everyone, followed them to behave similarly. Thus, social proof is primarily a social influence only (McMullan et al., 2022). However, social proof differs from direct influence and is based on individual motives and conformity to social customs to maintain social prestige and avoid social sanctions (Bhattacharyya & Bose, 2020).

Today, this phenomenon of social proof is more crucial in the age of social interactions through social media platforms. The arrival of social media creates a virtual world. To many, this opportunity enabled human actions and practices to look further into everyday lives, providing evidence known as social proof (Seo et al., 2018). More than that, the venture of social media into our lives made a social proof concept measurable through social media metrics such as likes and reviews by different customers (Ferreira et al., 2023; Kim et al., 2021). Thus, social media-generated data has provided some metrics to measure social proof's relevance and has shown different exposure to understanding the social proof theory in this digital age. In the virtual world of social media, the literature defines social proof as online social proof (Mathur et al., 2021), as these cues influence consumer behavior and attitude toward shared endorsement content by celebrities, influencers, and other user-generated content (Jennings et al., 2024).

The prime factors that serve as social proof consist of reviews and sentiments, expert endorsements/influencer advocacy, user-generated content, peer recommendations/affinity spaces, and social media mentions. Each play a pivotal role in influencing consumer behavior and product experiences, which are explained below with real-world examples.

Reviews and Sentiments

Social media platforms today serve as channels for customers to share their experiences with the product/brand through reviews and expressing their sentiments (Bhattacharyya & Bose, 2020). Customers with product usage experiences share their direct feedback on the social media platform, express their honest opinions on their own social media page, or express their feedback on the brands' social media page through reviews or drafting the sentiments in the comment box. Customers usually share their comments, such as ratings or testimonials, that help other consumers gauge the product's potential quality, usability, and credibility. Positive reviews received by brands help build trust among other potential consumers, while negative reviews deter a brand's potential buyers (Zhang et al., 2017). Therefore, reviews and sentiments play a critical role in social proof, acting as a mirror for brands to improve their offerings and product experiences.

- *Example*: A post receiving positive reviews and sentiments from customers on Amazon's page for highly-rated products builds trust and encourages potential buyers, which promises better product experiences. Sometimes, consumers share their purchases and reviews on social media platforms like Instagram.
- *Example:* Customers express bad experiences after booking the OYO hotel room services online on LinkedIn, where they share their sentiments of bad hotel places not reaching their expectations, leading to more negative experiences and deterring potential brand consumers.

Expert Endorsements/ Influencer Advocacy

Second, with the massive progress of social media platforms as advertising channels allowing two-way interaction between a brand and a consumer, endorsements have also garnered increasing attention. Today, the growth of users with massive followers on social media platforms such as Instagram has given a new rise to the influencer economy (Vrontis et al., 2021). The influencers are similar to celebrities who capitalize on their strengths in niche areas of content creation and share their endorsements or advocate the positive/negative aspects of the products (Kozinets et al., 2024; Salunke et al., 2025). This acts as social proof for the consumers as influencers are credible sources in consumers' minds and influence consumer decision-making. Thus, these brand endorsements by influencers or experts often sway consumers towards buying through added layers of authenticity and reliability, making the products and their experiences more desirable.

- *Example:* Kylie Jenner's Instagram page is a popular brand advocate, and her recommendations act as social proof in the fashion, beauty, and accessories segment for consumers due to her popularity and massive influence through her credible identity of product recommendations.
- *Example:* Mr. Beast's promotion of gaming apps on platforms such as YouTube increased download and user engagement as consumers admire the endorsing personality due to the quality of recommendations, usage experiences, and relevance through their expertise.

User-Generated Content

Platform users (also consumers of the product/brand) create content in various formats such as Images, videos, short reels, and many others to share their experiences associated with the product or indirectly infuse product-related content. Such instances are popularly called user-generated content and act as organic social proof related to product features such as quality or usability. They boost other consumers by amplifying reach and encouraging them (Mathur et al., 2021). Thus, social media platforms allow users to create authentic content and build social proof for the product to validate its functionality, inspiring creativity among the users and fostering consumer engagement.

- *Example:* The best example is the 'Starbucks Red Cup Challenge' where users post creative images of Starbucks holiday cups, share their experiences, and inspire other consumers to participate in boosting sales while fostering consumer engagement.
- *Example:* GoPro's Instagram page fosters collaborations with its customers by featuring video shots using their camera that inspire others to purchase and replicate those incredible experiences.

Peer Recommendations/ Affinity Spaces

Social media platforms have allowed consumers to make virtual friends, including their connections, like friends and families, but also make friends worldwide (Oliveri & Carpenter, 2024). Such platforms have also allowed building affinity spaces (virtual close groups of friends with the same interests) that enable them to share experiences related to some products or advocate a brand with their close friends virtually by building a sense of belonging and trust. These recommendations through peer members or affinity spaces are often viewed as credible social proof.

- *Example:* The Facebook open groups or Instagram groups of close friends that talk about fashion or beauty products serve as social proof in the form of user testimonials and influencer purchase decisions of the consumers.
- *Example:* Reddit's product-specific subreddit threads related to Apple products where users discuss Apple features and its exclusivity concerning satisfaction create trust among potential consumers.

Social Media Mentions

On social media, mentions (in the form of tags and hashtags) are widespread practices performed by users of the platforms, influencers, or brands, which serve as public acknowledgments of the product/brand (Wisernotify, n.d.). Such mentions act as social proof, amplifying the visibility and credibility of the product/brand from a trusted source. In such cases of mentions, viral mentions of the brand's groundbreaking work with positive connotations can garner consumers' attention to positive experiences. In contrast, the negative connotations of the brands/ products, such as bad product reviews, can lead to negative experiences in the minds of potential buyers.

- *Example:* Tesla's mentions on Twitter create a buzz for the brand related to Tesla's products, foster product awareness, and influence consumer decision-making. While a mention of Dairy Milk chocolate has a worm inside the Cadbury created negative experiences in consumers' minds.
- *Example:* Viral challenges of the Nike brand, encouraging users to share the post with #JUSTDOIT, boost brand engagements, and create a positive brand image in the consumers' minds.

Overall, these factors act as social proof, wherein leveraging the above factors through social media platforms can make the brand's product more appealing and trustworthy and foster a vibrant community among the brands. However, suppose social proof marks a negative sentiment or connotation for a brand/product through social proof factors. In that case, it can create a negative impression on the buyers, ultimately affecting their product experience.

4 The Intersection of FOMO and Social Proof: A Synergistic Effect

As discussed above, social proof and FOMO can influence consumer experiences and behavior independently. Their intersection on social media platforms creates a synergistic effect. The co-existence of FOMO and social proof, such as its evidence in influencer marketing, plays a pivotal role. For instance, an endorsement of a product by an influencer (perceived authority) validates the product's desirability (social proof). Also, it heightens the product purchase before the deal passes (FOMO). The best example is Kylie Jenner's stories on Instagram, which feature exclusive products with the statement, "Available for 24 h only." Such advertising campaigns on social media platforms such as Instagram generated immense traction. They validated the product (social proof) as it comes with the credibility of Kylie, and limited-time offers trigger FOMO. Thus, the co-existence of FOMO and social proof is pivotal in enabling better advertising campaigns while affecting consumer experiences and behavior. Such coexistence between FOMO and social proof leads to several mediating factors before allowing consumer experiences. These factors are social reassurance, social norms, emotional arousal, perceived urgency, perceived trust, and perceived value. Each of them are explained below.

Social Reassurance

When bombarded with promotional messages on social media, some consumers feel comfortable with their decision-making through social proof and FOMO, achieving social reassurance through observing the positive experiences of other consumers or endorsers (Zollo et al., 2021). Social proof helps present examples of consumers benefitting from the product, while FOMO amplifies the feeling that others are benefitting and the observer (consumer) is missing out on something. For example, when an influencer on Instagram posts about a skincare product with the caption, "Everyone is talking about XYZ miracle serum," positive reviews assure consumers. At the same time, the brand highlights "1 million satisfied users, limited time offer," reassures potential consumers that the product has been tried and tested.

Social Norms

Consumers depend on the acceptable and deemed expected behaviors in the social setting for their decision-making, thus bounded by the social norms (Goldstein & Cialdini, 2011). Social proof and FOMO both help consumers to validate social norms. Social proof reinforces social norms through the presentation of widespread participation, while FOMO amplifies conformity due to the fear of exclusion among consumers. For instance, fashion brands use social media campaigns such as "Everyone is rocking this season's must-have jacket" to nudge consumers toward purchase while making them feel that skipping the trend may make them feel left out.

Emotional Arousal

FOMO and social proof heighten consumer emotions such as excitement, joy, anxiety, and anticipation (e.g., Tan et al., 2024). This emotional arousal often leads consumers to impulse buying due to the urge to feel what others are experiencing with the product. However, this may not always lead to positive experiences with the product; sometimes, a consumer may regret buying the product because their expectations of the product differ. In such cases, though emotional arousal compels consumers to purchase impulsively, a product not meeting consumer expectations can lead to negative experiences. Thus, a brand should advertise the campaigns illustrating what consumers should expect, such as product quality. For example, a concert promising a great event to consumers uses social proof and FOMO to sell the tickets. Concert tickets sell out, but some consumers have negative experiences as the concert did not meet their expectations.

Perceived Trust

In social media, trust is crucial when consumers cannot physically examine the product (Van der Schyff & Floweday, 2023). Social proof builds trust among consumers through positive reviews, testimonials, social media mentions, and others, while FOMO adds a layer of urgency, making the product look more reliable. For example, Airbnb's super host badge and positive reviews received through user-generated content and testimonials on social media act as social proof. Pairing it with a layered message such as "the listing was booked 7 times in the past 24 h" adds a layer of urgency, compelling the consumers to act while making them trust the property.

Perceived Urgency

FOMO on social media directly leads to urgency and can be heightened if visual cues in the form of real-time updates are flashed on social media, representing the scarcity of products (Hodkinson, 2019). Some advertising campaigns on social media generally present social proof while utilizing countdown timers to buy the product. Such instances instill a sense of immediacy and magnify the product urgency among the consumers.

All these mediating factors stemming from the coexistence of social proof and FOMO play a crucial role in enabling greater product experiences among consumers. The combined influence of social proof and FOMO is multifaceted as they affect consumer product experiences from pre-purchase anticipation to helping them make decisions based on peer validation and fear of exclusion till post-purchase stages during satisfaction received from the product.

5 FOMO and Social Proof Effect on Product Experiences

Today, social media platforms shape consumer decision-making and behavior. Amid these, two socio-psychological constructs, FOMO and social proof, play a pivotal role in influencing consumers' product experiences. FOMO, a pervasive apprehension that other consumers have rewarding experiences, and social proof, the idea that people copy the actions of others in an attempt to reflect correct behavior, influences decision-making, emotions, and actions. These factors operate across three levels of consumer product experiences: cognitive, affective, and behavioral. The sub-section below presents how FOMO and social proof affect cognitive, affective, and behavioral experiences with real-world examples.

Cognitive Level Experiences

FOMO and social proof shape consumers' thoughts, perceptions, and understanding of a product through anticipation, comparison, and validation in the context of social media platforms. FOMO generally stems from time-limited offers, perceived scarcity, or consumers' anxiety about missing out on something valuable. These trigger cognitive biases in the consumer's mind and prioritize urgent purchases over other deliberations (Niu et al., 2022). A classic example is Apple, which launched its latest devices with pre-release teasers and limited pre-order slots. Here, the consumers experience cognitive load with constant evaluation of whether they can afford it or miss out on the latest product. Social proof, on the other hand, influences consumer perceptions through peer validation of product quality and desirability. When observing the positive experiences of other peer members, consumers often trigger cognitive experiences toward the product's reliability and quality. For example, when consumers observe hundreds of positive reviews and sentiments towards a product, they frequently shift their cognitive evaluations and experience positive notions about the product in the pre-purchase stage.

Affective Level Experiences

Consumers often experience several emotions during any product's pre-purchase, purchase, and post-purchase stages. Primarily, the affective level pertains to emotions and feelings related to the product (Eitan & Gazit, 2023). FOMO and social proof heavily drive affective-level experiences and often drive consumers towards purchase, satisfaction, and loyalty. FOMO usually leads to a series of emotions such as anxiety, envy, excitement, and others that amplify anticipation and perceived value of the product. Consumers experiencing excitement about grabbing a deal or anxiety about missing the overall product experience go through a halo effect, which means that the emotions often outweigh the objective product evaluation, such as the need for purchase, quality, and others. For example, the limited duration of the availability of skincare products on Instagram stories evokes a mix of anxiety and thrill among a potential buyer. Consumers who buy the product feel better emotions, while those who miss buying may have negative affective experiences during pre-purchase and purchase. However, in the post-purchase stage, consumers often experience negative emotions about the product and purchase decision if the product does not live up to expectations.

Similarly, social proof evokes positive emotions as peer member validation or influencer advocacy builds trust and reassurance and reduces the fear of skepticism. Emotional contagion is crucial as seeing the influencers or the peer member's validation fosters happy emotions, elevating the consumer's affective experiences. For example, a favorite influencer or close friend of a consumer advocating about the lipstick brand through shared positive testimonials builds trust and enthusiasm among the consumers. However, if the social proof talks about negative testimonials or mixed feedback, then the affective experiences among the consumers also drive some ambiguity for the product and may decide not to purchase it.

Behavioral Level Experiences

Consumers take actions based on social proof or FOMO, such as purchasing decisions, sharing the content with peer groups, or engaging with a brand to know more about its quality or reliability (e.g., Good & Hyman, 2021). Such actions are crucial indications of behavioral experiences. FOMO drives consumer actions toward immediately making purchase decisions through rational thinking or impulse buying due to fear of exclusion or urgency created by the advertised campaign. The classic example is sneaker drops by the Nike brand, wherein limited editions of sneakers are sold out within minutes or hours, driven by FOMO. Such experiences offered by exclusive brands provide better experiences if the brand lives up to consumer expectations. Second, social proof encourages behavioral experiences through the bandwagon effect, wherein the consumers often mimic the actions of the larger groups toward purchasing a product and experiencing the same aura of the social groups. For instance, a viral TitTok video showcasing a unique product with unique characteristics often encourages consumers to purchase a product due to social norms and reassurance. Additionally, if an influencer or TikTok star endorses the same product, it builds trust and credibility towards purchase among potential buyers.

Thus, FOMO and social proof act as a socio-psychological power that influences consumer product experiences at cognitive, affective, and behavioral levels. By leveraging these factors, brands can create a compelling advertising campaign infused with FOMO and social proof that will shape consumer perceptions, emotions, and actions. Whether an advertising campaign brings forward scarcity messaging, emotional appeal, or peer validation techniques, social proof and FOMO collectively shape the consumer journey, encouraging ordinary products to become must-have items in the minds of consumers.

However, this overall consumer journey and product experiences due to FOMO and social proof depends on three main factors: (a) Consumer involvement, (b) Socio-demographic features, and (c) Social media platforms and usage intensity. Each of them is explained in sub-sections below.

a. *Consumer involvement*: A degree of consumer interest in a product on a social media platform. Consumers with high involvement often seek more information, reviews, peer member validations, and recommendations with the effect of social proof and FOMO. For example, someone interested in buying a smartphone will look for more social proof and experience FOMO, fearing they would miss out on some essential features. At the same time, consumers who are less involved in purchasing a product may not be affected by social proof and FOMO factors more often or may not care for the same. For example, buying some turmeric power from a particular brand may not require social proof or may not generate anxiety due to its availability and consideration of daily-usage items.
b. *Socio-demographic features*: Age, income, education, and cultural background are pivotal in shaping how consumers perceive FOMO and social proof-related advertising campaigns on social media platforms. For instance, younger generations like Generation Z and millennials will be more susceptible to FOMO as they highly rely on social media such as Instagram for decision-making and follow the trends of social media peer users, influencers, and content creators. A teenager will be more pressured to purchase a trendy sneaker with limited-time offers as other peer members in his/her social group own the sneaker. Similarly, cultural factors can also amplify the social proof. Consumers in a collectivistic society like India will depend on social media platforms for social proof, such as validations through external reviews, but also focus on endorsements or advice from their community members, such as family/friends in the physical setting apart from online social proofs.
c. *Social Media Platform and Usage Intensity*: Finally, the type of platform and the time the consumer spends on a particular platform also magnifies the FOMO and social proof. Social media platforms like Instagram and TikTok rely heavily on visual content such as video reels that create an aspirational halo among consumers through curated lifestyle presentations that make certain products seem essential. For instance, an influencer on Instagram endorsing the latest lipstick shade may make consumers buy it to feel included in the social community. Similarly, the high usage intensity a consumer spends on TitkTok, almost 4–5 h, increases the exposure to viral trends and products, making consumers feel to follow the crowd, acting as validation and equally generating a feeling of FOMO.

Thus, though there are several FOMO and social proof factors used individually or in coexistence for advertising the products and enhancing the experiences, factors such as consumer involvement, socio-demographic characteristics, social media platforms, and usage intensity of consumers can intensify or de-intensify the impact of FOMO and social proof among consumers and ultimately the product experiences.

6 Conclusion

This chapter aimed at understanding FOMO and social proof's influence on product experience on social media platforms presents a comprehensive view of various factors and how these factors of FOMO and social proof affect the product experiences at cognitive, affective, and behavioral levels experiences. First, the chapter highlights the importance of FOMO and social proof with a grounded understanding from the previous studies, underscoring its importance and relevance in the social media age. Second, with real-world examples, it explains various factors encapsulated in the concept of social proof and FOMO, such as review, peer member validation, social comparison triggers, exclusive content, geo-tagged content, real-time engagement, social media mentions, user-generated content and influencers advocacy or endorsements which act as social proof or generate FOMO. Third, the chapter sheds importance on how FOMO and social proof's co-existence in social media campaigns can create a synergistic effect that provides social reassurance and perceived trust, creates perceived urgency, helps embrace social norms, and affects emotional arousal in consumers' minds. Fourth, by presenting a comprehensive outlook, the framework further explains how FOMO and social proof factors influence consumer experiences related to the product at three levels: cognitive, affective, and behavioral experiences. Fifth, despite the importance of FOMO and social proof in influencing consumer product experiences, the chapter presents that overall success depends on consumer involvement in the product, socio-demographic features, variety of social media platforms, and usage intensity of consumers. Finally, the chapter closes by explaining several real-world examples, enunciating how social proof and FOMO can not only create positive experiences during the pre-purchase to post-purchase stages but also facilitate negative experiences if the advertised campaign loaded with FOMO and social proof does not live the expectations of consumers. Thus, this chapter comprehensively explains the social proof and FOMO phenomena.

References

Aitamurto, T., Won, A. S., Sakshuwong, S., Kim, B., Sadeghi, Y., Stein, K., Royal, P. G., & Kircos, C. L. (2021, May). From fomo to jomo: Examining the fear and joy of missing out and presence in a 360 video viewing experience. In *Proceedings of the 2021 CHI conference on human factors in computing systems* (pp. 1–14).

Alves, H., Fernandes, C., & Raposo, M. (2016). Social media marketing: A literature review and implications. *Psychology & Marketing, 33*(12), 1029–1038.
Amblee, N., & Bui, T. (2011). Harnessing the influence of social proof in online shopping: The effect of electronic word of mouth on sales of digital microproducts. *International Journal of Electronic Commerce, 16*(2), 91–114.
Baumöl, U., Hollebeek, L., & Jung, R. (2016). Dynamics of customer interaction on social media platforms. *Electronic Markets, 26*, 199–202.
Bhattacharyya, S., & Bose, I. (2020). S-commerce: Influence of Facebook likes on purchases and recommendations on a linked e-commerce site. *Decision Support Systems, 138.*
Bui, M., Krishen, A. S., Anlamlier, E., & Berezan, O. (2022). Fear of missing out in the digital age: The role of social media satisfaction and advertising engagement. *Psychology & Marketing, 39*(4), 683–693.
Cengiz, H., & Şenel, M. (2024). The effect of perceived scarcity on impulse-buying tendencies in a fast fashion context: A mediating and multigroup analysis. *Journal of Fashion Marketing and Management: An International Journal, 28*(3), 405–425.
Cialdini, R., & Cialdini, R. (2007). *Influence: The psychology of persuasion.* https://cltr.nl/wp-content/uploads/2020/04/Robert-P-Cialdini-Influence-The-Psychology-of-Persuasion.pdf
Eitan, T., & Gazit, T. (2023). No social media for six hours? The emotional experience of Meta's global outage according to FoMO, JoMO and internet intensity. *Computers in Human Behavior, 138*, Article 107474.
Erlinda, V., & Fatmawati, I. (2025). Bibliometric analysis of publication trends in the Scopus database on the theme fear of missing out to consumers behavior. *Multidisciplinary Reviews, 8*(3), 2025070–2025070.
Ferreira, C., Robertson, J., Lam, J., & Vella, J. (2023). Expert reviews uncorked: Contrasting the differences in the language used in online reviews of white and red wine. *Journal of Wine Research, 34*(2), 140–154.
Flecha Ortiz, J. A., Santos Corrada, M., Perez, S., Dones, V., & Rodriguez, L. H. (2024). Exploring the influence of uncontrolled social media use, fear of missing out, fear of better options, and fear of doing anything on consumer purchase intent. *International Journal of Consumer Studies, 48*(1), Article e12990.
Goldstein, N. J., & Cialdini, R. B. (2011). Using social norms as a lever of social influence. In *The science of social influence* (pp. 167–191). Psychology Press.
Good, M. C., & Hyman, M. R. (2021). Direct and indirect effects of fear-of-missing-out appeals on purchase likelihood. *Journal of Consumer Behaviour, 20*(3), 564–576.
Hodkinson, C. (2019). Fear of Missing Out' (FOMO) marketing appeals: A conceptual model. *Journal of Marketing Communications, 25*(1), 65–88.
Jennings, F. J., Neville-Shepard, R., Jackson, D. B., Magusiak, A., & Sigrist, K. (2024). From fringe to mainstream: How celebrity endorsement on social media contributes to the spread of conspiracy theories. *Southern Communication Journal, 89*(2), 119–131.
Jiang, J., Lu, H., Yang, B., & Cui, B. (2015). Finding top-k local users in geo-tagged social media data. In *2015 IEEE 31st International Conference on Data Engineering*, 267–278.
Kim, I., Choi, Y. K., & Lee, S. (2021). How do consumers choose to click 'like' on luxury ads in social media? Role of envy, number of likes, and culture. *International Journal of Advertising, 40*(8), 1247–1264.
Kroeber, A., & C Kluckhohn. (1952). Culture: A critical review of concepts and definitions. In *Peabody Museum of Archaeology & Ethnology, Harvard University*. https://psycnet.apa.org/record/1953-07119-001
Kozinets, R. V., Gretzel, U., & Gambetti, R. (2024). *Influencer & creator: Business, cultura e pratica.* FrancoAngeli.
Lou, C., & Yuan, S. (2019). Influencer marketing: How message value and credibility affect consumer trust of branded content on social media. *Journal of Interactive Advertising, 19*(1), 58–73.
Lu, F. C., & Sinha, J. (2024). How social media usage and the fear of missing out impact minimalistic consumption. *European Journal of Marketing*, (ahead-of-print).

Mathur, S., Tewari, A., & Singh, A. (2021). Modeling the factors affecting online purchase intention: The mediating effect of consumer's attitude towards user- generated content. *Journal of Marketing Communications, 28*(7).

McMullan, K., Laurell, C., & Pitt, L. (2022). Managing the tensions in marketer-influencer relationships. *Business Horizons.*

Meyer, J. H., Friederich, F., Matute, J., & Schwarz, M. (2024). My money—My problem: How fear-of-missing-out appeals can hinder sustainable investment decisions. *Psychology & Marketing, 41*(11), 2677–2694.

Morsi, N., Sá, E., & Silva, J. (2024). Walking away: Investigating the adverse impact of FOMO appeals on FOMO-prone consumers. *Business Horizons.*

Niu, G. F., Shi, X. H., Yang, W. C., Jin, S. Y., & Sun, X. J. (2022). Can smartphone presence affect cognitive function? The moderating role of fear of missing out. *Computers in Human Behavior, 136*, Article 107399.

Oliveri, A. R., & Carpenter, J. P. (2024). Refreshing the affinity space concept: Evolving understandings of learning via social media platforms in an algorithmic age. *Information and Learning Sciences, 125*(9), 628–649.

Qin, Y. S. (2020). Fostering brand–consumer interactions in social media: The role of social media uses and gratifications. *Journal of Research in Interactive Marketing, 14*(3), 337–354.

Salunke, P., & Jain, V. (2022). Instagram marketing (2015–2021): A review of past trends, implications, and future research. *Exploring the latest trends in management literature*, 129–146.

Salunke, P., Jain, V., Eastman, J., Mishra, T., & Chakraborty, A. (2025). Decoding the effectiveness of social media influencers' endorsement on consumer behavior: An evidence-based approach. *Electronic Commerce Research*, 1–37.

Sánchez-Fernández, R., & Jiménez-Castillo, D. (2021). How social media influencers affect behavioural intentions towards recommended brands: The role of emotional attachment and information value. *Journal of Marketing Management, 37*(11–12), 1123–1147.

Seo, Y., Li, X., Choi, Y. K., & Yoon, S. (2018). Narrative transportation and paratextual features of social media in viral advertising. *Journal of Advertising, 47*(1), 83–95.

Sigurdsson, V., Larsen, N. M., Alemu, M. H., Gallogly, J. K., Menon, R. V., & & Fagerstrøm, A. (2020). Assisting sustainable food consumption: The effects of quality signals stemming from consumers and stores in online and physical grocery retailing. *Journal of Business Research, 112.*

Tan, P. L., Tjiptono, F., & Tan, S. Z. (2024). Fear more or fear no more: Examining the emotional and behavioral consequences of FOMO and JOMO. *Asia Pacific Journal of Marketing and Logistics, 37*(6).

van der Schyff, K., & Flowerday, S. (2023). The mediating role of perceived risks and benefits when self-disclosing: A study of social media trust and FoMO. *Computers & Security, 126*, Article 103071.

Van Dijck, J. (2011). Flickr and the culture of connectivity: Sharing views, experiences, memories. *Memory Studies, 4*(4), 401–415.

Van Maanen, P.-P., & Van Der Vecht, B. (2014). Development and evaluation of multi-agent models of online social influence based on Cialdini's principles. *Social Network Analysis and Mining, 4*, 1–12.

Vempati, S., Bhuma, M. K., & Fiaidhi, J. (2023). *Fear of missing out, social media engagement, smartphone addiction and distraction moderating role of tracking apps in the youth.* Authorea Preprints.

Vrontis, D., Makrides, A., Christofi, M., & Thrassou, A. (2021). Social media influencer marketing: A systematic review, integrative framework and future research agenda. *International Journal of Consumer Studies, 45*(4), 617–644.

Whalen, C. K., Henker, B., Ishikawa, S. S., Jamner, L. D., Floro, J. N., Johnston, J. A., & Swindle, R. (2006). An electronic diary study of contextual triggers and ADHD: Get ready, get set, get mad. *Journal of the American Academy of Child & Adolescent Psychiatry, 45*(2), 166–174.

Wisernotify. (n.d.). *What are social media mentions? | Importance & tracking strategies.* Bot Verification. https://wisernotify.com/marketing-term/social-media-mentions/

Wisernotify.com. (2025). *33 Impactful social proof statistics (2025)*. Bot Verification. https://wisernotify.com/blog/social-proof-statistics/

Yaputri, M. S., Dimyati, D., & Herdiansyah, H. (2022). The correlation between fear of missing out (fomo) phenomenon and consumptive behaviour in millennials. *Eligible: Journal of Social Sciences, 1*(2), 116–124.

Zhang, T., Abound Omran, B., & Cobanoglu, C. (2017). Generation Y's positive and negative eWOM: Use of social media and mobile technology. *International Journal of Contemporary Hospitality Management, 29*(2), 732–761.

Zollo, L., Carranza, R., Faraoni, M., Díaz, E., & Martín-Consuegra, D. (2021). What influences consumers' intention to purchase organic personal care products? The role of social reassurance. *Journal of Retailing and Consumer Services, 60*, Article 102432.

Measuring the Success of Social Media Presence with Google Analytics: From Clicks to Conversions

Mano Weligodapola and Chathurini Kumarapperuma

Abstract

Social media platforms function as vital instruments that deliver brand exposure to customers while simultaneously producing financial revenue. Organizations encounter difficulties in moving their social media assessment forward from basic metrics such as likes and shares because of extensive platform usage. Through Google Analytics, businesses can convert basic social media metrics into actionable business insights that prove direct business results. Businesses need to monitor meaningful performance indicators that encompass conversions and sales, and customer loyalty, instead of superficial metrics. The approach requires businesses to track meaningful performance indicators, which include conversions and sales, together with customer loyalty, instead of superficial metrics. The method presented in this chapter enables companies to enhance their social media strategies and generate quantifiable outcomes. The chapter includes expert advice and major company case studies of Coca-Cola and Airbnb and provides practical steps for implementing multi-channel attribution models. Marketers can use this guide to analyze user behavior while setting conversion targets and developing a data-driven social media marketing strategy. Social media success requires organizations to move beyond visibility because they must convert engagement metrics into quantifiable growth that supports marketing objectives and investment returns.

C. Kumarapperuma
SLIIT Business School, Sri Lanka Institute of Information Technology (SLIIT), Malabe, Sri Lanka
e-mail: chathurini.k@sliit.lk

M. Weligodapola (✉)
International Business University (IBU), Toronto, Canada
e-mail: mweligodapola@ibu.ca

© The Author(s), under exclusive license to Springer Nature Singapore Pte Ltd. 2026

N. S. Jayawardena et al. (eds.), *Digital Advertising and Consumer Behavior*, Management for Professionals, https://doi.org/10.1007/978-981-95-7809-2_5

1 Introduction

The digital world keeps transforming at a fast pace, yet social media has outgrown its basic communication function. Businesses depend on social media as an essential tool that helps them improve brand recognition and customer interaction and ultimately grow their revenue. Social media platforms, including Facebook and Instagram, alongside LinkedIn and X (formerly Twitter) have become essential channels for businesses to connect with diverse audiences because they have reached billions of active users worldwide. Does any organization truly measure its social media presence impact through metrics that extend past simple "likes" and "shares"? The following analysis explores the critical metrics and evaluation methods needed to measure social media program success. The document recommends that businesses move away from counting basic interactions while they focus on monitoring important outcomes, which Loftus (2012) defines as conversions. The research demonstrates how organizations can convert their unfiltered social media data into actionable insights through Google Analytics as their data-driven marketing solution. The gained insights lead to improved digital marketing approaches, which result in significant increases in return on investment (ROI) and enable better decision-making for sustainable business growth.

This chapter presents an all-encompassing view through statements from renowned experts in the field. The discussion presents current social media analytics patterns and practical marketing challenges with corresponding effective solutions. The chapter demonstrates Google Analytics optimization of social media initiatives through case studies of international businesses to achieve conversion increases. This chapter delivers an extensive guide for social media analytics success by analyzing bounce rates and session durations and multi-channel attribution, and user behavior flows. The chapter presents practical examples and expert direction with an organized plan to assist entrepreneurs and digital marketers in using Google Analytics for social media measurement.

The digital age has made social media platforms more closely linked to consumer behavior, so businesses must have precise methods to measure their social media marketing success. Real success occurs when social media interactions produce tangible business results instead of depending on metrics such as likes and shares, and follower counts. As one seasoned digital marketing expert succinctly stated, "*A thousand likes won't cover expenses; what truly counts is conversions.*" Modern marketing relies on social media as its core foundation because it allows businesses to reach their target audiences and increase brand visibility while generating revenue growth.

The main challenge emerges when organizations attempt to surpass basic metrics to establish accurate methods for measuring social media initiative effectiveness. Marketers need to surpass basic engagement metrics to understand how their social media activities affect organizational financial performance. A strategic and holistic monitoring system should be implemented to evaluate social media campaign ROI and track user behavior (Berger et al., 2023). Businesses that follow this approach will achieve measurable value from their efforts instead of accumulating empty vanity metrics.

The beverage industry leader, Coca-Cola demonstrates how social media can enhance brand engagement through its worldwide success. The "Share a Coke" campaign generated massive success through millions of social media interactions. Coca-Cola achieved exceptional success through its intentional application of Google Analytics to analyze campaign outcomes. The company moved away from measuring popularity through vanity metrics because it concentrated on tracking meaningful actions such as website traffic and product sales, and newsletter subscriptions generated from their social media efforts. The company achieved a better assessment of campaign value through its transition from measuring vanity metrics to measuring actual outcomes. Coca-Cola enhanced its brand position while leading the consumer goods market competition through its strategic approach. The data-driven approach demonstrates how social media engagement leads to concrete business achievements.

Web 2.0 technologies have revolutionized business-to-customer relationships through individualized marketing strategies according to Dwairi & Al-Khataybeh (2023). Marketers today possess extensive data resources that they can use to enhance their social media strategies and measure their effectiveness when used correctly. Measuring social media campaign impact requires data collection beyond basic metrics because it demands strategic alignment between data insights and marketing goals. Businesses need to stay flexible because social media platforms evolve continuously while learning effective methods to generate measurable results. A social media presence alone does not lead to business success because companies must convert their online visibility into quantifiable business expansion.

The travel industry leader Airbnb demonstrates how cross-platform analytics forms the foundation of its social media strategy. The company uses Google Analytics to monitor referral traffic from Facebook and Instagram, and Twitter to identify which channels produce the most conversions. The company's data demonstrates that Instagram draws younger travel customers, but LinkedIn succeeds in finding professional hosts. The gained insight allows Airbnb to make strategic budget decisions and optimize campaigns which achieve specific conversion targets that support its overall business objectives.

A Senior Performance Marketing Analyst pointed out that "*businesses should focus on actual lead conversion rates instead of vanity metrics when measuring success. The key performance indicator for your post's success should be website traffic that results in actual purchases rather than mere post likes*".

Social media delivers its greatest worth by creating genuine relationships, which produce concrete, quantifiable outcomes. Businesses should redirect their social media focus from trivial metrics such as likes and shares toward concrete results, including leads and conversions, because this approach maintains alignment with their business objectives. This method produces both higher ROI and enhanced digital strategy effectiveness.

Key Takeaways

- Organizations should shift their attention from monitoring meaningless social media metrics such as "likes" and "shares" to tracking meaningful outcomes that generate business growth, including conversions and sales, and customer engagement.
- Google Analytics enables companies to transform their social media data into actionable insights, which helps them optimize their campaigns to measure website traffic and lead generation, and actual purchase effects.
- The chapter demonstrates how businesses, including Coca-Cola and Airbnb, utilize social media analytics to enhance conversions through expert insights supported by real-world examples.
- The adoption of data-driven strategies enables Airbnb to customize its social media approach across platforms by modifying content and spending to achieve particular conversion objectives, which results in better audience engagement.

2 Social Media Metrics: From Vanity to Value

Evaluating the actual effects of social media presence on a company proves to be a challenging process. Businesses commonly focus their attention on monitoring "vanity metrics," which include follower counts and likes, and shares. The numbers show content engagement but fail to provide a complete understanding of social media's role in business success. The superficial metrics that create success illusions rarely produce meaningful outcomes such as increased sales and loyal customers, and an enduring brand worth. Srinivasan et al. (2016) emphasize that companies should move past superficial indicators to measure customer mindset metrics deeply. The company can enhance its marketing approach and forecast future brand success by implementing this approach.

As one experienced digital marketing strategist aptly puts it, "*Engagement metrics are like high-fives; they might feel great, but they don't guarantee a victory*." This analogy highlights the importance for businesses to dig deeper and critically evaluate their social media strategies. Are those likes, shares, and comments adding value to the business? Are they helping achieve broader marketing goals, such as generating leads, building brand awareness, or fostering customer loyalty? It's a reminder that surface-level engagement isn't enough; true success comes from aligning social media efforts with meaningful outcomes.

A digital marketing strategist explained that engagement metrics provide temporary satisfaction but do not ensure victory. The analogy demonstrates why businesses need to explore beyond surface-level metrics when assessing their social media strategies. The business value of likes, shares, and comments remains uncertain because they do not directly contribute to business growth. The metrics should assist businesses in reaching their marketing objectives, which include lead acquisition and brand visibility, and customer retention. The key to success lies in making social media efforts produce meaningful results rather than simply measuring superficial engagement metrics. According to a digital marketing consultant, *"Vanity metrics may inflate your social media ego, but they don't sustain a business. True success comes from analyzing data that connects engagement with outcomes like lead generation, sales, and customer loyalty."*

Nike serves as an excellent example that demonstrates how to successfully adapt to this transformation. The company maintains its focus on meaningful engagement rather than accumulating large numbers of likes and shares despite having millions of followers. Through Google Analytics, Nike monitors meaningful social media interactions that lead users to visit their online store and download their app and make purchases. Nike optimizes its marketing campaigns by measuring product views and sign-ups, and sales numbers to achieve better conversion rates. The company demonstrates that major corporations like Nike can prevent superficial metric fixation by measuring only the essential business outcomes.

To move beyond vanity metrics, businesses must zero in on key performance indicators (KPIs) that directly correlate with their specific marketing objectives. This might include metrics such as website traffic, lead generation, conversion rates, and ROI. As a marketing researcher explained it, *"It's not about how many people see your content; it's about how many take meaningful action. Likes won't pay the rent."* This shift requires marketers to create a reduced yet highly impactful set of performance metrics that drive real business value (Al-Dwairi & Al-Khataybeh, 2023).

Organizations across the board have started including essential social media metrics in their marketing dashboards to achieve better performance insights. Organizations have moved their attention from the short-term pleasure of following follower growth to measuring social media's actual impact on lead generation and customer acquisition, and revenue growth. The method enables businesses to develop strategies that produce meaningful outcomes that drive long-term success.

Expert interviews demonstrate the risks involved with excessive attention to vanity metrics. A digital strategist warned that, "*Getting stuck in the vanity metric loop is risky. While growing numbers feel good, they don't guarantee real business growth. Without tracking conversions, you're only skimming the surface.*" This underscores the need to not just collect data but interpret it in ways that support long-term goals. The absence of proven links between engagement metrics and business results makes even successful viral campaigns ineffective for delivering substantial outcomes.

Small business entities face additional challenges when they attempt to handle social media metrics. Without the resources and expertise of larger firms, small businesses face challenges in interpreting KPIs while developing effective strategies that produce meaningful results (Wu et al., 2024). According to a digital analytics expert, "*small businesses typically become overwhelmed by their data. The numbers present themselves to them, but they fail to understand how to convert this information into actionable steps, which results in unsuccessful marketing campaigns*".

The research targets the improvement of social media marketing approaches for teams working in small and medium-sized businesses (SMEs). The research delivers practical methods for data analysis which allows businesses to move away from meaningless metrics and focus on conversion-oriented targets that support their objectives. The expert emphasized that "*Your social media following represents a business opportunity rather than a popularity contest.*" Every business needs this fundamental change in perspective. A business reaches genuine success when its audience members perform particular actions, such as purchases and newsletter sign-ups, and customer loyalty development. Successful businesses emerge from the rest through their ability to analyze and adapt social media while using meaningful metrics for optimization in today's digital world.

Key Takeaways

- Businesses need to focus on performance metrics, which include conversions and sales, and customer loyalty, instead of vanity metrics such as likes and shares, because they do not measure real business value.
- The company Nike demonstrates this approach by monitoring significant actions including app downloads and purchases, instead of superficial engagement metrics to improve conversion rates and optimize their campaigns.
- Organizations need to track website traffic along with lead generation and ROI metrics because these metrics ensure social media efforts lead to revenue growth and customer acquisition.
- Small businesses that experience data overload from social media should concentrate on actionable metrics to develop better strategies that will support their long-term development.

3 Google Analytics: Unlocking the Power of Social Media Insights

Google Analytics serves as a strong analytical tool that delivers essential performance data about a business's social media presence. The platform monitors essential performance indicators, which include referral traffic data and engagement metrics such as time on site and bounce rates, and lead generation and conversion rates (Kim et al., 2021). As one digital marketing specialist puts it, "*Google Analytics is like a crystal ball; it reveals what's hidden, from traffic sources to conversion rates.*" Businesses should select their most effective social channels and content through data analysis to achieve maximum returns.

Businesses can enhance their marketing performance evaluation by linking their social media platforms to Google Analytics. The combination of Facebook advertising with Google Analytics enables businesses to monitor user interactions, including page duration and action completion rates, such as newsletter sign-ups and purchases. As one social media manager puts it, "*Knowing who visits your site isn't enough, you need to understand what they do once they're there. That's where the real value lies.*"

The e-commerce platform Shopify demonstrates effective customer journey tracking through its implementation of Google Analytics. The social media data integration with Shopify allows the platform to monitor the entire customer journey from ad clicks to purchase completion so it can optimize its strategies for better conversion rates. The company achieved higher profitability through its strategic focus on successful channels, including Facebook and Pinterest. Experts agree that Google Analytics serves as a tool for tracking user interactions with your brand while providing a roadmap for understanding these interactions. The detailed analysis enables businesses to surpass basic metrics and discover the complete worth of their social media initiatives.

Google Analytics provides social media users with its most significant benefit through its capability to monitor customer interactions across various touchpoints. A consumer will start by interacting with a brand on social media before searching for the product and finally purchasing on either the brand's website or app. Understanding this path helps businesses allocate resources more effectively and create strategies that drive conversions (Srinivasan et al., 2016). As a digital analytics expert explains, "*Google Analytics uncovers the hidden steps consumers take before converting. In today's multi-channel world, it's crucial to understand how social media contributes to the overall customer journey, not just as an entry point but as a key driver of meaningful interactions.*" Companies that analyze their touchpoints can determine which platforms produce better conversion rates, and they can use this information to enhance their omnichannel approach for improved results (Chaffey & Smith, 2023).

Businesses achieve superior results by implementing Google Analytics in their social media strategies because this approach enables them to measure actual performance instead of superficial metrics. Experts agree that analytics provides essential insights about user behavior, which transforms social media into a measurable growth driver.

Key Takeaways

- Google Analytics enables businesses to monitor referral traffic together with engagement and conversion metrics, which provides an advanced understanding of social media's effects on business results.
- Shopify and other companies track their customers through all touchpoints with Google Analytics to maximize their campaign effectiveness and boost conversion rates and profitability.
- The platform gives users an unambiguous understanding of customer actions by revealing which social platforms and content types lead to purchases and sign-ups.
- Businesses that track cross-channel interactions can improve their strategies and optimize resource use to achieve better results.

4 Social Traffic Sources: Identifying Top-Performing Platforms

Through Google Analytics businesses can monitor their website traffic origins to understand which social media channels produce the most value. One of the social media analysts explains that "*Knowing where your audience spends time is half the battle.*" Each social media platform targets a distinct audience purpose, so Instagram works best for B2C customer engagement and LinkedIn performs better for B2B business relationships. Understanding these differences is key to allocating resources wisely and maximizing ROI (Tsimonis et al., 2020).

An expert highlighted the value of platform-specific insights, saying, "*Every platform has its strengths, and Google Analytics helps pinpoint where your audience is most engaged. If LinkedIn drives conversions but Instagram doesn't, adjust accordingly.*" Businesses that track bounce rate and session duration, and conversion rates will discover which platforms generate the highest ROI. A digital strategist recommends that businesses should avoid spreading themselves too thinly across different platforms. Businesses should concentrate their resources on the specific platforms that actually produce meaningful outcomes.

Analyzing User Behavior: From Engagement to Action

The evaluation of social media success depends on monitoring user activities. The actual importance of understanding user actions after website clicks surpasses the importance of website traffic generation. Marketers use Google Analytics tools such as User Flow and Behavior Flow to create visual representations of how customers move from social media to their website. As one analyst puts it, "*Think of it as a treasure map; the real prize is converting users.*" The actual goal of conversion stands as the true treasure according to analysts.

An e-commerce expert emphasized that understanding user behavior following link clicks holds greater importance. "*The analysis of user behavior following link clicks matters more than getting users to click the link. Users will abandon the site if the experience does not meet their expectations*" (E-commerce expert). Users who experience high bounce rates tend to view the landing page as uninteresting or unrelated, which demonstrates the requirement for optimization (Tupikovskaja-Omovie, 2022).

The expert interviews show that success is not just about clicks or shares; it is about tracking the whole customer journey, from interacting with a social media post to acting on the website. As one digital marketing consultant puts it, "*Clicks are just the start. The real value lies in understanding how those clicks turn into leads or sales.*" Businesses should evaluate social media effectiveness by measuring lead generation and conversion rates to determine its impact on the customer journey. The analysis of user behavior following engagement helps businesses use their resources efficiently to achieve maximum marketing impact (Srinivasan et al., 2016).

Key Takeaways

- Google Analytics enables businesses to determine which social media platforms perform best through the analysis of bounce rate and session duration and conversion rates, which helps them direct their efforts toward platforms with the highest return on investment.
- The tools User Flow and Behavior Flow show how website visitors navigate after clicking through social media traffic, so businesses can maximize meaningful engagement and conversion rates.
- Businesses can improve their strategies by using platform-specific insights to direct their efforts toward channels that effectively support their lead generation and sales objectives.
- The complete customer journey analysis from social media contact to website actions helps businesses concentrate on conversion generation rather than just measuring basic click activity or superficial engagement.

5 Setting Conversion Goals: Making the Data Work for You

Google Analytics delivers its strongest capability through conversion tracking, which enables businesses to monitor specific goal-oriented actions, including sign-ups and purchases. Monitoring these conversions is crucial for measuring the ROI of social media campaigns (Bag et al., 2022). Businesses can assess their performance and make data-based strategy adjustments through the establishment of specific and actionable goals.

As one expert put it, "*Without clear goals, data is just noise. Conversion tracking turns that noise into actionable insights*" (Digital Marketing Expert). The industry widely accepts this concept because businesses understand that social media metrics become directionless when conversion goals remain undefined. Companies that track conversions can determine which platforms and campaigns perform best while identifying necessary adjustments. A data analytics consultant adds, "*It's not just about tracking sales, it's about understanding every touchpoint, like newsletter sign-ups or social shares, and how they impact the bottom line.*" This expanded viewpoint enables businesses to understand the complete worth of customer interactions and social media's role in their marketing process.

HubSpot demonstrates proper Google Analytics usage by monitoring different conversion goals which include form submissions and both demo requests and newsletter sign-ups. The approach reveals which social channels produce particular conversions while providing user behavior insights and pointing out strategy adjustment requirements. Digital marketers emphasize that goal setting requires continuous evaluation because goals need to adapt to changing campaigns and audience patterns. Businesses that update their goals regularly can convert unprocessed data into useful insights, which leads to improved decisions and higher ROI.

Key Takeaways

- The tracking capabilities of Google Analytics enable businesses to monitor essential conversions such as newsletter sign-ups and purchases to evaluate social media campaign ROI and develop data-based strategy enhancements.
- The lack of specific conversion targets makes social media metrics appear without direction. Businesses need to establish specific objectives that transform statistical data into actionable insights to determine their most successful platforms and campaigns.
- A successful conversion strategy requires monitoring both sales and content downloads and social shares because it helps organizations track the complete customer journey.
- Conversion goals need to adapt to changing campaigns and business priorities so social media data remains relevant for achieving maximum ROI.

6 ROI and Attribution Models: Proving the Value of Social Media

The calculation of social media investment returns remains a difficult task for digital marketers. Marketers face a major challenge when trying to turn social media engagement into quantifiable business results. Businesses can track their combined conversion impact across marketing channels through the attribution models provided by Google Analytics. The models deliver enhanced customer interaction insights that follow the entire customer journey from social media contact to purchase completion, thus allowing better evaluation of social media effectiveness (Bianchi, 2020).

One expert explained, "*Attribution models are crucial for understanding how all your marketing channels work together. Social media often acts as the first point of contact, but without a complete view, you might miss its real impact on driving conversions*" (Digital Marketing Strategist). The expert noted that using only the "last-click" model would minimize social media's influence because it frequently leads customers to brands during their early stages of engagement before they make purchases through different channels such as paid search or email. An analytics consultant noted that the channel performance analysis changes depending on whether you use first-touch, linear, or time-decay models. A multi-channel strategy enables businesses to track how social media contributes to conversions even when it does not result in the last conversion point. The last-click model would give all credit to email because it only tracks the final click, but a more comprehensive model would recognize Instagram's role in the customer's purchase journey.

Airbnb demonstrates the successful implementation of multi-touch attribution models to analyze social media ROI through its platform. The tracking system of Google Analytics enables Airbnb to monitor customer interactions across different touchpoints which helps evaluate social media's impact on both brand awareness and conversion rates. A Facebook ad from Airbnb leads a potential customer to search properties on Google before they book their stay through an email promotion. Through its time-decay attribution model, Airbnb provides more accurate conversion tracking by assigning value to each step in the customer journey.

Organizations must develop customized attribution models because various models function more effectively for different business objectives. Your business needs to understand customer pathways while selecting an attribution model that supports your organizational approach. The first-touch model stands as the optimal choice when brand awareness stands as your main business objective. The last-click model works best when you need to generate sales quickly. The experts in this chapter repeatedly emphasized that businesses must choose appropriate attribution models to accurately measure social media's impact on conversions and ROI.

Key Takeaways

- Google Analytics enables businesses to measure social media ROI through different attribution models, which show how various marketing channels contribute to conversions throughout the customer journey.
- The "last-click" model produces inaccurate results for social media impact measurement because it usually advances customer journey progression during the initial stages. Multi-touch models, which include "first-touch" and "time-decay" reveal social media conversion support more effectively than the last-click model because they demonstrate value beyond the final interaction point.
- Businesses should choose their attribution model based on their specific business objectives. The first-touch model works best for building brand awareness, but the last-click model works better for driving immediate sales. Organizations must select models that match their strategic goals and customer journey development patterns.
- Through multi-touch attribution Airbnb monitors the complete conversion journey of social media interactions to properly measure its impact on brand discovery and conversion rates.

7 Conclusion: A Data-Driven Approach to Social Media Success

The chapter demonstrates how Google Analytics functions as a critical tool to measure and enhance social media performance. Companies that use data can move past basic metrics such as likes and shares to focus on meaningful factors that create real value. The chapter offers actionable guidance by integrating expert insights with comprehensive social media metric analysis to turn data into successful strategies.

Digital marketing strategists confirm that "*Data without a strategy is just numbers.*" Organizations gain actual power through their numbers when they use them to make performance-enhancing decisions. Marketers need to monitor basic metrics such as engagement and traffic, together with advanced customer actions that result in conversions. Organizations should connect their social media activities to organizational targets through user pathway tracking between touchpoints and conversion marker establishment to enable continuous strategy adjustments.

A digital marketing specialist stressed that current digital marketing requires exactness. The key to modern marketing success involves identifying specific successful elements and their fundamental causes before performing continuous optimization to boost performance. Google Analytics allows businesses to monitor conversions and deploy attribution models that result in better ROI and market position.

The professionals in this chapter believed that businesses that excel at analytics will adapt better to market changes within the dynamic digital marketing environment. A social media manager explained it best by stating that "*Social media success is no longer dependent on random guesses.*" The foundation for strategy development today relies on data-driven insights which enable you to build plans that expand with your audience growth and their changing requirements.

The growing complexity of the digital world allows businesses that fully adopt analytics to become industry leaders and maximize their social media ROI.

References

Al-Dwairi, R. M. D., & Al-Khataybeh, M. (2023). Web 2.0 tools and service quality: The key to effective customer relationships in e-commerce environments. *2023 International Conference on Information Technology: Cybersecurity Challenges for Sustainable Cities, ICIT 2023 - Proceeding*, 827–831. https://doi.org/10.1109/ICIT58056.2023.10226159

Bag, S., Srivastava, G., Bashir, M. M. Al, Kumari, S., Giannakis, M., & Chowdhury, A. H. (2022). Journey of customers in this digital era: Understanding the role of artificial intelligence technologies in user engagement and conversion. *Benchmarking*, *29*(7), 2074–2098. https://doi.org/10.1108/BIJ-07-2021-0415

Berger, J., Moe, W. W., & Schweidel, D. A. (2023). What holds attention? Linguistic drivers of engagement. *Journal of Marketing, 87*(5), 793–809. https://doi.org/10.1177/00222429231152880

Bianchi, A. (2020). *Driving consumer engagement in social media* (1st ed.). Routledge. www.routledge.com/

Chaffey, D., & Smith, P. (2023). *Digital marketing excellence* (6th ed.). Routledge.

Kim, S., Chen, J., Cheng, T., Gindulyte, A., He, J., He, S., Li, Q., Shoemaker, B. A., Thiessen, P. A., Yu, B., Zaslavsky, L., Zhang, J., & Bolton, E. E. (2021). PubChem in 2021: New data content and improved web interfaces. *Nucleic Acids Research, 49*(D1), D1388–D1395. https://doi.org/10.1093/nar/gkaa971

Loftus, W. (2012). Demonstrating success: Web analytics and continuous improvement. *Journal of Web Librarianship, 6*(1), 45–55. https://doi.org/10.1080/19322909.2012.651416

Srinivasan, S., Rutz, O. J., & Pauwels, K. (2016). Paths to and off purchase: Quantifying the impact of traditional marketing and online consumer activity. *Journal of the Academy of Marketing Science, 44*(4), 440–453. https://doi.org/10.1007/s11747-015-0431-z

Tsimonis, G., Dimitriadis, S., & Omar, S. (2020). An integrative typology of relational benefits and costs in social media brand pages. *International Journal of Market Research, 62*(2), 216–233. https://doi.org/10.1177/1470785318822270

Tupikovskaja-Omovie, Z. (2022). Enhancing user experience in fashion m-retail: Mapping shopping user journey using google analytics, eye tracking technology and retrospective think aloud interview. *Fashion Practice, 14*(3), 352–375. https://doi.org/10.1080/17569370.2022.2129466

Wu, C. W., Botella-Carrubi, D., & Blanco-González-Tejero, C. (2024). The empirical study of digital marketing strategy and performance in small and medium-sized enterprises (SMEs). *Technological Forecasting and Social Change, 200*,. https://doi.org/10.1016/j.techfore.2023.123142

Enhancing the Online Shopping Experience with Virtual Reality and Augmented Reality Videos

H. M. Udanee Sachithra Rathnayake Samarasinghe, Umesha Dabare, and Ranitha Sachinthana Weerarathna

Abstract

Virtual Reality (VR) and Augmented Reality (AR) are rapidly emerging technologies combining digital and physical surroundings to provide extremely immersive and engaging user experiences. These technologies are progressively influencing the future of digital commerce by changing the way consumers interact with businesses and products. This chapter investigates the revolutionary power of VR and AR in altering the online buying experience by bridging the sensory and experiential gaps typically associated with e-commerce. These technologies improve customer engagement, boost confidence, and personalize the buying experience by utilizing immersive simulations and real-time product displays. The chapter looks into fundamental principles, actual applications, and the technology infrastructure necessary for successful execution. Taking real-world examples in a cross-industries approach representing beauty, fashion, automotive, and home decorations, it further explains how VR and AR influence consumer behavior and decision-making. Ultimately, these bring into light emerging trends and strategic opportunities, illustrating how these immersive technologies would drive innovation, strengthen brand loyalty, and shape the future of retail in a dynamic, digital marketplace.

H. M. U. S. Rathnayake Samarasinghe
Beacon International College, Singapore, Singapore
e-mail: udanee@beacon.edu.sg

U. Dabare · R. S. Weerarathna (✉)
SLIIT Business School, Sri Lanka Institute of Information Technology, Malabe, Sri Lanka
e-mail: ranitha.w@sliit.lk

U. Dabare
e-mail: umesha.d@sliit.lk

© The Author(s), under exclusive license to Springer Nature Singapore Pte Ltd. 2026
N. S. Jayawardena et al. (eds.), *Digital Advertising and Consumer Behavior*, Management for Professionals, https://doi.org/10.1007/978-981-95-7809-2_6

1 Introduction

With the evolution of digital e-commerce, online shopping is an everyday necessity and a rich culture of spending. Businesses must keep up with these changes with the aim of making the experience almost a replica of the joys incurred when shopping physically. A challenge businesses have to overcome is online shoppers experiencing disconnectedness due to the absence of sensory engagement which are offered by in-store experiences. The advancement of innovative technologies has brought Augment Reality (AR) and Virtual Reality (VR) into the picture, emerging as transformative technologies, drastically changing online retail practices. These technologies provide a connection among the physical and digital realms, letting consumers engage with products in previously unimaginable. Virtual reality positions consumers in simulated worlds, allowing them to navigate through virtual shopfronts and also evaluate products in realistic contexts with a live experience. Augmented Reality enriches digital aspects onto the physical retail environments, enabling consumers to view and sense products in a simulative setting, furniture within their residences or assess the appearance of clothing and cosmetics on their bodies, all via the interface of their smartphone or tablet. Together with that, this chapter begins with exploring the fundamental concepts of AR and VR, addressing its applications in retail and the role of enhancing the online shopping experience. From the ground aspects which influence consumer psychology to sky-high technology and immersive tools, here the discussion presents a comprehensive narration of how these two tech applications would redefine e-commerce and shape its future.

2 Concepts and Applications of AR and VR

Virtual Reality is "an immersive experience in a completely simulated environment, excluding everything in the physical "real" world," (BigCommerce, 2021). By wearing VR headsets like the Meta Quest or HTC Vive, customers are given the opportunity to virtually navigate stores, observe and inspect 3D models of products, or get engaged with exclusive experiences like virtual car test drives. For example, Audi's VR showroom allows users to experience a car's features interactively, enhancing confidence in their purchasing decision (Zeng et al., 2023). Moreover, VR is particularly useful in sectors where physical experience matters the most, such as real estate, automotive, and high-value retail products.

Augmented Reality adds to the physical world by introducing some digital elements on the real pictures via phones or tablets, therefore showcasing a visual of how the product would fit in the user's home or how it would look on them (Carmigniani et al., 2011). For instance, AR allows potential customers to place imaginary sofas within their homes as well as wear clothes and jewelry without actually changing them all from the comforts of their homes behind a screen. Both VR and AR seek to develop a more engaging shopping experience, enhancing interactivity that does not only give customers the ability to visualize the products but also interact with it, which online shopping does not offer. IKEA's AR app, IKEA Place, enables customers to visualize furniture within their homes before purchasing, minimizing the risk of dissatisfaction (Anthony, 2023). Similarly, Sephora's Virtual Artist app allows shoppers to virtually try on makeup, eliminating the need for physical samples and ensuring a hygienic and personalized experience (McKinsey & Company, 2023).

The success of VR and AR always depends upon the robust technological infrastructure, and it gets into dynamic changes and upgrades along the way. Considering the VR applications, it requires specialized hardware with high fidelity graphics and spatial audio to generate lifelike simulations. Compared to VR, AR is more mobile-friendly in providing solutions powered by real-time image recognition and machine learning algorithms. Tools like Unity and Unreal Engine facilitate the creation of realistic 3D environments and objects, while the advent of 5G networks has dramatically enhanced the speed and responsiveness of these applications (Wiederhold & Riva, 2023). These will transform shopping online by providing customized, interesting, and instructive experiences. Whether exploring a virtual showroom or checking out a product using AR, consumers will be better equipped to make educated selections, lowering return rates and increasing their connection with companies. As these breakthroughs progress, their potential applications will grow even further, defining the future of retail with unprecedented levels of involvement and participation.

3 Transforming the Shopping Experience: Interactive and Immersive

The application of VR and AR are revolutionizing the shopping experience, transforming the same into a more dynamic, interactive and immersive journey. These tools empower consumers by providing huge control over their engagement with products and services, allowing them to feel the sensory aspects of the physical shopping experience in the online space enriching convenience.

In the current context, the key aspects visible of these technologies are product visualization. AR lets customer position virtual items inside their retail environment's tangible surroundings, enabling them to view the appearance of a couch in their living room or assess how some sort of decorations look once these items are placed on wherever you want to. IKEA's augmented reality application, IKEA Place, demonstrates this functionality by enabling users to virtually "position" furniture within their residences, so markedly diminishing the ambiguity linked to substantial acquisitions (Anthony, 2023; Ozturkcan., 2021). In addition, the fashion and beauty sectors also refer to the same as mentioned above with the example taken with Sephora enhancing consumer confidence and satisfaction where L'Oreal use AR-powered virtual try-on features letting their customers experiment a wide array of makeup products on their faces via smartphone applications. Through these practices organizations can cultivate trust, confidence, and reduce uncertainty in purchasing.

Moreover, the immersive virtual environments enrich the customer experience via offering simulations comparable to in-store visits. A laboratory study on extended reality shopping demonstrated that VR could surpass traditional retail experiences in terms of hedonic enjoyment, even though there are certain challenges customers would face. Moreover, VR platforms enable users for a simulative experience to navigate virtual showrooms, examine products, and engage with them as if these were physically present in real-world. Audi's VR showroom allows buyers to "test drive" vehicles and personalize features, enhancing the purchasing experience (Zeng et al., 2023). These features not only improve the purchasing experience but also nurture deeper emotional bonds between consumers and the organizations. Another main feature of these technologies is their capacity to generate customized shopping experiences. Via the integration of machine learning algorithms, VR and AR platforms may customize settings and product suggestions according to individual taste and preferences. For instance, AR can recommend beauty hues according to skin tone, while VR can display curated products in a customized virtual boutique. This degree of customization is really impressive here as it enhances client happiness and fosters loyalty (Wiederhold & Riva, 2023).

Furthermore, VR and AR substantially diminish obstacles to interaction, allowing consumers to interactively examine things without any limitations. Conventional e-commerce depends on static photos and descriptions; however, these immersive technologies introduce a dimension of interactivity that enhances consumer engagement. Retailers like Alibaba have implemented VR shopping platforms that allow consumers to explore virtual shopfronts, engage with products, and finalize purchases all within a completely digital setting (Liew et al., 2023; Srivastava, 2024). This gamified shopping strategy strengthens the engagement on platforms and improves brand retention. Furthermore, VR and AR avoid decision-making difficulties by offering accurate, real-time and key information regarding product characteristics, dimensions, and functionality which are essential in making choices. By diminishing uncertainty, these technologies increase returns and cultivate confidence in online commerce. Shopify indicates that consumers utilizing AR capabilities are 40% more inclined to complete a purchase due to the confidence these products foster (Shopify, 2023).

These technologies have mostly influenced their capacity to replicate the cognitive and sensory aspects of physical buying on digital channels. It is noteworthy that AR and VR solve the constraints of conventional e-commerce by letting consumers engage with goods in a reasonable and contextually relevant way (Muruganantham & Kumar, 2024). These also open novel avenues for consumer customization, such as virtual co-design of products (Rane et al., 2023), in which buyers actively assist to match their purchases to their own taste. Brands are changing the e-commerce landscape and keep innovating with AR and VR by offering engaging and immersive experiences that satisfy the needs of tech-savvy consumers. These changes indicate a more interesting, customized, and futuristic retail paradigm.

4 Impact Towards Consumer Behavior

The integration of VR and AR in e-commerce transcends technological progress; it fundamentally alters customer behavior. These immersive technologies allow buyers to visualize, interact with, and customize products, effectively mitigating significant challenges of online buying, such as ambiguity, disengagement, and discontent. The outcome is an unparalleled degree of assurance in buying choices and a profound emotional bond with businesses, generating enduring loyalty.

Enhanced assurance using pragmatic visual representations is one of the most notable effects of VR and AR is its capacity to provide realistic, interactive representations of products. As mentioned above, the conventional e-commerce platforms depend on static photos and descriptions, resulting in client ambiguity over the size, color, or fit of products. As in the example associated with IKEA Place and Sephora, VR and AR permit consumers to interact with the brand in a more simulated environment where they can feel the product with a live simulation. These skills alleviate the cognitive difficulties of decision-making, facilitating more trust in customer decisions. By the way, low returns have historically been a hurdle in e-commerce, frequently due to discrepancies between product descriptions and actual products. On top of this, VR and AR substantially alleviate this problem by offering buyers a comprehensive and precise identification of the product prior to the stage where customers tend to purchase. A 2023 Shopify study revealed that augmented reality technologies reduced return rates by 25% in sectors like furniture and apparel, where fit and aesthetics are paramount (Artlabs, 2018; Shopify, 2023). This not only reduces expenses for businesses but also improves customer satisfaction, as consumers receive products that fulfil their expectations.

In addition to practical advantages, VR and AR engender a sense of surprise and exhilaration that conventional internet purchasing fails to replicate. Immersive experiences, such as navigating virtual showrooms or participating in gamified shopping events, transform the act of shopping into an interactive journey. Alibaba's VR shopping platform enables consumers to traverse stores digitally, engage with merchandise, and participate in exclusive events, thereby enhancing their emotional engagement in the company (Alibaba Cloud Community, 2024; Srivastava, 2024). This increased interaction fosters favorable connections with the brand, promoting repeat visits and acquisitions. Customization and brand fidelity personalization is fundamental to consumer loyalty, and VR and AR are adept at customizing experiences to individual preferences. By amalgamating AI with these technologies, merchants may establish exceptionally tailored shopping environments. Augmented reality technologies can suggest clothing styles or makeup tints based on the user's prior selections, whilst virtual reality environments can assemble virtual shopfronts showcasing products that correspond with the shopper's preferences (Wiederhold & Riva, 2023). This degree of personalization not only satisfies consumer expectations but also cultivates a sensation of uniqueness, rendering clients feeling esteemed and comprehended.

Extended engagement and increased conversion rates interactivity are a crucial element in maintaining client engagement. Further, VR and AR enhance user engagement on retail platforms by providing gamified and exploratory functionalities. A 2023 analysis by Shopify indicated that consumers utilizing AR capabilities spend 40% more time on platforms than typical e-commerce users, markedly enhancing the probability of purchase (Shopify, 2023). Furthermore, the experiential engagement facilitated by these technologies promotes impulsive purchasing, as consumers have a heightened emotional attachment to objects. Here, VR and AR experiences are intrinsically shared, promoting social engagement in the context of buying. Attributes such as virtual try-ons and gamified shopping environments motivate users to disseminate their experiences on social media, enhancing brand visibility. Moreover, the innovation of these technologies frequently generates discussion, resulting in spontaneous word-of-mouth marketing. Zeng et al. (2023) indicate that consumers who engage with augmented reality in online buying are 70% more inclined to endorse the brand to others, hence enhancing its reach and impact.

Confidence and openness trust is another pivotal element in customer behavior, and VR and AR augment it by removing uncertainty. These technologies enable consumers to examine products comprehensively, including magnifying textures, assessing functionality in virtual settings, or visualizing product integration into their life. Audi's VR showrooms allow buyers to personalize vehicles and experience virtual test drives, fostering confidence in both the product and the brand (Anthony, 2023). This transparency instills confidence in clients, increasing the likelihood of purchase completion and subsequent transactions. Facilitating Consumer Decision-Making VR and AR facilitate an explicit and engaging presentation of items, enabling consumers to make informed choices. This empowerment enhances confidence and alleviates the stress linked to buying, especially for high-value or intricate goods. Research indicates that consumers utilizing VR or AR tools experience more control and satisfaction, resulting in increased post-purchase loyalty (Srivastava, 2020).

Brands that embrace VR and AR are referred to as innovative and consumer-centric, enhancing their brand. Consumers are more inclined to exhibit brand loyalty towards companies that emphasize their expertise and utilize advanced technologies to fulfil their requirements. Wiederhold and Riva (2023) emphasize that immersive experiences offered by VR and AR enhance the probability of repeat purchases by 30%, linking consumers to these technologies to superior service and innovative practices. Sustainability and Ethical Considerations Ultimately, VR and AR facilitate sustainable shopping methods that increasingly impact customer behavior. These technologies diminish the necessity for actual samples, showrooms, and returns, hence minimizing the carbon footprint of retail operations. Environmentally concerned consumers are more inclined to endorse brands that implement such advances, hence enhancing loyalty.

5 Technological Infrastructure and Implementations

Hardware, software, network infrastructure, and system integration must all be included in a strong technological framework for VR and AR to be successfully implemented in e-commerce (Rane et al., 2023). The deployment of these technologies, which are designed to produce realistic and captivating shopping experiences, depends on the number of interrelated elements.

Hardware Requirements

Hardware is essential to deliver VR and AR experiences. To create immersive settings, high-performance VR devices like the Oculus Rift, HTC Vive, and PlayStation VR are necessary (Anthes et al., 2016).These gadgets frequently have controllers and sensors that track motion, allowing users to interact with virtual worlds with ease. The majority of contemporary smartphones and tablets with AR-capable platforms, such as Google's ARCore and Apple's ARKit, are adequate for AR, increasing its accessibility for a larger audience. Although less frequently utilized in retail environments, advanced AR glasses such as Microsoft HoloLens and Magic Leap offer extra functionalities for particular use cases.

Software and Development Platforms

Development platforms and software tools are equally important. Retailers may create realistic simulations for VR and AR apps by using platforms like Unity and Unreal Engine, which are commonly used to produce 3D models, animations, and interactive environments. Retailers may successfully incorporate augmented reality into their digital platforms assisted by AR-specific development kits like Vuforia, ARKit, and ARCore (Syed et al., 2023). By optimizing programs for a range of devices, these platforms enable developers to guarantee flawless user experiences.

3D Modeling and Content Creation

A key component of effective VR and AR implementations is high-quality 3D modeling. Customers can see products in virtual or augmented settings thanks to realistic, detailed, and lifelike 3D representations (Fathima & Sooda, 2023).To produce material optimized for several platforms, this calls for sophisticated image technologies and talented designers.By providing customers with a more realistic and engaging picture of their items, retailers who engage in the creation of 3D content gain a competitive advantage.

Internet Connectivity and Cloud Computing

Delivering seamless VR and AR experiences requires cloud infrastructure and fast internet connectivity. Because 5G networks provide high bandwidth, low latency, and quicker data transmission rates all essential for real-time rendering and interaction, their rollout is especially noteworthy. Retailers can effectively manage the massive amounts of data needed for VR and AR applications thanks to cloud computing systems like AWS and Google Cloud, which offer scalable storage and processing capability (Liew et al., 2023). The dissemination of VR and AR material across various geographic regions is further optimized using material Delivery Networks (CDNs).

Artificial Intelligence and Machine Learning

By facilitating customized purchasing experiences, artificial intelligence (AI) and machine learning increase the efficacy of VR and AR. In virtual worlds, AI can provide personalized recommendations by analyzing consumer behavior and interests (Rane et al., 2023).By improving object recognition and responsiveness, machine learning further enhances AR and VR give users a more engaging and dynamic experience.

Integration with E-commerce Platforms

VR and AR must work in unison with current e-commerce systems for a positive and significant impact. Connecting immersive technology to payment gateways, inventory management systems, and customer relationship management (CRM) tools is part of this. Integration improves consumer happiness and conversion rates by facilitating a seamless transition from virtual exploration to checkout. Retailers can easily integrate AR features into their platforms with the help of tools like Shopify AR and WooCommerce AR Viewer (Hatem et al., 2024).

User-Friendly Interfaces

The development of user-friendly interfaces is essential to the success of VR and AR in e-commerce. These user interfaces must be simple and easy to use, accommodating people with different degrees of technological expertise. Even inexperienced users may connect with these technologies with ease thanks to its responsive design, interactive features, and easy navigation.

Future Trends and Sustainability

It is anticipated that VR and AR technologies will play a bigger part in e-commerce as they develop further. Features like virtual try-ons and extensive product customization will be made possible by a wider adoption of AR through improved app and website capabilities. New developments like VR-powered social commerce combine e-commerce and social engagement by enabling users to shop in virtual settings with peers (Muruganantham & Kumar, 2024). Furthermore, by eliminating the need for physical showrooms and samples, these technologies help to reduce the carbon footprint associated with conventional retail operations.

6 Industry Examples

Through the creation of immersive, interactive, and customized consumer journeys, AR and VR technologies are revolutionizing both in-person and online buying. Detailed examples of each industry are provided below, complete with analysis.

Beauty and Cosmetics

Sephora Virtual Artist: Through 3D facial mapping technology, Sephora's AR feature enables consumers to visually test makeup on their cellphones. Before making a purchase, customers can try on different tones of lipstick, foundation, and other cosmetics. This feature has decreased return rates and given customers more confidence when choosing products. Sephora gives customers a customized shopping experience without requiring tangible goods by incorporating augmented reality (Lele, 2021). By bridging the gap between online and in-store buying, this invention increases conversions and engagement.

L'Oréal Virtual Makeup Try-On: Customers can virtually try on various beauty hues and products with AR (Javornik, 2016). By removing doubt in decision-making, the technology increases user engagement with the brand and boosts revenues. Unlike tangible items, AR encourages experimentation, which would be expensive and time-consuming. By providing customers with a clear idea of the applicability of the product, it increases customer happiness.

Fashion and Apparel

Nike unveiled Nike Fit, a cutting-edge innovation intended to solve the widespread problem of customers purchasing the wrong size shoes. To precisely assess the entire contour of both feet, this technology combines computer vision, data science, machine learning, AI, and recommendation algorithms. Users can get accurate size suggestions for various Nike shoe designs by using the camera on their smartphone to scan their foot (Patov, 2024). By guaranteeing a better fit, this individualized method seeks to increase consumer happiness by decreasing the possibility of returns and promoting a more customized purchasing experience. Nike lowers operating expenses associated with returns and increases customer trust in online shopping by tackling one of the major problems in online fashion retail: proper sizing (Cheng, 2019).

In an effort to engage younger customers and improve the in-store shopping experience, Zara launched a cutting-edge AR experience in 120 flagship locations worldwide in April 2018. Customers could examine virtual models exhibiting the newest designs by using the Zara AR app to point their cellphones at certain locations within the store, such as shop window displays, sensors, or mannequins. These talking and moving virtual models would give comprehensive details on the clothing goods and give users the choice to find the items in-store or make a straight purchase through the app (Hatem et al., 2024). The goal of this AR project was to satisfy younger consumers' digital inclinations by facilitating a smooth transition between online and offline buying. Zara's in-store AR features allow customers to point their smartphones at specific locations to see virtual models showcasing the latest clothing lines. This brings online shopping interactivity into physical stores. Zara combines digital and physical shopping experiences, encouraging customers to explore their offerings dynamically, thereby boosting in-store traffic and engagement (Sandler, 2018).

Furniture and Home Decor

Launched in September 2017, IKEA's IKEA Place app uses AR to let users virtually place life-size 3D models of furniture in their own homes. By allowing buyers to see how items will fit and seem in their homes before making a purchase, this innovation tackles frequent problems in furniture shopping, like size misjudgment and style mismatches. The app included more than 2,000 products when it first launched, with a primary concentration on larger living room furnishings like coffee tables, couches, armchairs, footstools, and well-liked floor-mounted storage options. Customers may choose a product, digitally arrange it in their room, and then buy it straight from the app or find it in-store. With 98% accuracy, the app's AR technology guarantees accurate scaling depending on room dimensions. This accuracy adds to the virtual placement's authenticity by enabling users to see details like fabric textures and the way light and shadow interact with furniture. IKEA hopes to close the gap between online and in-store shopping experiences by using this technology, giving customers a useful tool to help them make wise decisions and lowering the possibility of returns because of unanticipated fit or style difficulties. IKEA's dedication to using technology to improve the customer experience is demonstrated by the creation of IKEA Place, a noteworthy service innovation. IKEA enhances consumer pleasure and solidifies its position as a progressive leader in the retail sector by using augmented reality to solve real-world furniture shopping issues (Sandler, 2017).

Features such as voice shopping with Alexa, tailored suggestions, and an AR tool are some ways that Amazon's shopping app improves the online buying experience. Before making a purchase, consumers can see the real-world setting via simulation about how items like furniture and home décor will appear in their environments thanks to AR View. This creative method lowers the possibility of returns while also making decision-making easier. The app is a complete platform for easy and knowledgeable buying since it also incorporates safe payment methods, smooth navigation, and instant access to user evaluations.

Automotive Industry

BMW has led the way in incorporating cutting-edge technologies to improve driving dynamics and consumer experiences. Customers may explore BMW's newest models and services in a contemporary, interactive setting at the BMW Eurokars Experience Centre in Singapore, which is a digitally immersive environment that exemplifies the retail experience. BMW unveiled the M Mixed Reality experience worldwide, which combines virtual and real-world driving experiences. It lets drivers steer actual cars through scenes that have been digitally created, taking the driving experience to new, immersive levels. Furthermore, BMW's partnerships with businesses such as Holo-Light have resulted in the creation of Extended Reality (XR) applications, which streamline design and production processes by allowing experts to view and interact with vehicle components in AR. These programs demonstrate BMW's dedication to using cutting-edge technology to redefine automotive retail and driving experiences.

7 Future Trends and Opportunities

Immersive Virtual Stores: Retailers will increasingly create fully immersive VR stores where customers can shop as if they were in a physical location. These virtual stores can replicate the in-store experience, allowing shoppers to walk through aisles, interact with products in 3D, and make purchases within the virtual environment. Brands like Walmart and Alibaba are already trialing this, and it is likely to become a mainstream option, especially for global customers who want access to flagship stores without traveling.

Virtual Fitting Rooms and Try-Ons: One of the most impactful uses of AR in retail is virtual try-ons. Apparel and beauty brands will offer AR-powered fitting rooms, allowing customers to try on clothes, accessories, or makeup virtually. This lowers the need for physical stores while offering an engaging and practical solution for customers who want to see how products fit without having to order multiple sizes. This trend is likely to reduce return rates and boost consumer confidence in online shopping.

Social Shopping and AR-driven Collaboration: VR could bring a social element to online shopping, allowing friends or family members to shop together in a shared virtual space, even when these are miles apart. Additionally, AR can enable real-time collaboration between customers and sales supporters or stylists. Shoppers could obtain personal recommendations from remote experts via AR, making their shopping experience more interactive and personalized.

Virtual Pop-up Stores and Events Retailers: Customers can experiment virtual pop-up stores and product launches in VR environments. These events can attract large audiences without the geographic limitations of physical spaces, enabling retailers to create exclusive, time-limited shopping experiences. Virtual pop-up stores will be particularly appealing for fashion, tech, and luxury brands that want to create a buzz around new product releases.

8 Conclusion

The combination of VR and AR with online purchasing marks a paradigm shift in e-commerce, altering how customers engage with digital platforms and products as technology advances dramatically. This chapter examined how these technologies improve the shopping experience by making it more interactive, immersive, and personalized, therefore bridging the gap between physical and virtual retail practices. In other words, AR and VR applications have demonstrated outstanding yet possible capabilities to influence consumer behavior by solving particular issues in online shopping, such as ambiguity regarding product fit, quality, and usage.

As highlighted above, the technological infrastructure supporting these innovations continues to boom, enabling smoother implementations and broader adoption across industries. With real-world examples like IKEA's AR furniture placement app and Sephora's virtual try-on tools, it is evident that companies leveraging these technologies are not only driving consumer engagement but also setting new benchmarks for customer satisfaction and loyalty catering to online shopping platforms. These examples underscore the necessity for businesses to invest in technologies like AR and VR to keep competitive in an increasingly digital yet dynamic marketplace.

Furthermore, the chapter explored how these technologies influence customer behavior, ranging from increasing confidence in purchasing decisions to encouraging impulsive but educated purchases. This combined effect of affecting decision-making and emotional engagement highlights the significance of both AR and VR in transforming e-commerce shopping. The discussions also detailed future trends and opportunities in this industry, which would allow customers to access more personalized, inventive, and creative customer offerings with more ease.

Looking ahead, the growth of AR and VR in e-commerce is both promising and unstoppable. As developments in hardware, software, and connectivity continue to lower entry barriers, the bulk of businesses are likely to adopt these technologies, allowing more customers to enjoy interactive and immersive shopping experiences. This transition will not only change consumer expectations but will also create new opportunities for innovation in retail, marketing, and customer involvement.

Along the way, it has been proved that the future of online shopping lies in harnessing the full potential of AR and VR technologies. By offering unprecedented levels of interaction and immersion, these tools are aiming to revolutionize e-commerce practices, creating opportunities for businesses to forge deeper connections with their customers while delivering value in ways that were previously unimaginable. The ongoing advances in this space present a compelling opportunity for stakeholders to shape the next era of retail, ensuring its relevance and growth in an increasingly digital world.

References

Alibaba Cloud Community. (n.d.). *Alibaba rolls out deeper immersive luxury shopping experience in the metaverse*. https://www.alibabacloud.com/blog/alibaba-rolls-out-deeper-immersive-luxury-shopping-experience-in-the-metaverse_599369

Anthony, S. (2023). *Amazon's immersive shopping experience through VR/AR*. Signalytics. https://signalytics.ai

Artlabs. (2018). *Benefits of Shopify AR for small businesses*. https://artlabs.ai/blog/benefits-of-shopify-ar-for-small-businesses

BigCommerce. (2021). *Virtual reality in ecommerce: How does it work?* https://www.bigcommerce.com/articles/ecommerce/virtual-reality-ecommerce/

Carmigniani, J., Furht, B., Anisetti, M., Ceravolo, P., Damiani, E., & Ivkovic, M. (2011). Augmented reality technologies, systems and applications. *Multimedia Tools and Applications, 51*(1), 341–377. https://doi.org/10.1007/s11042-010-0660-6

Cheng, A. (2019, May 9). Nike unveils "a game-changing innovation": A fit feature to fix shoe sizing online and in-store. *Forbes*. https://www.forbes.com/sites/andriacheng/2019/05/09/this-new-nike-fit-feature-could-be-a-game-changer/

Hatem, F., Mirzah, N., Hamdoun, S. H., & Krasovska, H. (2024). Integration of programs for online shopping for users of Android devices. In *2024 35th Conference of Open Innovations Association (FRUCT)* (pp. 232–243). IEEE. https://doi.org/10.23919/FRUCT61870.2024.10516403

Javornik, A., Rogers, Y., Moutinho, A. M., & Freeman, R. (2016). Revealing the shopper experience of using a "magic mirror" augmented reality make-up application. In *Proceedings of the 2016 ACM conference on designing interactive systems* (pp. 871–882). https://doi.org/10.1145/2901790.2901810

Lele, A. (2021). *Factors influencing consumer loyalty in augmented reality beauty apps: Sephora virtual artist empirical study* (Doctoral dissertation). Toronto Metropolitan University.

Liew, S. Y., Rana, M. E., Hameed, V. A., & Safavi, S. (2023). Navigating the Retail 4.0 landscape: The transformative impact of cloud computing. In *2023 IEEE 21st Student Conference on Research and Development (SCOReD)* (pp. 499–507). IEEE. https://doi.org/10.1109/SCOReD60679.2023.10563349

McKinsey. (2023). *McKinsey technology trends outlook 2023*. https://www.mckinsey.com/capabilities/mckinsey-digital/our-insights/the-top-trends-in-tech-2023

Muruganantham, G., & Kumar, B. D. (2024). Augmented reality: Shaping the metaverse. In C. Krishnan, A. Behl, S. Dash, & P. D. Yadav (Eds.), *The metaverse dilemma: Challenges and opportunities for business and society* (pp. 33–52). Emerald Publishing Limited. https://doi.org/10.1108/978-1-83797-524-220241003

Ozturkcan, S. (2021). Service innovation: Using augmented reality in the IKEA Place app. *Journal of Information Technology Teaching Cases, 11*(1), 204–388. https://doi.org/10.1177/2043886920947110

Patov, A. (2024). *Customer experience (CX) at Nike: A case study in excellence.* Renascence.io. https://www.renascence.io/journal/customer-experience-cx-at-nike-a-case-study-in-excellence

Rane, N., Choudhary, S., & Rane, J. (2023). Enhanced product design and development using artificial intelligence (AI), virtual reality (VR), augmented reality (AR), 4D/5D/6D printing, Internet of Things (IoT), and blockchain: A review. https://doi.org/10.2139/ssrn.4644059

Sandler, E. (2018, April 16). Zara stores target millennials with augmented reality displays. *Forbes.* https://www.forbes.com/sites/emmasandler/2018/04/16/zara-stores-targets-millennials-with-augmented-reality-displays/

Shopify. (2023). *Impact of AR on conversion rates in e-commerce.* https://www.shopify.com

Srivastava, S. (2020). *AR/VR trends and predictions for 2020 & beyond.* Appinventiv. https://appinventiv.com/blog/ar-vr-trends/

Srivastava, S. (2024). *AR/VR trends and predictions for the upcoming years.* Appinventiv. https://appinventiv.com

Syed, T. A., et al. (2023). In-depth review of augmented reality: Tracking technologies, development tools, AR displays, collaborative AR, and security concerns. *Sensors, 23*(1), 146. https://doi.org/10.3390/s23010146

Wiederhold, B. K., & Riva, G. (2023). Emerging topics in VR/AR retail applications. *Cyberpsychology, Behavior, and Social Networking.*

Zeng, J. Y., Xing, Y., & Jin, C. H. (2023). The impact of VR/AR-based consumer experiences. *MDPI.* https://www.mdpi.com

Understanding Short Video Advertising in Digital Marketing Through Digital Analytics

Ajay Khatter, Hare Krishna Chaudhary, and Swati Sharma

Abstract

Short video advertising has become a pivotal element of digital marketing, fuelled by the widespread popularity of platforms like TikTok, Instagram Reels, and YouTube Shorts. This chapter aims to explore the effectiveness of short video ads by using digital analytics. It investigates how these ads engage audiences, comparing their impact to longer ad formats. The purpose is to offer insights into the elements that contribute to the success of short video ads and to understand their role in modern digital marketing strategies. To systematically review and analyse the effectiveness of short video ads, this chapter applies the PRISMA methodology. Through an in-depth exploration of historical context, theoretical frameworks, and empirical evidence, the chapter examines the key factors that make short video ads effective. The research evaluates various metrics, such as click-through rates and viewer interaction, to provide a comprehensive view of how these ads perform in comparison to traditional ad formats. The findings shows that short video ads excel at capturing attention and driving action due to their concise and impactful nature. Creativity, precise targeting, and strategic timing emerge as critical factors for maximizing their effectiveness. The analysis highlights that short video ads significantly outperform traditional ad formats in terms of engagement metrics. These ads resonate

A. Khatter (✉)
Faculty of Higher Education, William Angliss Institute, Melbourne, VIC, Australia
e-mail: Ajay.Khatter@angliss.edu.au

H. K. Chaudhary
Amity University, Noida, India
e-mail: hk2191chy@gmail.com

S. Sharma
Amity Institute of Travel and Tourism, Amity University, Noida, India
e-mail: ssharma3@amity.edu

© The Author(s), under exclusive license to Springer Nature Singapore Pte Ltd. 2026
N. S. Jayawardena et al. (eds.), *Digital Advertising and Consumer Behavior*,
Management for Professionals, https://doi.org/10.1007/978-981-95-7809-2_7

particularly well with mobile-first consumers, who prefer quick, on-the-go content consumption. As a result, short video ads are reshaping digital marketing strategies and driving greater engagement. This chapter underscores the growing importance of short video ads in the era of mobile-first consumers. Marketers must prioritize creativity, precise audience targeting, and timing to maximize the effectiveness of short video ads. The comparative analysis suggests that these ads are a more effective medium than longer formats for engaging users and prompting actions. However, limitations exist in terms of understanding the full scope of audience responses and the long-term impact of short video ads on brand loyalty. Future research should focus on exploring the evolving dynamics of short video advertising and how it continues to reshape the digital marketing landscape.

1 Introduction

Short video advertising has become a cornerstone of digital marketing strategies, transforming how brands connect with audiences in today's fast-paced, attention-scarce world. Platforms like TikTok, Instagram Reels, and YouTube Shorts have played a pivotal role in popularising this format, allowing companies to engage audiences through concise, visually appealing content (Addo et al., 2022). Unlike traditional advertising approaches, which often rely on lengthy storytelling, short video ads cater to modern viewers' preference for quick, easily digestible content, making them particularly effective for capturing attention and driving action (Xiao et al., 2023).This study leverages the PRISMA approach to systematically identify, evaluate, and synthesise relevant literature, providing a data-driven exploration of the effectiveness of short video advertising in digital marketing. By employing digital analytics, businesses gain critical insights into consumer behaviour, engagement metrics, and campaign performance, enabling them to optimise strategies for greater impact (Camilleri, 2020). Metrics such as views, clicks, engagement rates, and conversions offer valuable feedback, allowing marketers to refine their content and better target their audiences (Addo et al., 2022).

The rise of platforms like TikTok, Instagram Reels, and YouTube Shorts has reshaped consumer expectations, emphasising quick, engaging content that is easy to consume and share (Aydin et al., 2021). These platforms not only prioritise short-form videos but also provide tools to enhance user interaction, such as TikTok's Duet feature or Instagram's Reels Remix. As a result, brands now have fresh opportunities for creativity and storytelling, creating impactful narratives that resonate with audiences in seconds (Sutherland, 2024). Compared to conventional formats that often rely on extended narratives, short videos deliver immediate visual appeal and concise messaging, making them more effective at capturing attention and driving viewer engagement (Ge et al., 2021). This paper examines the efficiency of short video advertising through the lens of digital analytics, focusing on key areas such as engagement metrics, consumer responses, and the creative elements that contribute to their success. Digital analytics provides a precise, data-driven perspective on the effectiveness of these ads, empowering marketers to make informed decisions about content, timing, and audience targeting (Rosário & Dias, 2023). By understanding which types of content generate the best results, businesses can guide their campaigns with actionable insights, ensuring their strategies align with audience preferences and behaviours (Kamal & Aziz Bablu, 2022).

Despite the rapid adoption of short video advertising, more research is still needed into the strategic and psychological factors that drive engagement and conversion, specifically within short-form content. Much of the existing literature focuses on broader social media trends or long-form advertising, leaving a gap in understanding the unique capabilities and limitations of short videos. This study addresses this gap by systematically analysing the effectiveness of short video ads, with particular attention to audience engagement, creative strategies, and the role of digital platforms in enabling targeted consumer interactions. The findings aim to advance both theoretical understanding and practical applications in digital advertising. By exploring how short video ads leverage creativity, audience targeting, and data-driven decision-making, this research offers valuable insights for marketers looking to maximise the impact of their campaigns. As digital platforms and consumer preferences continue to evolve, short video advertising represents a powerful tool for brands to connect with their audiences in meaningful, memorable ways.

2 Literature Review

The Power of Short Video Ads in Digital Marketing

Short video ads have revolutionised digital marketing, capitalising on the growing consumer preference for rapid, engaging content (Yin et al., 2024). Platforms like TikTok, Instagram Reels, and YouTube Shorts have transformed how people consume media by emphasising brief, visually appealing formats designed for maximum engagement. These platforms have driven a shift from traditional, static content to dynamic, interactive content that resonates with audiences on a deeper level (Bhandari & Bimo, 2022). The adaptability of short video ads to changing consumer behaviour has made them an indispensable tool for marketers looking to build brand visibility and connect with their target audiences effectively (Meng et al., 2024).

Leveraging the AIDA Model for Short Video Ads

The AIDA model (Attention, Interest, Desire, Action) serves as a foundational framework for understanding the effectiveness of short video ads (Rabindranath & Singh, 2024). Each phase of AIDA is essential in driving consumer engagement:

Attention: The concise and visually rich nature of short video ads makes them particularly effective in capturing viewers' attention. Platforms like TikTok, designed for quick consumption, enhance this phase by promoting content that grabs users' focus within seconds (Belanche et al., 2020).

Interest: Once attention is captured, sustaining interest requires compelling narratives and dynamic visuals. Short videos excel at this by delivering high-impact messages tailored to the audience's preferences (Luo et al., 2022).

Desire: Effective short video ads build emotional connections with viewers, fostering a sense of desire for the product or service being advertised. The psychological appeal of well-crafted visuals and soundtracks enhances this phase (Poth, 2020).

Action: Clear and concise calls-to-action (CTAs) encourage viewers to take the desired steps, whether it's clicking a link, making a purchase, or sharing the video (Zheng et al., 2024).

Metrics as Indicators of Success

Metrics such as views, likes, shares, and conversion rates are critical in evaluating the success of short video ads. These engagement metrics are more indicative of audience interest and ad effectiveness than traditional measures like impressions (Tafesse & Wien, 2018). Short videos outperform traditional formats in capturing user interaction, with algorithms favouring content that generates high engagement levels (Fang et al., 2023). Platforms like TikTok have revolutionised content delivery by rewarding videos with higher retention and interaction rates. For example, a video that garners significant likes and shares is more likely to be promoted through the platform's algorithm, further increasing its visibility and impact (Trunfio & Rossi, 2021).

The Role of Digital Analytics in Short Video Advertising

Digital analytics has become an essential component of short video advertising, offering marketers detailed insights into consumer behaviour and ad performance (Shi et al., 2023). By analysing metrics such as engagement rates, click-through rates (CTR), and conversions, marketers can fine-tune their campaigns in real-time (Pauwels et al., 2023). This data-driven approach enables businesses to adapt quickly to audience preferences, optimising the relevance and reach of their content. The integration of analytics with short video ads allows for greater personalisation and targeting (Kshetri et al., 2024). For example, content tailored to specific demographics or interests consistently outperforms generic ads, as viewers are more likely to engage with material that feels relevant to their needs and preferences (Li et al., 2022).

Moreover, analytics tools provide insights into viewing patterns and engagement spikes, helping marketers identify what elements resonate most with their audiences. This iterative process of creating, analysing, and refining content ensures that short video ads remain impactful in a rapidly changing digital landscape (Willis, 2024).

Timing and Audience Targeting

The success of short video ads is not only dependent on content quality but also on strategic timing and audience targeting. Research shows that ads deployed during peak engagement periods achieve significantly higher interaction and conversion rates (Li et al., 2022). Platforms like Instagram and TikTok allow marketers to identify when their target demographics are most active, ensuring their ads reach audiences at the right moment (Ortiz et al., 2023). Audience segmentation further enhances ad effectiveness by enabling marketers to deliver personalised content to specific groups (Beauvisage et al., 2023). For instance, a younger audience on TikTok might respond well to humorous and fast-paced videos, while an older demographic on Instagram might prefer aesthetically pleasing and informative content. This level of customisation is critical in maximising the impact of short video ads.

The Psychological Appeal of Short Videos

Consumer psychology plays a crucial role in the success of short video ads. Visually appealing content is more likely to capture attention and be remembered, making it a powerful tool for brand messaging (Poth, 2020). Short videos, with their combination of striking visuals, engaging narratives, and emotional resonance, create a memorable experience for viewers (Pellegrino, 2024). Research also highlights the importance of storytelling in short video ads. Even within a limited timeframe, a well-crafted narrative can evoke emotions, build trust, and foster a connection with the audience. This emotional engagement increases the likelihood of viewers taking action, whether it's purchasing a product or sharing the ad with their network (Zhang et al., 2023).

Advantages Over Traditional Advertising

Compared to traditional advertising formats, short video ads offer several distinct advantages. They are less intrusive, more enjoyable, and better suited to the fast-paced nature of modern digital consumption (Dong et al., 2024). The brevity of these ads aligns with the limited attention spans of today's audiences, ensuring that the message is delivered effectively within seconds. Additionally, short video ads are optimised for mobile consumption, which accounts for the majority of online activity. Their adaptability to different screen sizes and orientations makes them highly accessible, further increasing their reach and effectiveness (Willis, 2024).

The Future of Short Video Advertising

As digital marketing continues to evolve, short video ads are poised to play an even more significant role (Varadarajan et al., 2022). The studies by Chaudhary et al. (2023, 2024, 2025), Divya Bose and Hare Krishna Chaudhary (2023), and Kumar and Chaudhary (2023) highlight the growing importance of sustainability, technology, and inclusivity in hospitality and food services. These trends align with the evolving role of digital marketing, where short video advertising, powered by analytics, can amplify eco-friendly practices and inclusivity messages. As businesses increasingly adopt responsible tourism and AI in operations, short video ads can effectively communicate their sustainability efforts to a broader audience. Advances in mobile technology and the growing influence of social media platforms have created an environment where concise, impactful content is highly valued (Alghamdi et al., 2023).Emerging trends, such as the integration of augmented reality (AR) and interactive elements into short video ads, are likely to enhance their appeal further. These innovations provide new opportunities for brands to engage with audiences in creative and immersive ways (Ruihao, 2021).

Furthermore, the use of artificial intelligence (AI) in digital analytics is set to revolutionise how marketers' approach short video advertising. AI-powered tools can analyse vast amounts of data to identify patterns, predict trends, and optimise ad performance, ensuring that campaigns remain relevant and effective in an increasingly competitive landscape (Addo et al., 2022). Short video ads have transformed digital marketing by delivering high-impact messages that resonate with modern audiences (Amiri et al., 2023). By leveraging frameworks like the AIDA model, incorporating detailed digital analytics, and emphasising personalisation and timing, marketers can maximise the effectiveness of these ads.

The combination of concise messaging, emotional resonance, and data-driven strategies makes short video ads a powerful tool for brands looking to build engagement and drive conversions (Zhang et al., 2024). As technology continues to advance, the potential for innovation in this space remains vast, ensuring that short video advertising will remain at the forefront of digital marketing for years to come.

3 Methodology

The selection process for this study was meticulously designed to ensure a robust and comprehensive review of the literature on short video advertising in digital media. To achieve this, the PRISMA (Preferred Reporting Items for Systematic Reviews and Meta-Analyses) methodology was employed. PRISMA offers a structured framework for systematically collecting, screening, and synthesising evidence, ensuring the review is thorough, focused, and high-quality. This approach provided the foundation for a rigorous analysis that addresses the dynamic and evolving nature of digital marketing. The process began with an extensive search for relevant academic articles. Keywords such as "short video advertising," "digital analytics," "engagement metrics," and "conversion rates" were used to query reputable databases, including Google Scholar, Scopus, and Web of Science. This initial effort yielded 150 articles. To refine the dataset, PRISMA guidelines were applied to eliminate duplicates and exclude non-English publications. This ensured the focus remained on accessible and relevant studies.

Next, the remaining 100 articles underwent a detailed screening process. The primary criterion was relevance, with a focus on identifying studies that directly addressed short video advertising and its interplay with digital analytics. Articles that explored unrelated topics, such as long-form content or traditional advertising, were removed. This phase reduced the sample size to 40 articles, each of which showed potential for contributing meaningful insights. In the final stage, the 40 articles were rigorously evaluated against predefined inclusion criteria. Studies that failed to provide substantial insights into key areas—such as engagement metrics, consumer behaviour, or best practices for short video content—were excluded. The ultimate selection included 20 high-quality articles. These studies were chosen for their direct relevance to the research objectives, focusing on critical aspects such as consumer engagement, actionable insights, and strategies for optimising short video advertising. This selection process was instrumental in grounding the study's findings in robust and credible evidence. The systematic use of PRISMA ensured that the review was not only comprehensive but also focused on the most relevant and impactful literature available. By narrowing the scope to studies that provide actionable insights into the effectiveness of short video ads, the research delivers meaningful contributions to the field of digital marketing. Moreover, the PRISMA methodology facilitated the identification of key themes and trends in the literature. This systematic approach enabled the study to develop a clear understanding of how short video ads drive engagement and conversions in digital media. The findings offer valuable insights for marketers seeking to refine their strategies and adapt to the fast-evolving landscape of digital marketing. Through this rigorous process, the study provides a well-rounded, evidence-based perspective on the transformative potential of short video advertising.

4 Findings

Increased Engagement Through Short Video Format

Short video content significantly boosts engagement rates by catering to modern viewers' preference for quick, digestible content. This format thrives on platforms like TikTok and Instagram, where users are accustomed to scrolling through rapid, visually stimulating videos. Compared to longer formats, short videos capture and retain attention more effectively, leading to higher retention rates and interaction. The concise structure of short films aligns seamlessly with user preferences on social media, making them an ideal tool for maintaining viewer interest and driving engagement. Research highlights that shorter videos outperform longer formats when it comes to grabbing attention, holding viewers' focus, and prompting interactions. Their brief and impactful nature encourages viewers to watch, like, share, and comment, creating a ripple effect of engagement across platforms. This quick-capture ability is particularly valuable in today's crowded digital landscape, where attention spans are short and content competition is fierce. As Willis (2024) points out, the concise style of short videos makes them inherently shareable and interactive, enhancing their appeal and effectiveness in reaching broader audiences.

Higher Conversion Rates Due to Clear Calls-To-Action

Short video ads excel at driving consumer action thanks to their ability to incorporate concise and effective calls-to-action (CTAs) directly into the content. These CTAs are strategically embedded to prompt immediate consumer responses, whether it's clicking a link, making a purchase, or signing up for a service. Studies consistently show that short video ads generate higher click-through rates (CTR) and conversions than static or text-based ads, mainly when the messaging is designed to evoke an emotional response or meet a specific consumer need. One of the key strengths of short video ads lies in their ability to deliver a clear and compelling value proposition within seconds. By addressing immediate consumer needs or appealing to their emotions, these ads are not only attention-grabbing but also action-oriented. Research by (Zheng et al., 2024) underscores that platforms like TikTok and Instagram, with their emphasis on quick and engaging content, are particularly effective for this type of advertising. Short videos, when combined with emotionally resonant messaging and well-placed CTAs, create a powerful tool for marketers to drive conversions at scale.

Enhanced Ad Performance Through Personalisation and Targeting

The integration of digital analytics has transformed the effectiveness of short video advertising by enabling personalised and targeted campaigns. Through data-driven audience segmentation, marketers can tailor ads to specific demographics, interests, and behaviours, resulting in more relevant and impactful content. Personalisation plays a critical role in increasing engagement, as viewers are more likely to interact with ads that feel directly relevant to them. Understanding consumer demographics and interests allows businesses to create content that resonates on a personal level, making the ads feel less intrusive and more aligned with individual preferences. Tailored content not only grabs attention but also fosters a sense of connection with the brand, increasing the likelihood of interaction and retention. Li et al. (2022) highlight how digital analytics empowers businesses to develop data-informed strategies that optimise content for specific markets, ensuring maximum impact.

Moreover, personalised short video ads are better equipped to address the diverse needs of audiences across different platforms. Whether it's tailoring messaging for a younger demographic on TikTok or creating visually appealing ads for Instagram's aesthetic-focused audience, personalisation ensures the content feels relevant and engaging. This level of customisation has proven to be a game-changer in improving the performance of short video advertising campaigns. A summary of the findings is presented in Table 1 below.

Table 1 Summary of the findings (*Source* Author's own work)

Finding	Metric	Insight
Engagement	Views, Likes, Shares	Short videos are great at holding attention and driving interactions, especially on TikTok and Instagram
Conversion	Click-Through Rate (CTR)	Clear, emotionally resonant calls to action in short videos encourage viewers to take action
Personalisation	Demographic Fit	Tailoring ads to match the interests and preferences of your audience makes them feel more relevant and engaging
Timing	Peak Interaction Times	Posting ads when your audience is most active leads to better visibility and stronger engagement
Creative elements	Visual Appeal, Storytelling	Eye-catching visuals and compelling stories make your brand memorable and more likely to be shared
Platform features	Interactive Tools	Using tools like TikTok Duet or Instagram Reels Remix encourages interaction and extends the ad's reach

5 Recommendations

To enhance the effectiveness of short video ads, incorporating creative elements such as vivid visuals and compelling storytelling plays a pivotal role in boosting audience recall. These elements not only capture attention but also foster a deeper emotional connection with viewers, making the content more memorable. Additionally, releasing ads during peak engagement periods on platforms like TikTok and Instagram maximises visibility and ensures the content reaches the widest possible audience. Leveraging platform-specific features, such as Instagram's Reels Remix or TikTok's Duet, further amplifies audience interaction and involvement (Muchitsch, 2024). The optimal length for short video ads is typically between six and fifteen seconds, striking a balance between brevity and impact (Yang & Zhai, 2022). Publishing ads during times of maximum platform engagement has been shown to boost interaction and visibility significantly. Strong visuals, a clear narrative, and a simple, uncluttered design are crucial in drawing the audience's attention and maintaining their involvement (Nicoli et al., 2022). These components are particularly effective when combined with interactive features like TikTok Duet and Instagram Remix, which encourage user-generated content and greater audience engagement (Shen, 2023).

Short video ads should prioritise delivering concise, high-impact messages with aesthetically appealing visuals. Such ads not only increase the likelihood of being remembered but also enhance the chances of being shared widely. To maximise their impact, brands should focus on communicating their value proposition within the first few seconds of the ad, ensuring clarity and relevance (Al-Subhi, 2022). Moreover, digital analytics data can be harnessed to customise short video ads based on specific consumer preferences and behaviours. This personalised approach significantly increases engagement and conversion potential (Chandra et al., 2022). Timing also plays a critical role in the success of short video ads, with studies consistently showing that ads placed during peak times yield higher engagement rates (Chen et al., 2024). By combining creative design, strategic timing, and data-driven customisation, marketers can maximise the effectiveness of their short video advertising campaigns.

Contribution to Theory

This study expands the application of the AIDA model to the realm of short video advertising, offering valuable insights into how attention—a crucial phase of the AIDA framework—is uniquely harnessed within short-form content. By examining the dynamic ways short video ads capture and sustain attention, this research adds depth to our understanding of engagement-driven models like AIDA and furthers the evolution of advertising theory. Short video ads bring a unique complexity to the process of engaging consumer attention, sparking interest, and motivating action within a matter of seconds. This study highlights how these ads align with each stage of the AIDA model, particularly emphasising the importance of the initial "attention" phase. Drawing on theories of consumer psychology, the findings suggest that visually compelling, personalised content is more effective in capturing and maintaining interest. This tailored approach not only grabs attention but also creates a pathway to desire and action, ensuring the ad's message resonates within the viewer's limited attention span.

By exploring the interplay between ad format, consumer attention, and engagement metrics, this study contributes to the ongoing discourse in digital advertising theory. It underscores the potential of short video ads as a powerful tool for modern marketers, blending creative storytelling with strategic, psychology-driven techniques to maximise impact.

Contribution to Practice

This study provides marketing practitioners with practical, evidence-based insights into crafting short video ads that drive engagement and conversions. By focusing on key elements like creativity, timing, and personalisation, marketers can create powerful advertisements that resonate with digital audiences. The findings emphasise the importance of creativity in capturing attention, while concise messaging ensures the content is clear and impactful within the limited time frame of short videos. Strategic timing is another critical factor, as delivering ads at the right moment can significantly enhance their effectiveness. For marketers seeking to maximise the potential of short video ads, this research offers actionable guidance. It highlights how digital analytics can be used to measure ad performance and tailor content to specific audience segments, ensuring a more personalised and relevant experience. By leveraging these insights, practitioners can develop highly targeted campaigns that align with audience behaviours and preferences. Moreover, this study underscores the value of data-driven decision-making in optimising short video ad strategies. By combining creative storytelling with analytics-based insights, marketers can produce ads that not only engage but also convert. In essence, this research serves as a roadmap for practitioners aiming to craft compelling, high-performing short video ads that stand out in today's fast-paced digital landscape.

Conclusion

The findings of this study highlight the immense potential of short video ads to capture the attention of digital audiences and drive higher conversion rates. These ads, when executed with creativity and precise targeting, can achieve remarkable success on platforms like Instagram Reels and TikTok, where brevity and impact are key. Short video advertising has emerged as a highly effective tool in digital marketing, enabling brands to engage audiences through dynamic, concise content tailored to specific preferences and behaviours. By leveraging digital analytics, marketers can refine their strategies to maximise ad performance, ensuring the right message reaches the right audience at the right time. This research underscores the importance of three core elements—timing, targeting, and creativity—in enhancing the effectiveness of short video ads. Creative storytelling, combined with data-driven personalisation, enables brands to cut through the noise and resonate with viewers in mere seconds. Furthermore, succinct messaging not only captures attention but also reinforces brand identity and encourages action. Future studies could explore the broader psychological impacts of short video ads on diverse consumer groups, including their influence on emotions, purchasing decisions, and long-term brand recall. Additionally, investigating how these ads perform across varying demographics and cultural contexts would provide deeper insights into their versatility. Ultimately, this paper emphasises that while short video ads hold immense promise for engagement, their success depends on strategic content creation and thoughtful execution tailored to the unique characteristics of each platform and audience.

Limitations and Future Investigation

One of the primary limitations of this study is its narrow focus on short video advertisements within a limited selection of digital platforms, specifically TikTok, Instagram Reels, and YouTube Shorts. While this approach provides valuable insights into the effectiveness of these popular platforms, it does not capture the broader landscape of digital advertising. The digital advertising ecosystem is vast and diverse, encompassing formats like interactive ads, live video ads, and even augmented reality experiences, which were beyond the scope of this research. By focusing solely on short video ads, the study might not fully account for emerging trends or alternative advertising strategies that are gaining traction in the digital space. Another significant limitation is the reliance on secondary data. While secondary data offers accessibility and a wealth of existing information, it might not capture the nuanced and evolving aspects of consumer behaviour. This reliance limits the depth of understanding of how audiences engage with and respond to short video ads in real time. To address these gaps, future research could expand the focus to include a broader range of digital advertising formats and platforms. Exploring interactive and live video ads could provide a more comprehensive view of the evolving digital advertising landscape. Additionally, future studies could incorporate primary data collection, such as consumer surveys or focus groups, to delve deeper into psychological impacts. Longitudinal studies examining the long-term effects of short video ads on consumer behaviour and brand loyalty would also contribute valuable insights to the field.

References

Addo, P. C., Akpatsa, S. K., Nukpe, P., Ohemeng, A. A., & Kulbo, N. B. (2022, July 3). Digital analytics approach to understanding short video advertising in digital marketing. *Journal of Marketing Theory and Practice, 30*(3), 405–420. https://doi.org/10.1080/10696679.2022.2056487

Al-Subhi, A. S. (2022, January 1). Metadiscourse in online advertising: Exploring linguistic and visual metadiscourse in social media advertisements. *Journal of Pragmatics, 187*, 24–40. https://doi.org/10.1016/j.pragma.2021.10.027

Alghamdi, A. M., Pileggi, S. F., & Sohaib, O. (2023). Social media analysis to enhance sustainable knowledge management: A concise literature review. *Sustainability, 15*(13), 9957. https://www.mdpi.com/2071-1050/15/13/9957

Amiri, A. M., Kushwaha, B. P., & Singh, R. (2023). Visualisation of global research trends and future research directions of digital marketing in small and medium enterprises using bibliometric analysis. *Journal of Small Business and Enterprise Development, 30*(3), 621–641. https://doi.org/10.1108/JSBED-04-2022-0206

Aydin, G., Uray, N., & Silahtaroglu, G. (2021). How to engage consumers through effective social media use—Guidelines for consumer goods companies from an emerging market. *Journal of Theoretical and Applied Electronic Commerce Research, 16*(4), 768–790. https://www.mdpi.com/0718-1876/16/4/44

Beauvisage, T., Beuscart, J.-S., Coavoux, S., & Mellet, K. (2023, 2024, October 1). How online advertising targets consumers: The uses of categories and algorithmic tools by audience planners. *New Media & Society, 26*(10), 6098–6119. https://doi.org/10.1177/14614448221146174

Belanche, D., Flavián, C., & Pérez-Rueda, A. (2020). Brand recall of skippable vs non-skippable ads in YouTube. *Online Information Review, 44*(3), 545–562. https://doi.org/10.1108/OIR-01-2019-0035

Bhandari, A., & Bimo, S. (2022, January 1). Why's everyone on TikTok now? The algorithmized self and the future of self-making on social media. *Social Media + Society, 8*(1), 20563051221086241. https://doi.org/10.1177/20563051221086241

Camilleri, M. A. (2020). The use of data-driven technologies for customer-centric marketing. *International Journal of Big Data Management, 1*(1), 50–63. https://doi.org/10.1504/ijbdm.2020.106876

Chandra, S., Verma, S., Lim, W. M., Kumar, S., & Donthu, N. (2022). Personalisation in personalised marketing: Trends and ways forward. *Psychology & Marketing, 39*(8), 1529–1562. https://doi.org/10.1002/mar.21670

Chen, Y., Chen, L., & Pan, Y. (2024, June 12). Social media influencer endorsement: the conditional effects of product attribute description in sponsored influencer videos. *Journal of Marketing Management, 40*(9–10), 675–703. https://doi.org/10.1080/0267257X.2024.2305748

Chaudhary, H. K., & Sharma, T. (2023). Efficient strategies for managing food waste in institutional catering: A comprehensive study. *PUSA Journal of Hospitality and Applied Sciences, 9*(2), 68–75. https://doi.org/10.48165/pjhas.2023.9.2.9

Chaudhary, H. K., Singh, M., & Ghosh, P. (2024). *Balancing act: Achieving carbon neutrality in star-rated hotels through net zero methodology and responsible tourism practices* (pp. 337–360). https://doi.org/10.2991/978-94-6463-437-2_24

Chaudhary, H. K., Singh, M., & Ghosh, P. (2025). The impact of green technology on guest safety: The mediating roles of responsible tourism practices and guest satisfaction. *Journal of Hospitality and Tourism Insights*. https://doi.org/10.1108/JHTI-09-2024-0953

Divya, B., & Chaudhary, H. K. (2023). Challenges and opportunities in scaling millet-driven cloud kitchen businesses: A comprehensive study. *EPRA International Journal of Multidisciplinary Research (IJMR)*, 155–164. https://doi.org/10.36713/epra15143

Dong, X., Liu, H., Xi, N., Liao, J., & Yang, Z. (2024). Short video marketing: What, when and how short-branded videos facilitate consumer engagement. *Internet Research, 34*(3), 1104–1128. https://doi.org/10.1108/INTR-02-2022-0121

Fang, J., Ni, Y., & Zhang, J. (2023). Value assessment of UGC short videos through element mining and data analysis. *Applied Sciences, 13*(16), 9418. https://www.mdpi.com/2076-3417/13/16/9418

Ge, J., Sui, Y., Zhou, X., & Li, G. (2021, August 19). Effect of short video ads on sales through social media: the role of advertisement content generators. *International Journal of Advertising, 40*(6), 870–896. https://doi.org/10.1080/02650487.2020.1848986

Kamal, M., & Aziz Bablu, T. (2022, April 7). Machine learning models for predicting click-through rates on social media: Factors and performance analysis. *International Journal of Applied Machine Learning and Computational Intelligence, 12*(4), 1–14. https://neuralslate.com/index.php/Machine-Learning-Computational-I/article/view/36

Kshetri, N., Dwivedi, Y. K., Davenport, T. H., & Panteli, N. (2024, April 1). Generative artificial intelligence in marketing: Applications, opportunities, challenges, and research agenda. *International Journal of Information Management, 75*, 102716. https://doi.org/10.1016/j.ijinfomgt.2023.102716

Kumar, A., & Chaudhary, K. H. (2023). Empowering diversity: Role of artificial intelligence in promoting gender inclusion within the hotel industry. *Social, Economic and Gender Inclusiveness in Tourism and Hospitality Industry*, 2–11.

Li, W., Jiang, M., & Zhan, W. (2022). Why advertise on short video platforms? Optimising online advertising using advertisement quality. *Journal of Theoretical and Applied Electronic Commerce Research, 17*(3), 1057–1074. https://www.mdpi.com/0718-1876/17/3/54

Luo, X., Tabassum, N., & Nayak, B. S. (2022). The AIDA model and the impact of TikTok video streaming on online shopping: A case study of TikTok. In B. S. Nayak & N. Tabassum (Eds.), *Modern corporations and strategies at work* (pp. 73–91). Springer Nature Singapore. https://doi.org/10.1007/978-981-19-4648-6_4

Meng, L., Kou, S., Duan, S., & Bie, Y. (2024, October 1). The impact of content characteristics of Short-Form video ads on consumer purchase Behavior: Evidence from TikTok. *Journal of Business Research, 183*, 114874. https://doi.org/10.1016/j.jbusres.2024.114874

Muchitsch, V. (2024, March 14). Sad girls on TikTok: Musical and multimodal participatory practices as affective negotiations of ordinary feelings and knowledges in online music cultures. *Popular Music and Society, 47*(2), 231–247. https://doi.org/10.1080/03007766.2024.2320589

Nicoli, N., Henriksen, K., Komodromos, M., & Tsagalas, D. (2022). Investigating digital storytelling for the creation of positively engaging digital content. *EuroMed Journal of Business, 17*(2), 157–173. https://doi.org/10.1108/EMJB-03-2021-0036

Ortiz, J. A. F., De Los M. Santos Corrada, M., Lopez, E., Dones, V., & Lugo, V. F. (2023, November 1). Don't make ads, make TikTok's: media and brand engagement through Gen Z's use of TikTok and its significance in purchase intent. *Journal of Brand Management, 30*(6), 535–549. https://doi.org/10.1057/s41262-023-00330-z

Pauwels, K., Peran, M., Shah, Z., Schnaidt, G., & Vercamer, D. (2023, September 1). Sponsored brands video rings up clicks and sales in the short and long run. *Journal of Marketing Analytics, 11*(3), 275–286. https://doi.org/10.1057/s41270-023-00237-3

Pellegrino, A. (2024). Memory: How it works and how to become "unforgettable" in a digital world. In A. Pellegrino (Ed.), *Decoding digital consumer behavior: Bridging theory and practice* (pp. 77–93). Springer Nature Singapore. https://doi.org/10.1007/978-981-97-3454-2_6

Poth, C. H. (2020, August 1). Prioritisation in visual working memory enhances memory retention and speeds up processing in a comparison task. *Cognitive Processing, 21*(3), 331–339. https://doi.org/10.1007/s10339-020-00967-7

Rabindranath, M., & Singh, A. K. (2024). Understanding advertising process: Models and theories. In M. Rabindranath & A. K. Singh (Eds.), *Advertising management: Concepts, theories, research and trends* (pp. 167–224). Springer Nature Singapore. https://doi.org/10.1007/978-981-99-8657-6_6

Rosário, A. T., & Dias, J. C. (2023, November 1). How has data-driven marketing evolved: Challenges and opportunities with emerging technologies. *International Journal of Information Management Data Insights, 3*(2), 100203. https://doi.org/10.1016/j.jjimei.2023.100203

Ruihao, Z. (2021, November 15). Analysis of short video marketing strategy and industry trend and suggestions to uploaders. Proceedings of the 2021 3rd International Conference on Economic Management and Cultural Industry (ICEMCI 2021).

Shen, Z. (2023). The platform revolution in interactive marketing: Increasing customer-brand engagement on social media platforms. In C. L. Wang (Ed.), *The Palgrave handbook of interactive marketing* (pp. 433–450). Springer International Publishing. https://doi.org/10.1007/978-3-031-14961-0_19

Shi, R., Wang, M., Liu, C., & Gull, N. (2023). The influence of short video platform characteristics on users' willingness to share marketing information: Based on the SOR model. *Sustainability, 15*(3), 2448. https://www.mdpi.com/2071-1050/15/3/2448

Sutherland, K. E. (2024). Producing videos that Pop. In K. E. Sutherland (Ed.), *Strategic social media management: Theory and practice* (pp. 503–562). Springer Nature Singapore. https://doi.org/10.1007/978-981-99-9496-0_16

Tafesse, W., & Wien, A. (2018, June 13). Implementing social media marketing strategically: An empirical assessment. *Journal of Marketing Management, 34*(9–10), 732–749. https://doi.org/10.1080/0267257X.2018.1482365

Trunfio, M., & Rossi, S. (2021, September 1). Conceptualising and measuring social media engagement: A systematic literature review. *Italian Journal of Marketing, 2021*(3), 267–292. https://doi.org/10.1007/s43039-021-00035-8

Varadarajan, R., Welden, R. B., Arunachalam, S., Haenlein, M., & Gupta, S. (2022, July 1). Digital product innovations for the greater good and digital marketing innovations in communications and channels: Evolution, emerging issues, and future research directions. *International Journal of Research in Marketing, 39*(2), 482–501. https://doi.org/10.1016/j.ijresmar.2021.09.002

Willis, M. (2024). Short video adverts: A modern and virtual form of advertising. In W. Ozuem, S. Ranfagni, & M. Willis (Eds.), *Digital transformation for fashion and luxury brands: Theory and practice* (pp. 107–131). Springer International Publishing. https://doi.org/10.1007/978-3-031-35589-9_6

Xiao, L., Li, X., & Zhang, Y. (2023, January 1). Exploring the factors influencing consumer engagement behavior regarding short-form video advertising: A big data perspective. *Journal of Retailing and Consumer Services, 70*, 103170. https://doi.org/10.1016/j.jretconser.2022.103170

Yang, Y., & Zhai, P. (2022, March 1). Click-through rate prediction in online advertising: A literature review. *Information Processing & Management, 59*(2), 102853. https://doi.org/10.1016/j.ipm.2021.102853

Yin, X., Li, J., Si, H., & Wu, P. (2024, January 1). Attention marketing in fragmented entertainment: How advertising embedding influences purchase decision in short-form video apps. *Journal of Retailing and Consumer Services, 76*, 103572. https://doi.org/10.1016/j.jretconser.2023.103572

Zhang, H., Mu, X., Yan, H., Ren, L., & Ma, J. (2023). A survey of online video advertising. *WIREs Data Mining and Knowledge Discovery, 13*(2), e1489. https://doi.org/10.1002/widm.1489

Zhang, N., Ruan, C., & Wang, X. (2024, August 6). You recommend, I trust: the interactive self-presentation strategies for social media influencers to build authenticity perception in short video scenes. *Information Systems Frontiers*. https://doi.org/10.1007/s10796-024-10523-9

Zheng, C., Ling, S., Cho, D., & Kim, Y. (2024). How social presence influences engagement in short video-embedded advertisements: The serial mediation effect of flow experience and advertising avoidance. *Journal of Theoretical and Applied Electronic Commerce Research, 19*(2), 705–724. https://www.mdpi.com/0718-1876/19/2/38

Immersive Product Demonstrations Through Metaverse Technology

Animesh Kumar Sharma and Rahul Sharma

Abstract

By combining immersive technologies like virtual reality (VR), augmented reality (AR), and three-dimensional (3D) virtual environments, the metaverse is transforming product displays. This chapter looks at how companies are using these tools to make immersive, captivating product demonstrations that give customers realistic, interactive experiences. The study employed VOSviewer to examine research trends in the field and the PRISMA (Preferred Reporting Items for Systematic Reviews and Meta-Analyses) technique to thoroughly investigate the body of existing literature data from 1994 to 2024. The chapter conducted a thorough analysis to examine how immersive product presentations in the metaverse are changing user engagement, customer behaviour, and conventional marketing tactics. This study emphasises how immersive visualisation influences purchase decisions by showcasing significant technical developments and case studies from a variety of industries, including real estate, automobile, and fashion. The chapter also covers the difficulties that organisations encounter, like the expense of using immersive technologies and possible privacy issues. Insights into potential future study areas are provided in the chapter's conclusion, with an emphasis on how these technologies may be further leveraged to enhance customer experiences and company outcomes in the digital marketplace.

A. K. Sharma (✉) · R. Sharma
Mittal School of Buisness, Lovely Professioinal University, Phagwara, Punjab, India
e-mail: mr.animesh@gmail.com; animesh.41800104@lpu.in

R. Sharma
e-mail: rahul.12234@lpu.co.in

© The Author(s), under exclusive license to Springer Nature Singapore Pte Ltd. 2026

N. S. Jayawardena et al. (eds.), *Digital Advertising and Consumer Behavior*,
Management for Professionals, https://doi.org/10.1007/978-981-95-7809-2_8

1 Introduction

As the digital world changes, businesses are constantly looking for new ways to connect with customers, display products, and influence buying choices (Lee & Lee, 2020; Mariani & Wamba, 2020). The use of the metaverse to create immersive product demonstration has been one of the most transformational developments in recent years (Bilgihan et al., 2024; Gandhi et al., 2024). This virtual universe, which seamlessly blends technology such as virtual reality (VR), augmented reality (AR), and three-dimensional (3D) surroundings, provides companies with an unprecedented chance to transcend traditional marketing methods and connect with customers in previously inconceivable ways. Companies may use the metaverse to produce fascinating, realistic, and interactive product demonstrations that change the way customers interact with brands and their goods (Bilgihan et al., 2024; Sridharan & Kumar, 2024).

The metaverse has transformed product presentation by allowing customers to interact with things in a virtual environment that seems real and responsive (Barrera & Shah, 2023; Mourtzis et al., 2022). This technology has important ramifications for marketing since it increases user engagement, changes customer behaviour, and provides a new viewpoint on the traditional sales funnel. The metaverse allows potential buyers to "experience" a product whether it's trying on virtual clothing, exploring the interior of a car, or visualizing how a piece of furniture would look in their home creating a deep emotional connection that mere photos or videos cannot replicate (Habil et al., 2024; Han et al., 2022; Yoo et al., 2023).

Immersive product demonstrations driven by the metaverse are poised to transform the way marketers convey value (Abrokwah-Larbi, 2024; Dwivedi et al., 2023). Visual immersion has a significant impact on consumer decision-making since people tend to base their purchases on detailed, memorable experiences made possible by metaverse technology (Mladenović et al., 2024; Shamim et al., 2024; Sun et al., 2023). However, like with any invention, organizations that use this technique confront hurdles. The financial costs of creating and deploying immersive technology may be substantial, and rising worries about data privacy in digital settings complicate matters. Still, as the metaverse evolves and becomes more accessible, it has the potential to become a key component of digital product promotion (Dwivedi et al., 2022; Nalbant & Aydın, 2023).

In an era where digital innovation is redefining every element of the customer experience, the metaverse has emerged as a game-changing tool for providing immersive product demonstration (Johri et al., 2024; Kumar et al., 2024; Schulte & Shemakov, 2024). Companies may now build previously imagined compelling and interactive product experiences using virtual reality (VR), augmented reality (AR), and three-dimensional (3D) virtual environments. The metaverse enables companies to create virtual showrooms, interactive exhibitions, and hyper-realistic simulations that allow buyers to engage with things as if they were physically present (Akbar & Agyei, 2024; Yaqoob et al., 2023). This advancement in digital interaction provides a more vivid and engaging experience than standard product displays or online purchasing interfaces (Kim et al., 2021; Lee et al., 2022).

Immersive product presentations powered by the metaverse are a new paradigm in customer interaction, pushing the limits of how customers see, interact with, and assess items (Alimamy & Jung, 2024; Shen et al., 2021). Consumers may now examine things from unique and individualized viewpoints, from digitally "trying on" a designer clothing to delving into the detailed features of a high-tech device (Chakraborty et al., 2021). The metaverse blurs the distinction between the physical and digital worlds, and when businesses incorporate these immersive technologies, they affect not just customer behaviour but also traditional marketing strategies (Chakraborty & Biswal, 2024; Hadi et al., 2024; Nair et al., 2024). Customers are no longer passively seeing a product; instead, they are part of an interactive journey that enriches, personalizes, and ultimately makes their experiences unforgettable (Khan, 2024).

This shift is more than just novelty; immersive product demonstrations in the metaverse have a substantial impact on customer decision-making processes (Gupta, 2023; Kaur et al., 2024; Xi et al., 2023). Visualizing a product in a vivid, interactive manner may instil a sense of ownership and a greater knowledge of its worth, dramatically influencing purchase intentions (Raja et al., 2024). A consumer, for example, may see how a 3D model of furniture fits into the layout, colours, and measurements of a room, decreasing ambiguity and increasing confidence in their purchase. Technological improvements in 3D modelling, spatial audio, and haptic feedback enhance these experiences, giving buyers a more comprehensive grasp of a product's features and advantages (Chen & Mu, 2024; Wedel et al., 2020).

However, as promising as these advancements are, they also present obstacles. Implementing immersive technology in the metaverse can be costly, necessitating significant expenditures in hardware, software, and specialized labour (Rafique & Qadir, 2024; Ud Din et al., 2023). Furthermore, these experiences present privacy concerns since they frequently demand access to sensitive user data, which might jeopardize customer trust if not handled properly (Alhitmi et al., 2024; Darvish et al., 2024). Despite these challenges, the potential for immersive product demonstration in the metaverse is apparent, and as the technology evolves, it is likely to become a vital aspect of current marketing tactics, delivering a competitive advantage to businesses prepared to embrace the digital future (Buhalis et al., 2023; Raji et al., 2024).

The fast evolution of metaverse technology has propelled immersive product presentations to the forefront of digital marketing innovation (Tyagi & Tyagi, 2024). However, considerable research gaps exist, necessitating a comprehensive PRISMA-based evaluation to fully comprehend the promise and limits of this method. Although virtual reality (VR), augmented reality (AR), and 3D modelling have all been explored individually in marketing, there has been little study on their combined impact when utilized in the metaverse to create seamless, interactive product experiences. A thorough examination of how these technologies interact is required, as current research lacks detailed insights into the specific consumer behavioral impacts, such as purchase intention, brand perception, and customer satisfaction, which immersive demonstrations may influence more effectively than traditional approaches. Furthermore, the limitations of implementing metaverse technology for marketing are understudied. While several studies note high prices, few go into detail about additional hurdles, including privacy issues, technological complexity, and the significant resource commitments needed. Furthermore, with technology in this field quickly advancing, there is no systematic evidence of how developments such as enhanced haptic feedback, high-resolution 3D images, and spatial audio increase the efficacy of immersive product presentations. This information is critical for understanding how technological improvements lead to richer, more engaging customer experiences. There is also a noteworthy paucity of research comparing traditional marketing approaches to metaverse-based product demonstration. Few studies provide direct comparisons or quantitative measurements, raising uncertainties regarding the exact benefits and drawbacks of using the metaverse for marketing. Furthermore, the privacy implications of immersive experiences are little understood, particularly in terms of consumer data collecting, security, and ethical problems. Given these research gaps, a PRISMA-based study would present a systematic synthesis of current findings, providing valuable insights into the practical applications, challenges, and ethical considerations of immersive product demonstrations via metaverse technology, ultimately guiding future research and strategic implementation.

In this in-depth study, we'll look at how immersive product demonstrations in the metaverse are changing the way businesses operate. We will look at how firms are employing VR, AR, and 3D environments to improve consumer engagement, how these demonstrations affect purchase behaviour and marketing methods, and the hurdles that come with implementing new technology. Through these perspectives, it becomes evident that the metaverse is more than just a virtual escapist place; it is also a great instrument for marketers to interact with their customers on a deeper, more immersive level.

Research Questions

The research questions were developed based on the extensive literature review.

RQ1: What have been the key research trends in the field of immersive product demonstrations through metaverse technology in the last three decades?

RQ2: What are the most influential countries and institutions contributing to research on immersive product demonstrations through metaverse technology?

RQ3: What are the most used keywords and themes in studies on immersive product demonstrations through metaverse technology?

RQ4: How has the publication trend of immersive product demonstrations through metaverse technology evolved geographically?

2 Research Methodology

This systematic review uses PRISMA (Preferred Reporting Items for Systematic Reviews and Meta-Analyses) criteria to assess the corpus of research on immersive product demonstration using metaverse technology (Asar et al., 2016). The purpose of this review is to identify, analyse, and synthesize studies on the use of immersive technologies in product marketing, specifically virtual reality (VR), augmented reality (AR), and three-dimensional (3D) virtual environments, with a focus on how they influence consumer behaviour, engagement, and purchase decisions.

Database Selection

This systematic review's source is Scopus, a large and internationally renowned database for academic research that includes peer-reviewed journals, conference papers, and other scholarly publications. Scopus is regarded as an excellent source due to its comprehensive coverage of multidisciplinary research, including digital marketing, technology, and innovation studies, which ensures a strong selection of relevant studies.

Eligibility Criteria

Specific qualifying criteria were devised to guarantee that only high-quality and relevant research was included. The research had to have been published in peer-reviewed journals, conference proceedings, or other academic sources that were Scopus-indexed. The study required to concentrate on immersive technologies like virtual reality (VR), augmented reality (AR), or 3D, particularly their application in product demonstrations inside the metaverse or virtual settings. Furthermore, research has to look at the effects of immersive product demonstrations on customer behaviour, engagement, buy intentions, and marketing efficacy, as well as technological improvements in metaverse platforms or tools used for product demonstration. Articles focusing on generic marketing methods that were not relevant to immersive or metaverse-based settings, as well as studies unrelated to product presentations or consumer involvement, such as theoretical papers or non-empirical research, were excluded from the review. Research that was unavailable in full-text or lacked adequate methodological rigor, such as reviews without a systematic search strategy or studies without empirical data, was also removed. Furthermore, research that was primarily concerned with non-commercial or non-business applications of metaverse technology was excluded.

Search Strategy and PRISMA Framework

To find all relevant studies in the Scopus database, a sophisticated search technique was created. The search strings were built using keywords related to immersive technologies and product demonstrations, including terms like "Immersive product demonstrations," "Metaverse technology," "Virtual reality product demonstrations," "Augmented reality product demonstrations," "3D virtual environments product marketing," "Customer engagement in metaverse," and "Impact of VR/AR on consumer behaviour." These keywords were merged using Boolean operators (AND, OR) to guarantee a comprehensive and exact search. The search was limited to English-language publications published between 1994 to 2024, with an emphasis on current research that captures the newest breakthroughs in metaverse technology. After identifying the extracted data, the second step of the data cleaning procedure was carried out, which rejected articles that were not published in English and were not journal or conference papers, as well as papers that were in press and had no author. In the third step, eventually ($N = 1440$), documents were included for further analysis (Fig. 1) (Donthu et al., 2021).

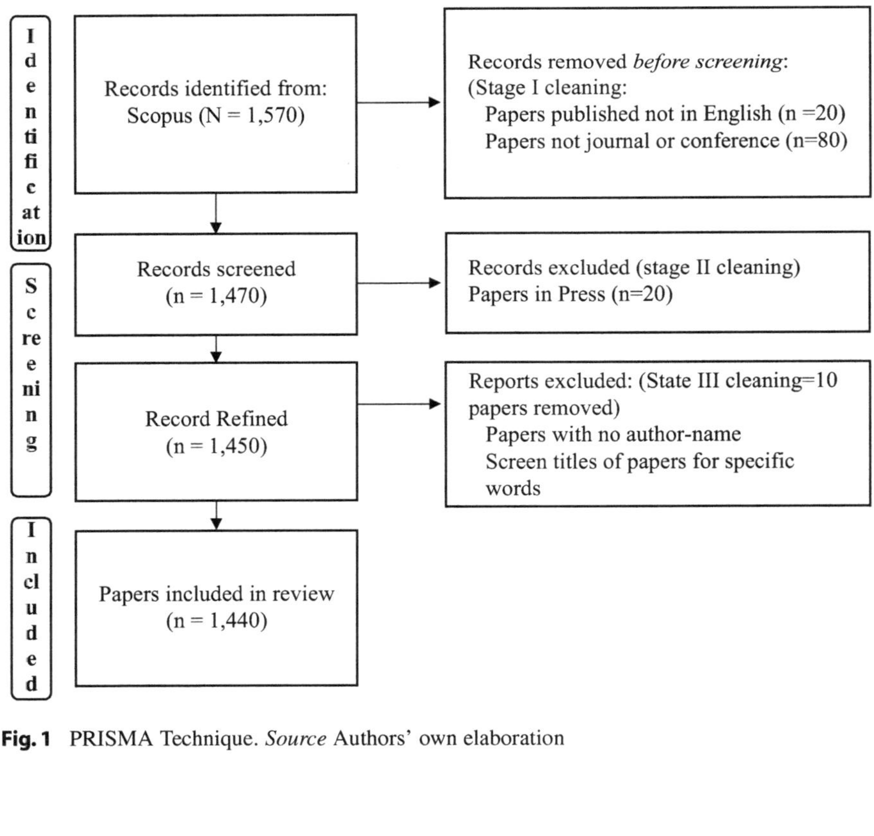

Fig. 1 PRISMA Technique. *Source* Authors' own elaboration

Data Analysis

The research landscape on Immersive Product Demonstrations using Metaverse Technology was studied using bibliometric indicators, which highlighted trends, key studies, and patterns of collaboration. The retrieved data was analysed using the VOSViewer software, which produced graphical representations of citation networks, co-authorship relationships, and keyword clusters. This enabled the identification of research interests, knowledge gaps, and major contributors to the field of adventure tourism entrepreneurship study. To be more specific, the study examined the yearly number of publications to identify trends, the most often referenced articles to highlight major research, and co-authorship networks to identify patterns of collaboration across writers, institutions, and nations. The term co-occurrence analysis was also used to identify field issues and trends.

3 Results

Post applying the PRISMA Technique for the analysis of data extracted from the database, 1,440 data was used for the analysis through the VOSviewer software. There are 704 (48.89%) articles, 283 (19.65%) conference papers, 234 (16.25%) review papers, 111 (7.71%) books, 102 (7.02%) book chapters, 2-2 (0.14%) conference review and ediotiral paper; 1-1 (0.07%) note and short surveys (Fig. 2).

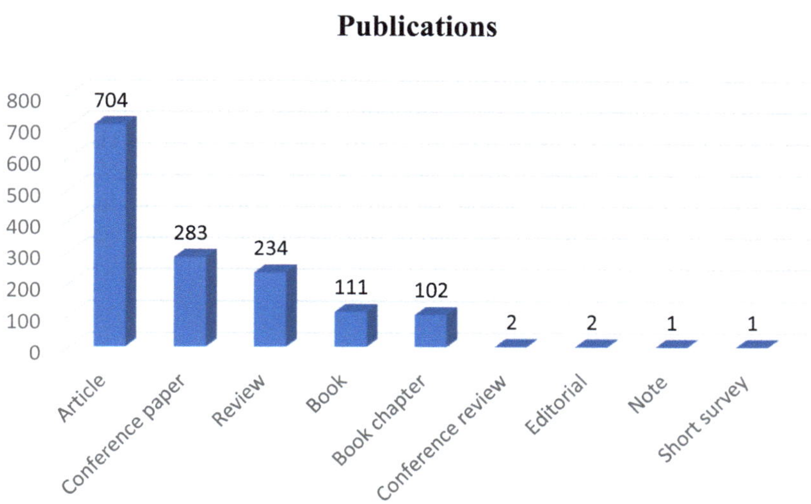

Fig. 2 Publications. *Source* Authors' own elaboration

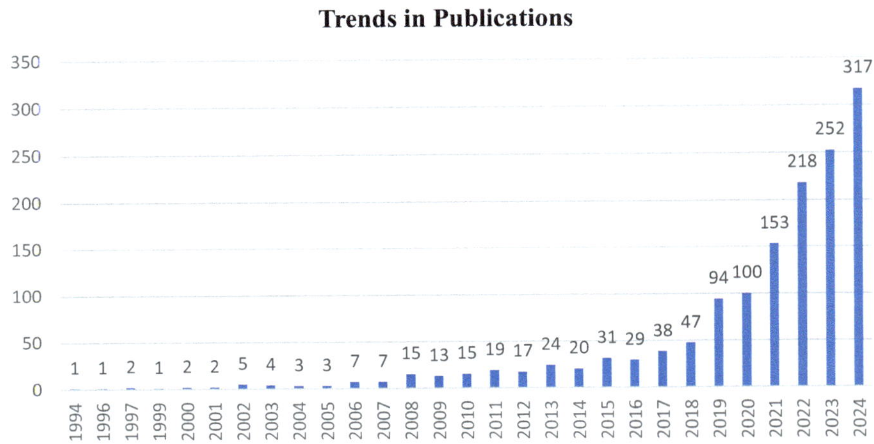

Fig. 3 Trends in Publications. *Source* Authors' own elaboration

Trends in Publications

Figure 3 shows the trends in the publications in the field of immersive product demonstrations through metaverse technology. Beginning with 1994 and 1996, there was little activity, with only one publication each year. Interest progressively increased, with occasional publishing surges, as in 2002 (5 publications) and 2006–2007 (7 publications per year). Significant growth began after 2008, with a noteworthy increase to 15 publications, followed by consistent rises each year. The number of publications increased considerably after 2015, rising from 31 to 94 in 2019. This tendency accelerated during the COVID-19 pandemic, with 100 publications in 2020, followed by 153 in 2021 and 218 in 2022. The trend persisted, with 252 publications in 2023 and an astonishing 317 in 2024. This trend highlights the increased emphasis on metaverse applications for product presentations, indicating the technology's growing incorporation into both academic and industrial spheres.

The Top Institutions

Figure 4 shows the number of publications by major academic and research institutions, highlighting their contributions to intellectual activity. CNRS (Centre National de la Recherche Scientifique) and Purdue University lead the list with 18 papers apiece, demonstrating their enormous research output. Aalborg University has 15 publications, followed by the University of Michigan in Ann Arbor, which has 14. Zhejiang University and the University of Hong Kong both have 13 publications, demonstrating their substantial academic presence.

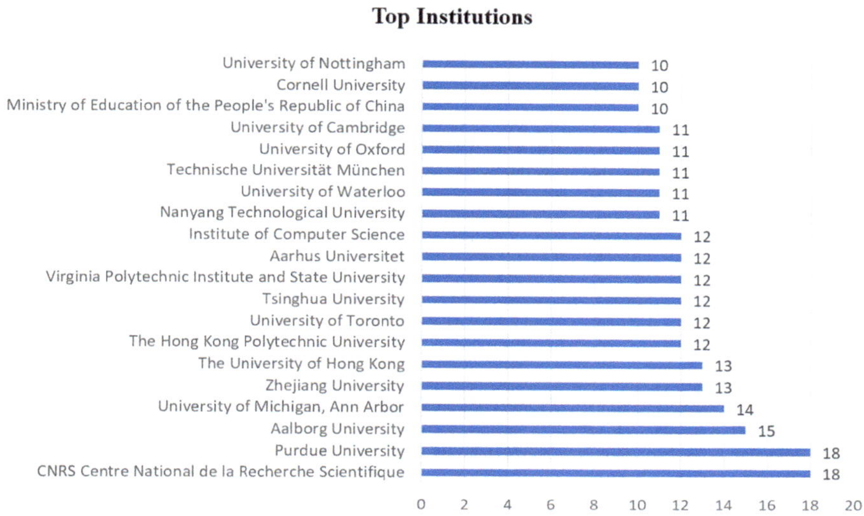

Fig. 4 Top institutions. *Source* Authors' own elaboration

The Hong Kong Polytechnic University, University of Toronto, Tsinghua University, Virginia Polytechnic Institute and State University, Aarhus Universitet, and the Institute of Computer Science all contributed 12 articles, demonstrating their strong research capacity. Nanyang Technological University, the University of Waterloo, Technische Universität München, the University of Oxford, and the University of Cambridge all have 11 publications, demonstrating their global academic importance. Finally, the Ministry of Education of the People's Republic of China, Cornell University, and the University of Nottingham, all with ten publications, complete the list of prolific producers to academic writing.

Top Country Publications

Figure 4 shows the twenty countries' publications published by various nations, emphasizing their contribution to a certain field of immersive product demonstrations through metaverse technology. The United States leads by a wide margin, with 403 publications demonstrating its supremacy in the subject. China is the second-largest contributor, with 217 publications, while the United Kingdom is third, with 188. Other significant providers are Germany (126), Canada (98), and Australia (93). France (64), Italy (57), Denmark (43), Spain (42) and the Netherlands (40) all make significant contributions. Among Asian nations, India (53), South Korea (49), Japan (37), Malaysia (33) and Taiwan (26) stand strongly. Scandinavian countries such as Finland (32) and Sweden (27) contribute value, as do New Zealand (29) and Switzerland (26). This statistic highlights worldwide engagement in research, with considerable contributions from both developed and emerging economies. Figure 5 demonstrated the density visualization of the publications of the top countries (Fig. 6).

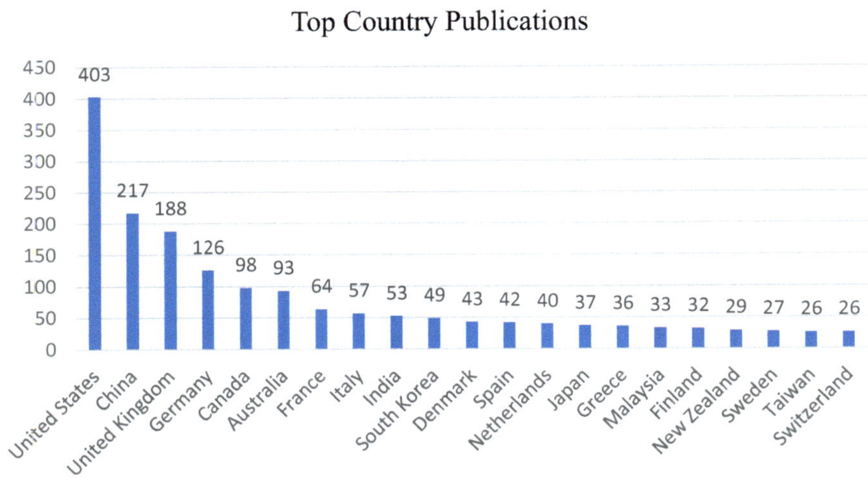

Fig. 5 Top country publications. *Source* Authors' own elaboration

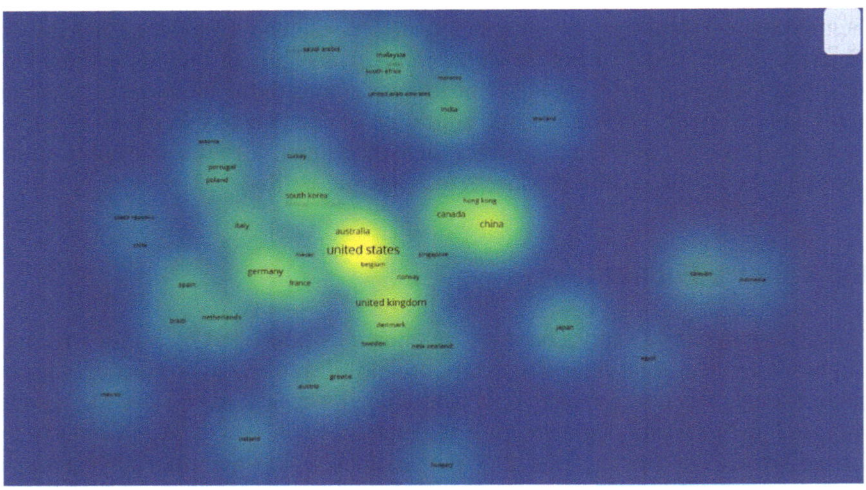

Fig. 6 Top country publications density visualization. *Source* VOSviewer

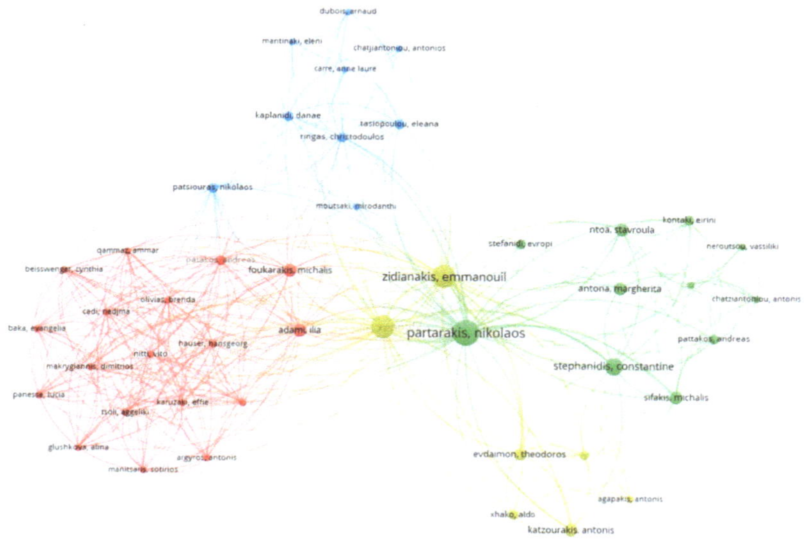

Fig. 7 Co-authorship Network Visualization. *Source* VOSviewer

Co-Authorship Analysis

Figure 7 shows the network visualization of the co-authorship analysis in immersive product demonstrations through metaverse technology. It shows that 'Partarakis, Nikolaos', 'Zidiankis, Emmanouil' and Stephanidis Constantine" are prominently connected in the study. Larger nodes, such as "Partarakis Nikolaos" and "Zidianakis Emmanouil," indicate a key or more prominent function in the network. The green cluster focuses on "Partarakis Nikolaos" and "Zidianakis Emmanouil." The red cluster contains tighter intra-connections, indicating significant internal collaboration, and is concentrated on other notable personalities such as "Adam Ilia." The blue cluster is smaller, indicating a less linked or isolated subnetwork.

Co-Occurrence of Keywords

Figure 8 shows the network visualization of the co-occurrence of keywords in immersive product demonstrations through metaverse technology. The network also highlights multidisciplinary themes, including links to sectors such as robots, human interaction, and medical education. This graph purports to depict research patterns throughout time, maybe taken from academic papers, and it emphasizes

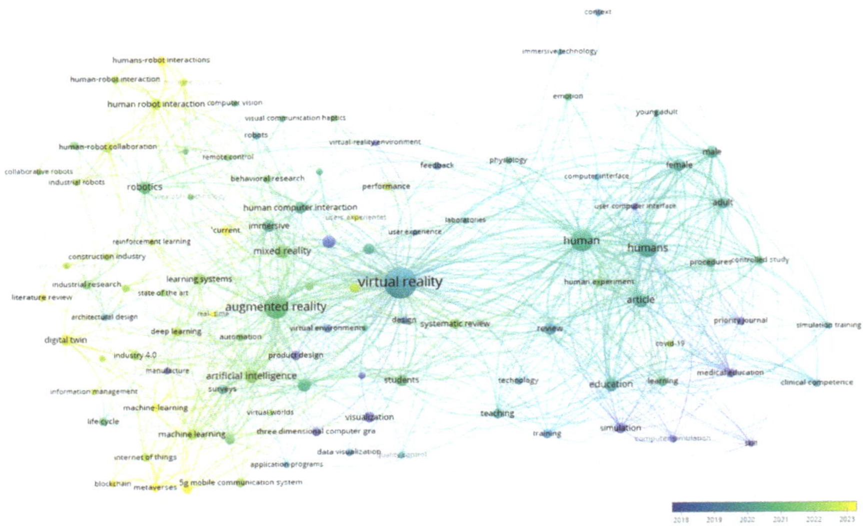

Fig. 8 Co-occurrence of keywords. *Source* VOSviewer

the connections between various technologies and intellectual topics. "Virtual reality" is the most central keyword and linked node, reflecting its importance in several related sectors. Emerging themes such as "metaverse", "5G mobile communication", and "digital twin" are linked to other technology-related subjects. Nodes are color-coded to denote groupings of similar themes. Green node, such as "augmented reality" and "machine learning," center on technology and industrial applications. Blue nodes, such as "humans," "education," and "simulation," are relevant to user experience, learning, and healthcare. Yellow nodes, such as "blockchain" and "metaverse," refer to developing technologies and systems.

Co-Citation Analysis

Figure 9 depicts a co-citation network from a bibliometric investigation on the topic of immersive product demonstration employing metaverse technology. Lines linking nodes denote co-citation links, which indicate that the two authors/publications are mentioned together in other works. The thickness of the lines represents the frequency of co-citations; bigger lines imply greater links or shared impact. Partarakis Nikolaos, Zidianakis Emmanouil, and Stephanidis Constantine are bigger and more central, implying that they are frequently co-cited and fundamental to the study.

Fig. 9 Co-citation analysis. *Source* VOSviewer

Bibliometric Coupling

Figure 10 shows the bibliographic coupling of the of immersive product demonstrations through metaverse technology. Authors such as "Ramani, Karthik," "Patrarkis, Nikolaos," and "Levine, Howard U." propose a core set of writers or works that are extremely significant to the study. Authors spread further away from the central cluster identify writers or research that are less closely related to the primary topics but have some common references. The core cluster is most likely indicative of fundamental research on immersive product demos and metaverse technologies, as it cites comparable essential articles. The outlying nodes and smaller clusters might reflect specialized applications or related study topics with weak connections to the core theme.

Fig. 10 Bibliometric coupling. *Source* VOSviewer

4 Thematic Map

The thematic map gives insight into research patterns and suggests subjects that require more investigation or are critical to the area. The thematic map for the current study was created using R studio's bibliometrics package to identify and depict themes based on their importance (centrality) and evolution (density). It has four quadrants: fundamental themes, emerging or diminishing themes, specialist themes, and motor themes. The thematic map (Fig. 11) is a graph that depicts the progression of several themes in a field. The Y axis represents the degree of development (density), while the X axis represents the level of importance (centrality).

Quadrant Analysis

For the current study the quadrant analysis is provided below.

Motor Themes*(High Centrality, High Density):* The study area focuses on highly developed motor topics. These subjects imply that they are important and active fields of research since they have considerable links with other themes (high centrality) as well as internal cohesion (high density). Themes with high centrality and density. These are well-developed and relevant to the research domain. The words

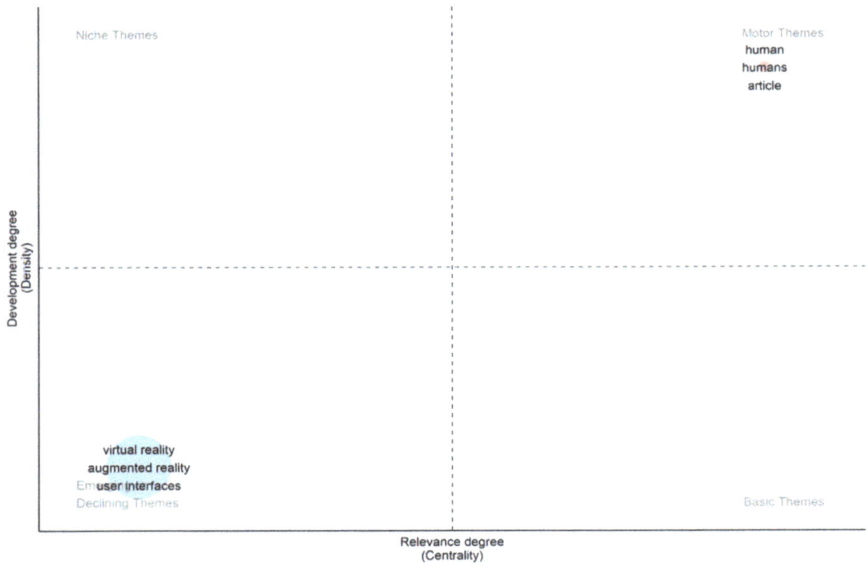

Fig. 11 Thematic Map. *Source* RStudio' Bibliometrics

"human," "humans," and "article" are clustered together on this map, indicating that they are central and developed.

Niche Themes*(Low Centrality, High Density):* Niche themes are highly focused and developed, but have little linkages to the wider academic area. These themes do not have a broad impact or applicability, but they are typically important for a certain subject or industry. Themes with great density but poor centrality. These are specific issues that have been thoroughly investigated but are not broadly related to other themes. This quadrant on the map is empty.

Emerging or Declining Themes*(Low Centrality, Low Density):* Themes with low centrality and density. These are either developing or diminishing research fields. Themes with low centrality and density. These are either developing or diminishing research fields. The terms "virtual reality," "augmented reality," and "user interfaces" appear on this map, indicating that they are undeveloped or are not fundamental to the study domain.

Basic Themes*(High Centrality, Low Density):* Basic themes are important to the field's structure since they have significant linkages to other study topics, yet they are undeveloped. These are usually basic concepts or techniques that support other subfields but require more study and exploration. Themes having significant centrality but low density. These are essential subjects that are vital but have not been thoroughly investigated. This quadrant on the map is empty.

5 Factorial Analysis

Figure 12 depicts a conceptual structure map produced from Multiple Correspondence Analysis (MCA). It is often used in bibliometric or thematic analysis to depict the associations between concepts, phrases, or keywords in a research dataset. The current study's factorial analysis is carried out using bibliometrics in R. Figure 12 shows a scatter plot graph for the factorial analysis. The two axes are designated "Dim 1 (83.4%)" and "Dim 2 (5.82%)". Dim 1 on the X-axis denotes the first primary dimension, accounting for 83.4% of the variation in the data. Dim 2 on the Y-axis represents the second principal dimension, explaining 2.6% of the variance. It emphasizes secondary patterns or differences between ideas. These two dimensions work together to position concepts in the conceptual space based on their similarities or co-occurrences in the dataset. It identifies the most significant contrasts between words or concepts. This graph has several points, each of which represents a word. The terms highlighted in red are all about virtual reality, metaverse, machine learning, deep learning, and immersive technologies. Each word's location on the graph is defined by its relationship to other words, and its placement might indicate similarities or differences with other words. Each triangle or label represents a term or notion derived from the data. Keywords that are closer together suggest a strong conceptual association or frequent co-occurrence in the dataset.

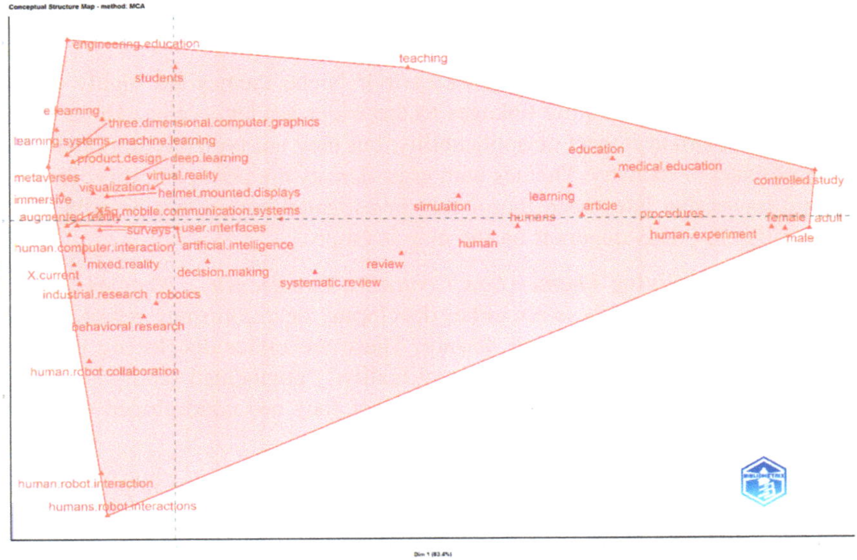

Fig. 12 Factorial analysis. *Source* RStudio' Bibliometrics

Clusters and Structure

The red shaded area connects related terms, forming conceptual groupings. Keywords in comparable categories have thematic commonalities. Terms such as "virtual reality," "augmented reality," "metaverses," and "machine learning" are grouped, showing a preference for immersive technology and AI-related applications. The terms "education," "medical education," "teaching," and "students" are clustered on the right, indicating educational or pedagogical topics. Keywords such as "human–robot interaction," "robotics," and "behavioural research" are clustered in the bottom left, indicating a concentration on robotics and human-technology collaboration. The horizontal axis (Dim 1) divides concepts into broad categories, such as technical/technological topics (left) and human-centered applications or research (right). The vertical axis (Dim 2) distinguishes subcategories within these topics, such as innovative technical concepts vs conventional or practical uses. Immersive technology and AI topics (e.g., virtual reality, machine learning, augmented reality) are clustered on the left, indicating a technical concentration. Education and human-centered studies (e.g., medical education, teaching, humans, publications) dominate the right, emphasizing applications in human-centric domains. Robotics research is organized at the bottom and focuses on interactions and collaboration between people and robots. This map gives insights into the examined dataset's theme arrangement and conceptual links, assisting researchers in identifying significant focus areas and thematic patterns.

6 Discussion

The current study's findings provide a comprehensive review of immersive product demonstration using metaverse technology, which can be compared to previous research to detect patterns and insights in this rapidly emerging field. This study finds a considerable increase in research into immersive technologies. This is consistent with previous study by Partarakis and Zabulis (2024), who discovered that metaverse technology has transformational potential in the immersive product demonstration sector. Both studies emphasize the relevance of these technologies in promoting healthcare, suggesting a consistent trend in the sector. The inclusion of "virtual reality", "artificial intelligence", "deep learning", and "augmented reality" as top keywords in the present study is consistent with previous findings, demonstrating the continuous relevance of these technologies in immersive product demonstration. This analysis of Influential Authors, Organizations, and Journals finds that authors like Partarakis, Nikolaos', 'Zidiankis, Emmanouil' and Stephanidis Constantine" as well as institutions like CNRS Centre National de la Recherche Scientifique, Purdue University and the Purdue University, make important contributions to the current research. This study's findings are similar to prior studies by Chakraborty et al. (2024) and Kim et al. (2021), who also recognized the importance of these aspects. The identification of these major entities highlights their crucial role in promoting metaverse research, implying a deliberate effort by top scholars and institutions to advance the subject. The most prominent motifs observed in this study were immersive visualization, virtual product presentation, and 3D modelling in immersive product demonstrations. This is supported by Barrera and Shah (2023), who emphasised the use of metaverse technology in the research. The co-authorship research demonstrates a high degree of collaboration among scholars, implying a dynamic exchange of ideas and multidisciplinary teamwork. This pattern of collaboration is established in studies by Dwivedi et al. (2022), who highlight the relevance of multidisciplinary research in virtual reality. The frequent co-authorship of prominent specialists emphasizes the collaborative aspect of metaverse research, which is essential for creativity and successful issue resolution in metaverse technology.

7 Implications

The implications of the bibliometric study on immersive product demonstrations through metaverse technology are discussed in the following section, categorized into theoretical and managerial aspects.

Theoretical Implications

The study gives vital insights that help to enhance and refine existing theories while also opening up new areas for future research. The potential of this study is to extend and refine consumer behavior theories such as the Theory of Planned Behavior (TPB) and the Technology Acceptance Model (TAM) in the context of immersive technologies, whereas these theories focus on understanding consumer decision-making and technology adoption in more traditional, non-immersive environments. The metaverse, on the other hand, offers a distinct, highly interactive, and compelling world that calls these established concepts into question. This study adds to existing consumer behavior theories by incorporating additional elements like immersion, presence, and virtual experience. By combining previous studies on metaverse-based product demonstration, the study can help to create a new paradigm of immersive marketing. This theoretical framework may encompass notions such as virtual brand experiences, interactive consumer touchpoints, and emotional involvement in ways that traditional marketing models have not fully explored. The study can also help to further theories of co-creation and consumer empowerment by demonstrating how immersive settings allow customers to actively participate with and influence the brand story rather than merely receiving marketing messages. In the field of consumer-technology interaction ideas, the study highlights the need to investigate the link between humans and technology in the context of the metaverse. Immersive technologies, such as VR and AR, allow consumers to interact with products and brands in ways that were not possible in older, more static internet settings. These technologies introduce new types of interaction design, in which consumers' emotional responses and interactive behaviors shape the consumer experience.

Managerial Implication

The study provides significant insights for managers and business leaders who want to use immersive technology, particularly the metaverse, to improve their product demonstration, marketing strategies, and consumer engagement. Companies that use virtual reality (VR), augmented reality (AR), and 3D virtual environments can create dynamic and fascinating experiences that allow customers to interact with products in new ways. Managers can use these immersive tools to provide interactive demonstration so that clients can "experience" things before making a purchasing decision. For example, in the automotive business, a virtual test drive might allow buyers to explore a vehicle's features and performance in a fully immersive environment. In retail, customers might virtually try on clothes or see furniture in their own houses. This type of hands-on, experiential marketing is likely to promote customer engagement, improve brand loyalty, and produce higher conversion rates. The metaverse provides a unique opportunity for managers to personalize the customer experience by tailoring virtual settings and interactions based on consumer data. Immersive product demonstration in the metaverse can have a major impact on purchasing decisions, which has important administrative implications. Managers should recognize that offering a highly immersive, interactive experience can assist reduce customer confusion during the decision-making process, resulting in improved conversion rates and increased revenue.

Managers should carefully assess the scale of their immersive marketing, the target demographic, and the resources required to create an engaging experience.

8 Conclusion

The study identifies a significant shift in how brands communicate with customers and display their products. As immersive technologies such as virtual reality (VR), augmented reality (AR), and three-dimensional (3D) virtual environments advance, the metaverse is emerging as an essential platform for businesses to provide highly engaging, interactive, and realistic product experiences. This technological advancement is profoundly transforming how businesses interact with their consumers and how customers make purchasing decisions, rather than simply improving product demonstration. Furthermore, the report stresses the need of incorporating these immersive experiences into an omnichannel strategy, ensuring that virtual product demonstrations complement and improve the overall consumer journey across several touchpoints. A seamless, multi-channel approach ensures that customers receive the same consistent, unified brand message whether they interact with the company in a physical store, on a website, or in a metaverse.

9 Limitations and Scope of Future Research

This research focuses on the use of immersive technologies such as virtual reality (VR), augmented reality (AR), and three-dimensional (3D) settings in the metaverse for commercial demonstrations. However, due to the quickly growing nature of immersive technology, new breakthroughs such as artificial intelligence (AI)-driven avatars and haptic feedback may have a greater impact on how people experience this product demonstration. This study does not include all upcoming technologies that could play an important role in improving metaverse experiences, allowing potential for future research to investigate these additional features. The study's methodology, which is based on the PRISMA approach and uses Scopus as the major database, provides a structured and targeted evaluation of relevant literature, but it may limit the range of findings. Scopus, while thorough, does not include all global publications, thus some pertinent research may have been missed. Future research could investigate industry-specific applications of metaverse technology to deliver more personalized recommendations. Future research can explore deeper into industry-specific uses for virtual product demonstrations. Healthcare, education, automotive, fashion, and real estate industries have all begun to investigate metaverse applications, but each has unique obstacles and potential with immersive technologies. Future research could look into how frequent exposure to VR and AR-based product demonstration influences consumers' attention spans, emotional responses, brand loyalty, and purchasing habits. Furthermore, academics might look at the potential psychological consequences, such as digital fatigue or over-reliance on virtual experiences, and what these mean for firms looking to build long-term consumer relationships through the metaverse.

References

Abrokwah-Larbi, K. (2024). Transforming metaverse marketing into strategic agility in SMEs through mediating roles of IMT and CI: Theoretical framework and research propositions. *Journal of Contemporary Marketing Science, 7*(1), 56–83. https://doi.org/10.1108/JCMARS-08-2023-0034

Akbar, A., & Agyei, B. A. (2024). Next-gen services innovation: Leveraging metaverse for unparalleled customer satisfaction in tourism industry. *Journal of Metaverse Business Designs*, *5*(1), 14–26. https://jmbd.org/index.php/home/article/view/22

Alhitmi, H. K., Mardiah, A., Al-Sulaiti, K. I., & Abbas, J. (2024). Data security and privacy concerns of AI-driven marketing in the context of economics and business field: An exploration into possible solutions. *Cogent Business & Management, 11*(1), 2393743. https://doi.org/10.1080/23311975.2024.2393743

Alimamy, S., & Jung, T. (2024). The AR cloud: Navigating metaverse augmentation technologies for enhanced co-creation of value within services. *Journal of Service Research,* 10946705241265752. https://doi.org/10.1177/10946705241265753

Asar, S. H., Jalalpour, S. H., Ayoubi, F., Rahmani, M. R., & Rezaeian, M. (2016). PRISMA; preferred reporting items for systematic reviews and meta-analyses. *Journal of Rafsanjan University of Medical Sciences, 15*(1), 68–80.

Barrera, K. G., & Shah, D. (2023). Marketing in the Metaverse: Conceptual understanding, framework, and research agenda. *Journal of Business Research, 155*, Article 113420. https://doi.org/10.1016/j.jbusres.2022.113420

Bilgihan, A., Leong, A. M. W., Okumus, F., & Bai, J. (2024). Proposing a metaverse engagement model for brand development. *Journal of Retailing and Consumer Services, 78*, Article 103781. https://doi.org/10.1016/j.jretconser.2024.103781

Buhalis, D., Leung, D., & Lin, M. (2023). Metaverse as a disruptive technology revolutionising tourism management and marketing. *Tourism Management, 97*, Article 104724. https://doi.org/10.1016/j.tourman.2023.104724

Chakraborty, D., Polisetty, A., & Rana, N. P. (2024). Consumers' continuance intention towards metaverse-based virtual stores: A multi-study perspective. *Technological Forecasting and Social Change, 203*, Article 123405. https://doi.org/10.1016/j.techfore.2024.123405

Chakraborty, U., & Biswal, S. K. (2024). Diffusion of innovation in Direct-to-Avatar (D2A): A study of immersive communication and branding in the metaverse. *Computers in Human Behavior,* 108318. https://doi.org/10.1016/j.chb.2024.108318

Chen, Y., & Mu, B. (2024). *Exploration of multimedia perception and virtual reality technology application in computer aided packaging design.* https://doi.org/10.14733/cadaps.2024.S25.141-155

Darvish, M., Bick, M., & Keresztyen, L. (2024). Exploring the potential of virtual immersive workspaces: Benefits, limitations, and implications. *California Management Review, 66*(4), 102–120. https://doi.org/10.1177/00081256241258494

Donthu, N., Kumar, S., Mukherjee, D., Pandey, N., & Lim, W. M. (2021). How to conduct a bibliometric analysis: An overview and guidelines. *Journal of Business Research, 133*, 285–296. https://doi.org/10.1016/j.jbusres.2021.04.070

Dwivedi, Y. K., Hughes, L., Baabdullah, A. M., Ribeiro-Navarrete, S., Giannakis, M., Al-Debei, M. M., Dennehy, D., Metri, B., Buhalis, D, Cheung, C. M. K., Conboy K., Doyle, R., Dubey, R., Dutot, V., Felix, R., Goyal, D.P., Gustafsson, A., Hinsch, C., …, & Wamba, S. F. (2022). Metaverse beyond the hype: Multidisciplinary perspectives on emerging challenges, opportunities, and agenda for research, practice and policy. *International journal of information management*, *66*, 102542. https://doi.org/10.1016/j.ijinfomgt.2022.102542

Dwivedi, Y. K., Hughes, L., Wang, Y., Alalwan, A. A., Ahn, S. J., Balakrishnan, J., Barta, S., Belk, R., Buhalis, D., Dutot, V., Felix, R., Filieri, R., Flavián, C., Gustafsson, A., Hinsch, C., Hollensen, S., Jain, V., Kim, J., Krishen, A. S., … & Wirtz, J. (2023). Metaverse marketing: How the metaverse will shape the future of consumer research and practice. *Psychology & Marketing, 40*(4), 750–776. https://doi.org/10.1002/mar.21767

Gandhi, M., Gaur, A., Kar, A. K., & Dwivedi, Y. K. (2024). Crafting user experiences in the metaverse: A design science study. *Technological Forecasting and Social Change, 209*, Article 123759. https://doi.org/10.1016/j.techfore.2024.123759

Gupta, P. (2023). Understanding consumer behavior in virtual ecosystems: Adoption of immersive technologies in metaverse among consumers. In *Handbook of research on consumer behavioral analytics in metaverse and the adoption of a virtual world* (pp. 130–152). IGI Global. https://doi.org/10.4018/978-1-6684-7029-9.ch007

Habil, S. G. M., El-Deeb, S., & El-Bassiouny, N. (2024). The metaverse era: Leveraging augmented reality in the creation of novel customer experience. *Management & Sustainability: An Arab Review, 3*(1), 1–15. https://doi.org/10.1108/MSAR-10-2022-0051

Hadi, R., Melumad, S., & Park, E. S. (2024). The Metaverse: A new digital frontier for consumer behavior. *Journal of Consumer Psychology, 34*(1), 142–166. https://doi.org/10.1002/jcpy.1357

Han, D. I. D., Bergs, Y., & Moorhouse, N. (2022). Virtual reality consumer experience escapes: Preparing for the metaverse. *Virtual Reality, 26*(4), 1443–1458. https://doi.org/10.1007/s10055-022-00641-7

Johri, A., Sayal, A., Chaithra, N., Jha, J., Aggarwal, N., Pawar, D., Gupta, V., & Gupta, A. (2024). Crafting the techno-functional blocks for Metaverse—A review and research agenda. *International Journal of Information Management Data Insights, 4*(1), 100213. https://doi.org/10.1016/j.jjimei.2024.100213

Kaur, J., Mogaji, E., Paliwal, M., Jha, S., Agarwal, S., & Mogaji, S. A. (2024). Consumer behavior in the metaverse. *Journal of Consumer Behaviour, 23*(4), 1720–1738. https://doi.org/10.1002/cb.2298

Khan, H. A. (2024). Innovative services, processes and product design crucial for enhancing customer experience. In *Marketing and design in the service sector: Enhancing customer experience* (pp. 63–81). Emerald Publishing Limited. https://doi.org/10.1108/978-1-83797-276-020241006

Kim, J. H., Kim, M., Park, M., & Yoo, J. (2021). How interactivity and vividness influence consumer virtual reality shopping experience: The mediating role of telepresence. *Journal of Research in Interactive Marketing, 15*(3), 502–525. https://doi.org/10.1108/JRIM-07-2020-0148

Kim, J., & Ha, J. (2021). User experience in VR fashion product shopping: Focusing on tangible interactions. *Applied Sciences, 11*(13), 6170. https://doi.org/10.3390/su14127110

Kumar, V., Ashraf, A. R., & Nadeem, W. (2024). AI-powered marketing: What, where, and how? *International Journal of Information Management, 77*, Article 102783. https://doi.org/10.1016/j.ijinfomgt.2024.102783

Lee, S. M., & Lee, D. (2020). "Untact": A new customer service strategy in the digital age. *Service Business, 14*(1), 1–22. https://doi.org/10.1007/s11628-019-00408-2

Lee, J., Yang, J., & Ha, C. (2022, June). How should we suggest colors to creators in the metaverse? In *International Conference on Human-Computer Interaction* (pp. 212–219). Springer International Publishing. https://doi.org/10.1007/978-3-031-06417-3_29

Mariani, M. M., & Wamba, S. F. (2020). Exploring how consumer goods companies innovate in the digital age: The role of big data analytics companies. *Journal of Business Research, 121*, 338–352. https://doi.org/10.1016/j.jbusres.2020.09.012

Mladenović, D., Ismagilova, E., Filieri, R., & Dwivedi, Y. K. (2024). MetaWOM–toward a sensory word-of-mouth (WOM) in the metaverse. *International Journal of Contemporary Hospitality Management, 36*(6), 2144–2163. https://doi.org/10.1108/IJCHM-04-2023-0474

Mourtzis, D., Panopoulos, N., Angelopoulos, J., Wang, B., & Wang, L. (2022). Human centric platforms for personalized value creation in metaverse. *Journal of Manufacturing Systems, 65*, 653–659. https://doi.org/10.1016/j.jmsy.2022.11.004

Nair, A. J., Manohar, S., Mittal, A., & Chaudhry, R. (2024). Unleashing digital frontiers: Bridging realities of augmented reality, virtual reality, and the metaverse. In *The metaverse dilemma: Challenges and opportunities for business and society* (pp. 85–112). Emerald Publishing Limited. https://doi.org/10.1108/978-1-83797-524-220241006

Nalbant, K. G., & Aydın, S. (2023). Development and transformation in digital marketing and branding with artificial intelligence and digital technologies dynamics in the Metaverse universe. *Journal of Metaverse, 3*(1), 9–18. https://doi.org/10.57019/jmv.1148015

Rafique, W., & Qadir, J. (2024). Internet of everything meets the metaverse: Bridging physical and virtual worlds with blockchain. *Computer Science Review, 54*, Article 100678. https://doi.org/10.1016/j.cosrev.2024.100678

Raji, M. A., Olodo, H. B., Oke, T. T., Addy, W. A., Ofodile, O. C., & Oyewole, A. T. (2024). Business strategies in virtual reality: a review of market opportunities and consumer experience. *International Journal of Management & Entrepreneurship Research, 6*(3), 722–736. https://doi.org/10.51594/ijmer.v6i3.883

Raza, A., Wasim, M., & Ishaq, M. I. (2024). Virtual reality-based product displays to inspire consumers' purchase intentions: An experimental study. *Journal of Business Research, 175*, Article 114540. https://doi.org/10.1016/j.jbusres.2024.114540

Partarakis, N., & Zabulis, X. (2024). A review of immersive technologies, knowledge representation, and AI for human-centered digital experiences. *Electronics, 13*(2), 269. https://doi.org/10.3390/electronics13020269

Schulte, P., & Shemakov, R. (2024). The future of digital infrastructure: Case studies of global corporate strategies in augmented reality. In *Global perspectives in the metaverse: Law, economics, and finance* (pp. 119–143). Cham: Springer Nature Switzerland. https://doi.org/10.1007/978-3-031-54802-4_7

Shamim, N., Gupta, S., & Shin, M. M. (2024). Evaluating user engagement via Metaverse environment through immersive experience for travel and tourism websites. *International Journal of Contemporary Hospitality Management*. https://doi.org/10.1108/IJCHM-10-2023-1590

Shen, B., Tan, W., Guo, J., Zhao, L., & Qin, P. (2021). How to promote user purchase in metaverse? A systematic literature review on consumer behavior research and virtual commerce application design. *Applied Sciences, 11*(23), 11087. https://doi.org/10.3390/app112311087

Sridharan, A., & Kumar, S. (2024). The impact of metaverse on businesses. In *The metaverse dilemma: Challenges and opportunities for business and society* (pp. 13–30). Emerald Publishing Limited. https://doi.org/10.1108/978-1-83797-524-220241002

Sun, Y., Lu, Y., Wang, B., & Fan, W. P. (2023). Like being there: How the soft VR technology could change consumers' initial decision-making. *Computers in Human Behavior, 146*, Article 107814. https://doi.org/10.1016/j.chb.2023.107814

Tyagi, M., & Tyagi, S. (2024). Consumer experience and decision-making in the metaverse: Marketing 2.0 beyond traditional boundaries. In *Consumer experience and decision-making in the metaverse* (pp. 57–77). IGI Global. https://doi.org/10.4018/979-8-3693-4167-4.ch004

Ud Din, I., Awan, K. A., Almogren, A., & Rodrigues, J. J. (2023). Integration of IoT and blockchain for decentralized management and ownership in the metaverse. *International Journal of Communication Systems, 36*(18), Article e5612. https://doi.org/10.1002/dac.5612

Wedel, M., Bigné, E., & Zhang, J. (2020). Virtual and augmented reality: Advancing research in consumer marketing. *International Journal of Research in Marketing, 37*(3), 443–465. https://doi.org/10.1016/j.ijresmar.2020.04.004

Xi, N., Chen, J., Gama, F., Riar, M., & Hamari, J. (2023). The challenges of entering the metaverse: An experiment on the effect of extended reality on workload. *Information Systems Frontiers, 25*(2), 659–680. https://doi.org/10.1007/s10796-022-10244-x

Yaqoob, I., Salah, K., Jayaraman, R., & Omar, M. (2023). Metaverse applications in smart cities: Enabling technologies, opportunities, challenges, and future directions. *Internet of Things*, 100884. https://doi.org/10.1016/j.iot.2023.100884

Yoo, K., Welden, R., Hewett, K., & Haenlein, M. (2023). The merchants of meta: A research agenda to understand the future of retailing in the metaverse. *Journal of Retailing, 99*(2), 173–192. https://doi.org/10.1016/j.jretai.2023.02.002

Machine Learning-Based Approach and Customer Segmentation: A Review

Van Hau Pham and McIver Thomas

Abstract

This chapter examines how machine learning (ML) has revolutionized customer segmentation, transforming traditional demographic and psychographic models into dynamic, data-driven frameworks. By highlighting advanced techniques such as K-means, hierarchical clustering, Gaussian mixture models, and density-based methods (e.g., DBSCAN), it underscores the strategic value of ML in uncovering granular customer insights. A narrative review of prominent ML clustering algorithms and emerging methods (including deep learning integration and hybrid models) is conducted. Case studies and practical applications illustrate how these frameworks scale and adapt to diverse business scenarios. Emphasis is placed on comparing algorithmic strengths, limitations, and suitability for different segmentation objectives. ML-driven segmentation enables hyper-personalized marketing by isolating nuanced customer segments often overlooked by traditional approaches. Real-time feedback loops enhance strategic decision-making and predictive accuracy, allowing businesses to anticipate evolving consumer behaviors. Nonetheless, algorithmic transparency, ethical concerns, and data privacy challenges require vigilant oversight and responsible implementation. By harnessing ML-based segmentation, organizations can boost engagement, loyalty, and profitability in an increasingly data-centric marketplace. Aligning these advanced techniques with robust ethical safeguards fosters consumer trust and strengthens competitiveness. The chapter provides a roadmap for integrating ML into segmentation strategies, demonstrating how responsible, innovative applications can drive sustainable business growth.

V. H. Pham (✉)
School of Applied Business, Unitec Institute of Technology, Auckland, New Zealand
e-mail: phamhau100598@gmail.com; vpham@unitec.ac.nz

M. Thomas
Department of Information Technology, Otago Polytechnique, Dunedin, New Zealand

© The Author(s), under exclusive license to Springer Nature Singapore Pte Ltd. 2026
N. S. Jayawardena et al. (eds.), *Digital Advertising and Consumer Behavior*,
Management for Professionals, https://doi.org/10.1007/978-981-95-7809-2_9

Abbreviations

ML	Machine Learning
EM	Expectation-Maximization
GMM	Gaussian Mixture Models
DBSCAN	Density-Based Spatial Clustering

1 Introduction

In a world characterized by increasing complexity and heightened competition across virtually every industry, understanding customers at a granular level has emerged as a non-negotiable priority (Armstrong et al., 2014). Technological advancements, global market expansions, and rapidly shifting consumer behaviours have made it more critical than ever for businesses to tailor their offerings to specific customer groups (Parsons et al., 2023). Against this backdrop, customer segmentation has become a cornerstone of modern marketing, product development, and customer service.

Customer Segmentation

At its core, customer segmentation involves systematically dividing a heterogeneous customer base into smaller, more homogeneous groups (Wijekoon et al., 2021). These groups, or "segments," are typically defined by shared attributes that can range from broad demographic features (e.g., age, income, or educational level) to intricate psychographic patterns (e.g., values, attitudes, and lifestyles). The essential function of segmentation is to help businesses recognize that no two customers are exactly alike; thus, a one-size-fits-all strategy is rarely effective (Hjort et al., 2013). Instead, segmenting allows companies to develop targeted marketing campaigns, design relevant products, and deliver personalized experiences that resonate more deeply with each subgroup.

Traditionally, segmentation relied on basic demographic variables—such as age and income—due to limited data and analytical tools (Kotler & Keller, 2016). Today's digital ecosystem allows marketers to incorporate diverse data sources—transactional logs, browsing behaviour, social media analytics, and psychographic attributes—leading to hyper-granular and dynamic segments (Liu et al., 2015). Yet this complexity also poses challenges. Deciding which variables to include, how to cluster them, and ensuring segments remain actionable and stable over time is nontrivial (Chen et al., 2019).

The Importance of Customer Segmentation

Customer segmentation is a critical strategic tool allowing businesses to refine their offerings for specific customer groups, bolstering organizational efficiency and market competitiveness. Figure 1 illustrates all potential key benefits of customer segmentation. By distinguishing one segment from another, firms can craft **tailored value propositions** that align more closely with each group's unique preferences, pain points, and motivations—an approach that generally results in higher satisfaction, loyalty, and long-term profitability (Osterwalder et al., 2015; Payne et al., 2017). This customization ensures, for example, that a streaming service can differentiate its messaging for film enthusiasts and sports fans, ultimately boosting engagement across both segments.

Beyond personalization, segmentation supports **efficient resource allocation**. In a competitive environment, organizations must deploy budgets judiciously; identifying the most profitable or strategically significant segments enables them to

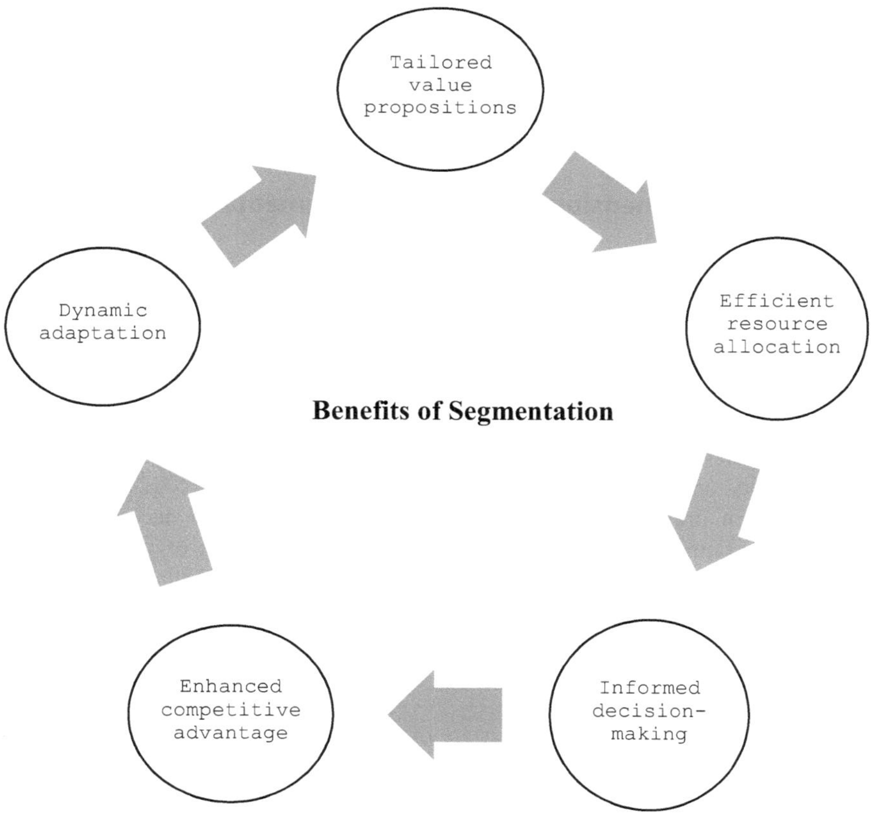

Fig. 1 Key benefits of customer segmentation. (*Source* Author's own work)

concentrate marketing spend and operational efforts where they will deliver the greatest return (Ailawadi & Farris, 2017). Rather than broadcasting untargeted campaigns, marketers can zoom in on the customer groups most likely to convert (Morgan et al., 2019).

Moreover, segmentation fosters **informed decision-making**. By examining how segments vary in spending patterns, channel preferences, or loyalty, businesses can tailor their strategies for maximum impact (Camilleri, 2018). For instance, if one cohort consistently responds to social media advertising while another prefers email newsletters, marketing teams can adapt their outreach and messaging accordingly, ensuring each group receives content that resonates with its specific habits (Hudak et al., 2017; Kumar, 2021).

In an increasingly crowded marketplace, segmentation also provides an **enhanced competitive advantage** (Yabs, 2014). Companies that understand customers' core needs can develop specialized offerings that others neglect, increasing brand affinity and reducing customers' likelihood of switching to competitors (Arnett, 2024). Finally, the importance of **dynamic adaptation** cannot be overstated. As technology evolves and consumer tastes shift, static segmentation models rapidly lose relevance; by contrast, agile, machine learning-powered segmentation frameworks allow for continuous realignment with emerging customer data (Mosaddegh et al., 2021). This ensures businesses remain relevant and proactive in meeting customer needs, cementing a lasting edge in the marketplace.

The Four Key Dimensions of Customer Segmentation

While segmentation can be executed through myriad variables, four core dimensions (geographic, demographic, psychographic, and behavioural) remain central in academic and practical frameworks (as depicted in Fig. 2) (Armstrong et al., 2014; Kotler & Keller, 2016).

Geographic Segmentation

This dimension addresses customers' location, examining regions, climate, population density, and urban versus rural residence (Schlegelmilch, 2022). Geographic nuances often influence consumer tastes, cultural norms, and accessibility. For example, e-commerce firms may prioritize different logistics or product assortments depending on a region's climate or infrastructure. With the increasing globalization of businesses, geographic segmentation helps reconcile cross-border differences in language, traditions, and purchasing power.

Demographic Segmentation

Who the consumer is lies at the heart of demographic segmentation. Variables typically include age, income, gender, education, and occupation (Kerin et al., 2020). Due to the ease of measurement, demographics remain the most commonly used basis for segmentation. While valuable, demographic data alone can

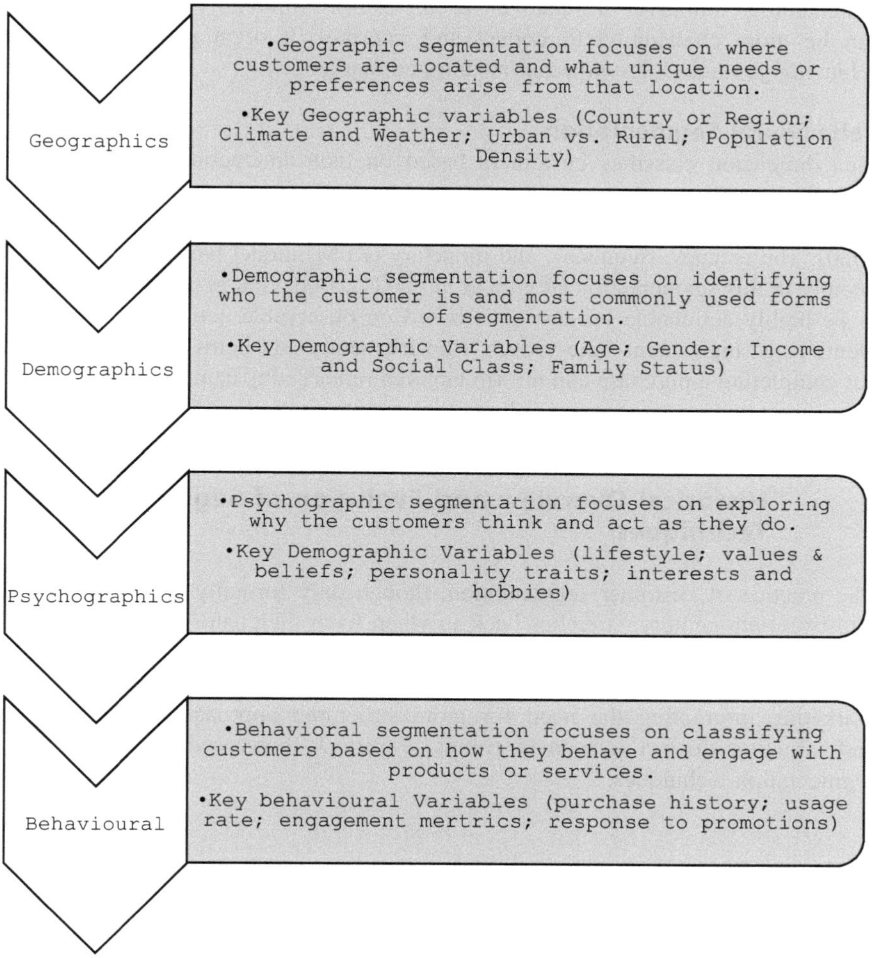

Fig. 2 Four key dimensions of customer segmentation. (*Source* Author's own work)

overlook bigger psychological or behavioural differences. Nonetheless, identifying basic demographic clusters often serves as an essential starting point for more sophisticated, multi-dimensional segmentation methods.

Psychographic Segmentation

Psychographic segmentation explores why consumers think and act in particular ways, focusing on values, personality traits, and lifestyle choices (Blömker & Albrecht, 2024). By examining these emotional and cognitive drivers, firms can shape brand narratives or product designs that resonate more deeply. For instance, environmentally conscious consumers may gravitate toward brands with robust sustainability initiatives (Luukkonen et al., 2024). Although psychographic data can be more challenging to collect and interpret, it often proves pivotal for achieving genuine differentiation in saturated markets.

Behavioural Segmentation

This dimension classifies customers based on their interactions with products, services, or communications, considering purchase frequency, channel usage, browsing history, and response to promotions (Maccarrone-Eaglen & Schofield, 2020). The recency, frequency, and monetary (RFM) model has been applied frequently in this segmentation (Rahim et al., 2021). Behavioural segmentation tends to be highly actionable because it is based on observable actions. For example, identifying "high intent" site visitors who frequently add items to their cart without completing a purchase can inform targeted remarketing campaigns designed to reduce cart abandonment rates (Murgado-Armenteros et al., 2021).

2 Historical Overview and Evolution of Segmentation Techniques

The practice of customer segmentation, though only formally recognized in the mid-twentieth century, stretches back to when local merchants maintained direct and personal relationships with their clients. As businesses expanded, personalized knowledge gave way to mass production and the adoption of undifferentiated marketing, prompting the need for more structured approaches to identifying and targeting distinct consumer groups. Figure 3 showcased the evolution of segmentation techniques.

Early Beginnings: Demographic and Geographic Segmentation

During the initial phases of segmentation, marketers primarily relied on demographic and geographic variables (Wedel & Kamakura, 2000). These data points

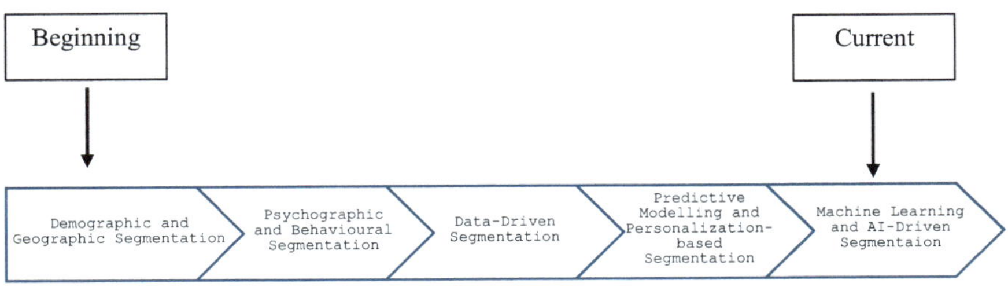

Fig. 3 Evolution of segmentation techniques. (*Source* Author's own work)

were readily available, straightforward to collect, and relatively simple to interpret (Kotler & Keller, 2016). They enabled a broad categorization of consumers according to region, age, gender, and other basic indicators that shaped consumption patterns and product preferences. Although such methods were rudimentary by contemporary standards, they constituted the foundation of systematic segmentation practice.

Psychographic and Behavioural Variables Enter the Picture

Later on, scholars and practitioners began recognising the limitations of solely demographic and geographic segmentation (Wedel & Kamakura, 2012). The inclusion of psychographic and behavioural metrics thus represented a pivotal advance in understanding the underlying drivers of consumer choice. Psychographic segmentation focuses on attitudes, values, and lifestyles, elucidating consumer behaviour motivations (Blömker & Albrecht, 2024). Behavioural segmentation, by contrast, categorizes consumers based on tangible actions, including purchase frequency, brand loyalty, and responsiveness to pricing (Maccarrone-Eaglen & Schofield, 2020). These methodologies enabled a richer and more nuanced view of the complex factors influencing customer behaviour.

The Rise of Data-Driven Segmentation

Subsequent developments in computing and data storage technologies precipitated a significant shift toward data-driven segmentation practices (Kotler & Keller, 2016). Statistical methods, such as factor analysis and cluster analysis, gave marketers and researchers the tools to draw insights from large-scale transactional records and survey data (Füller & Matzler, 2008; Ketchen & Shook, 1996). These analytical techniques bolstered the credibility and precision of segmentation, transitioning the field from predominantly intuitive or "gut-based" decision-making to more empirically grounded other data-intensive enterprises could now identify high-value or high-risk subgroups with approaches (Özemre & Kabadurmus, 2020).

The Advent of Predictive Modelling and Personalization

Later, predictive modelling augmented traditional segmentation techniques, empowering firms to anticipate future consumer behaviours based on historical and real-time data (Palmisano et al., 2008). This predictive capacity facilitated the rise of personalized marketing, in which each consumer was effectively treated as a unique "segment of one". E-commerce leaders, in particular, employed advanced recommendation algorithms to analyse individual users' browsing histories and purchase behaviours to generate customized product suggestions (Xiao & Benbasat, 2007). Personalization thus evolved from a theoretical aspiration to a widely adopted practice for increasing customer engagement and conversion rates.

Transition to Machine Learning and AI-Driven Segmentation

Contemporary segmentation methods rely extensively on machine learning (ML) and artificial intelligence (AI) to automate and refine the discovery of nuanced consumer subgroups (Armstrong et al., 2020, p. 98). These tools can detect subtle patterns within expansive datasets, enabling firms to identify emergent segments, predict evolving needs, and optimize targeting strategies in ways previously unattainable (Huang & Rust, 2021). This progression—from fundamental demographic categorizations to the current state of AI-driven hyper-personalization—reflects the broader growth in data availability and computational capacity (Ampountolas & Legg, 2021; Singh & Kaunert, 2024).

3 Machine Learning and its Role in Modern Customer Segmentation

The advent of machine learning (ML) has revolutionized this domain by streamlining and enhancing the segmentation process. ML-based systems accelerate the identification of targeted customer segments and reduce costs by automating significant portions of data preprocessing and analysis (Sahu, 2022). One of the primary distinctions between manual segmentation and ML-driven methods lies in the latter's ability to scale with increasing data volume. Whereas human-led approaches tend to slow down and incur higher expenses as the dataset grows, machine-learning algorithms typically exhibit improvements in accuracy and maintain efficiency under larger scales (De Bruyn et al., 2020).

A central strength of ML in customer segmentation is its capacity to detect intricate patterns and latent interrelationships within vast and multifaceted datasets (Armstrong et al., 2014). Techniques such as supervised learning, unsupervised learning (e.g., clustering), and semi-supervised approaches can uncover correlations that may not be readily apparent to human analysts (Taha, 2023). For example, a retailer might employ unsupervised learning methods—such as k-means clustering or hierarchical clustering—to group customers based on purchase frequency, basket size, preferred product categories, and even in-store movement patterns (Kasem et al., 2024). Machine learning models can reveal how specific shopper behaviours correlate with spending levels and store layout preferences by integrating data from sources like point-of-sale (POS) systems, loyalty programs, and in-store sensors (Inman & Nikolova, 2017). These insights enable data-driven decision-making to inform store design, product assortment, and promotional campaigns, enhancing overall marketing effectiveness.

From a marketing perspective, ML-based segmentation offers unprecedented agility in both strategy formulation and testing (Tsiptsis & Chorianopoulos, 2011). When marketing teams aim to trial several promotional tactics—personalized discounts, targeted email campaigns, or strategic product placements—machine learning systems can provide near-real-time feedback on which strategies perform best under given conditions (Leung et al., 2020). By analysing fine-grained customer responses, businesses can promptly identify successful approaches and eliminate ineffective ones. This iterative experimentation approach, facilitated by rapid ML-driven insights, is crucial in fast-paced retail environments, where consumer trends can shift within short time frames (Thaichon & Quach, 2023).

The implications of ML in customer segmentation extend beyond operational efficiency. Robust analytical methodologies increase the reliability of insights by reducing reliance on subjective judgments and conventional demographic assumptions (Ozan, 2018). Instead, ML algorithms capture customer data's behavioural, psychographic, and contextual nuances, leading to more accurate and flexible segment definitions (Kashwan & Velu, 2013). As the volume and variety of data continue to expand—encompassing social media interactions, mobile application usage, and sensor-generated data—ML stands poised to deliver more holistic customer views, bridging previously isolated data silos.

4 Key Clustering Techniques in Machine Learning-Based Customer Segmentation

This section explores advanced clustering and modelling techniques used in customer segmentation. It covers five prominent methods: K-means clustering, Hidden Markov Models (HMM), Agglomerative Hierarchical Clustering, Expectation-Maximization (EM) Clustering, and Density-Based Spatial Clustering (DBSCAN). The focus of this section is to provide an overview of each technique, comparing their practical implications rather than delving into mathematical equations or technical details. From that, the general reader could briefly understand each technique.

K-Means Clustering

Key Characteristics

K-means clustering is a partitioning algorithm that segments a dataset into k distinct, non-overlapping clusters. Each cluster is represented by its centroid, which is the mean position of all points within the cluster. This method is particularly effective for numerical data and assumes that clusters are roughly spherical and of similar sizes.

Process

The algorithm operates iteratively through the following steps:

- **Initialization**: Select k initial centroids, typically through random selection or using methods like K-Means++ to enhance convergence.
- **Assignment**: Assign each data point to the nearest centroid based on a chosen distance metric, commonly Euclidean distance.
- **Update**: Recalculate the centroids by computing the mean of all points assigned to each cluster.
- **Iteration**: Repeat the assignment and update steps until cluster assignments stabilize or a maximum number of iterations is reached.

Evaluation and Application in Customer Segmentation

K-Means is a computationally efficient and scalable clustering algorithm, making it ideal for large datasets. Its simplicity allows for ease of implementation and interpretability, enabling marketers to identify actionable customer groups like "premium" versus "casual" shoppers. However, it requires predefined cluster numbers, assumes isotropic clusters, and is sensitive to outliers and centroid initialization, which may yield suboptimal results. K-Means is widely applied in customer segmentation based on spending behaviour, purchase frequency, and demographics. Kansal et al. (2018) demonstrated its effectiveness in categorizing customers by annual spending and visit frequency, helping businesses optimize engagement and profitability through targeted strategies (Table 1).

Agglomerative Hierarchical Clustering

Key Characteristics

Agglomerative Hierarchical Clustering is a bottom-up approach that builds a hierarchy of clusters by progressively merging the most similar pairs of clusters. Unlike partitioning methods, it does not require pre-specification of the number of clusters. The result is represented as a dendrogram, a tree-like diagram that illustrates the nested grouping of data points.

Process

The algorithm proceeds through the following steps:

- **Initialization**: Treat each data point as an individual cluster.
- **Distance Computation**: Calculate inter-cluster distances using a chosen linkage criterion (e.g., single, complete, average, Ward's method).
- **Merging**: Combine the two closest clusters based on the linkage criteria.
- **Updating**: Recompute the distance matrix to reflect the newly formed clusters.
- **Iteration**: Repeat the merging and updating steps until all points are consolidated into a single cluster.

Table 1 Case study on applying K-means clustering in customer segmentation (Kansal et al., 2018)

Perpectives	Details
Objective	Segment a retail customer base using K-means clustering to uncover distinct customer groups and enable targeted marketing strategies
Dataset features	– **Feature 1**: Annual spending average – **Feature 2**: Annual visit frequency – **Number of records**: 200
Preprocessing	– Standard scaling applied to normalize data – Removed potential outliers to minimize distortion of clustering results
Optimal cluster selection	– Elbow method used to determine k = 5 – Evaluated within-cluster sum of squares (WCSS) for varying k
Algorithm steps	1. Initialize centroids (randomly or via K-means++) 2. Assign data points to the nearest centroid (Euclidean distance) 3. Update centroids 4. Repeat until centroids stabilize
Cluster segments	– **Target customers**: High spending, high frequency – **Careless shoppers**: Low spending, high frequency – **Sensible buyers**: Balanced spending and frequency – **Standard customers**: Moderate spending and frequency – **Occasional buyers**: Low spending, infrequent visits
Insights	– "Target customers" could be incentivized through loyalty programs – "Occasional buyers" suitable for re-engagement campaigns – "Careless shoppers" present upselling opportunities
Strengths of K-means	– Fast processing and scalable to larger datasets – Intuitive and visually interpretable clustering results – Clear, actionable segment definitions
Challenges identified	– Assumes spherical clusters, which may not reflect actual data patterns – Sensitive to centroid initialization; results varied with random starts – Outliers impacted centroid calculations, necessitating preprocessing
Visualization	2D scatter plot with clusters represented by distinct colours for interpretability and stakeholder communication
Conclusion	K-means clustering effectively segmented the customer base, enabling tailored strategies. Future work should explore additional features and predictive analytics integration

(*Source* Author's own work)

- **Dendrogram Cutting**: Select the desired number of clusters by cutting the dendrogram at a specific level.

Evaluation and Application in Customer Segmentation

Agglomerative Hierarchical Clustering is a flexible method for exploring hierarchical relationships in customer data. It detects diverse cluster shapes and relationships by utilizing various distance metrics and linkage methods, offering intuitive visualizations like dendrograms to guide segmentation decisions. This approach is particularly useful for uncovering nested customer structures, such as identifying sub-segments within "premium" or "budget" categories. However, its computational intensity and sensitivity to linkage and metric choices can lead to suboptimal outcomes. A study by Afzal et al. (2024) highlights its practical application, revealing hierarchical customer relationships and providing actionable insights for tailored marketing strategies and resource allocation (Table 2).

Table 2 Case study on applying agglomerative hierarchical clustering in customer segmentation (Afzal et al., 2024)

Perpectives	Details
Objective	Segment mall customers using agglomerative hierarchical clustering to identify meaningful groups based on demographics and spending behaviour
Dataset features	– **Features used**: Age, annual income ($K), spending score (1–100), and gender (numerically encoded)
Preprocessing	– Standardization applied to numerical features (e.g., annual income and spending score) for uniform scaling
Clustering approach	– Hierarchical clustering applied at three levels: 1. **Univariate clustering**: Based solely on "annual income" 2. **Bivariate clustering**: Combined "annual income" and "spending Score" 3. **Multivariate clustering**: Incorporated all features for a comprehensive segmentation
Visualization methods	– **Dendrograms**: Used to visualize hierarchical relationships in clustering – Scatter plots provided insights into cluster distributions at each level
Results	– Univariate and bivariate clustering revealed meaningful distinctions among customers based on income and spending patterns – Multivariate clustering captured more nuanced relationships using all features, such as age and gender
Validation	– The clustering structure was evaluated visually using dendrograms and scatter plots. No explicit external or internal validation metrics were provided in the document
Implications for strategy	– While specific segments were not named, clusters suggest actionable opportunities based on income and spending levels, such as targeting high-income, high-spending customers for premium services or re-engaging low-spending customers
Strengths	– Hierarchical clustering revealed nested relationships among data points – Flexible across various feature combinations (univariate, bivariate, multivariate)
Limitations	– No quantitative validation of clusters was discussed in the document – Computationally intensive and challenging for large datasets – Results depend on chosen distance metrics and linkage methods
Conclusion	Agglomerative hierarchical clustering demonstrated its utility in uncovering patterns and relationships among mall customers. Insights gained can inform targeted marketing strategies

(*Source* Author's own work)

Expectation-Maximization (EM) Clustering (Gaussian Mixture Models)

Key Characteristics

Expectation-maximisation clustering, often implemented through Gaussian Mixture Models (GMMs), is a probabilistic approach that models the data as a mixture of several Gaussian distributions. Unlike K-Means, EM Clustering allows for clusters with varying shapes, sizes, and covariance structures, providing a more flexible framework for data segmentation.

Process

The EM algorithm involves the following steps:

- **Initialization**: Define initial parameters for each Gaussian component, including means, covariances, and mixing coefficients.
- **Expectation (E-step)**: Compute the posterior probabilities that each data point belongs to each Gaussian component.
- **Maximization (M-step)**: Update the parameters of the Gaussian components to maximize the likelihood of the data given the current posterior probabilities.
- **Iteration**: Alternate between the E-step and M-step until convergence is achieved.

Evaluation and Application in Customer Segmentation

EM Clustering offers flexibility in modelling diverse shapes and sizes, including elliptical clusters with varying orientations and variances. Its probabilistic framework enables soft assignments, allowing data points to belong to multiple clusters with different degrees of membership, which is beneficial in capturing overlapping customer behaviours. This capability makes it ideal for uncovering complex structures within datasets. However, EM Clustering requires prior knowledge to specify the number of components and is sensitive to initialization, potentially leading to convergence at local optima. Additionally, its reliance on Gaussian distribution assumptions may limit its applicability to certain real-world datasets. In customer segmentation, EM Clustering is valuable for identifying segments with varying shapes and overlapping behaviours. Hariguna and Chen (2024) applied Gaussian Mixture Models (GMM), an EM implementation, to segment retail customers. The study identified distinct purchasing behaviour groups, enabling targeted pricing strategies and maximizing gross income (Table 3).

Density-Based Spatial Clustering (DBSCAN)

Key Characteristics

Density-Based Spatial Clustering of Applications with Noise (DBSCAN) is a clustering algorithm that identifies clusters as contiguous regions of high point density, separated by regions of low density. It does not require the specification of

Table 3 Case study on applying Gaussian Mixture Models (GMM) in customer segmentation (Hariguna & Chen, 2024)

Aspect	Details
Objective	Segment retail customers using GMM to identify purchasing behavior patterns and develop targeted pricing strategies to maximize gross income
Dataset and features	– **Records**: 1000 retail transaction records – **Attributes**: Unit price, quantity, total amount, payment methods, product categories, and customer demographics
Preprocessing	– One-hot encoding applied to categorical features (e.g., product line, payment method) – Standardization of numerical features (e.g., unit price, quantity) – Dataset checked for missing values; none were found
Algorithm parameters	– **Cluster count**: Determined using Bayesian information criterion (BIC), optimal $k = 10$ – **Convergence**: Achieved in 18 EM iterations
Clustering approach	– Data points assigned to clusters based on highest posterior probability from the fitted GMM – Each cluster represented as a Gaussian distribution
Identified segments	– **Segment 0**: Bulk buyers of lower-priced items, generating high gross income – **Segment 1**: Buyers of high-priced items in small quantities, yielding the highest average purchase value – **Segment 2**: High frequency of returns (negative average purchase values) – Other segments showed varying product preferences, spending behaviours, and payment method patterns
Evaluation metrics	– **Silhouette scores**: Training score of 0.175 and testing score of 0.015, indicating moderately defined clusters with room for improvement
Insights and strategies	– **Pricing strategies**: Premium pricing for high-value customers (e.g., segment 1); discounts and bundles for price-sensitive customers
Limitations	– Sensitivity to BIC for determining cluster count – Moderate silhouette scores indicated room for better-defined clusters – Initial pricing strategies required refinement to achieve positive outcomes
Results and impact	– Provided actionable segmentation insights for tailoring pricing strategies – Initial strategies led to a mixed impact on gross income, suggesting further optimization was needed
Conclusion	GMM effectively segmented customers and provided detailed behavioural insights but required iterative refinement of pricing strategies for better results

(*Source* Author’s own work)

the number of clusters in advance and is adept at discovering clusters of arbitrary shapes while simultaneously identifying outliers as noise.

Process

DBSCAN operates through the following steps:

- **Neighbourhood Definition**: For each data point, determine the number of neighbours within a specified radius (ϵ).
- **Core Points Identification**: Points with a number of neighbors exceeding a minimum threshold (*minPts*) are designated as core points.
- **Cluster Formation**: Core points and their reachable neighbors form clusters.
- **Outlier Detection**: Points not reachable from any core points are classified as outliers.

Evaluation and Application in Customer Segmentation

DBSCAN excels in identifying clusters of arbitrary shapes and is robust against outliers, ensuring that anomalies do not distort results (Van Hau et al., 2025). It eliminates the need for pre-specifying clusters, making it adaptable. However, its performance depends on careful tuning of ϵ and minPts, challenging without domain knowledge. It also struggles with datasets of varying densities and may be computationally intensive for large datasets. DBSCAN effectively identifies natural density-based groupings in customer segmentation, such as concentrated purchase behaviours or geographic clusters. It isolates outliers like extreme spenders, enabling targeted strategies. For example, Hossain (2017) demonstrated its use in segmenting customers based on spending behaviour, identifying clusters and flagging outliers for tailored marketing (Table 4).

Comparative Analysis and Selection Criteria

Selecting the most appropriate clustering or modelling technique for customer segmentation involves considering various factors, including data characteristics, computational resources, desired granularity, and specific business objectives. Figure 4 illustrates the selection guidelines for choosing appropriate clustering techniques. The following comparative analysis highlights the suitability of each method under different scenarios (Table 5):

5 Implications and Future Directions

Implications

This chapter highlights the significance of ML-based customer segmentation techniques over traditional methods, utilizing advanced clustering algorithms like K-Means, DBSCAN. These methods extract actionable insights from complex

Table 4 Case study on applying DBSCAN in customer segmentation (Hossain, 2017)

Perpectives	Details
Objective	To apply DBSCAN for customer segmentation using the wholesale customers dataset to group customers based on spending behavior and identify outliers
Dataset and features	– **Source**: Wholesale customers dataset (UCI machine learning repository) – **Attributes used**: Annual spending on six product categories
Preprocessing	– Feature normalization was applied to ensure uniform scaling of variables
Algorithm parameters	– ϵ: Distance radius for defining neighbourhoods – **MinPts**: Minimum number of points required to form a cluster – Parameters were selected through experimentation for optimal clustering
Clustering approach	– DBSCAN categorized points as core, border, or noise based on density – Core points formed clusters when connected through neighbors
Results	– DBSCAN identified distinct customer clusters based on spending behavior – Noise points were identified as outliers with unique characteristics
Validation	– Clusters were evaluated visually and interpreted based on spending categories
Strengths	– DBSCAN effectively identified clusters of varying shapes and sizes. – It was robust in identifying outliers
Limitations	– Sensitivity to parameter choices (ϵ\epsilonϵ and MinPts) required careful tuning – Computational intensity increased with larger datasets
Implications	– Clusters provided actionable insights into customer behavior – Outliers highlighted customers with unique spending patterns for further analysis
Conclusion	DBSCAN successfully segmented customers, providing meaningful groupings and identifying outliers for potential targeted strategies

(*Source* Author's own work)

datasets, enabling organizations to customize communication strategies and allocate resources efficiently. By targeting high-value customer clusters or addressing attrition risks, these techniques enhance engagement, loyalty, and business growth (Mogaji et al., 2021).

Advanced methodologies, such as Hidden Markov Models (HMMs) and Expectation-Maximization (EM) Clustering, improve predictive analytics by capturing temporal dynamics and probabilistic patterns. They support forecasting future customer needs and managing anomalies like fraud through techniques like DBSCAN. Hierarchical clustering further identifies sub-segments, offering nuanced insights for product development and service customization. Rigorous data preparation, algorithm selection, parameter tuning, and continuous validation ensure actionable insights aligned with organizational goals.

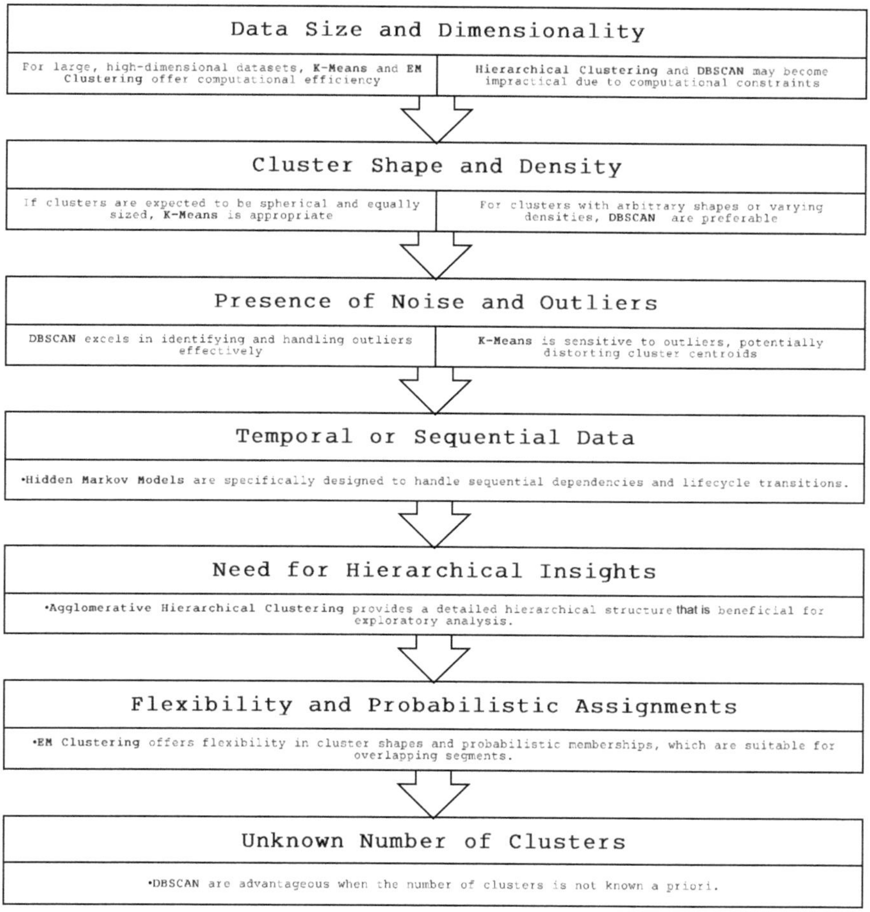

Fig. 4 Selection guidelines. (*Source* Author's own work)

Research Directions

Emerging research focuses on integrating deep learning frameworks like autoencoders with clustering algorithms to capture non-linear relationships in high-dimensional data (Berahmand et al., 2024). The rise of real-time data from IoT devices has spurred interest in online and incremental clustering methods for dynamic updates (Eslami et al., 2024; Quach et al., 2022). Combining clustering with predictive analytics enhances decision-making, enabling churn prediction and customer lifetime value estimation (Gadgil et al., 2023). Explainable AI (XAI) within clustering clarifies groupings, fostering trust and broader adoption (Arrieta et al., 2020). Ethical considerations, such as fairness and privacy, are prompting fairness-aware clustering and differential privacy techniques(Hermann,

Table 5 Comparison between clustering technique

Technique	Best Suited For	Advantages	Limitations
K-means clustering	Large datasets with well-separated, spherical clusters	Computationally efficient, simple implementation, easy interpretability	Requires pre-specification of k, assumes spherical clusters, sensitive to outliers
Hidden Markov models (HMM)	Sequential or time-based customer data, lifecycle modelling	Captures temporal dynamics, probabilistic handling of uncertainty, lifecycle insights	Complex implementation, requires specification of hidden states, susceptible to local optima
Agglomerative hierarchical clustering	Exploratory analysis revealing hierarchical relationships and sub-clusters	Reveals nested structures, flexible with distance metrics and linkage criteria, intuitive visualization through dendrograms	Computationally intensive for large datasets, irrevocable merging, sensitive to linkage choice
Expectation-maximization (EM) clustering	Data with overlapping clusters and varying shapes and sizes	Flexible cluster modelling, probabilistic memberships, accommodates diverse cluster shapes	Requires pre-specification of components, sensitive to initialization, assumes Gaussian distributions
Density-based spatial clustering (DBSCAN)	Data with arbitrary-shaped clusters and presence of outliers	Detects arbitrary shapes, robust to outliers, no need for pre-specified cluster number	Parameter sensitivity struggles with varying densities, computationally intensive

(*Source* Author's own work)

2022). Hybrid and ensemble methods improve outcomes, while visualization tools and dimensionality reduction simplify interpreting high-dimensional clustering results. These advancements aim to refine clustering methodologies for diverse applications.

6 Conclusion

Customer segmentation has become indispensable for organizations navigating today's competitive and complex markets. This chapter highlights the transformative impact of machine learning (ML) in enhancing segmentation, offering precision, scalability, and adaptability previously unattainable with traditional methods. ML-driven approaches empower businesses to analyse large-scale datasets, uncover intricate patterns, and develop tailored strategies to meet diverse consumer needs effectively. The exploration of key ML techniques, including K-means clustering, hierarchical clustering, Gaussian mixture models, and DBSCAN, demonstrates their practical applications and strategic advantages in segmenting customer bases. These methodologies enable businesses to move beyond static demographic variables, capturing behavioural, psychographic, and contextual nuances that drive consumer decisions. Moreover, the integration of ML with predictive analytics enhances forecasting capabilities, allowing organizations to anticipate customer preferences and optimize resource allocation.

References

Afzal, A., Khan, L., Hussain, M. Z., Hasan, M. Z., Mustafa, M., Khalid, A., Awan, R., Ashraf, F., Khan, Z. A., & Javaid, A. (2024). *Customer segmentation using hierarchical clustering.* 2024 IEEE 9th International conference for convergence in technology (I2CT).

Ailawadi, K. L., & Farris, P. W. (2017). Managing multi-and omni-channel distribution: Metrics and research directions. *Journal of Retailing, 93*(1), 120–135. https://doi.org/10.1016/j.jretai.2016.12.003

Ampountolas, A., & Legg, M. P. (2021). A segmented machine learning modeling approach of social media for predicting occupancy. *International Journal of Contemporary Hospitality Management, 33*(6), 2001–2021. https://doi.org/10.1108/IJCHM-06-2020-0611

Armstrong, G., Adam, S., Denize, S., & Kotler, P. (2014). *Principles of marketing.* Pearson Australia.

Armstrong, G., Denize, S., Volkov, M., Adam, S., Kotler, P., Ang, S. H., Love, A., Doherty, S., & van Esch, P. (2020). *Principles of marketing* (8th ed.). Pearson.

Arnett, D. B. (2024). Market segmentation strategy, target markets, and competitors: A resource-advantage theory perspective. *Journal of Marketing Management, 40*(13–14), 1269–1285. https://doi.org/10.1080/0267257x.2024.2391367

Arrieta, A. B., Díaz-Rodríguez, N., Del Ser, J., Bennetot, A., Tabik, S., Barbado, A., García, S., Gil-López, S., Molina, D., & Benjamins, R. (2020). Explainable artificial intelligence (XAI): Concepts, taxonomies, opportunities and challenges toward responsible AI. *Information Fusion, 58*, 82–115. https://doi.org/10.1016/j.inffus.2019.12.012

Berahmand, K., Daneshfar, F., Salehi, E. S., Li, Y., & Xu, Y. (2024). Autoencoders and their applications in machine learning: A survey. *Artificial Intelligence Review, 57*(2), 28. https://doi.org/10.1007/s10462-023-10662-6

Blömker, J., & Albrecht, C.-M. (2024). Psychographic segmentation of multichannel customers: Investigating the influence of individual differences on channel choice and switching behavior. *Journal of Retailing and Consumer Services, 79*, 103806. https://doi.org/10.1016/j.jretconser.2024.103806

Camilleri, M. A. (2018). *Market segmentation, targeting and positioning.* Springer.

Chen, H., Zhang, L., Chu, X., & Yan, B. (2019). Smartphone customer segmentation based on the usage pattern. *Advanced Engineering Informatics, 42*, 101000. https://doi.org/10.1016/j.aei.2019.101000

De Bruyn, A., Viswanathan, V., Beh, Y. S., Brock, J. K.-U., & Von Wangenheim, F. (2020). Artificial intelligence and marketing: Pitfalls and opportunities. *Journal of Interactive Marketing, 51*(1), 91–105. https://doi.org/10.1016/j.intmar.2020.04.007

Eslami, E., Razi, N., Lonbani, M., & Rezazadeh, J. (2024). Unveiling IoT customer behaviour: Segmentation and insights for enhanced IoT-CRM strategies: A real case study. *Sensors, 24*(4), 1050. https://doi.org/10.3390/s24041050

Füller, J., & Matzler, K. (2008). Customer delight and market segmentation: An application of the three-factor theory of customer satisfaction on life style groups. *Tourism Management, 29*(1), 116–126. https://doi.org/10.1016/j.tourman.2007.03.021

Gadgil, K., Gill, S. S., & Abdelmoniem, A. M. (2023). A meta-learning based stacked regression approach for customer lifetime value prediction. *Journal of Economy and Technology, 1*, 197–207. https://doi.org/10.1016/j.ject.2023.09.001

Hariguna, T., & Chen, S. C. (2024). Customer segmentation and targeted retail pricing in digital advertising using gaussian mixture models for maximizing gross income. *Journal of Digital Market and Digital Currency, 1*(2), 183–203. https://doi.org/10.47738/jdmdc.v1i2.11

Hermann, E. (2022). Leveraging artificial intelligence in marketing for social good—An ethical perspective. *Journal of Business Ethics, 179*(1), 43–61. https://doi.org/10.1007/s10551-021-04843-y

Hjort, K., Lantz, B., Ericsson, D., & Gattorna, J. (2013). Customer segmentation based on buying and returning behaviour. *International Journal of Physical Distribution & Logistics Management, 43*(10), 852–865. https://doi.org/10.1108/IJPDLM-02-2013-0020

Hossain, A. S. (2017). *Customer segmentation using centroid based and density based clustering algorithms*. 2017 3rd International conference on electrical information and communication technology (EICT).

Huang, M.-H., & Rust, R. T. (2021). A strategic framework for artificial intelligence in marketing. *Journal of the Academy of Marketing Science, 49*, 30–50. https://doi.org/10.1007/s11747-020-00749-9

Hudak, M., Kianičková, E., & Madleňák, R. (2017). The importance of e-mail marketing in e-commerce. *Procedia Engineering, 192*, 342–347. https://doi.org/10.1016/j.proeng.2017.06.059

Inman, J. J., & Nikolova, H. (2017). Shopper-facing retail technology: A retailer adoption decision framework incorporating shopper attitudes and privacy concerns. *Journal of Retailing, 93*(1), 7–28. https://doi.org/10.1016/j.jretai.2016.12.006

Kansal, T., Bahuguna, S., Singh, V., & Choudhury, T. (2018). *Customer segmentation using K-means clustering*. 2018 International conference on computational techniques, electronics and mechanical systems (CTEMS).

Kasem, M. S., Hamada, M., & Taj-Eddin, I. (2024). Customer profiling, segmentation, and sales prediction using AI in direct marketing. *Neural Computing and Applications, 36*(9), 4995–5005. https://doi.org/10.1007/s00521-023-09339-6

Kashwan, K. R., & Velu, C. (2013). Customer segmentation using clustering and data mining techniques. *International Journal of Computer Theory and Engineering, 5*(6), 856. https://doi.org/10.7763/IJCTE.2013.V5.811

Kerin, R., Steven, H., & William, R. (2020). *Marketing* (14th ed.). McGraw-Hill Education.

Ketchen, D. J., & Shook, C. L. (1996). The application of cluster analysis in strategic management research: An analysis and critique. *Strategic Management Journal, 17*(6), 441–458. https://doi.org/10.1002/(SICI)1097-0266(199606)17:6<441::AID-SMJ819>3.0.CO;2-G

Kotler, P., & Keller, K. L. (2016). *Marketing management* (15th Global ed.). Pearson Education.

Kumar, A. (2021). An empirical examination of the effects of design elements of email newsletters on consumers' email responses and their purchase. *Journal of Retailing and Consumer Services, 58*, 102349. https://doi.org/10.1016/j.jretconser.2020.102349

Leung, K. H., Mo, D. Y., Ho, G. T., Wu, C.-H., & Huang, G. Q. (2020). Modelling near-real-time order arrival demand in e-commerce context: A machine learning predictive methodology.

Industrial Management & Data Systems, 120(6), 1149–1174. https://doi.org/10.1108/Imds-12-2019-0646

Liu, Y., Li, H., Peng, G., Lv, B., & Zhang, C. (2015). Online purchaser segmentation and promotion strategy selection: Evidence from Chinese E-commerce market. *Annals of Operations Research, 233*(1), 263–279. https://doi.org/10.1007/s10479-013-1443-z

Luukkonen, R., Närvänen, E., & Becker, L. (2024). Consumer collectives in the circular economy: A systematic review and research agenda. *Sustainable Production and Consumption, 45*, 281–293. https://doi.org/10.1016/j.spc.2024.01.006

Maccarrone-Eaglen, A., & Schofield, P. (2020). Compulsive buying among young adults: A behavioural segmentation. *Young Consumers, 21*(1), 57–76. https://doi.org/10.1108/YC-02-2019-0958

Mogaji, E., Adeola, O., Hinson, R. E., Nguyen, N. P., Nwoba, A. C., & Soetan, T. O. (2021). Marketing bank services to financially vulnerable customers: Evidence from an emerging economy. *International Journal of Bank Marketing, 39*(3), 402–428. https://doi.org/10.1108/IJBM-07-2020-0379

Morgan, N. A., Whitler, K. A., Feng, H., & Chari, S. (2019). Research in marketing strategy. *Journal of the Academy of Marketing Science, 47*(1), 4–29. https://doi.org/10.1007/s11747-018-0598-1

Mosaddegh, A., Albadvi, A., Sepehri, M. M., & Teimourpour, B. (2021). Dynamics of customer segments: A predictor of customer lifetime value. *Expert Systems with Applications, 172*, 114606. https://doi.org/10.1016/j.eswa.2021.114606

Murgado-Armenteros, E. M., Parrilla-González, J. A., & Medina-Viruel, M. J. (2021). What does the olive oil tourist value at the destination? A criterion for olive oil tourism segmentation. *International Journal of Gastronomy and Food Science, 25*, 100378. https://doi.org/10.1016/j.ijgfs.2021.100378

Osterwalder, A., Pigneur, Y., Bernarda, G., & Smith, A. (2015). *Value proposition design: How to create products and services customers want.* Wiley.

Ozan, Ş. (2018). *A case study on customer segmentation by using machine learning methods.* 2018 International conference on artificial intelligence and data processing (IDAP).

Özemre, M., & Kabadurmus, O. (2020). A big data analytics based methodology for strategic decision making. *Journal of Enterprise Information Management, 33*(6), 1467–1490. https://doi.org/10.1108/JEIM-08-2019-0222

Palmisano, C., Tuzhilin, A., & Gorgoglione, M. (2008). Using context to improve predictive modeling of customers in personalization applications. *IEEE Transactions on Knowledge and Data Engineering, 20*(11), 1535–1549. https://doi.org/10.1109/Tkde.2008.110

Parsons, E., Maclaran, P., Chatzidakis, A., & Ashman, R. (2023). Contemporary issues in marketing and consumer behaviour. *Routledge.* https://doi.org/10.4324/9781003201151

Payne, A., Frow, P., & Eggert, A. (2017). The customer value proposition: Evolution, development, and application in marketing. *Journal of the Academy of Marketing Science, 45*(4), 467–489. https://doi.org/10.1007/s11747-017-0523-z

Quach, S., Thaichon, P., Martin, K. D., Weaven, S., & Palmatier, R. W. (2022). Digital technologies: Tensions in privacy and data. *Journal of the Academy of Marketing Science, 50*(6), 1299–1323. https://doi.org/10.1007/s11747-022-00845-y

Rahim, M. A., Mushafiq, M., Khan, S., & Arain, Z. A. (2021). RFM-based repurchase behavior for customer classification and segmentation. *Journal of Retailing and Consumer Services, 61*, 102566. https://doi.org/10.1016/j.jretconser.2021.102566

Sahu, M. K. (2022). Machine learning for personalized marketing and customer engagement in retail: Techniques, models, and real-world applications. *Journal of Artificial Intelligence Research and Applications, 2*(1), 219–254.

Schlegelmilch, B. B. (2022). Segmenting targeting and positioning in global markets. In *Global marketing strategy: An executive digest* (pp. 129–159). Springer. https://doi.org/10.1007/978-3-030-90665-8_6

Singh, B., & Kaunert, C. (2024). Future of digital marketing: Hyper-personalized customer dynamic experience with AI-based predictive models. In *Revolutionizing the AI-digital landscape* (pp. 189–203). Productivity Press. https://doi.org/10.4324/9781032688305

Taha, K. (2023). Semi-supervised and un-supervised clustering: A review and experimental evaluation. *Information Systems, 114*, 102178. https://doi.org/10.1016/j.is.2023.102178

Thaichon, P., & Quach, S. (2023). Artificial intelligence for marketing management. *Routledge.* https://doi.org/10.4324/9781003280392

Tsiptsis, K. K., & Chorianopoulos, A. (2011). Data mining techniques in CRM: Inside customer segmentation. *Wiley.* https://doi.org/10.1002/9780470685815

Van Hau, P., McIver, T., Robertson, K., & Thaichon, P. (2025). Effective customer segmentation using the recency, frequency, and monetary framework, combined with density-based clustering. *Journal of strategic marketing*, 1–23. https://doi.org/10.1080/0965254X.2025.2571534

Wedel, M., & Kamakura, W. A. (2000). Market segmentation: Conceptual and methodological foundations. *Springer Science & Business Media.* https://doi.org/10.1007/978-1-4615-4651-1

Wedel, M., & Kamakura, W. A. (2012). *Market segmentation: Conceptual and methodological foundations* (Vol. 8). Springer Science & Business Media. https://doi.org/10.1007/978-1-4615-4651-1

Wijekoon, A., Salunke, S., & Athaide, G. A. (2021). Customer heterogeneity and innovation-based competitive strategy: A review, synthesis, and research agenda. *Journal of Product Innovation Management, 38*(3), 315–333. https://doi.org/10.1111/jpim.12576

Xiao, B., & Benbasat, I. (2007). E-commerce product recommendation agents: Use, characteristics, and impact. *MIS Quarterly, 31*(1), 137–209. https://doi.org/10.2307/25148784

Yabs, J. K. (2014). Market segmentation strategies used as competitive advantage tool: A case of chloride exide Kenya limited. *Journal of Economics and Sustainable Development, 5*(26), P42–P48.

Marketing with Generative Artificial Intelligence: Applications, Opportunities, Challenges, and Research Agenda

Animesh Kumar Sharma and Rahul Sharma

Abstract

Generative Artificial Intelligence (GAI) is transforming marketing by allowing unprecedented levels of personalization, operational efficiency, and scalability. The purpose of this study is to explore the applications, opportunities, and challenges of marketing with generative artificial intelligence. A qualitative research methodology was employed, utilizing semi-structured interviews with industry experts. Data analysis using NVivo highlighted ten critical themes, including personalization, content optimization, automation, ethical considerations, transparency and accountability. The findings exhibit GAI's role in reshaping marketing strategies and provide insights into managerial implications. GAI strengthens customer experience by enabling predictive capabilities and streamlining operations, while challenges such as implementation costs, skill gaps, and data integration remain barriers. The study emphasizes the importance of ethical AI practices to build consumer trust, alongside upskilling teams to employ GAI's potential effectively. This study provides a comprehensive framework for leveraging GAI in marketing while addressing associated challenges, paving the way for future research on its transformative impact on customer-centric marketing practices. This study concludes with a research agenda to investigate GAI's evolving role in marketing, aiming to guide future theoretical advancements and industry applications.

A. K. Sharma (✉) · R. Sharma
Mittal School of Buisness, Lovely Professioinal University, Phagwara, Punjab, India
e-mail: mr.animesh@gmail.com; animesh.41800104@lpu.in

R. Sharma
e-mail: rahul.12234@lpu.co.in

© The Author(s), under exclusive license to Springer Nature Singapore Pte Ltd. 2026
N. S. Jayawardena et al. (eds.), *Digital Advertising and Consumer Behavior*,
Management for Professionals, https://doi.org/10.1007/978-981-95-7809-2_10

1 Introduction

Generative Artificial Intelligence (AI) has quickly emerged as a transformative tool across multiple industries, altering how businesses approach marketing (Kshetri et al., 2024). Using strong algorithms and machine learning models, generative AI allows for the generation of original content, designs, product ideas, and tactics with minimal human intervention (Shneiderman, 2020). In marketing, this technology is breaking new ground by going beyond standard data analysis and predictive models to actively develop engaging, tailored, and powerful content that resonates with target audiences. Generative AI applications in marketing range from dynamic ad creation to customer care chatbots, automated social media content development, and even improved customer segmentation. With natural language processing (NLP) technologies and picture generation, marketers can now create text, graphics, and multimedia content that seems highly personalized to individual tastes (Wen & Laporte, 2024). This transition has created chances for marketers to engage customers on a deeper, more personalized level, save operating expenses, and improve campaign inventiveness (Patil et al., 2024).

Furthermore, generative AI is transforming the way marketers plan and optimize their operations. With AI-powered technologies capable of extracting insights from massive datasets, brands can make data-driven decisions at previously unthinkable granularity and speed (Vidhya et al., 2025). This is a new era in which the balance between human creativity and computer intelligence is being fine-tuned to enhance marketing success. Marketing has always relied on innovation and adaption to new technologies. From the advent of digital advertising to social media marketing and big data analytics, each revolution has altered how organizations engage with their customers. Another transformational force, Generative Artificial Intelligence (AI) is about to change marketing (Kumar et al., 2024). Generative AI, which encompasses technologies such as language models (e.g., ChatGPT) and picture generation models (e.g., DALL-E), provides a huge step forward in terms of content production automation, customer experience enhancement, and brand personalization (Bandi et al., 2023). Generative AI systems, which rely on massive datasets and powerful machine learning architectures, use advanced algorithms to generate new material with little human intervention (Rane, 2023). Unlike typical AI models, which only recognize patterns or classify data, generative AI produces unique, creative outputs such as text, art, music, and even videos (Ooi et al., 2023). This feature provides marketers with previously unheard-of chances to engage people, generate personalized messaging, and scale campaigns. As consumers' expectations for quick, relevant, and personalized experiences rise, generative AI offers tools that are not only powerful but also flexible to a wide range of marketing demands.

Generative AI systems such as ChatGPT, DALL-E, and Midjourney have empowered marketers by automating content generation, enabling hyper-personalization, and optimizing production processes for scalable marketing campaigns (More, 2024). Deloitte research from 2023 shows that GenAI considerably improves content marketing, with early adopters experiencing an average return on investment (ROI) of 12%. GenAI technologies assist marketers manage the rising demand for tailored, high-quality content, which has climbed 1.5 times between 2022 and 2023. This technology helps firms to produce timely, relevant content on a large scale, freeing up resources for more strategic, high-value tasks. Furthermore, firms who use GenAI save an average of 11.4 hours per week, indicating its effectiveness in increasing productivity (Deloitte Digital, 2023). According to a HubSpot poll conducted in 2023, 77% of marketers say GenAI is crucial for personalization since it improves customer experience and buyer engagement (HubSpot, 2023). As a result, marketers can concentrate on strengthening client relationships using insights gleaned from AI-driven analytics. This emphasis on personalization is shared by marketers, who report that AI-powered tactics enable them to create tales that strongly resonate with their target audiences. According to Deloitte's research, 65% of organizations are concerned about potential legal and ethical issues, highlighting the importance of cautiously integrating AI technologies into marketing.

The objective of this study is to explore the applications, opportunities, and challenges of generative AI in marketing, culminating in a research agenda to guide future academic and industry exploration.

2 Review of Literature

Generative Artificial Intelligence (AI) has received a lot of attention in recent years, thanks to its potential to autonomously develop and customize material. Generative AI technologies can generate unique text, photos, and videos by using techniques such as deep learning, Natural Language Processing (NLP), and image production (Sengar et al., 2024). These capabilities have opened up new marketing opportunities, notably in terms of increasing customer involvement, automating content development, and maximizing personalization efforts.

Content Generation and Automation

Content generation is one of the most important applications of generative AI in marketing, with models such as GPT-3 and DALL-E having a considerable impact (Haleem et al., 2022). These AI systems produce human-like writing and imagery, allowing marketers to automate a wide range of content, including product descriptions, social media postings, and adverts (Jaiswal et al., 2020). Ma and Sun (2020) found that generative AI can help with dynamic content marketing, allowing firms to respond swiftly to trends and consumer preferences. This automation minimizes the time and expense of content creation, allowing firms to expand their marketing operations effectively. Furthermore, Whittaker et al. (2021) discovered that AI-generated content frequently performs similarly to human-created material in terms of customer engagement. However, they warn that relying too heavily on AI may jeopardize authenticity, underlining the importance of strategic control.

Another significant advantage of generative AI is its ability to customize at scale; studies suggest that customers respond more positively to content that appears to be tailored to their needs (Baek & Kim, 2023).

Personalization and Customer Engagement

Generative AI improves personalization by evaluating and predicting customer behavior patterns in real time. AI tools enable brands to engage consumers on a deeper level by delivering personalized recommendations and tailored communications (Haleem et al., 2022). According to Gao et al. (2023), generative AI has a double influence on customization: it improves the relevancy of marketing communications and saves the time required to execute personalization methods. This is consistent with the findings of Huang and Rust (2021), who discovered a significant increase in customer satisfaction and retention rates for firms employing generative AI-powered personalization in their marketing. Kim et al. (2022) also investigate AI-driven chatbots and virtual assistants. These applications use generative models to imitate human-like conversations, providing 24-hour customer service and tailored interactions. According to research, consumers value the convenience of AI-assisted services, especially when they give accurate and contextually appropriate responses (Nirala et al., 2022). However, Castillo et al. (2021) warn that too scripted or mechanical interactions might harm brand perception, implying that AI-powered interactions require constant improvement to be effective.

Generative AI for Visual Content and Advertising

Generative AI's impact extends to visual marketing and advertising, where technologies like as GANs (Generative Adversarial Networks) are used to generate realistic images and visuals. According to Dwivedi et al. (2021), marketers are increasingly adopting AI-generated graphics to engage audiences on social media and other digital channels. These technologies enable the creation of unique, brand-aligned images without requiring considerable creative resources, which is especially beneficial for small and medium-sized firms. Furthermore, GAN-generated graphics can be updated in real time based on user feedback, providing a high level of adaptability in visual marketing. In digital advertising, generative AI helps with A/B testing and ad optimization by developing several ad variations and tracking their performance in real time. This enables marketers to identify the most effective messaging and images for various customer categories (Davenport et al., 2020). However, some studies show that using AI-generated graphics might lead to brand consistency issues, since models may not fully represent the brand's aesthetic or cultural nuances without rigorous human guidance.

Ethical Considerations and Limitations

Despite its benefits, the use of generative AI in marketing creates ethical and practical questions. According to Salminen et al. (2022), one major concern is data privacy, as generative models require a large amount of data to function properly. The growing requirement for user data to train these models can lead to privacy violations if not handled correctly. Furthermore, there is a possibility of producing false content, such as deepfake adverts or manufactured testimonials, which could undermine customer trust. A study by Campbell et al. (2022) also emphasized the possible loss of human authenticity in marketing communications, implying that customers may find it difficult to trust AI-generated material, especially if they believe it lacks a human touch. These considerations highlight the necessity of openness and ethical norms in the use of AI for marketing, with some academics suggesting a "human-in-the-loop" method to maintain authenticity (Häußermann & Lütge et al., 2022).

The literature on generative AI in marketing shows that this technology has transformative potential for content generation, personalization, and customer interaction. However, like with any strong technology, implementation must be approached with caution, balancing innovation and ethical considerations. The rapid improvements in generative AI indicate that its influence in marketing will rise, but organizations must be aware of its limitations and guarantee transparency in their AI-driven initiatives.

3 Research Methodology

This study utilizes a qualitative research approach to accomplish the research objectives (Qu & Dumay, 2011). The research conducted semi-structured interviews with marketing professionals who had at least five years of experience.

Interview Design

The semi-structured interviews were designed to elicit complete replies from participants so that the themes can be explored in further depth (Kallio et al., 2016). The interview questions that were prepared included the topics related to the Applications of Generative AI in Marketing; benefits, challenges and limitations of generative AI for marketing; and the trends and areas of research in the field based on the literature review.

Sampling Technique

Purposive sampling was used on LinkedIn to choose participants with more than or equal to five years of expertise in digital marketing (Barratt et al., 2015). More than

80 interview proposals were sent, with a focus on job variety in digital marketing through the online professional networking platform of LinkedIn in Delhi and NCR in India.

Data Collection and Analysis

37 respondents gave a positive response to the interview out of the total sent invitations. A total 29 digital marketers participated in the interview process, while 9 respondents had denied taking part in the interview, citing their other urgencies. The face-to-face interview was conducted with respondent at their given time and place. The average interview session lasted about 40–50 minutes with each respondent. All the answers were coded and analysed in the qualitative research software NVivo 12.0 (Allsop et al., 2022). Thematic analysis was used to examine the transcribed information from the interviews, as this technique can provide crucial themes and patterns about the usage, possibilities, obstacles, and prospective future research topics of generative AI in marketing.

Data Analysis

The demographic profile of the sample for the study is shown in Table 1. The sample characteristics indicates the distribution of males and females across different age groups and education levels, as well as their industry positions and experiences.

4 Result and Analysis

After analysing the data in NVivo, the following 10 themes based on the number of occurrences were identified, as shown in Table 2.

Personalization and Customer Engagement

Generative AI's role in creating personalized experiences like tailored adverts, product recommendations, and targeted content is critical to increasing user engagement. By evaluating user data, AI helps brands communicate with customers in ways that are relevant, timely, and meaningful.

Content Creation and Channel Optimization

The influence of generative AI on content generation across several platforms, including social media and email marketing, enables efficient development and optimization. AI solutions enable marketers to swiftly create, test, and change

Table 1 Sample characteristics

Variables	Frequency	Percentage (%)
Gender		
Male	22	75.86
Female	7	24.14
Age group (years)		
31–40	11	37.93
41–50	13	44.83
51–60	4	13.79
Above 60	1	3.45
Position		
Chief marketing officer	3	10.34
Digital marketing professionals	12	41.38
Marketing manager	9	31.04
Digital marketing analyst	5	17.24
Education		
Graduate	3	10.34
Postgraduate and above	26	89.66
Experience (years)		
5–10	10	34.47
11–15	14	48.29
Above 15	5	17.24

Authors' own elaboration

Table 2 Identified themes

Themes	Number of occurrences
Personalization and customer engagement	62
Content creation and channel optimization	58
Scalability and operational efficiency	53
Challenges in implementation and skill requirements	51
Automation and impact on team productivity	42
Effectiveness in personalization of advertising	36
Case studies and success stories in AI-driven marketing	31
Customer experience enhancement through predictive capabilities	26
Efficiency gains from AI vs. traditional approaches	16
Transparency, accountability, and ethical AI use	10

Authors' own elaboration

content, allowing them to target different audience segments more successfully across media.

Scalability and Operational Efficiency

AI's scalability in high-demand marketing situations enables teams to manage larger campaigns and worldwide markets with minimum resource strain. AI also automates repetitive procedures, allowing marketers to manage larger volumes and streamline operations without raising labor.

Productivity and Time Savings

Generative AI boosts productivity by automating mundane tasks like data analysis, A/B testing, and simple content production. This decreases the workload for marketing teams, allowing them to concentrate on strategic responsibilities and developing creativity.

Ethics, Transparency, and Trust

Data privacy, transparency, and responsibility are all major ethical considerations in the marketing use of artificial intelligence. Marketers are tackling these issues by publicly describing AI usage to customers, ensuring compliance with privacy laws, and conducting audits to avoid bias and retain confidence.

Challenges in Implementation and Skill Requirements

High costs, technological obstacles, and the requirement for specialized expertise are significant impediments to AI adoption. Organizations encounter challenges with data integration, compatibility, and data quality, all of which are critical for AI performance. Upskilling employees and obtaining appropriate resources are also key components of a successful AI implementation.

Automation and Impact on Team Productivity

AI's automation capabilities reduce time spent on routine operations, enhancing team productivity and allowing for shorter turnaround times for marketing efforts. This enables teams to more effectively manage resources, with an emphasis on innovation and strategic planning.

Effectiveness in Personalization of Advertising

The capacity of generative AI to develop highly personalized commercials and make real-time campaign updates improves the precision of advertising efforts. Marketing campaigns and customer response rates can be dramatically improved by targeting certain audience segments with appropriate adverts.

Case Studies and Success Stories in AI-Driven Marketing

Concrete examples of effective AI applications in marketing help to demonstrate AI's use. Case studies highlight AI's success in enhancing customer experience, increasing sales, and creating memorable interactions that resonate with customers across multiple sectors.

Customer Experience Enhancement Through Predictive Capabilities

AI's capacity to forecast client demands enables proactive involvement, resulting in smoother and more intuitive experiences. Generative AI allows brands to anticipate user preferences, making consumer experiences more frictionless and engaging.

Efficiency Gains from AI vs. Traditional Approaches

Generative AI beats traditional marketing strategies by increasing campaign speed, accuracy, and efficacy, resulting in higher returns and making it an appealing alternative for forward-thinking marketers.

Transparency, Accountability, and Ethical AI Use

Transparency and accountability in AI-driven campaigns help to address ethical concerns, as marketers take steps to ensure that AI-generated content is consistent with brand values and consumer expectations.

Discussion

Various themes emerge when discussing the impact of generative AI on marketing, emphasizing its revolutionary role in personalizing client engagement, expanding operations, increasing productivity, and resolving ethical problems. The findings are consistent with past research on AI in marketing, providing both validation and expansion of previously recognized concepts.

Personalization and Customer Engagement

Generative AI's capacity to develop personalized interactions across digital platforms is critical to modern marketing strategies. Marketers emphasized that AI-driven personalization boosts consumer engagement, which is consistent with previous study by Sheth et al. (2022), who discovered that customers are more inclined to engage with firms that provide relevant, individualized content. The latest findings contribute to this knowledge by demonstrating AI's real-time adaptability, which allows brands to adjust quickly to client preferences, hence improving the user experience.

Content Creation and Channel Optimization

The increased efficiency in content generation across marketing channels is consistent with the findings of Dwivedi et al. (2023), who found that AI speeds content production while maintaining quality. Marketers today use generative AI to efficiently adjust content across different platforms, indicating that AI has not only maintained but actually boosted the rate of content production since previous studies. This indicates a trend away from traditional content generation methods and toward more dynamic, data-driven approaches, proving that generative AI is critical to multi-channel marketing success.

Scalability and Operational Efficiency

Scalability in AI-powered marketing settings has emerged as a crucial benefit, allowing marketers to manage high-demand campaigns more easily. Earlier research, such as Aldoseri et al. (2024), stressed AI's ability to scale operations, particularly in digital-first companies. Current findings support this, demonstrating that generative AI helps brands to address various client needs across global marketplaces without requiring a linear increase in resources. This operational scalability demonstrates a strategic benefit, particularly for large enterprises with a diverse customer base.

Productivity and Time Savings

The influence of generative AI on productivity through the automation of repetitive jobs is well known, and current findings support this. According to previous research by Budhwar et al. (2023), automation is a huge time-saver for marketing teams, allowing them to focus on strategy. Today's digital marketers claim even greater productivity gains, showing that generative AI technologies have developed in their capabilities, producing more sophisticated, accurate, and user-friendly results than previously.

Ethics, Transparency, and Trust

Recent research shows that ethical problems such as transparency, data protection, and responsibility are becoming increasingly important in AI marketing. This theme expands on previous research by Hermann (2022), which highlighted the hazards of bias and lack of transparency in AI applications. The recent findings suggest that marketers are actively taking steps to address these challenges, such as revealing AI use in customer interactions and enforcing tougher data privacy regulations. This proactive strategy indicates a rising industry-wide commitment to preserving consumer trust while embracing AI.

Challenges in Implementation and Skill Requirements

The constraints of applying AI, such as high prices and skill gaps, are consistent with previous research by Dwivedi et al. (2021), which identified the necessity for specific skills in AI adoption. While some marketers have been able to easily integrate AI, smaller businesses continue to suffer resource limits, indicating that while AI usage is growing, accessibility concerns persist. Today's findings underline the importance of upskilling and investing in AI knowledge to fully realize the potential of generative AI, particularly for smaller and medium-sized businesses.

Automation and Impact on Team Productivity

Marketing teams continue to profit from the automation of routine jobs, with generative AI outperforming traditional marketing tactics in terms of efficiency. Prior research, such as that conducted by Al Naqbi et al. (2024), indicated that AI might increase efficiency by reducing manual tasks. Current studies confirm that generative AI not only automates activities but also helps marketers with creative processes by freeing up time, allowing for a more imaginative approach to marketing.

Effectiveness in Personalization of Advertising

Personalized advertising is one of the most notable advantages of generative AI, with current research revealing higher engagement rates and improved targeting accuracy than traditional methods. These findings build on Sands et al. (2024) research, which demonstrated AI's potential to improve advertising efficacy through customized messaging. The evolution of real-time adaption emphasizes AI's role in answering individual audience demands quickly, making advertising more effective and customer centric.

Case Studies and Success Stories in AI-Driven Marketing

Numerous AI success stories in marketing support the findings of previous studies, such as McKinsey's (2021) report on the practical benefits of AI in retail and e-commerce. The current findings offer similar case-based insights, illustrating AI's practical performance in raising revenue, optimizing user experiences, and automating customer care. The consistency of case study findings across sectors demonstrates generative AI's effectiveness as a strategic tool for producing measurable objectives (John et al., 2023).

Customer Experience Enhancement Through Predictive Capabilities

The capacity of generative AI to improve consumer experience by forecasting demands is a significant advantage, according to marketers today. This study builds on previous research, such as Cillo and Rubera (2024), who emphasized predictive capabilities as a cornerstone to tailored customer experiences. Generative AI's predictive capacity enables brands to provide proactive assistance and relevant recommendations, resulting in a more seamless and delightful customer journey.

Efficiency Gains from AI vs. Traditional Approaches

The significant efficiency gains found by digital marketers support previous studies' results that generative AI significantly outperforms traditional methods. In keeping with Berman and Vetrivel et al. (2024) research, which found a 30–50% boost in efficiency with AI, today's marketers perceive even larger increases in speed, accuracy, and content effectiveness, highlighting AI's ongoing evolution and success in decreasing resource needs.

Transparency, Accountability, and Ethical AI Use

Current research confirms that openness and accountability in AI-powered advertising are critical for preserving consumer trust. Earlier research, such as that conducted by Floridi and Cowls (2019), emphasized the need of transparency, and today's marketers are seen applying these values by actively assessing AI results and ensuring campaigns adhere to ethical rules. This persistent emphasis on ethical behaviors underscores the industry's shift toward responsible AI use.

5 Implications

This study contributes to academic research and corporate operations. The findings will provide a full understanding of how generative AI is changing the marketing landscape, emphasizing both potential benefits and concerns that demand attention.

Theoretical Implications

The results of this study on the usage of generative AI in marketing have important theoretical implications for understanding artificial intelligence's expanding role in customer interaction, content production, and operational efficiency. The findings also add to existing marketing theories by giving new insights into the practical application of generative AI tools, highlighting its transformational potential across multiple disciplines. These implications open up new lines of research and theoretical advancement in marketing, consumer behavior, and technological adoption. This study promotes consumer engagement theory, content marketing theories, and automation.

Managerial Implications

The outcomes of this study on generative AI in marketing provide useful insights for managers across a variety of marketing activities. These insights can help influence marketing strategy, operational decisions, and the proper use of AI technologies. Managers should prioritize integrating generative AI tools to improve customer engagement tactics. To effectively integrate AI in customer engagement, managers must invest in AI platforms that can analyse and understand customer data in real time. Managers should also ensure that AI systems are customer-centric, with an emphasis on offering relevant, timely, and personalized interactions that foster long-term relationships. Managers should use AI to better segment audiences, resulting in focused marketing that is more likely to connect with each group. Managers may utilize AI to automate repetitive operations like data analysis, reporting, and content updates, freeing up important time for their staff to work on more strategic projects. Managers should implement AI solutions that automate both content creation and administrative processes, giving marketing teams more time for creativity and strategy development. Managers must be proactive in resolving these problems to maintain consumer trust and avoid negative responses. Managers should develop ethical norms for AI use within their organizations. Managers must balance the costs and benefits of using AI tools and ensure that their teams have the requisite competence to effectively integrate and manage these technologies. Managers should also stay current on advances in AI technology to guarantee that their marketing processes remain competitive. Managers should prioritize AI systems that allow for easy output tracking and monitoring, ensuring that any flaws are identified and addressed as soon as possible.

Practical Implications

This study's findings on the usage of generative AI in marketing equip practitioners with useful insights. Practitioners should use generative AI to provide highly tailored and interactive customer experiences. AI may be used to modify communications, goods, and content to each customer's tastes, resulting in real-time, personalized engagements. To do this, practitioners can link AI platforms with their customer relationship management (CRM) systems, allowing for real-time analysis of client data to promote tailored engagement. Regular updates to the AI models based on customer input and behavioural patterns will help to refine and improve customisation. AI helps marketers to properly segment their customers and provide targeted adverts to certain groups. Practitioners can utilize generative AI to find high-value audience segments based on demographics, habits, and interests, resulting in more successful ad targeting and budget allocation. Practitioners must be proactive in resolving ethical issues associated to AI, particularly data protection and transparency. AI should be implemented in a way that protects consumers' privacy and data rights. Clear transparency regarding AI's role in content generation, personalization, and automated communication can help to develop consumer trust.

6 Conclusion

This study investigated the role and impact of generative AI in marketing, emphasizing its revolutionary potential for increasing customer engagement, personalizing content, and optimizing operations. This study identified key themes that highlight the value that generative AI brings to modern marketing practices, such as the ability to deliver highly personalized customer experiences, improve scalability, and automate routine tasks, all of which increase team productivity. These findings also revealed important difficulties, such as ethical and privacy issues, operational limits, and a skills gap among marketing teams, all of which must be addressed for successful AI implementation. The study's findings are consistent with earlier research that has recognized generative AI's expanding role in allowing more data-driven, customer-centric marketing. However, our study goes beyond this by focusing on the practical, ethical, and operational aspects that marketers confront when implementing AI in the real world. The study specifically focuses on how AI might expedite content creation and personalization while emphasizing the significance of openness and accountability to create consumer confidence. Unlike prior studies, which frequently focus primarily on technological benefits, this study takes a comprehensive approach, assessing both the opportunities and restrictions that generative AI brings to marketing operations. The findings of this study have major theoretical and managerial consequences, providing vital counsel for firms seeking to appropriately adopt AI. Practically speaking, the study provides tangible measures for marketers to incorporate AI into their strategy, enhance performance, and uphold ethical standards. As generative AI evolves, marketers must take a balanced approach that maximizes AI's possibilities while minimizing its limitations. This allows firms to remain competitive, sensitive to customer wants, and equipped to manage the ethical difficulties that AI brings to the marketing scene. Generative AI presents both disruptive opportunities and problems for marketers.

7 Limitations and Scope of Future Research

This study is based on self-reported data from marketing professionals, which may have biases such as social desirability or recollection bias. Participants' comments may have either inflated or underestimated the usefulness of generative AI. Future research could benefit from using objective performance data, such as AI-driven campaign analytics, to validate these findings. The study is largely concerned with the viewpoints of marketing professionals and does not cover customer reactions to AI-generated content and engagement techniques. Consumer impressions are essential in determining the efficacy and ethical acceptability of AI-powered marketing. Future research should look at customer reactions to AI personalization and transparency practices to present a more balanced picture. Although this study highlights the necessity of ethical and transparent AI practices, it does not go into detail about the precise tactics needed to effectively operationalize responsible AI. Future studies might investigate best practices, frameworks, and organizational policies that enable teams to adopt ethical AI, with an emphasis on case studies from firms that have successfully implemented responsible AI programs. Future research should focus on longitudinal studies that track the progress of generative AI in marketing and investigate how emergent technologies, such as responsible AI frameworks, affect customer perceptions and marketing outcomes over time.

References

Al Naqbi, H., Bahroun, Z., & Ahmed, V. (2024). Enhancing work productivity through generative artificial intelligence: A comprehensive literature review. *Sustainability, 16*(3), 1166. https://doi.org/10.3390/su16031166

Aldoseri, A., Al-Khalifa, K. N., & Hamouda, A. M. (2024). AI-powered innovation in Digital transformation: Key pillars and industry impact. *Sustainability, 16*(5), 1790. https://doi.org/10.3390/su16051790

Allsop, D. B., Chelladurai, J. M., Kimball, E. R., Marks, L. D., & Hendricks, J. J. (2022). Qualitative methods with Nvivo software: A practical guide for analyzing qualitative data. *The Psychiatrist, 4*(2), 142–159. https://doi.org/10.3390/psych4020013

Baek, T. H., & Kim, M. (2023). Is ChatGPT scary good? How user motivations affect creepiness and trust in generative artificial intelligence. *Telematics and Informatics, 83*, 102030. https://doi.org/10.1016/j.tele.2023.102030

Bandi, A., Adapa, P. V. S. R., & Kuchi, Y. E. V. P. K. (2023). The power of generative ai: A review of requirements, models, input–output formats, evaluation metrics, and challenges. *Future Internet, 15*(8), 260. https://doi.org/10.3390/fi15080260

Barratt, M. J., Ferris, J. A., & Lenton, S. (2015). Hidden populations, online purposive sampling, and external validity: Taking off the blindfold. *Field Methods, 27*(1), 3–21. https://doi.org/10.1177/1525822X14526838

Budhwar, P., Chowdhury, S., Wood, G., Aguinis, H., Bamber, G. J., Beltran, J. R., et al. (2023). Human resource management in the age of generative artificial intelligence: Perspectives and research directions on ChatGPT. *Human Resource Management Journal, 33*(3), 606–659. https://doi.org/10.1111/1748-8583.12524

Campbell, C., Plangger, K., Sands, S., & Kietzmann, J. (2022). Preparing for an era of deepfakes and AI-generated ads: A framework for understanding responses to manipulated advertising. *Journal of Advertising, 51*(1), 22–38. https://doi.org/10.1080/00913367.2021.1909515

Castillo, D., Canhoto, A. I., & Said, E. (2021). The dark side of AI-powered service interactions: Exploring the process of co-destruction from the customer perspective. *The Service Industries Journal, 41*(13–14), 900–992. https://doi.org/10.1080/02642069.2020.1787993

Cillo, P., & Rubera, G. (2024). Generative AI in innovation and marketing processes: A roadmap of research opportunities. *Journal of the Academy of Marketing Science, 53*(3), 684–701. https://doi.org/10.1007/s11747-024-01044-7

Davenport, T., Guha, A., Grewal, D., Bressgott, T. (2020). How artificial intelligence will change the future of marketing. *Journal of the Academy of Marketing Science, 48*, 24–42. https://doi.org/10.1007/s11747-019-00696-0

Digital, D. (2023). *Generative AI and productivity: A game-changer for businesses.* Deloitte Insights. https://www.deloittedigital.com/au/en/insights/perspective/how-data-ai-crm-trust-could-transform-your-business.html

Dwivedi, Y. K., Hughes, L., Ismagilova, E., Aarts, G., Coombs, C., Crick, T., et al. (2021). Artificial intelligence (AI): Multidisciplinary perspectives on emerging challenges, opportunities, and agenda for research, practice and policy. *International Journal of Information Management, 57*, 101994. https://doi.org/10.1016/j.ijinfomgt.2019.08.002

Dwivedi, Y. K., Kshetri, N., Hughes, L., Slade, E. L., Jeyaraj, A., Kar, A. K., et al. (2023). Opinion paper: "so what if ChatGPT wrote it?" multidisciplinary perspectives on opportunities, challenges and implications of generative conversational AI for research, practice and policy. *International Journal of Information Management, 71*, 102642. https://doi.org/10.1007/s40171-023-00356-x

Gao, B., Wang, Y., Xie, H., Hu, Y., & Hu, Y. (2023). Artificial intelligence in advertising: Advancements, challenges, and ethical considerations in targeting, personalization, content creation, and ad optimization. *SAGE Open, 13*(4), 21582440231210759. https://doi.org/10.1177/21582440231210759

Haleem, A., Javaid, M., Qadri, M. A., Singh, R. P., & Suman, R. (2022). Artificial intelligence (AI) applications for marketing: A literature-based study. *International Journal of Intelligent Networks, 3*, 119–132. https://doi.org/10.1016/j.ijin.2022.08.005

Häußermann, J. J., & Lütge, C. (2022). Community-in-the-loop: Towards pluralistic value creation in AI, or—Why AI needs business ethics. *AI and Ethics, 2*(2), 1–22. https://doi.org/10.1007/s43681-021-00047-2

Hermann, E. (2022). Leveraging artificial intelligence in marketing for social good—An ethical perspective. *Journal of Business Ethics, 179*(1), 43–61. https://doi.org/10.1007/s10551-021-04843-y

Huang, M. H., & Rust, R. T. (2021). Engaged to a robot? The role of AI in service. *Journal of Service Research, 24*(1), 30–41. https://doi.org/10.1177/1094670520902266

HubSpot. (2023). *The state of artificial intelligence in marketing: Insights and trends.* HubSpot Research. https://blog.hubspot.com/marketing/state-of-ai-report

Jaiswal, D. P., Kumar, S., & Badr, Y. (2020). Towards an artificial intelligence aided design approach: Application to anime faces with generative adversarial networks. *Procedia Computer Science, 168*, 57–64. https://doi.org/10.1016/j.procs.2020.02.257

John, M. M., Olsson, H. H., & Bosch, J. (2023). Towards an AI-driven business development framework: A multi-case study. *Journal of Software: Evolution and Process, 35*(6), e2432. https://doi.org/10.1002/smr.2432

Kallio, H., Pietilä, A. M., Johnson, M., & Kangasniemi, M. (2016). Systematic methodological review: Developing a framework for a qualitative semi-structured interview guide. *Journal of Advanced Nursing, 72*(12), 2954–2965. https://doi.org/10.1111/jan.13031

Kim, S., Jang, S., Kim, S., Tithe, T. A., Hellol, H. I., Das, P., & Arif, S. (2022). AI-DRIVEN CHATBOTS AND VIRTUAL ASSISTANTS. *International Journal of Grid Computing & Applications, 16*(1/2), 1–19. https://doi.org/10.5121/ijgca.2025.16202

Kshetri, N., Dwivedi, Y. K., Davenport, T. H., & Panteli, N. (2024). Generative artificial intelligence in marketing: Applications, opportunities, challenges, and research agenda. *International Journal of Information Management, 75*, 102716. https://doi.org/10.1016/j.ijinfomgt.2023.102716

Kumar, V., Kotler, P., Gupta, S., & Rajan, B. (2024). EXPRESS: Generative AI in marketing: Promises, perils, and public policy implications. *Journal of Public Policy & Marketing, 07439156241286499.* https://doi.org/10.1177/07439156241286499

Liv, N., & Greenbaum, D. (2020). Deep fakes and memory malleability: False memories in the service of fake news. *AJOB Neuroscience, 11*(2), 96–104. https://doi.org/10.1080/21507740.2020.1740351

Ma, L., & Sun, B. (2020). Machine learning and AI in marketing—Connecting computing power to human insights. *International Journal of Research in Marketing, 37*(3), 481–504. https://doi.org/10.1016/j.ijresmar.2020.04.005

McKinsey & Company. (2021). *The state of AI in 2021: Transformations in retail and e-commerce.* https://www.mckinsey.com/capabilities/quantumblack/our-insights/global-survey-the-state-of-ai-in-2021

More, A. B. (2024). Generative AI: The impact, possibilities, and difficulties. In *Generative AI and implications for ethics, security, and data management* (pp. 17–46). IGI Global. https://doi.org/10.4018/979-8-3693-8557-9.ch002

Nirala, K. K., Singh, N. K., & Purani, V. S. (2022). A survey on providing customer and public administration based services using AI: Chatbot. *Multimedia Tools and Applications, 81*(16), 22215–22246. https://doi.org/10.1007/s11042-021-11458-y

Ooi, K. B., Tan, G. W. H., Al-Emran, M., Al-Sharafi, M. A., Capatina, A., Chakraborty, A., et al. (2023). The potential of generative artificial intelligence across disciplines: Perspectives and future directions. *Journal of Computer Information Systems, 65*(1), 1–32. https://doi.org/10.1080/08874417.2023.2261010

Patil, D., Rane, N. L., & Rane, J. (2024). Future directions for ChatGPT and generative artificial intelligence in various business sectors. *The Future Impact of ChatGPT on Several Business Sectors* 294–346. https://doi.org/10.70593/978-81-981367-8-7_7

Qu, S. Q., & Dumay, J. (2011). The qualitative research interview. *Qualitative Research in Accounting & Management, 8*(3), 238–264. https://doi.org/10.1108/11766091111162070

Rane, N. (2023). ChatGPT and similar generative artificial intelligence (AI) for building and construction industry: Contribution, opportunities and challenges of large language models for industry 4.0, industry 5.0, and society 5.0. *Opportunities and Challenges of Large Language Models for Industry, 4.* https://doi.org/10.2139/ssrn.4603221

Salminen, J., Jung, S. G., Kamel, A. M. S., Santos, J. M., & Jansen, B. J. (2022). Using artificially generated pictures in customer-facing systems: An evaluation study with data-driven personas. *Behaviour & Information Technology, 41*(5), 905–921. https://doi.org/10.1080/0144929X.2020.1838610

Sands, S., Campbell, C., Ferraro, C., Demsar, V., Rosengren, S., & Farrell, J. (2024). Principles for advertising responsibly using generative AI. *Organizational Dynamics, 4*, 1–9. https://doi.org/10.1016/j.orgdyn.2024.101042

Sengar, S. S., Hasan, A. B., Kumar, S., & Carroll, F. (2024). Generative artificial intelligence: A systematic review and applications. *Multimedia Tools and Applications* 1–40. https://doi.org/10.1007/s11042-024-20016-1

Sheth, J. N., Jain, V., Roy, G., & Chakraborty, A. (2022). AI-driven banking services: The next frontier for a personalised experience in the emerging market. *International Journal of Bank Marketing, 40*(6), 1248–1271. https://doi.org/10.1108/IJBM-09-2021-0449

Shneiderman, B. (2020). Human-centered artificial intelligence: Three fresh ideas. *AIS Transactions on Human-Computer Interaction, 12*(3), 109–124. https://doi.org/10.17705/1thci.00131

Vetrivel, S. C., Arun, V. P., Saravanan, T. P., & Maheswari, R. (2024). Harnessing AI for next-generation service marketing. In *Integrating AI-driven technologies into service marketing* (pp. 265–298). IGI Global. https://doi.org/10.4018/979-8-3693-7122-0.ch015

Vidhya, J., Sarulatha, N., Bruce, A., Yogeshwaran, R., & Aarthi, K. (2025). Societal impact and cultural implications. In *Exploring Generative AI with Computational Intelligence* (pp. 113–132). CRC Press.

Wen, Y., & Laporte, S. (2024). EXPRESS: Experiential narratives in marketing: A comparison of generative AI and human content. *Journal of Public Policy & Marketing*, 07439156241297973. https://doi.org/10.1177/07439156241297973

Whittaker, L., Letheren, K., & Mulcahy, R. (2021). The rise of deepfakes: A conceptual framework and research agenda for marketing. *Australasian Marketing Journal, 29*(3), 204–214. https://doi.org/10.1177/1839334921999479

Ethical Concerns in the Field of Artificial Intelligence and Data Analytics in Insurance Industry

Pawan Pant, Kaushal Kishore Mishra, Bhaskara Srinivas, and Azmee Zaheer

Abstract

This chapter analyses ethical considerations in data analytics, which holds great promise for changing corporate operations, strengthening risk management plans, and boosting customer experiences in the quickly evolving insurance market. However, as the use of data-driven technology grows, there is a growing need to address ethical issues related to data collecting, analysis, and use. The organisation of the chapter is based on key ethical values, including responsibility, openness, fairness, privacy, and informed consent are all included in the framework, which draws its principles from the literature review on ethics, data governance, and regulatory compliance. An empirical study with descriptive statistical analysis using tools correlation, regression and ANOVA has been carried out to find the relationships between the different sets of variables, viz. transparency in data analytics practices and stakeholder trust; ethical training and awareness programs for employees and moral decision-making in data analytics processes; and data breaches and privacy incidents. A sample size of 345 IT professionals and students from the tri-city of Chandigarh over three months from January to March 2024 has been administered for data analysis. From the empirical study, it has been established that there is a highly positive correlation between transparency in data and trust in stakeholders. It has also been observed that ethical training and awareness programs for employees have a positive influence on ethical decision-making in data analytics processes. We have found that organisations that prioritise privacy by design principles exhibit greater resilience to data breaches and privacy incidents.

P. Pant · K. K. Mishra (✉) · B. Srinivas · A. Zaheer
Chandigarh University, Mohali, India
e-mail: kkmsitmbbk@gmail.com

© The Author(s), under exclusive license to Springer Nature Singapore Pte Ltd. 2026

N. S. Jayawardena et al. (eds.), *Digital Advertising and Consumer Behavior*,
Management for Professionals, https://doi.org/10.1007/978-981-95-7809-2_11

1 Introduction to Ethical Considerations

The ethical aspects of data utilisation have gained prominence in the quickly changing world of data analytics within the insurance sector. Insurance companies face moral conundrums relating to responsibility, transparency, fairness, permission, privacy, and fairness as they use big data analytics to spur innovation and obtain a competitive edge (Floridi, 2019; Boyd & Crawford, 2012; Kitchin, 2014). Beyond legal and regulatory compliance, ethical failings in data analytics affect stakeholder relationships, trust, and reputation (Mittelstadt et al., 2016). Therefore, for insurers to successfully negotiate the intricate convergence of data, technology, and ethics, they must comprehend and handle ethical issues (Floridi & Taddeo, 2016).

According to Diakopoulos and Friedler (2016), there is pressure to compromise between individual rights that uphold society's ideals and data-driven insights from insurers. Although opacity in algorithms and data processing techniques may hide biases in potential discrimination outcomes, transparency is necessary to build trust and make informed choices (O'Neil, 2016). To achieve justice in insurance analytics, one should be attentive to the existence of biases in algorithmic models as well as historical data; this means that there is an urgent need for the implementation of measures aimed at bias identification and reduction (Barocas & Selbst, 2016). Lastly, the ethical imperative of privacy requires keeping private and sensitive information from being released and respecting people's right to own their data (Solove, 2006). However, the growth of methods for data collection and the development of advanced analytics poses a threat to traditional notions of permission and privacy (Acquisti, 2009).This Article provides an overview of the ethical issues surrounding the use of data analytics in the insurance sector. This Article attempts to give the insurer the frameworks and the information needed to navigate through the ethical complications of alchemy by clarifying certain important ethical principles and estimating their consequences for decision-making processes. Insurers can, through adopting a multi-dimensional approach toward data analytics that combines regulatory compliance, organisational culture, and the involvement of stakeholders, move toward a responsible and ethical approach towards data analytics that encourages trust and integrity and enhances societal values (Floridi et al., 2018).

2 Theoretical and Foundational Underpinnings of Ethics in Data Analytics

Foundational Ethical Principles

Fundamental ethical values shine as a ray of hope in the vast and complex world of algorithmic decision-making and data-driven insights within the constantly evolving data analytics domain of the insurance industry (Floridi, 2019). Among these are transparency, equity, responsibility, privacy, and permission- all the foundations of ethical and responsible data practices in the insurance analytics industry. Transparency calls for openness and clarity in procedures and techniques supporting data gathering, processing, and use (Diakopoulos & Friedler, 2016). In order to do so, insurers may illuminate the complexities of algorithms and data sources, thereby building trust and enabling stakeholders to understand the consequences of data-driven decisions (Mittelstadt et al., 2016). Another key principle is fairness, which addresses bias and discrimination in data and algorithms that minimise them so that outcomes are fair for everyone (Barocas & Selbst, 2016; Dwork & Mulligan, 2013). This essentially means that the biases developed during the algorithmic design and from historical data will be addressed through ongoing consciousness and proactive methods.

The closest concept to openness and fairness is probably accountability. This is the recognition of responsibility, as well as the existence of systems that monitor and provide remedies (Floridi et al., 2018). Accountability, as one holds each other accountable for the social effects of their data analytics activities, should be an element of ethical governance for insurers. Privacy in the current electronic age is a fundamental right focused on the importance of safeguarding individuals' autonomy and dignity and personal information integrity by Solove (2006). Beyond the fulfilment of legal requirements, the privacy aspects involve moral obligations toward respecting persons' right to privacy and lowering the possibility of data use misbehaviour in the context of insurance analytics.

Finally, permission includes autonomy, which restates people's rights to control how their data is used and to make informed decisions about how it is collected and processed (Acquisti, 2009). However, in the era of pervasive data collection and omnipresent analytics, meaningful consent is difficult to get; hence, creative ways to empower people in the data ecosystem are needed.

Informed Consent and Data Ownership

Informed consent is a fundamental ethical concept in the insurance analytics space. It respects the autonomy of individuals and their rights to control the use of their data, as well as well-informed decision-making processes when it comes to the collection and use of the said data (Floridi, 2019). However, meaningful permission in a complex ecosystem of data and opaque data practices poses challenges. In order to give individuals autonomy and preference for privacy, insurers need to take initiatives so that people are informed about the goals, scope, and consequences of the data collection and processing process (Acquisti, 2009). Moreover, as Diakopoulos and Friedler (2016) pointed out, informed consent is not only legally required but also ethically; it underlines how important it is to respect people's autonomy and dignity in a data-driven society. On one hand, the clarity of communication, together with people having the power to give consent and make decisions based on data sharing and utilisation, makes clear and simple procedures about consent in place for insurance organisations to implement (Mittelstadt et al., 2016). Further, data ownership adds complexities in the field of insurance analytics since it poses rights issues as well as people's sovereignty over their respective data (Solove, 2006). This will allow individuals to have a sense of control over how their personal information is collected, used, and shared. Insurers, on the other hand, can still collect and process data for legitimate business purposes (Barocas & Selbst, 2016). For that reason, insurers need to strike a balance between what is required for the well-being of the individuals involved and the utility of the data (Floridi et al., 2018). By giving high priority to informed permission and the exercise of data ownership rights, insurance companies can maintain their moral principles by gaining the trust of their policyholders and fostering a culture of data stewardship and accountability (Oh, 2007).

In this regard, the rights of people to data self-governance and self-control of their personal information mean data ownership, and informed consent is a concept that is central to ethics within the insurance analytics domain (Floridi et al., 2018). To enable people to make decisions regarding their data, insurers should provide transparent information that is clear, concise, and accessible regarding the purposes and the effects of data collection and processing (Diakopoulos & Friedler, 2016). Also, informed consent must always communicate and interact with individuals to help them exercise their rights and choices in the use and sharing of their data (O'Neil, 2016). Conversely, data ownership raises complex questions of moral issues in regard to people's relationship to their data (Barocas & Selbst, 2016). Individuals retain control over their data, hence the right to control and direct its use, even though insurers may collect and process data for business purposes (Mittelstadt et al., 2016). Insurers must, therefore, solve the moral dilemma of the utility of data and human liberty to respect people's rights to access, update, and delete their data as necessary (Acquisti, 2009). To demonstrate commitment to best practices for moral data handling and increase consumer confidence, insurers must ensure informed consent and respect the rights of ownership in data.

Ethical Decision-Making

There are various ethical decision-making frameworks that insurance companies must use to deal with numerous moral dilemmas that have arisen from using insurance analytics (Jobin et al., 2019). According to Floridi et al. (2018), the frameworks provide systematic ways of assessing the moral implications of data activities and assist decision-makers in making defensible choices. One of these frameworks is the principle-based approach that is used to evaluate the ethical aspects of data analytics activities. It is based on solid ethical principles like transparency, fairness, and privacy (Mittelstadt et al., 2016). This makes it easier for insurance firms to spot potential risks and prepare mitigation strategies with diligent application of such principles to specific scenarios and situations. Another consequentialist model is used to assess the data practices and decisions based on the effect generated by the stakeholders on society's welfare (Diakopoulos & Friedler, 2016). Such a strategy would weigh the potential benefits and drawbacks of the data analytics projects and look to activities that maximise the benefits and minimise the drawbacks. Virtue ethics frameworks also highlight the development of moral qualities in decision-making, such as honesty, integrity, and empathy (Barocas & Selbst, 2016). Through virtue ethics frameworks, businesses can imbue insurers with ethical awareness and individual character so they make morally sound decisions when things become complex and confused. In conclusion, the ethical decision-making frameworks provide systematic approaches towards the solutions to moral dilemmas in the insurers, proper data practices and integrity, as well as confidence in insurance analytics (Richterich, 2018).

Ethical decision-making frameworks are critical to helping guide insurers through the complexity of ethical dilemmas in insurance analytics, giving them systematic approaches to examining, evaluating, and resolving ethical considerations (Floridi, 2019). The most popular deontological approach is the rule of obligation, duty, or ideal regardless of consequences (O'Neil, 2016). In this context, the assessment of insurers will consider the best data practices in light of whether they fulfil the legal and ethical standards, such as respect for rights (Howells, 2019). Moreover, in data analytics activities, the rights-based approach emphasises the protection of essential freedoms and rights such as autonomy and privacy (Acquisti, 2009). When employing this paradigm, the insurer will favour activities that promote and protect individuals' rights, even at the cost of short-term expense or restriction of the use of data (Yamaguchi et al., 2023). Also, the ethical decision-making process usually employs participatory methods and stakeholder engagement that allow insurers to incorporate stakeholder values and preferences into the decision-making processes and seek feedback from diverse perspectives (Floridi et al., 2018). Integrating the views and interests of stakeholders into the activity can help the insurers make their data analytics activity more legitimate and ethical (Osoba et al., 2019). Overall, ethical decision-making frameworks allow insurers to systematically address ethical dilemmas, promote moral awareness and accountability, and retain moral standards in insurance analytics (Stahl et al., 2022).

Promoting Ethical Culture and Leadership

Ethical culture and leadership play a significant role in the journey of the insurance industry toward ethical data analytics because it ensures that ethical principles are deeply rooted within the beliefs and practices of a company (Floridi, 2019). It means that all those norms, attitudes, and actions that can make individuals or organisations make ethical choices and behave well in a moral sense are comprised of the concept of an ethical culture (Floridi et al., 2018). Insurers need to foster a culture that highly values the discussion of moral issues and incorporates such in day-to-day operations, which means opening lines of communication and teaching staff how to make ethical decisions (Mittelstadt et al., 2016). As role models and moral custodians, leaders establish the standard for moral behaviour in organisations (Barocas & Selbst, 2016). The executives and management teams in the insurance sector should be the epitome of moral behaviours, foster a culture of accountability, and provide explicit expectations about moral behaviour (O'Neil, 2016). Ethical leadership also includes the empowerment of staff to express the ethical dilemmas, developing avenues through which unethical activities should be reported and through which moral questions would be inputted in a strategic-making process (Acquisti, 2009). At the culmination, these result in granting sustainability and a long-term ability for insurance analytics initiatives to prevail and prosper (Himes, 2019). Insurers can set an environment upholding ethical values while promoting trust and the interest of various stakeholders through ethical culture and leadership (Kristijono et al., 2022).

Promoting an ethical culture and leadership in the insurance sector ensures the integrity of data analytics processes, builds trust among the stakeholders, and assures compliance with regulatory requirements (Floridi et al., 2018). The establishment of an ethical culture at the organisational level can be promoted through organisational leaders who focus on making ethical considerations in the decision-making process (Mittelstadt et al., 2016). This will be at all levels of the organisation, with open communication and organisational goals aligned with ethical standards (Diakopoulos & Friedler, 2016). Funding by leaders for ethical training programs for staff and tools for improving ethical decision-making is also significant, as proposed by Barocas and Selbst (2016). Systems of accountability will be needed to get ethical lapses dealt with promptly and transparently by ethical leadership, as urged by O'Neil (2016). Leaders can foster an atmosphere where ethical considerations are ingrained in the business culture by modelling ethical behaviour and holding others and themselves accountable for respecting ethical standards (Acquisti, 2009). Insurance companies can also encourage inclusivity and diversity among their workforces because different viewpoints lead to more substantial, more moral decision-making processes (Floridi, 2019). Utilising these endeavours, insurance companies can develop a leadership and ethical culture that not only reduces risks but also stimulates innovation, builds confidence, and improves the standing of the insurance sector overall.

3 Objectives of the Study

The following are the objectives of the study considering the theoretical and foundational underpinnings of ethics in data analytics ethics–

1. To study the impact of transparency in data analytics practices on stakeholders' trust.
2. Analyze how ethical employee training and awareness programmes for employees influence ethical decision-making during the data analytics process.
3. To analyse how the emphasis on data privacy leads to data breaches and privacy incidents.

4 Review of Literature and Hypotheses on Data Privacy and Regulation

Transparency and Accountability

The ethical principles of the insurance industry about data analytics are based on transparency and accountability, which underlines responsibility, openness, and clarity in data activities (Floridi et al., 2018; Zwitter & Elden, 2018). In order for stakeholders to be able to understand and analyse these mechanisms thoroughly, insurers must open up procedures, techniques, and algorithms in data collection, analysis, and decision-making processes (Diakopoulos & Friedler, 2016). Openness will ensure the alleviation of concerns about algorithmic obscurity and latent biases as the insurer is sure to win the hearts of all stakeholders, regulators, and clients (Mittelstadt et al., 2016). In addition, openness enhances responsibility in that the data activities of the insurer can be duly monitored and assessed (Floridi, 2019). It then entails accountability, meaning taking responsibility for the implications of bringing data analytics into society while enacting mechanisms of complaint and remedy (Barocas & Selbst, 2016). Therefore, holding decision-makers liable for their actions and the results during the process of data analytics will cause insurers to embrace proactiveness in supporting accountability as an ethical value. By encouraging responsibility and transparency, insurers may uphold moral principles and instil trust among their stakeholders while also establishing a responsible culture of data governance within the insurance sector (United Kingdom, 2023).

Transferring ethical use of data in analytics is therefore called for in insurance specifically, given the growing complexity and dependence on algorithms and models involving machine learning (O'Neil, 2016). According to Floridi et al. (2018), open methods allow stakeholders, be they the policyholders or regulatory authorities, to understand why such and such decisions have been taken, thereby letting the stakeholders assess the legitimacy and the fairness of the decision. In addition, transparency allows the detection of possible biases or mistakes that may arise in the process of working with data analytics, thus eliminating them (Diakopoulos & Friedler, 2016). Accountability results in integrity and trust within the insurance industry because of the requirement for businesses to be responsible for the results of their data-driven decisions (Floridi, 2019). Insurance companies can demonstrate their commitment to moral values as well as increase customer satisfaction and regulatory compliance by embracing accountability and transparency (Mittelstadt et al., 2016). In simple words, ethical data governance requires accountability and transparency when dealing with the complexity of analytics, and the insurer projects integrity and trust in business operations. All these reviews will be put together to develop the first hypothesis, which is as follows: H1: Greater transparency in data analytics practice is positively related to stakeholders' trust.

Fairness and Bias Mitigation

Fairness and bias mitigation stand out among ethical requirements for the realm of analytics as applied in insurance practice (Barocas & Selbst, 2016). Floridi et al. (2018) define fairness as treating people equally within various demographic classes and avoiding aggravation and perpetuation of already existing imbalances due to data-informed decision-making. Nevertheless, biases in algorithmic decision-making and inbuilt biases within data are also likely to interfere with operations conducted in data analytics (Mittelstadt et al., 2016; Liu & Wang, 2019). In dealing with such challenges, insurance companies need to make use of measures to reduce biases throughout the lifecycle stages, from collection and preprocessing to the actual development and deployment (Diakopoulos & Friedler, 2016). This entails intense data checks for bias sources and the use of fairness-aware methods in algorithmic models that ensure equal outcomes (O'Neil, 2016; Wang & Kosinski, 2018). To further reduce the risk of unconscious biases and promote the creation of fair and unbiased algorithms, insurance companies should also ensure that their data analytics teams are diverse and inclusive (Floridi, 2019). By taking bias and fairness as serious concerns and attacking both aggressively, insurers may respect moral standards, foster relationships with their stakeholders, and ensure data analytics procedures produce results that are fair to all stakeholders.

The ethical standards of fairness and reduction of prejudice are of utmost relevance in the insurance industry's embrace of data analytics (Barocas & Selbst, 2016). Being fair means that each person gets the same treatment and outcome regardless of their history or demographic features (Floridi et al., 2018). On the other hand, data analytics may perpetuate or exacerbate the existing biases in the data or those created by algorithmic decision-making processes (Mittelstadt et al., 2016). This way, insurers need to start playing offensively by addressing these biases at every stage of data lifecycles. Therefore, it involves the evaluation of data sets for a possible source of bias or mistake and correction, applying fair methods and algorithms (Diakopoulos & Friedler, 2016). Thirdly, insurers should also focus highly on diversity and inclusion in their teams for data analytics to minimise the likelihood of latent biases in algorithmic decision-making. This can be achieved by creating various points of view and experiences. (Floridi, 2019). Insurance organisations may maintain ethical principles, produce stakeholder trust, and contribute to the attainment of more equitable and balanced outcomes in insurance analytics by actively working to eradicate fairness and bias mitigation. The second hypothesis, which the above reviews will help support, is presented below:Hypothesis H2: Ethical training and employee awareness programs positively influence the ethical decision-making process in analytics.

Privacy and Data Protection

Privacy and data protection are extreme ethical concerns in the domain of insurance analytics, constituting the rights of people in how their data is gathered, used, and shared (Solove, 2006). The widespread use of gathering data and the development of high-powered analytics tools have made insurance firms navigate a complex tapestry of legal regulations and moral duties for sensitive data (Koops et al., 2017). Not only does it entail legal observances, such as the Health Insurance Portability and Accountability Act (HIPAA) or the General Data Protection Regulation (GDPR), but also the moral obligation toward the respect and dignity of people's autonomy (Floridi et al., 2018). To reduce risks to personal privacy rights and to preserve the reputation of insurers, there is a need to ensure that data protection measures deter illegal access, disclosure, and misuse of personal data (Barocas & Selbst, 2016). In addition, privacy-enhancing techniques and technologies—like data minimisation, encryption, and anonymisation—are necessary to minimise privacy risks and people's acceptance of responsible management of data (Acquisti, 2009). With privacy and data protection, insurers respect moral principles, build consumer trust, and lessen the possibility of adverse social effects from data breaches or misuse.

Besides being legally required, privacy and data protection are moral imperatives that require insurers to take preventative action and give them serious thought (Floridi, 2019). People should expect insurers to handle vast amounts of personal data responsibly and securely, such as health records, financial information, and demographic data (Mittelstadt et al., 2016). In this case, the responsibility of ensuring the integrity and security of this data is with the insurer, meaning it should not be open to illegal access, alteration, or disclosure. Moreover, ethical considerations involving privacy are not just about the enforcement of rules but more generalised ethical obligations toward respect for autonomy and privacy choices (Diakopoulos & Friedler, 2016). Insurance companies must adopt a privacy-by-design approach and consider privacy issues in the design stage when developing and deploying data analytics systems (Floridi et al., 2018). Insurance companies can reduce the risk of privacy violations and demonstrate commitment to ethical data governance by embedding privacy-enhancing features, including data anonymisation and encryption, in their activities (Acquisti, 2009). Besides that, insurance companies should be honest and open about their practices when communicating with policyholders on issues of data, hence providing individuals with the freedom to decide whether their data will be used or not and promoting an ethical culture. Third **Hypothesis** Keeping these reviews in view, the Third hypothesis is presented below-H3. Organisations with privacy-by-design principles would have a higher resilience against data breaches and privacy incidents.

5 Research Methodology and Analysis

An empirical study with descriptive statistical analysis using tools like correlation, regression, and ANOVA was carried out to ascertain the relationships between the various sets of variables—transparency in data analytics practices and stakeholder trust, ethical employee training and awareness programmes and ethical decision-making in data analytics processes, and data breaches and privacy incidents. A sample size of 345 IT professionals and students from the Chandigarh tri-city was gathered over three months, from January to March 2024, for data analysis. The analyses as per the objectives are given below.

Impact of Transparency in Data Analytics Practices on Stakeholders' Trust.

Hypothesis (H1): There is a positive correlation between transparency in data analytics practices and stakeholder trust.

It is evident from Tables 1, 2, and 3 that 52.2% of respondents out of 345 are in favour of high transparency in data, whereas 43.5% of respondents favour a very high trust rating for stakeholders. From Tables 4 and 5, we can see the correlation value between transparency in data and stakeholders' trust is .854. The significance level is less than .05. Hence, the alternate hypothesis is accepted. It infers that there is a very high correlation between transparency in data and stakeholders' trust.

Influence of Ethical Training and Awareness Programs for Employees on their Ethical Decision-Making in Data Analytics Processes.

Table 1 Descriptive statistics (e.g., mean, standard deviation) for transparency and trust ratings

		Transparency in data	Trust stakeholder
N	Valid	345	345
	Missing	0	0
Mean		3.3478	3.9565
Std. error of mean		0.04665	0.06454
Std. deviation		0.86646	1.19877

Table 2 Transparency in data

		Frequency	Per cent	Valid percent	Cumulative percent
Valid	Very low transparent	30	8.7	8.7	8.7
	Moderately transparent	135	39.1	39.1	47.8
	High transparent	180	52.2	52.2	100.0
	Total	345	100.0	100.0	

Table 3 Trust stakeholder

		Frequency	Per cent	Valid Percent	Cumulative Percent
Valid	Very low trust	30	8.7	8.7	8.7
	Moderately trust	75	21.7	21.7	30.4
	High trust	90	26.1	26.1	56.5
	Very high trust	150	43.5	43.5	100.0
	Total	345	100.0	100.0	

Table 4 Descriptive statistics of transparency in data and stakeholder's Trust

	Mean	Std. deviation	N
Transparency in data	3.3478	0.86646	345
Trust stakeholder	3.9565	1.19877	345

Table 5 Correlations between transparency in data and stakeholder's trust

		Transparency in data	Trust stakeholder
Transparency in data	Pearson correlation	1	0.854**
	Sig. (2-tailed)		0.000
	The sum of squares and cross-products	258.261	305.217
	Covariance	0.751	0.887
	N	345	345
Trust stakeholder	Pearson correlation	0.854[a]	1
	Sig. (2-tailed)	0.000	
	The sum of squares and cross-products	305.217	494.348
	Covariance	0.887	1.437
	N	345	345

**. Correlation is significant at the 0.01 level (2-tailed)

Hypothesis (H2): Ethical training and awareness programs for employees positively influence ethical decision-making in data analytics processes.

From Table 8, The F ratio in the ANOVA analysis is 26.742, and the significance level is less than .05. Hence, the alternate hypothesis is accepted. It is further inferred here that ethical training and awareness programs for employees have a positive influence on ethical decision-making in data analytics processes. From Table 9, the predictive power of ethical training on ethical decision-making while controlling for relevant variables (e.g., education level, job role) is also positive because the beta value is .269, which is positive Tables 6 and 7.

Impact of Prioritizing Data Privacy on Data Breaches and Privacy Incidents.

Table 6 Relationship between participation in ethical training programs and ethical decision-making

	Sum of Squares	df	Mean square	F	Sig.
Between groups	21.509	1	21.509	26.742	0.000
Within groups	275.882	343	0.804		
Total	297.391	344			

Table 7 Regression analysis to assess the predictive power of ethical training on ethical decision-making while controlling for relevant variables (e.g., education level, job role)

Model		Unstandardised coefficients		Standardised coefficients	t	Sig.
		B	Std. Error	Beta		
1	(constant)	3.196	0.147		21.770	0.000
	Participate in ethical training	0.569	0.110	0.269	5.171	0.000

[a]. Dependent Variable: Ethical Decision making

Table 8 The relationship between privacy by design principles and the occurrence/severity of data breaches and privacy incidents

		prioritise privacy by design	resilience to data breaches and privacy incidents
Prioritise privacy by design	Pearson correlation	1	0.103
	Sig. (2-tailed)		0.057
	The sum of squares and cross-products	314.348	40.435
	Covariance	0.914	0.118
	N	345	345
Resilience to data breaches and privacy incidents	Pearson correlation	0.103	1
	Sig. (2-tailed)	0.057	
	The sum of squares and cross-products	40.435	493.043
	Covariance	0.118	1.433
	N	345	345

Hypothesis (H3): Organizations that prioritise privacy by design principles exhibit greater resilience to data breaches and privacy incidents.

It is evident from Table 9 a and b that the correlation value between prioritising privacy by design and resilience to data breaches and privacy incidents is .103, and the significance level is more significant than .05. Hence, the alternate hypothesis is rejected. It infers that there is a very low correlation between prioritising privacy by design and resilience to data breaches and privacy incidents. The F value is 3.657, and the significance level is further greater than .05. Hence, the alternate hypothesis is rejected. It is therefore inferred that prioritised privacy by design principles practised by organisations exhibit lesser resilience to data breaches and privacy incidents.

Table 9 Regression analysis is used to determine if there is a significant correlation between the level of privacy by design implementation and the frequency or severity of data breaches/incidents. (ANOVA)

Model		Sum of squares	df	Mean square	F	Sig.
1	Regression	5.201	1	5.201	3.657	0.057[b]
	Residual	487.842	343	1.422		
	Total	493.043	344			

[a]. Dependent Variable: resilience to data breaches and privacy incidents
[b]. Predictors: (Constant), prioritise privacy by design

6 Conclusion: Ethical Imperatives for Data Alchemy

From the findings above, it has been observed that there is a very high correlation between transparency in data and stakeholders' trust. The ethical training and awareness programs for employees have a positive influence on ethical decision-making in data analytics processes. The predictive power of ethical training on ethical decision-making while controlling for relevant variables (e.g., education level, job role) is also positive because the beta value is .269, which is positive. Also, the prioritised privacy by design principles practised by organisations exhibit lesser resilience to data breaches and privacy incidents.

Ethical considerations become essential requirements in the constantly changing field of insurance analytics, influencing the direction and results of data alchemy projects. Big data analytics' revolutionary potential in the insurance sector offers hitherto unheard-of chances for creativity, effectiveness, and enhanced client experiences. However, these potentials also come with ethical obligations to make sure that data-driven activities respect the values of accountability, openness, fairness, privacy, and consent (Floridi et al., 2018). To maximise the benefits of data alchemy and improve risk management tactics, insurers must be cautious in defending the rights and interests of all parties involved, including policyholders, staff members, and the general public (Mittelstadt et al., 2016). Frameworks for ethical decision-making give insurers a methodical way to deal with the problematic moral conundrums that arise from insurance analytics, allowing them to strike a compromise between morality and business goals (Diakopoulos & Friedler, 2016). Fostering trust, integrity, and accountability in data processes is made possible by cultivating an ethical culture and leadership inside firms (Barocas & Selbst, 2016). Placing high importance on ethical principles at every stage of the data lifecycle-from collection and analysis to decision-making and distribution-will help insurance companies reduce risks, build stakeholder trust, and support the ethical and long-term development of data alchemy in the business (Acquisti, 2009). Moral imperatives work as guiding concepts that emphasise the importance of moral conduct, honesty, and the welfare of society in pursuing data-driven excellence in insurance analytics.

In conclusion, moral obligations can be said to be guiding lights in the dynamic world of data alchemy within the insurance industry. Insurance firms have to navigate a rugged terrain of ethical issues as they capitalise on big data analytics to ensure that data-driven procedures adhere to the values of accountability, openness, and fairness (Floridi, 2019). The ethical implications of data analytics are beyond legal compliance with social norms and values. This demands a proactive commitment to responsible data governance and moral decision-making (O'Neil, 2016). Ensure that insurers establish an ethical culture with risk reductions for data exploitation or abuse that would give stakeholders trust through transparency, fairness, and privacy throughout a data lifecycle, as proposed by Barocas & Selbst in 2016. Ethical leadership at all levels is also required to set the moral bars in business and to drive integrity and accountability in institutions (Floridi et al., 2018). Moral guidelines that direct insurers toward ethical and sustainable data activities that support the interests of people and society at large are known as ethical imperatives. This is especially true as the insurance industry continues to embrace data alchemy as a catalyst for innovation and growth.

Acknowledgements We express our heartfelt gratitude to all those who have helped in this research by providing their input directly or indirectly through their research works as references or direct input as respondents. We express our heartfelt indebtedness to the almighty God, who has given us the strength to complete the research work.

References

Acquisti, A. (2009). Privacy in electronic commerce and the economics of immediate gratification. In *Proceedings of the 10th International Conference on Electronic Commerce* (pp. 21–21).

Barocas, S., & Selbst, A. D. (2016). Big data's disparate impact. *California Law Review, 104*(3), 671–732.

Boyd, D., & Crawford, K. (2012). Critical questions for big data: Provocations for a cultural, technological, and scholarly phenomenon. *Information, Communication & Society, 15*(5), 662–679.

Diakopoulos, N., & Friedler, S. A. (2016). How to hold algorithms accountable. *Harvard Kennedy School Misinformation Review, 1*(1).

Dwork, C., & Mulligan, D. K. (2013). It's not privacy, and it is not fair. *Theoretical Inquiries in Law, 14*(1), 1–32.

Floridi, L. (2019). The logic of information: A theory of philosophy as conceptual design. Oxford University Press.

Floridi, L., Cowls, J., Beltrametti, M., Chatila, R., Chazerand, P., Dignum, V., et al. (2018). AI4People—An ethical framework for a good AI society: Opportunities, risks, principles, and recommendations. *Minds and Machines, 28*(4), 689–707. https://doi.org/10.1007/s11023-018-9482-5

Floridi, L., & Taddeo, M. (2016). What is data ethics? *Philosophical Transactions of the Royal Society A: Mathematical, Physical and Engineering Sciences, 374*(2083), 20160360.

Himes, H. E. (2019). *Bargaining for Security: The Rise of the Pension and Social Insurance Program of the United Steelworkers of America, 1941–1960.* https://doi.org/10.33915/etd.3917

Howells, G. (2019). Protecting consumer protection values in the fourth industrial revolution. *Journal of Consumer Policy, 43*(1), 145–175. https://doi.org/10.1007/s10603-019-09430-3

Jobin, A., Ienca, M., & Vayena, E. (2019). The global landscape of AI ethics guidelines. *Nature Machine Intelligence, 1*(9), 389–399.

Kitchin, R. (2014). The Data Revolution: Big Data, Open Data, Data Infrastructures and Their Consequences. SAGE Publications Ltd.

Koops, B. J., Leenes, R., & Bertolini, A. (2017). Privacy and security in the age of big data: A comparative analysis of four legal frameworks. *Computer Law & Security Review, 33*(2), 216–234.

Kristijono, N. H., Pramono, R., Supratikno, H., Sudibjo, N., & Juliana, N. (2022). Ethical decisions of leaders in sustainable investing to promote sustainable development. *International Journal of Sustainable Development and Planning, 17*(1), 13–28. https://doi.org/10.18280/ijsdp.170102

Liu, K., & Wang, H. (2019). Ethical issues in big data analytics: A stakeholder perspective. *Journal of Business Ethics, 156*(2), 441–461. https://doi.org/10.1007/s10551-018-3922-y

Mittelstadt, B. D., Allo, P., Taddeo, M., Wachter, S., & Floridi, L. (2016). The ethics of algorithms: Mapping the debate. *Big Data & Society, 3*(2), 2053951716679679. https://doi.org/10.1177/2053951716679679

Mittelstadt, B. D., Fairweather, N. B., & McBride, N. (2016). The ethics of data mining: A systematic literature review. *ACM Computing Surveys (CSUR), 48*(1), 10.

Mittelstadt, B. D., & Floridi, L. (2019). The ethics of big data: Current and foreseeable issues in biomedical contexts. *Science and Engineering Ethics, 25*(3), 631–647.

Mittelstadt, B. D., Russell, C., & Wachter, S. (2019). Explaining explanations in AI. *Communications of the ACM, 62*(7), 56–63.

Oh, E. (2007). *Natural hazards, the state and insurance: risk, responsibility and promises of (in)security*. https://doi.org/10.22215/etd/2007-08562

O'Neil, C. (2016). Weapons of math destruction: How big data increases inequality and threatens democracy. Broadway Books.

Osoba, O., Boudreaux, B., Saunders, J., Irwin, J., Mueller, P., & Cherney, S. (2019). Algorithmic equity: A framework for social applications. *In RAND Corporation eBooks*. https://doi.org/10.7249/rr2708

Richterich, A. (2018). *The Big Data Agenda: Data Ethics and Critical Data Studies*. https://doi.org/10.16997/book14

Solove, D. J. (2006). A taxonomy of privacy. *University of Pennsylvania Law Review*, 477–560.

Stahl, B. C., Schroeder, D., & Rodrigues, R. (2022). Ethics of artificial intelligence. *In Springer Briefs in research and innovation governance*. https://doi.org/10.1007/978-3-031-17040-9

United Kingdom. (2023). *IMF Country Report, 2023*(252), 1. https://doi.org/10.5089/9798400248627.002

Wang, Y., & Kosinski, M. (2018). Deep neural networks are more accurate than humans at detecting sexual orientation from facial images. *Journal of Personality and Social Psychology, 114*(2), 246–257.

Yamaguchi, S., Atarashi, T., Okada, A., Nasu, S., Yamauchi, T., Arase, Y., Aizawa, T., Nangaku, M., & Kadowaki, T. (2023). Impact of the COVID-19 pandemic on health check-ups: A Nationwide questionnaire survey in 639 healthcare facilities in Japan Society of Ningen Dock. *JMA Journal, 6*(3) https://doi.org/10.31662/jmaj.2023-0040

Zwitter, A., & Elden, L. (2018). Ethical considerations of big data: Challenges and opportunities. In *Big Data Challenges* (pp. 99–119). Springer.

Dr. Pawan Pant is working as an Associate Professor of Management at the University School of Business, Chandigarh University, Mohali, Punjab. He has published eight research papers, one national and one international journal. He has 11 years of teaching experience and worked as an Assistant Manager (Purchase) at Pacific Industries Ltd., Udaipur (Rajasthan), for one year. His area of specialisation is Economics.

Prof. (Dr.) K. K. Mishra is working as a Professor of Marketing at the University School of Business, Chandigarh University, Mohali, Punjab. He has published 54 national and international research papers in Scopus-indexed journals and book chapters and presented 31 papers at national and international conferences. He has four patent rights and three copyrights. He has 25 years of teaching and research experience. He has supervised two PhD scholars. He has twice qualified for UGC NET in Management. He has received the Best Faculty Award three times from the Indian Institute of Materials Management, National Head Quarters, Mumbai, in 2009, 2016 and 2018, respectively. He has been conferred the Best Paper Award for the paper titled "Harnessing AI: Unveiling Educators' Intentions and Synergy in Education", presented at the eighth International Conference on Information System Design and Intelligent Applications (ISDIS 2024) in Dubai, UAE, in 2024. He has chaired technical sessions of international conferences organised by the Indian Institute of Materials Management, Mumbai, in 2016 and 2018 and OP Jindal University Raigarh, in 2022 and 2023. He did his PhD in "Strategy formulation for marketing services in rural Uttar Pradesh" from Uttar Pradesh Rajarshi Tandon University, Allahabad.

Dr. Bhaskara Srinivas is a seasoned professional with a rich blend of industry and academic experience. With Nine years of industry expertise under his belt and 3.5 years of dedicated teaching as an Assistant Professor in the Management Department of the University School of Business, Chandigarh University, Mohali, Punjab, and his area of specialisation is Human Resource Analytics, Human Resource Management, organisation behaviour, ethical leadership, etc. Dr. Bhaskara Srinivas is a versatile individual who is well-versed in various facets of his field.

Dr. Azmee Zaheer is an Assistant Professor at the University School of Business, MBA department, Chandigarh University, Gharuan, Punjab. She has completed her PhD and MPhil in Management from Babasaheb Bhimrao Ambedkar University (A Central University) Lucknow, Uttar Pradesh. She received a Gold Medalist for M.phil's exemplary work. She has four years of research experience, 3.5 years of corporate experience in marketing, and 2.5 years of academic experience in marketing. She has also contributed to various research journals like Scopus, Web of Sciences, UGC Care, and Edited Book and has participated in multiple national and international seminars.

The Role that Gaming Features Play in Increasing Viewer Engagement in the Field of Digital Marketing

Udgam Mishra, Uttam Mishra, Keshav Prasad Gadtaula, and Achyut Gyawali

Abstract

This chapter explores how digital marketing experiences become more engaging by incorporating gaming elements that offer points, challenges, and rewards. The current digital landscape makes it challenging for traditional marketing methods to capture consumers' attention. Issues in modern marketing can be addressed through gamification, which blends various game elements with non-game experiences to foster interactive engagement. This section describes how psychological concepts meet social needs and achievements in successful gamification. The global brands Starbucks, Duolingo, and Nike use gamification methods to establish relationships with consumers for improved selling to active audiences. This research considers recent AI and AR innovations that enable brands to produce interactive experiences that are addressed to users. AI programs design tailored challenges around user profiles, and AR allows borderlessness between digital data and physical space. Ethical gamification deployment entails overcoming traps such as audience weariness, as well as accessibility and ethical issues with data security and excessive rewarding. Marketers can use gamification to build long-term relationships with consumers by balancing creativity with ethical practice. This leads to practical recommendations for developing inclusive marketing tactics, avoiding fraud, and adapting to trends. In doing so, it allows brands to be differentiated within competitive markets and builds meaningful connections with target consumers.

U. Mishra · K. P. Gadtaula · A. Gyawali
Tribhuvan University, Biratnagar, Nepal

U. Mishra (✉)
Purbanchal University, Biratnagar, Nepal
e-mail: 1mishrauttam@gmail.com

© The Author(s), under exclusive license to Springer Nature Singapore Pte Ltd. 2026
N. S. Jayawardena et al. (eds.), *Digital Advertising and Consumer Behavior*, Management for Professionals, https://doi.org/10.1007/978-981-95-7809-2_12

1 Introduction

Organisations must design a strategic framework for capturing and maintaining consumers' attention in the digital world. Digital media platforms have revolutionised all aspects of modern human life (Brubaker, 2020). The process of reaching and maintaining customer attention towards business ventures remains the same. Blending advertisements with social media posts as well as persistent notifications created a loss of consumer attention and rendered traditional methods of promotion ineffective. With this highly competitive landscape, brands need not just visibility within the market to survive, but also to foster deep consumer relationships that go beyond superficial interaction.

Digital marketing plays an important role in gamification. Considered a powerful tool in non-game worlds, gamification implements game functionality through point programs, scoring systems, and challenges to improve user commitment while encouraging actions and maintaining customer connections (Oliveira et al., 2024). By harnessing the principles of play, brands can convert static content into vibrant, interactive experiences that engage audiences and promote ongoing interaction. The emergence of gamification signifies a wider transformation in the marketing landscape. Conventional advertising, which depends on unidirectional communication, is supported by approaches that emphasise interactive engagement, customisation, and active user involvement (Remondes et al., 2024). For example, consumers, especially Millennials and Generation Z, seek marketing approaches that reflect their digital behaviours. These people have grown up in the world of video games, mobile apps, and interactive media, with a background for the easy acceptance of gamification.

For marketers, gamification refers to a powerful set of tools which angles these trends. Game-like elements intrinsically include interactions with human psychology; there is an inherent appeal to the need for achievement, competition, and socialisation. When properly done, gamification raises the level of engagement and creates emotional connections between brands and customers. For instance, Nike's NikePlus app captivates users by granting them points, challenges, and social competition as rewards for accomplishing fitness goals. The Coca-Cola "Share a Coke" marketing initiative made consumption more engaging by encouraging customers to locate specific branded bottles and consequently increased product exposure and customer interaction (Chan, 2024). Essential gamification transforms ordinary consumers into active consumers. The use of gamified content produces active engagement among users, whereas typical ads lead only to passive or immediate forgetfulness. It instils a feeling of ownership as if the consumer seems to be able to 'call brands out' on their turf. Gamification also introduces a sense of community and achievement, which are the valuable attributes of long-term brand loyalty. A sense of accomplishment that derives from them as they gather points, complete challenges, or even climb up the ranking ladder makes them want to share more (Wilson, 2024).

The significance of gamification extends beyond its immediate effect on engagement. Global spending on digital advertising is expected to surpass $800 billion by 2026 and brands must set themselves apart in an increasingly saturated market. Gamification offers a distinct differentiation option, crafting memorable experiences from conventional campaigns. New technologies such as AR, VR, and AI are gradually gaining popularity in mainstream life, and possibilities for gamified experiences will continue to grow (Emrich, 2024). With the development of digital marketing, gamification has become an essential resource, attracting attention and enhancing engagement and brand loyalty.

This chapter explored how game design elements can increase viewers' engagement in digital marketing. First, it provides a theoretical basis for gamification, rooted in psychology and behavioural science. An overview of the development of gamification with simple reward mechanisms for more sophisticated and engaging campaigns was provided. Moreover, this chapter offers practical recommendations on how to use gaming features on major platforms to achieve improved outcomes. Moreover, it examines the case studies of prominent brands to demonstrate the practical implementation and success of gamification. This chapter also investigates new trends and potential future pathways in gamification, emphasising technologies such as blockchain, artificial intelligence, and metaverse technology. These innovations transform how brands interact with consumers, facilitating highly personalised and immersive experiences. Nonetheless, this chapter also discusses obstacles and ethical issues, including concerns regarding data privacy, excessive gamified content, and the possibility of manipulative tactics. In other words, this chapter aims to prove that gamification is not a hype, but a game-changing strategy in digital marketing. By adding gaming aspects to their strategies, companies can establish substantial, active, and long-term relationships with their customers.

2 Theoretical Foundations of Gamification

Gamification

Gamification, a term popularised by Deterding et al. (2011), refers to the use of game mechanics such as points, badges, and leaderboards in a non-gaming environment to enhance user engagement and motivation (Tembulkar, 2024). Unlike traditional marketing techniques, which typically focus on passive content consumption, gamification transforms the user experience into a more active experience. This approach aligns with natural human tendencies towards accomplishments, competition, and socialisation. An example is the mobile fitness app Strava, which encourages users to compete by tracking their activities and personal records, and giving them badges.

Viewer engagement is a complicated term used to measure consumers' level of interaction with digital content. This encompasses numerical measures, such as click-through rates, time spent on content, and shares, along with qualitative aspects such as emotional connection and brand recognition. Gamification helps increase feelings of engagement because it can build active participation, making interactions much more rewarding and meaningful (Abdel Halim, 2025). Additionally, social media platforms such as Instagram use gamified features including polls, quizzes, and interactive stories, which can help brands build more personal relationships with their audiences.

Digital Marketing

Digital marketing refers to various methods through which products and services are sold on the Internet (Dwiandini, 2024). Gamification is gaining prominence as customers desire fun and personal experience. Traditional advertising methods, such as banner advertisements, are being pushed aside by gamification, which offers users fun and interactive experience. An ideal example is Duolingo, which employs game-like elements, such as streaks and progress tracking, to engage users and keep them interested.

3 Relevant Theories on Digital Marketing

Online marketing is a platform in which various efforts are made to sell products or services utilising online platforms. As customers wants and needs continue to change, gamification has emerged as one of the prime determinants of interactivity and personalisation in brand experience. There is a trend where the conventional advertising media like banner advertisements are being replaced by gamification techniques that are focused on delivering experiences that are closely associated with consumers' passion for entertainment and social interaction. Duolingo is perhaps the most compelling example of this movement as it entails the involvement of the users through embracing game-like functionalities that track their streaks and achievements. The uses and Gratifications Theory is a theory that has its roots in empirical research to explain consumer media choice behaviour (Keelson et al., 2024). Gamification marketing is underpinned by this theory through the creation of entertainment and valuable activities aimed at meeting various consumer needs. In addition, platforms such as LinkedIn and other social media platforms incorporate gamification features, such as endorsements or badges, to address the requirements of recognition and accomplishment of employees' work within the workplace.

Flow theory, as Csikszentmihalyi (1990) describes, states that high-level engagement in an activity reduces distractions and negative affect. In Internet marketing, gamification not only builds interesting brand experiences through interactive processes but is also used to build interactive brand experiences through interactive elements. The flow state is the concentration of attention on an activity with clearly defined and achievable goals. By adding instant feedback requirements, gamification deepens flow experiences through challenges, such as test capability and enjoyment limits. Learning systems like Kahoot enhances learning achievement through designing questions that are challenging but not beyond response limits, thereby sustaining student engagement. Flow theory, as argued by Csikszentmihalyi (1990), states that high-level engagement in an activity reduces distractions and negative affect. In Internet marketing, gamification not only creates interactive brand experiences through interactive processes, but also develops interactive brand experiences through entertaining processes. The state of flow is defined as the state of sustained attention to an activity with clear and achievable goals. With the addition of instant feedback demands, gamification strengthens the flow experience through the challenges of testing capacity and fun threshold. Online learning tools, such as Kahoot, improve learning achievement by preparing questions that are challenging but within response limits, thereby sustaining students' involvement. Technology Acceptance Model, proposed by Davis et al. (1989), is a general model employed to examine technology adoption. The model illustrates that ease of use and usefulness are fundamental factors that drive new technology adoption. These variables are important factors that affect consumer behaviour towards gamification and online marketing tools within the research context.

Deci and Ryan (2012) self-determination theory posits that autonomy, competence, and relatedness are fundamental human needs that give rise to intrinsic motivation. In my research, these elements contribute to the understanding of how gamification in digital marketing generates engagement and motivation through the provision of fundamental needs. Competence is achieved through the provision of rewards for accomplishments such as points or badges. Autonomy is given to users by allowing them to have control over their activities, for example, avatar design or challenge choice. Relatedness is fostered by enabling interaction with others, e.g., competition on leaderboards or sharing achievements.

4 Psychological Principles of Gamification

Gamification uses intrinsic and extrinsic motives to facilitate participation. Intrinsically, the user gets personal satisfaction from overcoming a challenge or achieving his/her goal, while extrinsically, there is a tangible reward, like discounts and exclusive content. A Fitbit system uses one of these dual approaches: giving badges when the users reach specific fitness achievements-intrinsic, and discounting health-related products. Malott's (2021) principle of operant conditioning explains how rewards reinforce behaviour. Gamified marketing leverages this by providing positive reinforcement at points, badges, and levels. Starbucks Rewards, for example, uses a tiered loyalty system where customers earn stars for purchases, creating a cycle of reinforcement that encourages frequent visits.

Gamification cognitively increases the level of challenge through problem solving, decision-making, or strategising; this kind of environment provokes mental effort and deeper emotional investments. For example, some challenges in gamified e-learning platforms include feedback loops that are necessary for active participation and attention maintenance. Social interaction is one of the major bases of gamified experience. The methods for satisfying these human needs, which depend on community recognition, include leaderboards, multiplayer challenges, and social sharing. A good example is Nike's running clubs, which leveraged gamified social competition to build both camaraderie and competitiveness among users.

5 Expanding Gamification's Theoretical Relevance

Gamification as Behavioural Design

Gamification extends beyond engagement to influence consumer behaviour. Concepts from behavioural economics, such as loss aversion and the endowment effect, are being more tightly incorporated into these gamified marketing strategies (Nussenbaum & Hartley, 2024). For example, apps such as Duolingo use streaks to tap into loss aversion and urge users to continue their daily activities in order to avoid losing streaks.

Neuropsychological Effects

Neuropsychological studies indicate that gamification mostly activates reward centres in the brain, because attaining goals or receiving rewards provokes dopamine release. This provides good feedback, enhances satisfaction, and promotes further interactions. VR platforms amplify this by placing users in gamified environments to trigger emotions.

6 Evolution and Types of Gaming Features in Digital Marketing

Historical Overview of Gamification in Marketing

Gamification, as a formalised concept, gained prominence in the early 2010s, but its roots can be traced back much further. Early marketing efforts incorporated game-like mechanics, such as loyalty programs, in the 1980s. These programs rewarded repeat purchases with redeemable points for discounts or gifts, thus laying the foundation for gamification. For example, airlines introduced frequent flyer programs that incentivise loyalty through tiered rewards.

The digital revolution in the late 1990s and the early 2000s marked a turning point. The rise of the internet and mobile devices has provided new opportunities for interactive and scalable gamified experiences. Brands began experimenting with basic online games and reward systems to engage customers. McDonald's monopoly campaign, launched in the 1980s but revitalised in digital formats, became a blueprint for blending traditional games with marketing objectives. By the mid-2000s, the proliferation of social media and smartphones revolutionised gamification. Platforms such as Facebook have enabled brands to create viral campaigns, whereas mobile apps have introduced real-time engagement through location-based features and push notifications. The launch of Foursquare in 2009 exemplified this shift, as users earned badges and rewards for "checking in". By the 2010s, gamification had grown into a multilevel promotional channel. Now, enabled by AR, VR, or AI, technologies even allow brands to be more personalised in their interactivity with their customers via game activities. Pokémon GO demonstrated what could be done with location-based AR, while Duolingo popularized game-like learning through progress tracking, streaks, and leaderboards. Currently, gamification is among the most critical features of digital marketing, because it opens up new ways to increase engagement, retention, and loyalty.

7 Gaming Features in Digital Marketing

Points Systems

Point systems are likely to have the highest usage among the gamification elements. They reward users for certain actions such as making purchases, sharing content, or completing tasks. Usually, these points can be converted into rewards such as discounts, special products, or experiences. Examples include Starbucks Rewards, in which customers earn stars for every purchase they make and which can be exchanged for free drinks and food items. This creates a feeling of achievement, and promotes repeated engagement.

Competition and Leaderboards

Leaderboards introduce some sort of competition, whereby users can compete with the performance of others. This feature taps into the basic human desire for social status and recognition. Such examples are represented by Strava, who uses leaderboards to show running or cycling achievements to encourage participants to improve their performance and boost their frequency.

Challenges and Quests

Challenges and requests induce users to perform certain activities. In general, these features include achievements or rewards that provide feelings of progression. Brands such as Nike use challenges in the Nike Run Club app to allow users to join virtual races or to achieve fitness goals. These activities will not only engage them but also build a brand's value for health and fitness.

Badges and Achievements

The platform acknowledges user progress through achievements and badges when users meet predetermined goals or complete tasks. Participation on these virtual platforms is motivated by symbolic tokens that represent accomplishments. The professional networking site LinkedIn uses badges to show users' skill sets and qualifications, which helps them grow professionally, while promoting increased platform interaction.

Progress Bars and Levels

Progress bars and levels shape the user's progress and make it achievable. Both are very good at long-term motivational effects, because they simplify larger goals into smaller steps. For example, the language learning app Duolingo uses progress bars to track daily goals and levels, as a measure of overall mastery.

Virtual Economies and Rewards

Virtual economies deal with the digital currencies or goods that users obtain, spend, or trade. This system adds a strategic element to the gamified experience and involves investments in certain strategic moves. Virtual economies have become mainstream through games such as Fortnite, which have been increasingly adopted by brands. For example, on different e-commerce platforms, one obtains points that can be used for exclusive products or other types of discounts.

Customization and Avatars

Customisation allows users to create and tailor their experiences by building avatars or changing their virtual surroundings. Their ability to do so strengthened their emotional involvement and commitment. Online game sites such as Roblox illustrate a model in which users can create their own avatars and world models, which have been successfully applied in entertainment marketing campaigns.

Storytelling & Narration

Narrative-driven gamification involves telling a story about the user's experience. Campaigns with a narrative will help make brand messages more memorable and interactive, too. The Coca-Cola "Happiness Quest" engagement campaign allows users to engage in a game by completing storylines for rewards and sharing positive experiences.

Applications Across Industries

Retail-gamified loyalty programs are routinely deployed by retailers to stimulate repeat purchase. Sephora's Beauty Insider program provides tiered rewards, and apps like Klarna gamify shopping through exclusive deals and personalised recommendations.

Fitness and Wellness

They also use gamified features, such as challenges, leaderboards, and badges, which allow users to break out of their daily routines and attempt to reach their health goals through apps, such as MyFitnessPal and Fitbit. These features keep users engaged, making fitness tracking fun and fulfilling.

Education

Gamified learning is a popular educational trend that facilitates and improves learning. Platforms like Kahoot! Quizizz gamified learning using points, badges, and leaderboards. First, these tools were tested in a classroom or corporate training programme. An increasing number of financial apps are adding gamified features to promote savings and investment. For example, Qapital utilises visual progress bars and goal-setting challenges to make saving for specific goals easier for customers.

Entertainment and Media

Streaming platforms and media companies have adopted gamification for engagement optimisation. For example, Spotify personalises its playlists and rewards by listening to milestones using badges and prompting users to explore them.

Upcoming Features gaming

Gamification has a wide scope and has become a trend toward technological improvement. Which of the following technological advancements brings immersive experiences, merging digital and physical realities? Whether it is AI-driven personalisation for more tailored gamified experiences or the new age of digital ownership via blockchain non-fungible tokens (NFTs), the metaverse continues to evolve.

8 Implications for Marketing Practice

Gamification in Digital Marketing: Gamification is an exciting and innovative approach marketers use to enhance engagement, retention, and traction. However, game-like elements are insufficient for creating a successful campaign. Therefore, to maximise gamification, marketers need a strategic approach to implement gamification according to the goals of their brand and audience. The first element of gamification adoption had specific goals. Marketers must not be blinded to what they are trying to achieve, design website traffic, app downloads, or customer retention. For instance, the exercise brand Peloton utilises gamification elements to develop brand loyalty by providing users with challenges and milestones linked to its larger goal of health and shared experiences in a community. Gamification techniques must be aligned with the interests and behaviours of the target audience. Younger audiences, especially Gen Z and Millennials, tend to respond well to social competition and rewards, whereas older audiences tend to lean more towards functionality and ease of use. Designing gamified user experiences by combining these two elements and audience research is crucial. Gamified features should reinforce a brand's values and identity rather than detract from them (Papangeli & Fredmark, 2024). For instance, a luxury brand may use exclusive high-quality virtual rewards to maintain its premium image, whereas a playful, youth-focused brand may incorporate vibrant competitive games.

9 Gamification in Marketing to Drive Engagement

Loyalty programs are among the best possible uses of gamification. Brands use these to incentivise repeat purchases and drive loyalty through points, rewards, and tiered benefits. Starbucks' rewards have a tiered structure that has become increasingly rewarding, encouraging consumers to spend more time to access exclusive benefits. Dopamine is an attention-grabbing neurotransmitter that promotes interest and evokes an emotional bond between the brand and the consumer.

Interactive content turns passive social content viewers into active participants. Beauty brands, including L' Oréal, have adopted virtual features that allow users to experiment with makeup products. This creates an entertaining interactive experience. However, users are more likely to convert because they can make informed purchase decisions. Gamification ties in social engagement encourage users to share their achievements and to participate in community activities. While not all campaigns have to game-fy this way, a brilliant case of slightly gamifying a campaign and going viral is the recent #IceBucketChallenge that leveraged social sharing to increase ALS awareness. This framework includes leaderboards, collaborative tasks, social media challenges, and any form of gamification that provides a sense of community and promotes customer loyalty.

Time-sensitive gamification creates an urgency for users to take immediate action such as flash sales or limited-time rewards. Amazon and other e-commerce platforms employ countdown timers to generate conversions during their sales events. Typically, fitness apps for men face weekly challenges and unique rewards throughout the week to ensure that users do not become bored. Artificial intelligence can allow brands to tailor gamified experiences according to user behaviour and preferences. For example, Netflix uses AI to recommend programming and reward users for achievements, such as total hours watched or finishing a series. Personalisation helps make gamified content more relevant, engaging, and impactful. AR technologies can provide gamified experiences even richer by linking real and digital worlds. Retailers such as IKEA use AR to give users a preview of how furniture might look in their homes, creating a gamified shopping experience that increases customer satisfaction and buyer confidence.

10 Applications Across Marketing Channels

Social Media Marketing

Social media platforms provide ideal conditions for gamified campaigns, because both platforms operate through viral mechanisms and user engagement. The interactive features of Instagram polls, together with Snapchat filters and TikTok challenges, help brands establish fun connections with their audience. The fitness brand launched a TikTok dance challenge, which serves as a product marketing method to engage users who have become active creators of new content.

Email Marketing

The application of gamification techniques has produced new vitality in the existing email-marketing strategies. Your promotional emails will receive greater attention through interactive gaming features, attracting users to spin the wheel game or to scratch off their rewards. The fashion retailer ASOS sends gamified email campaigns to users, offering special discounts that enhance customer interaction and business revenue.

Mobile Apps

Mobile apps provide unique interfaces for gamified engagement. To keep users glued, in-app notifications, geolocation-based achievements and incentives are important. Fitness apps based on Fitbit use these elements to promote daily activities, whereas language-learning apps, such as Duolingo, keep users on board with streak counts and progress tracking.

E-commerce Platforms

Gamified features, such as virtual try-ons, personalised suggestions, and loyalty programs can enhance online shopping experiences. Sephora's Beauty Insider program is a great example of how gamification can improve customer retention and encourage repeat purchases.

Ethics of Gamification

The vast potential of gamification is accompanied by ethical challenges which marketers must address in order to maintain customer trust and reputation. Gamification techniques can effectively motivate users to remain compatible with their knowledge deficits. The use of streaks and rewards as incentives leads users to adopt addictive patterns without their understanding. Companies must develop strategies that positively affect customers' health outcomes. Personalised gamified experiences depend on user data collection; however, brands must protect this information by being transparent about their data protection measures. Customers become reluctant to share details when they hear data leaks from the companies. The entertainment features of gamified content must have a proper balance with its operational effectiveness. Brands that provide too many secondary functions lose their valuable core communications and degrade their assessment of the program value.

11 Measuring the Impact of Gamification

To evaluate the success of gamified campaigns, marketers must track key performance indicators (KPIs) such as:

1. Engagement Metrics: Click-through Rates, Time Spent, and Social Share
2. Retention Rates: Frequency of user interactions.
3. Conversion Rates: The percentage of users who take desired actions, such as purchases or sign-ups.
4. Customer Feedback: Surveys and reviews that gauge user satisfaction with gamified features.

12 Case Studies and Applications

Gamification has evolved as a potential marketing tool for digital platforms. It has been used across multiple sectors from retail and fitness to education, entertainment, and finance. Case studies identified brands that introduce gaming features to drive engagement, build customer loyalty, and meet marketing goals.

1 Nike: NikePlus Nike Run Club

Nike's most impactful marketing achievements stem from its gamified operations in which the Nike Plus loyalty program connects to the Nike Run Club app. Using NikePlus, users are intrinsically motivated to spend money buying and advocating Nike products. Participants can accumulate points through their membership activities to unlock unique benefits, including first access to new product releases and customised fitness plans. Within the Nike Run Club app, users gain access to social leaderboards and virtual prizes together with competitive features. Users have the opportunity to participate in running competitions based on 10 thousand and 20 thousand steps, because these events help them gain virtual badges toward their targets. The system builds personal user drives, and establishes a social group of fitness users. Brand loyalty strengthened alongside user interactions with Nike products and their services became the result.

2 Starbucks: Starbucks Rewards Program

The Starbucks Rewards customer loyalty program achieved gamification success by increasing customer returns and loyalty retention rates. Customers who join Starbucks Rewards accumulate stars from their transactions, enabling them to claim free drinks, food products, and company-branded merchandise. The reward system provides different benefits which motivate consumers to spend more money on accessing new advantages in the program. The program introduces double-star days during specific seasonal events, which creates momentary excitement along with a sense of urgency among participants. The gamified Starbucks Rewards demonstrate how brand-customer habit formation occurs through gamified approaches. Starbucks' app integration enables users to monitor their achievements, receive specific deals, and participate in interactive marketing activities that elevate their total customer journey.

3 Pokémon GO: Location-Based Augmented Reality

Niantic's Pokémon GO is one of the most famous examples of successful location-based gamification through the integration of real-world spaces with digital gameplay experiences. Pokémon GO players complete missions outdoors using their mobile devices to locate Pokémon in real-world locations. This behaviour drives them to travel to different places and interact socially. The marketing buzz of the app attracted customers to sponsored locations such as McDonald's and Starbucks, who utilised this visitor increase to promote their products. Through this campaign, the company demonstrated that AR and gamified features could lead people to actively participate in the physical space and simultaneously generate brand visibility at the same time. The spectacular success of Pokémon Go fuelled special interest in applying game mechanisms to location-based market elements across various commercial domains Table 12.2.

Table 12.1 Overview of industry-specific applications of gamification

Industry	Gamified program/Example	Key gamification features	Impact/Outcome
Retail	Sephora's beauty insider	Points, tiered rewards, interactive features	Increased customer loyalty and repeat visits
Fitness	Fitbit and Strava	Badges, challenges, leaderboards	Encouraged regular participation and competition
Education	Duolingo	Streaks, progress bars, achievement badges	Improved engagement and learning satisfaction
Entertainment	Spotify's wrapped	Personalised insights, social sharing	Enhanced user satisfaction and brand connection
Finance	Qapital and acorns	Visual progress, gamified goal-setting	Boosted user motivation to save and invest

13 Industry-Specific Applications of Gamification

Sephora's program, Beauty Insider, brings gameification elements to the consumer purchase experience by rewarding both spending and usage levels. Points are earned with every dollar spent, which can be traded for priority access to limited offers, priority access to sales, and extra perks. The tiered system of the program entails that customers spend more money to gain additional perks. Additionally, Sephora features interactive elements within its app and virtual try-ons using augmented reality (AR). These gameified elements improve the purchasing experience and reinforce customer and brand loyalty.

Exercise apps such as Strava and Fitbit add game-like functionality to encourage people to achieve fitness and health targets. Physical exercise is tracked using Fitbit, and badges and praise are offered to achieve certain targets, such as covered miles or calories burned. It has functionality that enables users to compete with or against one another, competing against or cooperating with one another, thus fostering a sense of togetherness and competitiveness. Comparing performance at specific routes with one another across the world and playing in a cooperative competitive environment are functionalities that users find delectable. These functionalities intensify the competitiveness of fitness tracking and motivate users to develop sustainable habits.

Duolingo, a language-learning app, is a perfect example of gamification in education. The app uses streaks, progress bars, and achievement badges to attract and motivate the users. Duolingo content is broken down into bite-sized chunks, with rewards for achieving daily goals or moving through levels. Duolingo's gamified approach to learning has made language learning easy and fun, with more than 500 million downloads worldwide. This phenomenon demonstrates how gamification turns mundane, boring work into thrilling and interesting experiences.

In the context of content gamification, Spotify's annual wrapping project creates custom summaries of users' listening tastes. Users are given an extensive review of their regularly played songs, loved artists, and the most popular genres depicted both creatively and interactively. Spotify helps facilitate the distribution of these wrapped summaries as material for wider social media campaigns, thus enhancing the visibility of the campaign. This is a good example of how content gamification increases brand loyalty. The recognition of personal tastes deepens user involvement and improves engagement across platforms.

A good example is Qapital, which allows users to set savings targets and automatically trigger deposit schedules based on certain behaviours including rounding transaction amounts. The combination of milestone incentives and visual representations of progress creates sustained motivation. Similarly, Acorns encourages small investments through gamification to make portfolio growth more visible. All these features help make financial planning accessible, especially to those with low to middle incomes who would otherwise find the topic intimidating.

McDonald's monopoly campaign was one of the first examples of implementing gamification elements for the worldwide promotion of products. The campaign combines traditional gaming methods with modern digital features, making it compatible with a wide range of mobile applications. Customers collect game pieces with their purchases, qualifying for a variety of awards, including free food and large amounts of money. The game component of this program effectively sustains consumers' purchasing habits and creates a feeling of expectation. McDonald's monopoly is a promotional exercise that seamlessly marries nostalgia with modern ideas.

14 Emerging Trends and Future Directions in Gamification

As technology develops and consumer expectations change, gamification evolves, thereby providing new opportunities for brands to attract viewers. Technologies Approaching Gamified Marketing: AI, AR, VR, Blockchain, and Metaverse, discussed these developments and their significance for the future of gamification in this section.

Artificial Intelligence (AI)

AI transforms gamification by enabling brands to offer personalised experiences. Using user data analytics, AI can gain an understanding of preferences, provide personalised rewards, modify challenges according to skill levels, and cater to individual preferences. The dynamic personalisation of gamified experiences enhances engagement, making it more realistic and enjoyable. Netflix and other companies use AI to provide tailored content recommendations and celebrate milestones in the usage of that system (in a friendly manner), such as finishing a show or watching a certain number of hours. Similarly, fitness apps can adjust challenges to ability so that goals remain attainable while still in demand. AI chatbots can gamify customer service by converting conversations into quizzes, puzzles, or interactive tasks. For instance, a retail chatbot may provide discounts to complete a trivia challenge involving a brand's products. AI can also offer immediate feedback to users, helping reinforce behaviour and elevate the overall gamified experience. Educational applications such as Duolingo use AI technology to comprehend user knowledge and create custom learning plans that increase retention and progress.

15 Augmented Reality (AR) and Virtual Reality (VR) in Gamification

Augmented and virtual reality technologies are expanding the scope of gamification, providing immersive experiences that bridge physical and digital worlds. These technologies enable users to interact in ways that traditional marketing cannot provide brands with entirely new ways of attracting specific audiences. Retailers such as Sephora and IKEA use AR to allow users to try makeup or view furniture in their homes. Gamification enhances the shopping experience and reduces buyer resistance. Pokémon GO's use of AR showed the potential for gamification to promote real-world engagement. Other brands, including tourism boards, have used these strategies to establish scavenger hunts and interactive tours in cities. Brands can create stories that are driven by gamification, which places users in immersive VR environments. For instance, car manufacturers such as Mercedes-Benz launched virtual showrooms, allowing users to explore cars in a gamified environment. VR is used more frequently in corporate training, in which gamified simulations allow employees to practice real-world scenarios in safe environments. Walmart employed virtual reality gamification to prepare employees to handle Black Friday crowds.

16 Blockchain and Non-Fungible Tokens (NFTs)

As more games are created around web3 elements, we see that blockchain technology paves the way for secure and transparent systems that revolve around digital ownership. Rather, unique digital assets, such as non-fungible tokens, have taken the world by storm and are increasingly used in gamified campaigns. Brands can create limited-edition NFTs as prizes for gamification For example, if a fashion brand wants to perform a 1–2-week challenge to provide exclusive items to users, it may face challenges. Blockchain: Blockchain technology ensures transparency in gamified loyalty programmes. This allows users to securely track their rewards and transactions. This fosters trust and motivates individuals to be more involved. Blockchain can also be used to build decentralised virtual economies in which users can trade digital goods earned through gamified interactions. Virtual economies that significantly boost user involvement are best illustrated by gaming platforms, such as Decentraland.

The Metaverse

Metaverse represents a shared virtual space that users connect through avatars during sharing activities. This emerging platform will deliver the next-generation approach for gamified marketing. The combination of augmented reality functions and virtual reality content through blockchain technology provides brands with innovative methods for creating lively interactive engagement between themselves and consumers. Metaverse platforms enable businesses to create branded spaces in which users can participate in challenges, attend events, or shop for products in gamified virtual environments. Metaverse enables gamification to acquire social features through implementation. Brands can develop multiplayer games, collaborative challenges, and live metaverse events. Users in metaverse gamified commerce systems receive digital currency and rewards to exchange experiences that include virtual items, physical products, and purchase opportunities. Users who reach specific milestones in virtual gameplay would gain access to special discounted items and limited-time exclusive products.

17 Emerging Consumer Behaviours

The growing dominance of digital natives in the marketplace drives changes that transform marketing approaches through the requirements for customised experiences and interactive content. The new trend in audience consumption involves younger generations choosing interactive media over traditional static advertising formats. The transformation of marketing messages into playable content through a gamification strategy satisfies user preferences. Customers tend to prefer awards which provide real value or match their personal values. Brands that provide custom incentives and social responsibility programs achieve higher market success rates. Public knowledge of ethical and privacy issues related to customer data grows daily among consumers. Any successful gamification system depends on clear communication and sincere interactions between brands and clients.

18 Challenges and Ethical Considerations

Gamification creates significant opportunities to improve brand loyalty, yet it causes specific implementation difficulties for market operators. The popularity of gamified marketing methods produces multiple issues that encompass both viewer exhaustion and privacy violations, together with emotional manipulation confrontations. A review of such challenges follows, together with recommendations for their solutions.

19 Challenges in Gamified Marketing

1 **Audience Fatigue and Over-Saturation**

As a result, with gamification making its way into every industry, consumers may become accustomed or even desensitised to gamified elements. Treatment with leaderboards, badges, points, etc., with similar mechanics can lead to diminishing marginal returns. For example, when several brands in the same industry adopt the same approach, they become redundant, diminishing the impact of such campaigns. To fight fatigue, marketers must continually evolve and develop new and creative types of gamification. By integrating personalisation and unique narratives along with emerging technologies such as AR and VR, bid managers can hold the attention of users and create campaigns that set themselves apart from the rest.

2 **Accessibility Barriers**

More advanced gamified experiences (e.g. those leveraging AR, VR, or blockchain) may not be available to every audience. The data show that some demographic groups are excluded because of the high cost of devices or limited technological literacy, leading to an unbalanced starting point. Brands must create gamified experiences that include everyone and provide simplified versions for those who may not be on the latest technology. For instance, VR applications may target tech-savvy users, but a complementary mobile-friendly version can maintain accessibility for more users.

3 **Measurement and ROI Challenges**

It can be challenging to measure the return on investment (ROI) for gamified campaigns. Although metrics such as clicks, shares, and time spent are measurable, few find a clear link between these and tangible business outcomes, such as sales or customer retention. Marketers should set clear KPIs that take gamification beyond their walls, tying them to higher-level business goals. A balance of qualitative feedback with quantitative metrics can lead to greater wholeness in success evaluation.

4 **Maintaining User Interest Over Time**

Maintaining engagement in gamified initiatives, especially campaigns that run over the long term, is another approach. Once users complete the available challenges or maximise rewards, they lose the incentive to continue. Regularly update with new content, levels, or challenges, and seasonal or time-limited events to keep the user returning. For example, gaming apps often bring limited-time prizes or seasonal challenges to keep things exciting.

20 Ethical Considerations in Gamified Marketing

Data Privacy and Security

Many gamified experiences depend on user data aggregates to customise content or monitor progress. However, collecting too much data or not clarifying policies may stir up privacy concerns. Consumers are concerned about how their data is being used, especially if brands are leaving themselves open to issues with regulations such as the General Data Protection Regulation (GDPR). Brands need to specify what data is collected, how it will be used, and what measures are in place to protect user information. The need for opt-in consent and compliance with data protection laws.

1 Psychological Manipulation

Some gamification tactics exploit the psychological principles behind things, such as loss aversion or habit formation, in ways that can be considered underhanded. Streaks can also add unnecessary pressure or guilt when users fail to maintain them. Gamification is performed ethically; however, it values user well-being. Brands require experience that serves users and offers them fulfilling benefits rather than taking advantage of their vulnerabilities. Including the ability to pause and avoid penalising streaks helps to reduce unnecessary stress.

2 Inclusivity and Fairness

Another crucial factor that gamification considers is the diversity of the user groups. For example, inaccessibility to rewards for users in specific regions or the non-availability of a specific physical ability required for tasks can drive away some part of the audience. Inclusive design practices must be followed when the content is gamified. Virtual rewards or experiences can be tailored to diverse cultural, regional, and physical environments.

3 Ethical Marketing Practices

Some brands may gamify to distract themselves from the less-attractive features of a product or service. For example, gamified features can distract individuals from high costs, hidden fees, and other negative characteristics. Transparent and honest marketing practices align with ethical gamification. Gamified campaigns should align with the relevant core values of the brand and offer real user value, and marketers should be mindful of this.

21 Balancing Entertainment and Responsibility

Gamification involves a balance between entertainment and responsibility. Moving past the threshold where users are "engaged", marketers need to tread carefully so that they do not take advantage of and isolate them. Clarify the purpose of the gamified elements, rules of participation, and user data that will be used. Gamification experiences for users. Value-added offerings of entertainment, education, or tangible rewards. Test with Users in Everyone: Regularly test with both regular users and other vital user groups to ensure that gamified elements are enjoyable, fair, and ethical. The input is used to further refine the campaigns. Users can learn how a gamified system operates. For example, how points can be accumulated and how rewards can be redeemed. This creates trust and reduces misunderstandings. Gamification can create awareness of social issues and encourage audiences to donate to the cause or participate in socially responsible shopping or sustainable behaviours. Apps that reward eco-responsibility, such as cutting carbon emissions or recycling, tie involvement to socially engaging results.

22 Conclusion

Gamification has transformed online business, in terms of how companies engage consumers. Having previously been passive advertizing, it is now dynamic and interactive business experiences which indirectly involve consumers throughout the buying process with point schemes, leader boards, challenges, and other game-type functionality. This meets the increasing requirement for personalization, interactivity, and contextually related engagement, especially from younger, technology-conscious consumers. Gamification leverages human psychology, engaging intrinsic and extrinsic drivers of behavior to propel user activity. A variety of theories, such as Uses and Gratifications Theory, Flow Theory, and Self—Self-Determination Theory, provide primary theoretical foundations that enhance the effectiveness of the approach. Leveled, structured gamified experiences forge intense emotional connections, satisfying audience psychologies of achievement, autonomy, and social belonging, yielding highly engaged behavior.

Why should a company pursue gamification? Renowned global brands like Nike, Starbucks, and Duolingo demonstrate that gamification can be adapted to any business model. Whether promoting fitness goals, fostering consumer loyalty, or making language learning enjoyable, gamification can be tailored to various niches, transforming sectors from retail to education to finance to entertainment. Emerging technologies—such as AI, AR, VR, blockchain, and the metaverse—expand the possibilities of gamification. This innovation unlocks hyper-personalised, immersive experiences that blend the physical and digital realms. For instance, AR—enabled virtual try—ons and VR—based simulations illustrate how technology can enhance engagement in gamified marketing campaigns.

Nevertheless, several constraints inherent with gamification have the potential to hinder engagement and minimize interaction, most noticeably, audience weariness. The existence of access issues with regards to gamification can lead to an environment with a lot more consumerism than engagement. For brands to abide by ethical standards, there is a need to emphasize inclusivity, transparency, and users' well-being. There is a need for designers to establish trust with a brand because ethical gamification is all about infusing long-term meaning in brands. The future of gamification will be about connecting evolving consumer behaviors to an evolving technology landscape. All marketing in the future across all media platforms will be driven by trends like AI-driven personalization and gamification-driven sustainability. With these advancements, brands can become more competitive and robust. Gamification's benefits extend beyond merely engaging an audience immediately, including long-term benefits like deeper brand loyalty, longer retention, and improved ROI. The revolution makes consumer-brand interaction vivid and not boring, thus revolutionizing the interaction between brands and consumers. Gamification routines encourage sharing and collaboration, commemorating moments of success for the users and collaborating to achieve shared objectives, which increase the visibility of campaigns.

Gamification cannot be considered a short-run fad but as consumer behavior business as a normative practice. It eclectically integrates innovation, technology, and consumer trends, thus becoming one of the best methods of generating interest and developing long-lasting relationships. As a core component of successful advertising campaigns within an increasingly changing digital era, its ability to combine entertainment, utility, and innovation is a core component of maintaining momentum under dispersed consumer attention. Its powerfulness, however, to a large extent depends on its practice, hence ethical issues, adaptability to emerging technologies, and compatibility with consumer tastes are essential attributes determining maximal involvement. Because gamification is greater than a methodology, it is now a paradigm that redefines business-to-consumer relationships, digital transformation's emphasis on engagement has voice through it as a responsive model for creating deep connections and maintaining sustainable brand loyalty.

References

Abdel Halim, N. (2025). The impact of Gamification on brand engagement and loyalty: A study of brand events. *Journal of Design Sciences and Applied Arts, 6*(1), 38–62.

Brubaker, R. (2020). Digital hyperconnectivity and the self. *Theory and Society, 49*, 771–801.

Chan, E. Y. (2024). Consumer behavior in practice. Springer, 1007, 978-3.

Csikszentmihalyi, M. (1990). *Flow: The psychology of optimal experience.* Harper & Row.

Davis, F. D., Bagozzi, R. P., & Warshaw, P. R. (1989). Technology acceptance model. *Journal Management Science, 35*(8), 982–1003.

Deci, E. L., & Ryan, R. M. (2012). Self-determination theory. *Handbook of Theories of Social Psychology, 1*(20), 416–436.

Deterding, S., Dixon, D., Khaled, R., & Nacke, L. (2011). From game design elements to gamefulness: Defining gamification. *Proceedings of the 15th International Academic MindTrek Conference*, 9–15. https://doi.org/10.1145/2181037.2181040.

Dwiandini, A. (2024). The use of social media influencers as a digital marketing strategy in generation Z. *JHSS (Journal of Humanities and Social Studies), 8*(1), 057–063.

Emrich, T. (2024). *The next dimension: How to use augmented reality for business growth in the era of spatial computing*. John Wiley & Sons.

Keelson, S. A., Bruce, E., Egala, S. B., Amoah, J., & Bashiru Jibril, A. (2024). Driving forces of social media and its impact on tourists' destination decisions: A uses and gratification theory. *Cogent Social Sciences, 10*(1), 2318878.

Malott, R. W. (2021). *Principles of behavior*. Routledge.

Nussenbaum, K., & Hartley, C. A. (2024). Understanding the development of reward learning through the lens of meta-learning. *Nature Reviews Psychology*, 1–15.

Oliveira, M., Abelha, A., Sousa, R., & Peixoto, H. (2024). Gamification in mobile applications: Techniques, benefits and challenges. *Procedia Computer Science, 251*, 678–683.

Papangeli, D., & Fredmark, I. X. (2024). *Gamified Brand Building: Brand Empowerment in Video Games.*

Remondes, J., Madeira, P., & Alves, C. (Eds.). (2024). *Connecting with consumers through effective personalization and programmatic advertising*. IGI Global.

Tembulkar, A. (2024). Gamification as an influencer for consumer behavior and engagement. In *Marketing and Gamification* (pp. 41–56). Routledge.

Wilson, M. (2024). *Relational Marketing: Case Studies and Best Practices in Multisensory Design, Gamification and Empathetic Communication to Cultivate Brand Experiences.*

Leveraging Machine Learning for Enhanced Online Marketing Activities

Pratiksha Jha, Vivek Aggarwal, and Ujjwal Kalra

Abstract

In today's digitally connected marketplace, the use of machine learning (ML) in online marketing has shifted from being a novel enhancement to a core necessity. This chapter explores the growing significance of ML technologies in reshaping how businesses interact with customers, manage operations, and develop strategies in e-commerce. It focuses on real-world applications of various machine learning models such as decision trees, neural networks, support vector machines, and ensemble methods to highlight how they support more informed decision-making and customised user experiences. The chapter places strong emphasis on practical implementations. It begins with a detailed discussion of personalised recommendation engines, which have evolved to consider individual preferences, browsing patterns, and contextual factors. It then moves into the realm of dynamic pricing, where algorithms adapt prices in real time based on demand, competition, and consumer behaviour. In addition, the chapter highlights how businesses are using ML to forecast sales, manage inventory efficiently, and reduce both surplus and shortages in stock. Security and customer trust are also explored through the lens of fraud detection systems powered by ML, which can identify suspicious activities with high precision. The chapter also examines customer service innovation through AI-driven chatbots that understand natural language, helping companies provide faster, more responsive support. Beyond that, it investigates how customer segmentation and sentiment analysis help marketers design more relevant campaigns and understand consumer emotions more deeply. This chapter does more than explain technology it connects these tools to business impact. Through examples and clear analysis,

P. Jha (✉) · U. Kalra
School of Business and Management, Christ University, Bengaluru, India
e-mail: pratikshajha09@gmail.com

V. Aggarwal
School of Business, Galgotias University, Greater Noida, India

© The Author(s), under exclusive license to Springer Nature Singapore Pte Ltd. 2026
N. S. Jayawardena et al. (eds.), *Digital Advertising and Consumer Behavior*,
Management for Professionals, https://doi.org/10.1007/978-981-95-7809-2_13

it demonstrates how machine learning helps businesses remain agile, customer-focused, and competitive. The goal is to show not just what ML can do but how it can be thoughtfully applied to meet evolving consumer expectations in a fast-paced digital economy.

1 Introduction

Commerce has been transformed through digital transformation, and how businesses and consumers operate has changed for good. In the world of e-commerce platforms that are growing in scale and complexity, the ability to understand and predict customer behaviour has become a fundamental part of a successful business in such a competitive environment. Machine learning (ML) in online retail has become a powerful enabler of innovation to process extensive data and derive actionable insights. Businesses can use sophisticated algorithms to provide more personalised, efficient, and secure shopping experiences and gain customer satisfaction and business growth (Fedorko et al., 2022).

The data that defines e-commerce success is the ability to make informed decisions. Every click, search, and purchase leaves a trail of valuable information from customers behind. Machine learning algorithms transform this data into functional patterns that allow businesses to predict trends, determine consumers' preferences, and react to the dynamics. This chapter explores how Random Forests, Decision Trees, K-nearest neighbours, Neural Networks, and Support Vector Machines are being used to revolutionise critical e-commerce functions and how businesses do business with their customers. Personalised recommendations are one of the most significant impacts of ML in e-commerce (Gupta & Pathak, 2014).

Traditional recommendation systems are no longer limited to giving you product suggestions but instead analyse your browsing histories, purchase habits, and even real-time behaviour to provide you with the most relevant and **personalised recommendations** possible (Kashyap et al., 2022). These systems are improved by advanced algorithms such as deep learning models, which can incorporate other complex factors such as season and geographic location. For instance, if the right platforms are used, Amazon can use these techniques to recommend products to users individually, leading to engagement and sales (Fig. 1).

Another opportunity where ML has transformed is in **dynamic pricing**. Using real-time data on customer demand, competitor pricing, and actual historical trends, ML algorithms let businesses behave dynamically by adjusting prices whenever needed. That's how it is done so that the cash flow during peak periods, such as holiday sales, is not hampered, but the customers are satisfied. Algorithms such as Gradient Boosting Machines (GBMs) and reinforcement learning models allow e-commerce platforms to react to sudden market fluctuations on real-time takers by developing more agile pricing strategies (Gupta & Bansal, 2020).

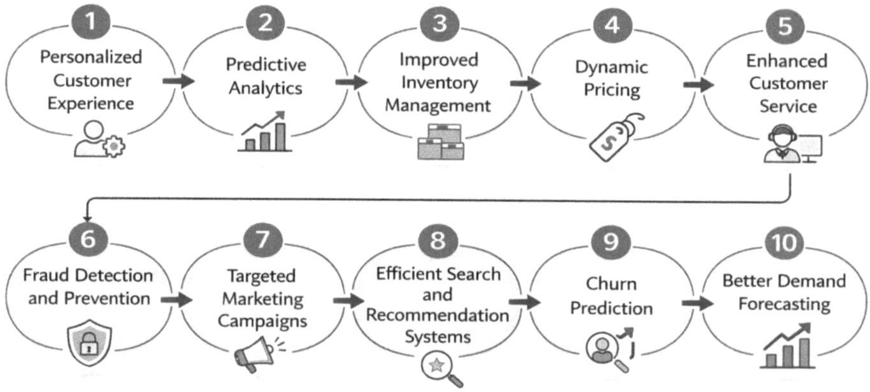

Fig. 1 Key advantages of utilizing machine learning in e-commerce. *Source* Authors

Even **sales forecasting and inventory management** have arrived at a prompt with machine learning. It is essential to have good forecasting to keep sufficient inventory and prevent stock out or overstocking. Long Short-Term Memory (LSTM) networks are algorithms that pronounce seasonal patterns and promotional effects, help the company optimise its supply chain, and minimise operational costs. That way, customers always get exactly what they're looking for, boosting satisfaction and loyalty (Singh, 2024).

Nevertheless, the exceptionally high development of online shopping has also amplified the risk of fraud and, in addition, requires strong fraud surveillance frameworks because they can hinder both merchants and consumers. They analyse transaction data for anomalies within the framework of ML techniques, such as Neural Networks and Random Forests (Alsayat, 2023; Samrat, 2022). These systems act as a shield for businesses and consumers to alert unusual behaviours like abnormal purchasing patterns or transactions from unusual locations. The security is further furthered with real-time fraud detection, making e-commerce platforms seem more trustworthy and confident (Samrat, 2022).

Regarding customer service, **AI-powered chatbots** have made an enormous difference. Chatbots that use NLP models like GPT and BERT fit the description of these, giving immediate, reliable responses to customer questions to mitigate reliance on human agents. As you keep interacting with them in the past, they learn and keep improving to answer complex questions in a way that makes sense, making the support experience as seamless and prompt as possible. The next big thing in this space is voice commerce and virtual assistants, where customers can shop hands-free and access support with minimal friction (Fedorko et al., 2022).

It is demonstrated that machine learning can also play a key role in **targeted marketing and consumer segmentation** in e-commerce. Businesses group customers based on behaviours, preferences, and purchasing history, using techniques such as K-Means Clustering and DBSCAN. That allows for hyper-personalized marketing campaigns that drive engagement and conversions. Beyond providing quantifiable statistics, sentiment analysis brings another level of insight as you leverage customer feedback, social media posts, or reviews to understand customer sentiment and help businesses adjust their strategy accordingly.

As we live in an era when consumer expectations are on a higher note than at any other time, machine learning is more than just a tool–it is a need. Using the power of ML, businesses can not only meet but exceed customer needs to create loyalty and fuel growth in a competitive environment. In this chapter, we will dig deep into these transformative technologies and take you through how they could play a key role in transforming e-commerce by exploring these transformative technologies. Additionally, this chapter examines the **research methodologies** behind these advancements. Through case studies of feature engineering data preparation model selection and evaluation processes, we can develop a comprehensive understanding of the factors that influence machine learning and drive the success of e-commerce. Techniques like this aid in demonstrating the importance of coordinating technology with operational tasks in order to create more individualized, effective, and safe shopping experiences.

2 Advanced Personalized Recommendations

In order to enhance the user experience by making recommendations for goods and content that are uniquely tailored to each user, contemporary e-commerce platforms rely on the art of personalized recommendation systems. The strength of these systems lies in a set of strong algorithms that attempt to interpret user behaviour and predict what a user would wish to buy or look at next. Deep learning, matrix factorization, and collaborative filtering are some of the methods that make these systems successful. Collaborative filtering compares people with similar tastes and looks at what other items are related to the product under consideration in order to find trends in what customers have done with the product. Matrix factorization, on the other hand, reveals hidden correlations between users and products by breaking down large users of individual interaction datasets into smaller, easier handleable elements. Highly sophisticated neural networks, known as deep learning, are able to learn intricate behaviours like browsing habits and past purchases (Kashyap et al., 2022).

One problem for these systems is the cold start problem, the situation where there is little data about a new user or product. To this end, platforms employ a cocktail of methods, including using demographic information or going directly to content-based approaches where recommendations are driven by product attributes rather than user behaviour. For instance, Amazon excels at item-based collaborative filtering, where other items for purchased items are suggested. Deep Learning is used in Spotify to generate personalised playlists, and Netflix merges a few approaches to keep users involved with content.

It's not enough, technology alone. These systems work only to an extent, and understanding human psychology is essential for their success. There's a higher likelihood that people will trust or engage with recommendations when they feel that they're relevant and in mind. A person's pleasure may be lowered by cognitive biases they may encounter, such as choice overload (being overwhelmed by too many options). Platforms like Netflix and Amazon have stepped up to the plate and are making a concerted effort to provide users with a comprehensive understanding of what is happening on the site. Furthermore, these systems feature feedback loops. For instance, they may ask users to rate content or items, which will be utilized to improve and further refine recommendations later on.

The use of generative AI models in personalized recommendations is another fascinating development. More than just making product suggestions, these sophisticated algorithms are able to create completely new experiences from the ground up. For example, they can create highly customized advertisements, write product descriptions that are unique to each user, or even forecast the emotional effects of specific recommendations. This results in a type of personalization that becomes aware of both your desires and emotions (Kumar et al., 2024).

In the end, personalized recommendation systems are changing the way we shop, watch and listen. They bring forward a seamless journey where every interaction counts, even as you stumble on to a new favourite movie or discover the perfect product at the perfect time. As artificial intelligence gets more sophisticated, these systems are going to be even more accurate in predicting not just what users explicitly want but what users don't want explicitly, but also what they don't know that they want. In fact, the future of e-commerce is about connecting, creating experiences, and letting shoppers experience you—and not just your products.

3 Dynamic Pricing Algorithms and Strategies

Since dynamic pricing is now an essential requirement for e-commerce companies and others who can modify the prices in real-time based on various factors, it makes its way onto the scene today. These strategies are based on the core of advanced machine learning (ML) algorithms, which analyse large volumes of data to set the most optimal price points. Gradient Boosting Machines (GBMs) are very effective in price prediction, as GBMs consider a series of factors and variables, such as consumer decisions. Support Vector Machines (SVMs) "round off", therefore, by applying marketing price strategy (which comes from data) based on past behaviour to be able to make a "price decision", which will be based on evidence (Gupta & Pathak, 2014).

Reinforcement learning is especially suited for dynamic pricing systems since it learns by interacting. The models approximate a market in that they can learn the most optimal pricing policies for adjusting their prices over time depending on the changing market. Ride-sharing services, e.g., Uber, employ surge pricing to associate supply and demand. Fares go up when there is high demand and limited supply—the more the fares go up, the more the drivers are willing to hit the road, and the better the customers are served with rides. Dynamic pricing also allows retailers to use information like customers' browsing history, annual shopping patterns, and even social media patterns to set prices. It also yields the maximum profit but also has the effect that the pricing strategy appears fair, i.e., the customer perceives other customer's valuation reflected in the price (Gupta & Pathak, 2014; Singh, 2024).

Dynamic pricing strategies depend heavily on real-time factors. Prices may be altered to competitive-based price changes, unforeseen changes due to consumer demand, and general economic factors such as inflation or market trends. (Gupta & Pathak, 2014). Through their price algorithms, retailers continuously adjust these factors, enabling them to respond quickly to changes in the market. It is aware that it offers incredibly low pricing for goods that no one wants to purchase.

The dynamic pricing model is a popular strategy that aims to increase algorithm efficiency for customer pleasure. A business can use algorithms to be profitable and competitive, but it must also evaluate how these prices are found. Both businesses and customers benefit from dynamic pricing as long as there is a sound pricing strategy and transparency. Companies that employ artificial intelligence (AI) and machine learning (ML) for pricing will continue to come up with new and creative approaches to optimize their pricing strategy in the face of market competition (Gupta & Pathak, 2014).

Dynamic pricing is fraught with difficulties; however, if customers believe in an unfairly high markup, however true it may be, when demand is high, these tactics can appear unfair. If this is true, enterprises in the area are on the cusp of becoming more open and ethical regarding pricing. To reduce that risk, companies can pre-emptively disclose prices of items and use fairness-aware algorithms. Some companies are thinking about complementary methods, e.g. the use of subscription models, where a provider delivers a regular level of value and thereby provides a drive to greater long-term customer loyalty.

4 Predictive Sales Forecasting and Inventory Management

The twenty-first-century e-commerce and retail business heavily relies on predictive sales forecasting and inventory control. Advanced technology predicts future sales trends in these systems and ensures that the business has the correct inventory levels. Accuracy in predicting sales enables savings in costs, prevents stockouts, and leads to better customer satisfaction as these companies are able to deliver when and where they want.

Sales forecasting is a big part of machine learning. This is mainly due to techniques such as Long Short Term Memory (LSTM) networks that are purely effective in the long-term cycle analysis or the sales pattern, e.g. the Christmas weekend cycle or purchase patterns of holidays. For example, traditional statistical models such as ARIMA (Autoregressive, Integrated, Moving Average) are robust for short-term predictions of time series data with clear seasonality. Finally, many businesses use these methods in combination with what is called ensemble models since the combination results in higher accuracy in their forecasts. Economic conditions, weather patterns, and consumer sentiment data to make them as reliable as possible. For example, companies modify inventory when there is an economic downturn or a core event that triggers a change in consumer behaviour (Gupta & Bansal, 2020).

While realising these systems is not easy! It is also possible for data collection errors to happen; seasonal patterns can be perverse, and often, manufacturers have given rise to bizarre spikes in demand from unexpected promotional events. Businesses should tackle these issues because they pre-process their data carefully, removing errors and putting in external factors like holidays or marketing campaigns. This helps businesses better balance supply and demand, which lowers overstocking and inventory shortages.

Premium products can be identified with the use of predictive analytics. These well-liked products can be sold by retailers without making room for less well-liked ones. It serves to reduce waste and overstocking. Moreover, supply chain management has advanced with cloud-based websites for real-time inventory tracking. By offering real-time stock information, they help businesses keep a tight ship and react swiftly to shifting customer demands. Blockchain technology and the Internet of Things (IoT) have the potential to revolutionize inventory management. When combined, they seem much more imaginative. Real-time monitoring of IoT devices and the collection of inventory data across warehouses are both possible with smart sensors (Gupta et al., 2022; Treiblmaier, 2018).

Blockchain technology ensures the authenticity and trackability of supply chain transactions and ensures businesses and consumers of the process provenance. Together, sensing technologies create a transparent and resilient supply chain that ensures that products are available at times customers want them while also remaining trustworthy and accountable (Gupta & Pathak, 2014). Businesses can employ these advancements to improve operations, which will enhance the overall consumer experience. Predictive sales forecasting and inventory management ensure that products are constantly available, delivery times are shortened, and expenses are minimized. They are a significant step in building a retail system that is more customer-focused, responsive, and efficient.

5 Fraud Detection and Prevention Systems

In e-commerce, where there are numerous transactions every day, fraud detection and prevention are essential. Machine learning techniques are used by fraud detection systems to identify and stop fraudulent activity. The primary foundation of fraud detection systems is supervised learning, which uses training data to determine whether a transaction is fraudulent or legitimate to classify unseen transactions as such (Samrat, 2022) For example, suppose you have the data where you already know where the fraud is or have already trained the models on the historical data. The models will then be able to identify similar patterns in subsequent transactions. On the other hand, unsupervised learning offers a crucial abnormality detection function by automatically detecting anomalous behavior in transaction semantics without the need for labeled data. Their ability to identify or create new fraud concepts—like unusual transaction locations or extended spending periods—sets them apart.

Fraud detection systems frequently employ ensemble approaches to increase system dependability. To increase accuracy, they use a range of models, including decision trees, neural networks, and simple algorithms. For instance, a decision tree may be used to classify a transaction in a high-risk category, while a neural network may be used to evaluate a complex data pattern. Together, they can create a system that can identify the smallest indications of fraud that could be missed by a single algorithm. Numerous systems employ real-time monitoring to identify anomalous activity, including high transaction rates or recurrent unsuccessful login attempts, and subsequently implement risk-prevention strategies. (Ray, 2022).

Protecting companies is only one aspect of fraud detection, but it is also about integrity with the others. Customers aren't going to remain loyal to your platform if they don't perceive that their transactions are secure. Fraud prevention on these platforms is successful as an alert is immediately provided the moment abnormal events take place to take prompt measures and avoid these losses. For instance, real-time alerts could be sent to customers by financial institutions if unusual transactions pass through, letting the customers immediately verify or void the activity.

However, fraudsters will always find new ways to exploit vulnerabilities, which leaves businesses on the front foot with adaptive machine learning (ML) systems. Yet these systems are designed by learning, based on emerging threats, on new data to guarantee they can work for new threats. Due to the fact that fraud patterns are increasing in sophistication and frequently focus on the newest technology or human mistake, that is why it is so essential. Businesses keep up to date on the situation by updating their models so that they maintain strong defences (Xu & Liu, 2024).

Fake reviews can also be fought using collaboration. Each of the above parties has to take action with the others to build a prevention package. A collaborative approach to security is one that includes things like multiple factor authentication (MFA), combining technologies such as biometrics and SMS codes or email confirmations, for example, to add extra security layers. In addition to using the traditional methods for securing your online accounts, such as passwords, you're also using biometric methods like fingerprints or facial recognition to lock down your accounts, meaning it's harder for unauthorised users to gain access.

Algorithms using state-of-the-art Machine Learning models and some of the technologies currently being implemented, such as blockchain, may revolutionise the landscape of fraud prevention systems for the next generation. However, the blockchain provides us with an irrefutable record of transactions, and it is almost impossible to alter the data (Xu & Liu, 2024). Real-time ML (machine learning) based anomaly detection coupled with this yields a highly effective system that can detect and repair threats before they reach victims. Furthermore, by investing in such technologies, not only can businesses deal better with their operational security, but it can also lead to developing trustable and loyal customer groups by delivering a secure and pleasant shopping experience to them (Jakkula, 2022).

Those e-commerce platforms that are to be resilient need to focus on innovative approaches that address the ever-changing cyber enemies, e.g., sophisticated fraud detection systems, adaptive learning systems, and federation across organisational boundaries. This is not just a matter of preventing fraud; it is a matter of making a better, more trustworthy ecosystem for consumers and companies.

6 Enhanced Customer Support with AI-Powered Chatbots

Artificial intelligence (AI) based chatbots have changed customer support in e-commerce, offering faster, more tailored and streamlined communication. Thanks to powerful natural language processing (NLP) models like GPT (Generative Pretrained Transformer) and BERT (Bidirectional Encoder Representations from Transformers), these chatbots can handle these complex queries. Conversational AI is different from earlier rule-based systems, as it can interpret context, deal with many flavours of communication and provide human-like interactions. Therefore, they are extremely useful for e-commerce platforms, where the success of the e-commerce platform largely rests on customer satisfaction, quality, and service speed (Carole et al., 2024; Kashyap et al., 2022).

There are several methods to improve the user experience with a chatbot. They could provide product recommendations based on a user's tastes and history. All of the above applies to their capacity to manage logistical chores such as order tracking, return processing, and addressing commonly requested questions. Chatbots automate basic tasks, reducing the strain on human TCS and allowing them to focus their abilities on more essential client demands. The fact that permits faster resolution results to eventually deliver a higher degree of customer satisfaction (Fedorko et al., 2022). Such systems have been adopted by high-end e-commerce websites like Amazon and many others to streamline their customer service process.

Customer service must eventually shift from interactive chatbot engagements to more advanced technologies like virtual assistants or phone commerce. Voice-enabled AI systems are becoming more and more common, and Amazon Alexa and Google Assistant are revolutionizing the purchasing experience. In fact, users may place orders, check them, and even pay for them by simply speaking to these devices. These developments make shopping easier and reduce tension, both of which are crucial for retaining and gaining new customers.

It's one of the most promising advancements in chatbot technology sentiment analysis. By measuring customer emotional reactions in conversations with chatbots, it's possible to adjust responses to feel more empathetic and practical (Wen et al., 2023).Suppose that a chatbot notices a tone/language of frustration or dissatisfaction and that it responds to either the problem or any further action immediately or by escalation to a live agent. It allows you to adopt an emotionally intelligent approach to your customers, which helps them feel valued and boosts the trust of the customers on the platform.

Furthermore, chatbot integration with the CRM (Customer Relationship Management) system enables businesses to explore new ways of understanding consumer behaviour more deeply. The analysis of chatbot dialogue provides companies insight into what customers value, how they buy, and what frustrates them customers. They then can pick more personal marketing approaches, how to make recommendations about products to other folks or campaign for promotions. AI chatbots, together with CRM, enhance not only operational efficiency but also customer relationships (Singh, 2024).

Since conversational AI is in its infancy, its universe has led to the redefining of not only customer service but also interaction. As technology developments continue, future systems can have AR virtual product demonstrations, as well as predictive analytics to predict customer needs before they are spoken. Businesses that adopt these technologies for customer support will not only offer better than what has ever been seen before but also create benchmarks of customer satisfaction. With its structure has come the customer, the experience where convenience, personalisation, and emotional intelligence do not exist in conflict but rather at their best complementarity (Fig. 2).

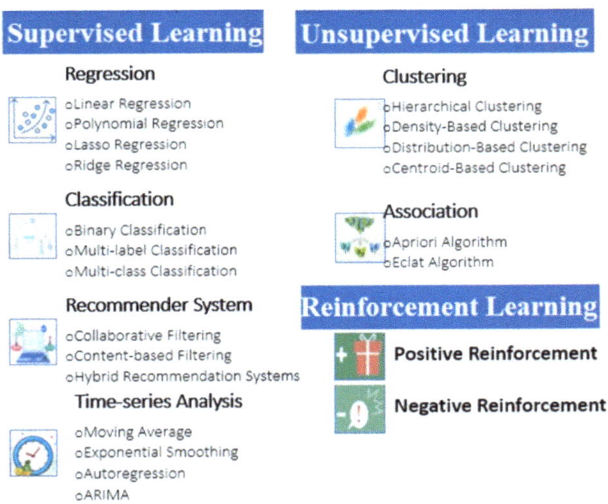

Fig. 2 Machine learning in e-commerce (adapted from Bharadwaj, 2025)

7 Data-Driven Marketing and Consumer Segmentation

It has revolutionized how businesses talk to consumers; it is impossible to do so through traditional mass marketing, and the results have been great. The core of this change is segmentation, according to customers' behaviour, preferences and demographics. This process is based on the application of machine learning techniques, which involves reading lots of data to interpret the figures.

An example is **K Means Clustering**, where Consumers are grouped according to a similar set of characteristics, e.g. purchase history, browsing behaviour or product preference. (Gupta & Pathak, 2014) The method allows businesses to understand diverse customer sets and apply different marketing strategies. Next is **DBSCAN (Density-Based Spatial Clustering of Applications with Noise)**, which finds clusters of consumer behaviour without explicit limits. Especially when finding a niche market or outliers.

Hierarchical clustering is a further step and more sophisticated technique that splits consumers into groups according to their similarity into nested groups. The defining aspect of this methodology is its ability to provide a highly granular and layered picture of the customer base, and, therefore, it becomes more straightforward to target some of the smaller subparts of that customer base. In addition, **sentiment analysis** has become an irreplaceable means of learning about consumers' emotions. Business people can study customer ratings, social media postings, or comments to determine customer satisfaction and identify the need for emotional responses to adapt their plans. (Gupta & Pathak, 2014; Singh, 2024).

Natural consumer segmentation encompasses **hyper-personalization**. Among these approaches, sophisticated segmentation techniques that generate extremely individual marketing messages for individual customers are used as a tool. Amazon and Netflix do it phenomenally because they introduce the ability to use machine learning algorithms to make product recommendations and their corresponding content for a specific user. For instance, Netflix leverages viewing history and tastes to propose series similar to a user's preference, and Amazon uses purchase history to advise items following the best previous purchase (Gupta & Pathak, 2014; Kashyap et al., 2022).

Despite how these advancements will lead to involvement and attachment, it is also a necessity that organisations address consumers' concern for data, as well as ethical marketing. Significantly, when regulations such as the GDPR (General Data Protection Regulation) rise, it proves the necessity for transparency in their collection, storage, and application. The business can build trust if they openly share their activities with the data and maintain ethical compliance (Gupta & Pathak, 2014).

Predictive analytics is another powerful addition to customer segmentation. Businesses may be able to meet future customer needs by combining segmentation strategies with predictive models. For instance, predictive analytics determines when a customer is most likely to place an order or show interest in a certain product based on past purchasing patterns. Instead of only reactively selling the right goods or services, businesses may utilize it to increase revenue and improve customer happiness.

The goal of data-driven marketing is to turn unprocessed data into actionable insights. Furthermore, when analytics methods develop further, more concealed consumer behavior will be found. It is possible to develop a new marketing strategy, for example, by knowing not only what products customers buy, but also the factors that influence their purchasing decisions. When knowledge and innovative innovations are combined, businesses may build enduring relationships with their target audiences and progressively increase customer loyalty (Xu & Liu, 2024).

With the digital sphere changing rapidly, the future of data-driven marketing consumer segmentation will define how unique and personalised customer engagement will be. It is the companies where resources are invested in more advanced segmentation methods that act with ethics and are always at the customer's centre that are most likely to succeed in increasingly competitive markets.

8 Sentiment Analysis for Consumer Insights

Sentiment analysis has become a must-have for any business that wants to understand consumer opinion and create or improve its strategy. Sentiment analysis stems from the idea of processing text information (social media, customer review, survey response) through sound natural language processing (NLP) and machine learning methods to identify text information's emotional and hedonistic feelings. They help businesses figure out how you feel about them or their products, services or brand to help them tweak their offerings and make data-driven decisions (Alsayat, 2023).

Various sentiment analysis techniques are helpful, such as sentiment classification, which categorises text as positive, negative or neutral sentiment. But beyond the detection of polarity, an advanced step is needed: quantifying the intensity of opinions and aspect-based sentiment analysis, which is a subdivision of the feedback to measure the opinions about specific product attributes. For instance, aspect-based sentiment analysis can also be used by a clothing retailer to learn whether a customer is happier with the quality of their fabrics or their delivery time. Precisely in this manner, companies can have this awareness and effectively respond to particular challenges and, in general, improve customer satisfaction (Saleem et al., 2021; Zhang et al., 2023).

Sentiment Analysis can also be employed in **social listening**, which is a practice of monitoring who you are communicating with on media and platforms and what they are saying about you. The company can analyse this data to follow public opinion, discover trends, and react accordingly. For instance, in a business, there may be a sudden surge in positive emotion following the rollout of a new product, indicating their success, or a surge in negative emotion over a particular feature that needs to be addressed urgently (Wen et al., 2023).

Brand management can't be done without sentiment analysis. Brand image plays a critical role in competitive markets, and using sentiment analysis to monitor shifts in public perception is a field strategy that has evolved within the brand sphere. For example, if negative sentiment rises, it could indicate dissatisfaction, and the company is alerted, taken action, and investigated and addressed before escalation. A brand's reputation is safeguarded by its upbeat, proactive measures and the resultant trust and brand loyalty (Saleem et al., 2021). Sentiment analysis can also be applied for **crisis management**, **public relations**, and beyond traditional uses. Businesses can play the right chords and read minds when it comes to doing optimistic trend forecasting at an early stage. They can also be proactive in reacting before the rise of disinformation or a negative impact on reputation. For example, a food delivery service is aware that customers are becoming increasingly irritated by extended wait times and will attempt to reduce anger by prioritising the enhancement of logistics. Now more than ever, it's crucial to have the ability to respond quickly to new issues that come up in the digital world (Alsayat, 2023; Zhang et al., 2023).

Sentiment Analysis, enhanced by modern NLP techniques, can include integration of **multilingual data**. It is crucial for businesses who operate in international marketplaces to be able to understand the sentiment of people from various cultural and language backgrounds. To meet the needs of a particular target audience, marketing professionals or groups, for instance, may use sentiment analysis across several marketplaces to decide on their messaging and the product strategy or alternative strategy they will adopt (Saleem et al., 2021). The strength of sentiment analysis will only increase with the strength and accessibility of ML and NLP. In the context of predictive analytics, the adoption of real-time sentiment analysis technology would enable the company to foresee customer reactions and take preventive measures. Sentiment analysis paired with prediction models to analyze the customer's response to a price manipulation or, for example, the introduction of a new product may be considered a case-in-point example.

Above all, sentiment analysis is an analytical instrument that can provide businesses with useful information about their customers to enable them to make better decisions, strengthen their connections, and stay ahead of the competition. It goes beyond just discovering what your customers think. Businesses become responsive and customer-focused leaders in their sectors when they incorporate sentiment information into all aspects of their operations, from marketing and crisis management to product creation.

9 Conclusion

E-commerce's playing field is currently leveled by machine learning. E-commerce is adopting machine learning techniques to give companies the resources and skills they need to make the best choices possible, based on a sound framework for decision-making and an excellent workplace experience. You can see from this chapter that it's more than just a tool; it's an enormous game changer. What sets it apart is that companies can use it to discover hidden patterns and make sense of large volumes of data, which allows them to foresee customer behavior with incredible clarity.

Through personalized recommendations that take into account customer preferences and dynamic pricing methods that set revenue at ideal levels at the moment, machine learning is changing the way that key elements of e-commerce operate. Without being constrained by a competitive market, companies can develop increasingly sophisticated client experiences using collaborative filtering, deep learning, and reinforcement learning. These developments highlight the ways in which consumer-focused and business-minded strategies can be combined to the shared advantage of all.

In the field of sales forecasting and inventory management, LSTM networks and ARIMA, among other few machine learning models, can assist keep businesses running. Companies can reduce expenses while increasing customer satisfaction by examining seasonal metrics, promotional impacts, and real-time data. Predictive analytics also ensures that supply chains can adjust to changing demand for an optimal shopping experience. Examples of supervised and unsupervised learning algorithms include those used in online shopping security and fraud detection systems. These solutions protect businesses from financial loss and provide consumers confidence that transactions are secure. Machine learning developments to address sophisticated threats, such as real-time monitoring and anomaly detection, have also resulted in the adoption of multi-factor authentication.

This study further examined at how AI-powered chatbots transformed relations with clients. Chatbots use both natural language processing models, such as GPT and BERT, to provide multilingual context-aware interaction, which can increase client engagement. Together with sentiment analysis, these technologies represent the next wave of business innovation, enabling companies to interact with their clients in a productive and empathetic manner.

Businesses can now bypass consumer segmentation and customisation in marketing thanks to machine learning. Businesses can target certain client groups with precision using prediction models and clustering algorithms, which increases customer loyalty and engagement. Additionally, sentiment analysis may support the success of these projects by giving them insight into public opinion and enabling them to respond by modifying their plans in real time without jeopardizing their brand image.

With the increasing integration of machine learning, e-commerce will continue to impress with its possibilities. Through the use of contemporary technologies like blockchain and the Internet of Things, the material aims to further improve operational efficiency, transparency, and chain confidence while revealing new facets of the interplay between the three supply chain factors. When combined with real-time analytics and flexible algorithms, this innovation chain will produce unprecedented levels of customer satisfaction and business outcomes.

E-commerce machine learning techniques have ultimately resulted in an ecosystem that is fueled by dynamism and data. By adopting these technologies, businesses may offer individualized, safe, and speedy online shopping experiences.

Predictive machine learning will continue to play a significant role in innovation and won't slow down anytime soon, enabling such growth to simply navigate this dynamic market environment and satisfy the growing demands of customers.

References

Alsayat, A. (2023). Customer decision-making analysis based on big social data using machine learning: A case study of hotels in Mecca. *Neural Computing and Applications, 35*(6), 4701–4722. https://doi.org/10.1007/s00521-022-07992-x

Carole, K. S., Armand, T. P. T., & Kim, H. C. (2024). Enhanced experiences: Benefits of AI-powered recommendation systems. In *2024 26th international conference on advanced communications technology (ICACT)* (pp. 216–220) https://doi.org/10.23919/ICACT60172.2024.10471918

Fedorko, R., Král̆, Š., & Fedorko, I. (2022). Artificial intelligence and machine learning in the context of E-commerce: A literature review. In (S. V. K. B. K. W. L. Sharma H.) (Ed.), *Communication and intelligent systems* (pp. 1067–1082). Springer. https://doi.org/10.1007/978-981-19-2130-8_82

Gupta, A. K., Dash, S., Aggarwal, V., & Yadav, P. D. (2022). Critical success factors influencing the success of SMEs. In *Proceedings - 2022 3rd International Conference on Computation, Automation and Knowledge Management, ICCAKM 2022.* https://doi.org/10.1109/ICCAKM54721.2022.9990271.

Gupta, R., & Pathak, C. (2014). A machine learning framework for predicting purchase by online customers based on dynamic pricing. *Procedia Computer Science, 36*, 599–605. https://doi.org/10.1016/j.procs.2014.09.060

Gupta, T., & Bansal, S. (2020). Machine learning algorithms for predictive analytics in E-commerce. *International Journal of Science and Research (IJSR), 9*(8), 1550–1557. https://doi.org/10.21275/sr24302212009

Jakkula, A. R. (2022). Personalizing shopping experiences with machine learning. *Journal of Technological Innovations, 3*(3) https://jtipublishing.com/jti/article/download/52/259

Kashyap, A. K., Sahu, I., & Kumar, A. (2022). Artificial intelligence and its applications in E-commerce–a review analysis and research agenda. *Journal of Theoretical and Applied Information Technology, 100*(24), 7347–7365. https://www.jatit.org/volumes/Vol100No24/12Vol100No24.pdf

Kumar, A., Mudgal, A., Yadav, A. L., & Sharma, A. (2024). Cloudsuggest: Enhancing e-commerce with personalized recommendations. In *2024 IEEE international conference on computing, power and communication technologies (IC2PCT)* (pp. 763–766). https://doi.org/10.1109/ic2pct60090.2024.10486797

Saleem, H., Muhammad, K. B., Nizamani, A. H., & Saleem, S. (2021). Data science and machine learning approach to improve e-commerce sales performance on the social web. *International Journal of Advanced Research in Engineering and Technology (IJARET), 12*(4), 12–16. https://doi.org/10.34218/IJARET.12.4.2021.040

Samrat, R. (2022). Fraud detection in E-commerce using machine learning. *BOHR International Journal of Advances in Management Research, 1*(1), 7–14. https://doi.org/10.54646/bijamr.002

Singh, G. (2024). Mapping consumer behaviour on E-commerce platform through AI. *International Journal of Advances in Engineering and Management (IJAEM), 6*, 1097. https://doi.org/10.35629/5252-060410971116

Wen, Z., Lin, W., & Liu, H. (2023). Machine-learning-based approach for anonymous online customer purchase intentions using clickstream data. *Systems, 11*(5), 255. https://doi.org/10.3390/systems11050255

Xu, Z., & Liu, S. (2024). Decoding consumer purchase decisions: Exploring the predictive power of EEG features in online shopping environments using machine learning. *Humanities and Social Sciences Communications, 11*(1). https://doi.org/10.1057/s41599-024-03691-1

Zhang, X., Guo, F., Chen, T., Pan, L., Beliakov, G., & Wu, J. (2023). A brief survey of machine learning and deep learning techniques for E-commerce research. In *Journal of Theoretical and Applied Electronic Commerce Research, 18*(4), 2188–2216. Multidisciplinary Digital Publishing Institute (MDPI). https://doi.org/10.3390/jtaer18040110.

The Contribution of 3D Video Advertisements for Sports Marketing: A Scoping Review

Buvaneswari Pallikuppam Sachithanandan, Rajakrithiga Ganesan, and Aishwaryaa Velayutham

Abstract

The diverse nature of 3D video advertisements has made its presence ubiquitous, appearing across devices and large displays in sports arenas. With the development of new-age technologies, digital advertising has become far easier. This study aims to identify and synthesize the current literature that signifies the contribution of 3D video advertisements for sports marketing. For this purpose, a scoping review was conducted using the five-stage framework developed by Arksey and O'Malley. A total of 19 records encompassing conceptual and empirical studies were selected using the PRISMA protocol for full-text review. Key concepts explored in these studies include augmented reality, virtual reality, extended reality, mixed reality, animation, and 360° videos for advertising. These studies were focused on varied sports marketing themes, such as sports broadcasting, sports sponsorship, in-game advertising, esports, and different types of sports, including football, car racing, tennis, golf, and baseball. Key variables, theories, methodological approaches, and future research areas included in the existing literature were discussed. Several studies found that using 3D video-enabled advertisements for sports marketing is effective and recommend it to gain strategic advantage, cover more audience, and generate more revenue.

B. . P. . Sachithanandan (✉) · R. . Ganesan · A. . Velayutham
University of Madras, Chennai, India
e-mail: cvcpsb@gmail.com

R. . Ganesan
e-mail: rajakrithiga1@gmail.com

A. . Velayutham
e-mail: aishwaryaa.official26@gmail.com

© The Author(s), under exclusive license to Springer Nature Singapore Pte Ltd. 2026
N. S. Jayawardena et al. (eds.), *Digital Advertising and Consumer Behavior*, Management for Professionals, https://doi.org/10.1007/978-981-95-7809-2_14

1 Background

Since the inception of digital advertising, various new advertising formats have been developed (Faruk et al., 2021; Lütjens et al., 2022; Quach et al., 2022; Sundar et al., 2017) by advertisers and designers alike (Wang et al., 2024). With the development of digitally stimulating 3D video elements, Augmented Reality (AR), Virtual Reality (VR), Extended Reality (XR), Mixed Reality (MR), 3D animation, Computer-Generated Imagery (CGI), and 360° videos have become more prevalent (Burton & Schlieman, 2021; Jayawardena et al., 2023a, 2023b; Otto & Rumpf, 2018) in both indoor and outdoor advertising settings. This change in customers' advertisement viewing has brought a paradigm shift in building customer experiences (Stalder, 2011). Tailoring advertisements to customers' preferences (Higgins et al., 2018; Quach et al., 2020; Thaichon et al., 2016), disguising the commercial intent of advertisements (Hudders et al., 2017; Meenaghan, 2001), actively involving the customers (Hudders et al., 2017; Stewart et al., 2019), and reducing advertisement annoyance (Violante et al., 2019) have been made possible with these new age technologies.

Recently, novel technologies have been used across various fields, and sports marketing is no exception (Otto & Rumpf, 2018; Tsuji, 2015). Sports marketing encompasses promoting products and services through sports and promoting sports-related products and services directly to sports fans and participants (Lee et al., 2021). The scope of sports marketing is continually evolving, incorporating new marketing techniques and adapting to changing consumer preferences (Fullerton & Merz, 2008; Goebert, 2020). It has significant potential to be elevated through 3D video technology in capturing viewer attention and creating interactive viewing experiences (Goebert & Greenhalgh, 2020; Lupinek et al., 2021). Staying in trend with these technologies, sports marketers have adopted various 3D video-enabled advertisement formats for in-stadium advertising, in-game advertising (IGA), esports, etc. (Lee et al., 2021; Lupinek et al., 2021; Regret Iyer et al., 2022; Wang & Yao, 2020).

Many studies have explored various aspects of these topics individually. However, it is essential to take a comprehensive approach to understand the broader scope of sports marketing (Fullerton & Merz, 2008). Scoping reviews are ideal for mapping the scope of a body of literature by synthesizing findings from different studies, identifying trends, highlighting areas requiring further exploration, and determining whether a more detailed systematic review is required (Behl et al., 2024; Munn et al., 2018; Colquhoun et al., 2014). Therefore, the present study attempts to synthesize the evidence on 3D video advertisements' contribution to sports marketing. Consequently, the objectives guiding the research work are: (a) to identify and collate available evidence on the contribution of 3D video advertisements for sports marketing, (b) to summarize the key concepts, themes, and methodological approaches of relevant studies, and (c) to synthesize potential knowledge gaps and provide directions for future research.

2 Methods

Given the complexity of conducting and reporting a scoping review and the need to be consistent with similar studies, commonly used structured frameworks were considered. The present review follows the five-step framework that Arksey and O'Malley (2005) developed with enhancements proposed by Levac et al. (2010). Following the same, the contents to be included in each step are explained under the five-stage approach: (1) identifying the research question, (2) identifying relevant studies, (3) study selection, (4) charting the data, and (5) collating, summarizing, and reporting the results (Arksey & O'Malley, 2005).

Identifying the Research Question

The research questions (RQ) that direct a scoping review must be broad and ensure clarity in inquiring about the studies' concepts, methods, and outcomes (Colquhoun et al., 2014). The present study includes the following research questions:

RQ1 What evidence exists on 3D video advertisements' contribution for sports marketing?

RQ2 Which key concepts, themes, and methodological approaches characterize studies on 3D video advertisements for sports marketing?

RQ3 What are the identified knowledge gaps and future research directions for 3D video advertisements in sports marketing?

Identifying Relevant Studies

In this stage, a search plan was formulated as suggested by Colquhoun et al. (2014), specifying where to search, which terms and sources to use, the period specified for the study, and the language restrictions drawn for the records. The search was conducted in October 2024, and records indexed in the Scopus database were considered, including the key terms relevant to 3D video advertisements and sports marketing. Key terms mentioned in the search query include 3D video, augmented reality, virtual reality, immersive video, 360° video, extended reality, mixed reality, animation, and any applicable variations of these terms available specifically in the title, abstract, and/or keywords. To restrict the results to sports-related advertisements, a criterion was set such that terms related to sports marketing, sports sponsorship, sporting events, sports promotion, esports, and any alternative terms used in the text were identified. Resultantly, 203 hits were established. As scoping reviews have a broader scope, no restrictions were made to the document sources and subject areas at this stage. Articles, books, conference papers, book chapters, proceedings, conference reviews, and grey literature from all subject areas were included in the initial research. Given that this is a relatively new topic with emerging technologies in the sports context, records published in the past 20 years, i.e., 2004 to 2024 and in English, were planned for consideration.

Study Selection

Study selection is an iterative process that requires refining the search strategy and reviewing the records for study inclusion (Colquhoun et al., 2014). The 203 records identified through the initial search were imported into a reference management software, Zotero, to check for any duplication of results. No duplication of data was identified. As suggested by several authors, the inclusion/ exclusion criteria (Table 1) were applied to the records, and those that could be immediately excluded were removed (Jayawardena et al., 2024; Lange et al., 2025). Subsequently, records published before 2004 (n = 04) and in other languages (n = 03) were excluded, yielding 196 records. Titles and abstracts of the identified records were reviewed for eligibility based on their relevance to the context and the inclusion/exclusion criteria. As a result, 184 records were excluded, and 12 records were included for full-text review. During this process, 07 additional records indexed in the Scopus database were identified through hand-searching references, searching available grey literature, and conducting other targeted searches based on the inclusion/exclusion criteria. These records were included to ensure comprehensive topic coverage and supplement the initial search results. The authors considered the 19 records for the final full-text review. The study selection process is consolidated using Preferred Reporting Items for Systematic Reviews and Meta-Analyses (PRISMA) flowchart (Fig. 1) to provide a comprehensive view of the number of records identified, screened, and included for the final review (Jayawardena et al., 2024; Moher et al., 2009).

Table 1 Inclusion and exclusion criteria

Inclusion criteria	Exclusion criteria
Records released from 2004 to 2024	Records released before 2004
Records published in English	Records published in any other languages
All types of document sources indexed in Scopus	Database other than Scopus
Addressed all the dimensions of 3D video advertisements for sports marketing: • 3D video element (s) • Advertisements/commercials/promotion • Sports marketing context (esports, sports broadcasts, sports sponsorship, etc.)	If either of these dimensions are met: • Focused only on conventional video formats or static components • Specific to 3D sports but not about advertisements

Source Authors' compilation

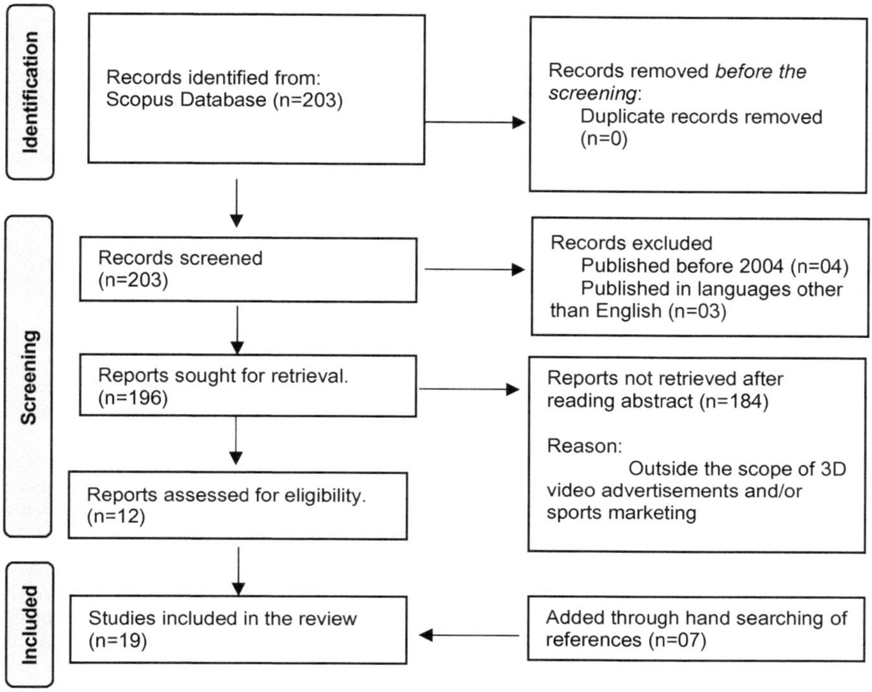

Fig. 1 PRISMA flowchart of the literature search process. *Source* Authors' compilation

Charting the Data

This step involves extracting the required information to answer the research questions. Information extracted from each record includes publication source (author names and year of publication), study setting (country, area, or region where the research was conducted), 3D video advertisement studied, research objectives related to the topic, theoretical perspectives, methodological approaches, and key contributions.

Collating, Summarizing, and Reporting the Results

All authors reviewed the 19 records, and the information extracted from each record was organized and tabulated (Table 2) in the results section of this paper. The findings of each record were further collated and discussed in the study. Quality assessment was not conducted, as scoping reviews aim to map the breadth of existing literature rather than critically appraise individual study quality (Finlay et al., 2022; Pham et al., 2014).

Table 2 Summary of the selected records

Reference and study setting	Type of 3D video advertisement	Research objectives related to the topic	Theory	Method/ research design	Key contributions
Uhm et al. (2024) Far East Asian region	VR	To explore how VR sports advertisements increase empathy and understand the relationship between empathy, sense of presence, and attitudes toward advertisements and brands	Embodiment theory, transportation theory	Empirical	VR sports advertisements evoke embodied empathy in viewers, leading to stronger emotional connections with athletes and more favourable attitudes toward advertisements and brands
Lee and Zhou (2023) United States	VR	To investigate the impact of different media types (VR vs. 2-D screen) on emotional and cognitive responses while watching sports content	Dynamic human-Centered communication system theory	Empirical	VR enhances attention to primary sports content but negatively affects memory recall for brand placements compared to 2-D screens. The high cognitive demands of VR limit resources for peripheral information, and the head movements required to view advertisements complicate processing. VR boosts main event memory but impairs recall of advertisements

(continued)

Table 2 (continued)

Reference and study setting	Type of 3D video advertisement	Research objectives related to the topic	Theory	Method/ research design	Key contributions
Goebert et al. (2022) United States	AR	To explore consumer attitudes and behavioural intentions towards AR-enhanced sports broadcasts	Elaboration likelihood model	Empirical	Consumers may be more receptive to AR technology than expected, making the broadcast more lucrative to sponsors and advertisers
Regret Iyer et al. (2022) Russia and Qatar	VR and 360° video	To explore how VR and 360° video are utilized in pre-game content produced by different organizations, specifically focusing on themes and immersive qualities of the sports content	NR	Qualitative content analysis	The VR and 360° video content identified four main themes: Stadium design, technology, facilities, and locality

(continued)

Table 2 (continued)

Reference and study setting	Type of 3D video advertisement	Research objectives related to the topic	Theory	Method/ research design	Key contributions
Oh et al. (2022) South Korea	VR	To investigate the effects of viewing type (2D vs. VR with and without interruptions) and time lapses on telepresence, flow experience, and spectatorship satisfaction in sports media consumption	Flow theory	Experimental	VR spectatorship (VRS) improves telepresence, flow, and satisfaction compared to traditional 2D viewing. Flow experience was enhanced in VRS with interruptions compared to VRS without interruptions, making it practical to increase advertising revenue
Lupinek et al. (2021) N/A	VR	To develop a conceptual framework for understanding IGA congruity in VR sports video games and its impact on consumer behaviour	IGA congruity framework, limited-capacity model of attention	Conceptual	A balanced integration of interactivity, intrusion, realism, and telepresence in VR gaming can lead to favourable consumer attitudes toward IGA, improved brand recognition, and sales activation

(continued)

Table 2 (continued)

Reference and study setting	Type of 3D video advertisement	Research objectives related to the topic	Theory	Method/ research design	Key contributions
Lee et al. (2021) N/A	VR and AR	To explore how VR and AR can be effectively integrated into sports marketing strategies and understand the implications of these technologies on consumer engagement and brand awareness	NR	Opinion-based literature	VR in IGA boosts brand awareness and fosters a positive mindset toward advertisements, leading to increased sales activation. These technological advancements provide marketers with novel methods to reach and engage customers
Burton and Schlieman (2021) N/A	360° video (component of XR)	To investigate users' impressions and attitudes toward XR technologies for sponsorship activation and the viability of 360° video integration as an experiential component of sponsor messaging	NR	Qualitative content analysis	360° activations enable brands to engage and promote unique, authentic, or appealing user experiences. Brands must create 360° video advertisements highlighting attitudinal benefits rather than relying on VR's immersive or interactive elements

(continued)

Table 2 (continued)

Reference and study setting	Type of 3D video advertisement	Research objectives related to the topic	Theory	Method/ research design	Key contributions
Wang and Yao (2020) United States	VR	To examine the impact of telepresence and user control on the effectiveness of embedded billboard advertisements in a VR car racing game	Limited cognitive capacity model	Experimental	VR gaming did not enhance brand recall or recognition but increased price estimation for advertisements displayed thrice. Telepresence and active control influence purchase intentions, with players in VR conditions showing higher purchase intentions than viewers
Javed et al. (2020) NR	Animation	To examine how types of advertisements (static, animated, and animated with sound) affect visual attention and revisit different content types	NR	Experimental	Due to their moving elements, animated advertisements with sound increased visual attention and revisits. Sports-related advertisements attracted less attention compared to shopping and political advertisements

(continued)

Table 2 (continued)

Reference and study setting	Type of 3D video advertisement	Research objectives related to the topic	Theory	Method/ research design	Key contributions
Goebert and Greenhalgh (2020) United States	AR	To investigate the acceptance of sports marketing AR advertising and examine the applicability of the TRAM framework in predicting sports consumer behaviour on AR activations	Self-determination theory, technology acceptance model, technology readiness and acceptance model (TRAM)	Empirical	AR's visual appeal strongly influences fans' usage intentions and word-of-mouth, while perceived ease of use has no significant impact. It validates TRAM as a robust framework for AR in sports marketing
Wedel et al. (2020) N/A	AR and VR	To explore how VR enhances consumer experiences and evaluate the current state of VR in marketing research and practice	Consumer information processing model	Conceptual	They identify the increasing use of VR in sports broadcasting to promote products and highlight product placement in virtual sports environments to contextualize products in desirable ways

(continued)

Table 2 (continued)

Reference and study setting	Type of 3D video advertisement	Research objectives related to the topic	Theory	Method/ research design	Key contributions
Otto and Rumpf (2018) Germany	Animation	To investigate the impact of animation intensity of sponsorship signage on sports viewers' attention and examine viewers' visual confusion due to high animation intensity	Saliency-based visual attention model	Experimental	Higher animation intensity in sponsorship signage increases sports viewers' attention without significantly causing visual confusion
Seo et al. (2018) South Korea	Animation	To examine how animation in esports advertisements impacts viewer attention and how this effect varies between battle and non-battle scenes in gameplay	Limited-capacity model of attention	Experimental	Animation in esports advertisements has a more substantial impact on fixation duration during less busy gameplay (non-battle scenes) than during busier gameplay (battle scenes), with the moderating role of gameplay intensity on viewer attention to advertisements

(continued)

Table 2 (continued)

Reference and study setting	Type of 3D video advertisement	Research objectives related to the topic	Theory	Method/ research design	Key contributions
You et al. (2017) N/A	MR	To investigate the real-time content creation and on-site mobile calibration interfaces of SelfieWall, an MR advertising platform, and some typical real-world deployment	(attention, interest, desire, and action) AIDA model	Conceptual	The SelfieWall platform effectively uses MR to capture the attention of passersby in events and venues with large crowds, such as sporting events. It also motivates users to share their experiences on social media, increasing brand visibility and awareness
Sung and Park (2017) South Korea	VR	To investigate the effects of VR advertisements on attitude toward advertisement, focusing on the moderating role of affective consumer involvement in sports	NR	Experimental	A positive relationship between the content type of VR advertisement and attitude toward advertisement is moderated by affective consumer involvement in sports

(continued)

Table 2 (continued)

Reference and study setting	Type of 3D video advertisement	Research objectives related to the topic	Theory	Method/ research design	Key contributions
Tsuji (2015) N/A	Animation	To examine how animated brand logos enabled by virtual technology contribute in the global setting	NR	Conceptual	Animation in virtual advertisements, such as brand logos displayed next to scoreboards or behind home plates, effectively captures viewer attention and reinforces brand visibility in global sports sponsorship
Breuer and Rumpf (2015) NR	Animation	To assess the impact of colour and animation on sports viewers' attention to sponsorship signage	Opponent colour processing theory, Feature integration theory, motion effect theory	Experimental	Colour and animation significantly impact sports viewers' attention. However, animation can create visual confusion for television sports viewers and may reduce the intended sponsorship effects
Tsuji et al. (2009) United States	Animation	To analyse the effects of animation, repetition, involvement, and team identification on brand awareness during a professional baseball game broadcast	Social identity theory	Experimental	While animation did not significantly affect brand awareness, repetition of brand exposure notably impacted recall and recognition

Source Authors' compilation
NR Not Reported, *N/A* Not Applicable

3 Results

Summary of the Selected Records

Table 2 presents the scoping review results for the 19 selected records. Records included 15 articles, two book chapters, one conference paper, and one editorial. A comprehensive overview of the study characteristics and synthesis of results addresses the first objective.

Study Characteristics

The summary of records selected for scoping review signifies a steady increase in publications, particularly over the past five years, with the highest activity occurring in 2020. Several authors have consistently published in this field, including Goebert C, Greenhalgh GP, Lee HW, Rumpf C, and Tsuji Y, suggesting a continued focus on related research areas over time. The study settings include 20 occurrences across several distinct countries/regions. The United States appears most frequently, with 05 occurrences, followed by South Korea ($n = 03$). Few records did not report their study setting ($n = 08$) or did not apply to the context (conceptual papers, opinion-based literature). Other countries where studies were conducted include Russia, Qatar, Germany, and Far East Asia.

Synthesis of Results

The review of 19 records highlights how 3D technologies such as VR, AR, animation, 360° video, and MR enhance advertising effectiveness. VR advertisements foster empathy and emotional connections, promoting positive brand perception and increased sales (Lee et al., 2021; Uhm et al., 2024). While VR's high cognitive demands improve focus on main events, they may reduce peripheral recall and memory of advertisements (Lee & Zhou, 2023). Enhanced user flow and telepresence boost viewing satisfaction and advertisement revenue, promoting favourable consumer attitudes toward IGA (Lupinek et al., 2021; Oh et al., 2022; Tsuji, 2015). VR experiences also increase price estimates, with telepresence and game control significantly influencing purchase intentions (Wang & Yao, 2020). Additionally, VR's use in sports broadcasting and virtual product placement showcases products in engaging settings, enhancing brand visibility (Wedel et al., 2020). Furthermore, affective engagement strengthens the relationship between VR advertisement content and viewer attitudes (Sung & Park, 2017). These technological advancements offer marketers innovative ways to engage consumers (Lee et al., 2021). AR's visual appeal enhances user engagement and promotes word-of-mouth, increasing broadcast value and strengthening audience connections (Goebert & Greenhalgh, 2020; Goebert et al., 2022). Animated advertisements, especially those with sound, attract more attention than static advertisements, effectively capturing viewer focus

(Javed et al., 2020). However, animation can sometimes cause visual confusion (Otto & Rumpf, 2018). In esports, animated advertisements improve viewer fixation during non-battle scenes, with repeated exposure enhancing brand recall (Seo et al., 2018). 360° activations engage users through immersive experiences, helping brands achieve campaign goals and highlight attitudinal benefits (Burton & Schlieman, 2021). MR advertisement platforms, such as SelfieWall, effectively capture attention and encourage social media interaction, creating engaging and interactive experiences for audiences (You et al. 2017). New technologies provide marketers with advanced tools to engage consumers, influence attitudinal responses, and drive purchase intentions, positioning 3D advertising as a powerful strategy for enhancing user engagement, emotional connections, and brand visibility in sports marketing.

4 Discussion

This section synthesizes the key concepts and sports marketing themes researched in the evidence, highlighting the methodological approaches, key variables, theories, and analytical tools employed. It also discusses the areas identified by previous studies as directions for future research.

Summary of Evidence

Following the PRISMA protocol to summarize the evidence, the second objective of this research is addressed. The key concepts explored include VR (n = 09) as the most prominent 3D video advertising element, followed by animation (n = 06), AR (n = 04), 360° videos (n = 02) as a component of XR, and MR (n = 01), enabling viewers to engage with sports content in innovative ways, enhancing how advertisements connect with audiences. Their usage across diverse sports marketing themes, such as sports broadcasting (Goebert et al., 2022; Wedel et al., 2020), sports sponsorship (Breuer & Rumpf, 2015; Burton & Schlieman, 2021; Tsuji, 2015), IGA (Lee et al., 2021; Lupinek et al. 2021; Seo et al., 2018), esports (Seo et al., 2018), and varied types of sports including football, car racing, tennis, golf, and baseball (Otto & Rumpf, 2018; Sung & Park, 2017; Tsuji et al., 2009; Uhm et al., 2024; Wang & Yao, 2020) highlight the expanding role of 3D technologies for advertising to enhance viewer engagement in sports marketing context. Key variables presented in the literature are categorized into cognitive, emotional, and behavioural dimensions. Cognitive variables such as attention, memory, telepresence, technology readiness, and brand awareness (Goebert, 2020; Javed et al., 2020; Lee & Zhou, 2023; Lupinek et al., 2021; Wang & Yao, 2020) highlight how viewers process and retain information. Emotion-based variables like attitude, empathy, sense of presence, arousal, and personal experience (Lee & Zhou, 2023; Oh et al., 2022; Uhm et al., 2024) reflect the emotional impact of 3D advertisements on audiences. Variables oriented to understanding behaviour, including involvement, purchase intention, word-of-mouth, and spectatorship (Goebert, 2020; Oh et al., 2022; Sung & Park, 2017; Wang & Yao, 2020) focus on viewer actions and responses influenced by the advertisement. Variables, such as attention, memory, involvement, telepresence, and attitude, signify their role in evaluating advertisement effectiveness. These variables provide marketers with comprehensive insights into how customers interact with 3D video advertisements. Theories such as the limited-capacity model of attention, elaboration likelihood model, motion effect theory, embodiment theory, and transportation theory provided a strong conceptual foundation for these investigations (Breuer & Rumpf, 2015; Goebert et al., 2022; Seo et al., 2018; Uhm et al., 2024). The evidence included empirical, experimental, and conceptual studies, with common methods such as eye-tracking technology (Javed et al., 2020; Otto & Rumpf, 2018) to measure fixation count and period, surveys, and lab experiments (Goebert et al., 2022; Oh et al. 2022). University students were the predominant population sampled, and analyses frequently employed were analysis of variance (Lee & Zhou, 2023; Tsuji et al., 2009; Wang & Yao, 2020), structural equation modelling (Goebert & Greenhalgh, 2020; Uhm et al., 2024), and thematic content analysis (Burton & Schlieman, 2021; Regret Iyer et al. 2022). These theoretical perspectives, varied study designs, and analyses enable sports marketers and advertisers to refine targeting strategies, improving advertisement effectiveness and return on investment.

Areas Identified for Future Research

This section addresses the third objective by synthesizing the knowledge gaps identified in the reviewed literature and exploring directions for future research. It is recommended that future studies should explore diverse age groups, genders, and cultural backgrounds (Sung & Park, 2017; Uhm et al., 2024), different levels of sports involvement (Uhm et al., 2024), homogeneous psychographic segments (Goebert et al., 2022), and conduct studies among real sports fans within wider populations (Otto & Rumpf, 2018). Future variables for investigation should include different technology adoption factors (Goebert, 2020), levels of cognitive involvement in sports (Wang & Yao, 2020), purchase intention (Seo et al., 2018; Uhm et al., 2024), the impact of negative branding on sports advertising effectiveness, and various animation formats (Breuer & Rumpf, 2015). In terms of experimental stimuli, research should explore different types of sports (Goebert et al., 2022; Lee & Zhou, 2023), famous brands for recall and recognition tests (Wang & Yao, 2020), and authentic sports sponsorship brands (Otto & Rumpf, 2018). Uhm et al. (2024) suggested that research should be conducted in real-time to capture the natural behaviours, while Goebert et al. (2022) opined to carry out similar experiments in a controlled laboratory for better precision and control over the variables. Additionally, future studies could utilize equipment such as eye-tracking devices (Lee & Zhou, 2023), mobile eye-tracking

(Breuer & Rumpf, 2015), and eye-tracking integrated into VR head-mounted displays, such as the HTC VIVE Pro Eye with Tobii analytical software (Lupinek et al., 2021), to enhance data collection and analysis. Frameworks like the VR IGA congruity framework (Lupinek et al., 2021) and the limited cognitive capacity model (Wang & Yao, 2020) should also be tested and validated. These gaps highlight the need for comprehensive approaches in future studies to deepen understanding and application of 3D video advertisements for sports marketing-based research.

5 Conclusion

This scoping review examined the role of 3D video advertisements, including AR, VR, animation, and 360° videos, in sports marketing. Using the Arksey and O'Malley framework (2005), 19 records from the Scopus database were analysed to chart research objectives, key concepts, theoretical perspectives, methodological approaches, findings, and identified research gaps. Results demonstrated the significant impact of 3D video advertisements in enhancing consumer engagement, brand loyalty, and experiential marketing while highlighting underexplored areas, such as the impact of negative branding on sports advertising effectiveness (Breuer & Rumpf, 2015; Regret Iyer, 2022).

The study provides practical implications for marketers, suggesting best practices to improve these technologies for campaigns and including customers' feedback to improve advertisement effectiveness. However, the review was limited to a single database and focused only on 3D video elements used in advertising for sports marketing. Future research should investigate 3D video advertisements across other industries and cultural contexts. Areas identified for future research as collated through the synthesis could also be studied. A systematic review with quality assessment could further refine these findings and establish evidence-based guidelines for using 3D video advertisements effectively.

Author Contributions All authors contributed equally to the research and/or publication of this chapter.

Funding The authors have not received any financial support for the research, authorship, or publication.

Availability of Data and Materials All data and materials used in this scoping review are available from journals and databases.

Competing Interests The authors declared no potential competing interests in the research, authorship, or publication of this chapter.

References

Arksey, H., & O'Malley, L. (2005). Scoping studies: Towards a methodological framework. *International Journal of Social Research Methodology, 8*(1), 19–32.

Behl, A., Pereira, V., Nigam, A., Wamba, S., & Sindhwani, R. (2024). Knowledge development in non-fungible tokens (NFT): A scoping review. *Journal of Knowledge Management, 28*(1), 232–267.

Breuer, C., & Rumpf, C. (2015). The impact of color and animation on sports viewers' attention to televised sponsorship signage. *Journal of Sport Management, 29*(2), 170–183.

Burton, N., & Schlieman, T. (2021). User response to extended reality sponsorship activations on social media: Exploring impressions of GoPro's use of 360 video in marketing. *Journal of Interactive Advertising, 21*(2), 93–107.

Colquhoun, H. L., Levac, D., O'Brien, K. K., Straus, S., Tricco, A. C., Perrier, L., Kastner, M., & Moher, D. (2014). Scoping reviews: Time for clarity in definition, methods, and reporting. *Journal of Clinical Epidemiology, 67*(12), 1291–1294.

Faruk, M., Rahman, M., & Hasan, S. (2021). How digital marketing evolved over time: A bibliometric analysis on Scopus database. *Heliyon, 7*(12), e08603, 1–10.

Finlay, A., Robinson, E., Jones, A., Maden, M., Cerny, C., Muc, M., Evans, R., Makin, H., & Boyland, E. (2022). A scoping review of outdoor food marketing: Exposure, power and impacts on eating behaviour and health. *BMC Public Health, 22*(1), 1431.

Fullerton, S., & Merz, G. R. (2008). The four domains of sports marketing: A conceptual framework. *Sport Marketing Quarterly, 17*(2), 90–108.

Goebert, C. (2020). Augmented reality in sport marketing: Uses and directions. *Sports Innovation Journal, 1*, 134–151.

Goebert, C., Greenhalgh, G., & Dwyer, B. (2022). A whole new ball game: Fan perceptions of augmented reality enhanced sport broadcasts. *Computers in Human Behaviour, 137*, 107388.

Goebert, C., & Greenhalgh, G. P. (2020). A new reality: Fan perceptions of augmented reality readiness in sport marketing. *Computers in Human Behaviour, 106*, 106231.

Higgins, S. F., Mulvenna, M. D., Bond, R. B., McCartan, A., Gallagher, S., & Quinn, D. (2018). Multivariate testing confirms the effect of age–gender congruence on click-through rates from online social network digital advertisements. *Cyberpsychology, Behaviour and Social Networking, 21*(10), 646–654.

Hudders, L., De Pauw, P., Cauberghe, V., Panic, K., Zarouali, B., & Rozendaal, E. (2017). Shedding new light on how advertising literacy can affect children's processing of embedded advertising formats: A future research agenda. *Journal of Advertising, 46*(2), 333–349.

Javed, Y., Al Qahtani, E., & Shehab, M. (2020). *The impact of advertisements on user attention during permission authorization.* In HCI International 2020—Late breaking papers: User experience design and case studies. 22nd HCI international conference, HCII 2020, Copenhagen, Denmark, July 19–24 2020 proceedings (Vol. 22, pp. 722–739).

Jayawardena, N. S., Behl, A., Nedungadi, P., Jones, P., & Raman, R. (2024). Integration of technology and marketing activities among service SMEs in emerging economies: A scoping review. *Journal of Global Information Management, 32*(1), 1–27.

Jayawardena, N. S., Ross, M., Quach, S., & Grace, D. (2023a). An investigation of visual comprehension in memory for 360-degree video advertisements amongst adolescents. *Asia Pacific Journal of Marketing and Logistics, 35*(7), 1789–1812.

Jayawardena, N. S., Thaichon, P., Quach, S., Razzaq, A., & Behl, A. (2023b). The persuasion effects of virtual reality (VR) and augmented reality (AR) video advertisements: A conceptual review. *Journal of Business Research, 160*, 113739.

Lange, S., Bolt, G., Vos, S., & Völker, B. (2025). Inclusion of the marginalized: The case of sport participation: A scoping review. *Journal of Global Sport Management, 10*(3), 431–463.

Lee, H. W., Brison, N. T., Cho, H., Pyun, D. Y., & Ratten, V. (2021). Adopting new technologies in sports marketing. *Frontiers in Sports and Active Living, 3*, 777841.

Lee, M., & Zhou, X. (2023). Real-time psychophysiological approaches to explore emotional and cognitive processing of VR-mediated sports. *International Journal of Sports Marketing and Sponsorship, 26*(2), 238–253.
Levac, D., Colquhoun, H., & O'Brien, K. K. (2010). Scoping studies: Advancing the methodology. *Implementation Science, 5*, 1–9.
Lupinek, J. M., Yoo, J., Ohu, E. A., & Bownlee, E. (2021). Congruity of virtual reality in-game advertising. *Frontiers in Sports and Active Living, 3*, 728749.
Lütjens, H., Eisenbeiss, M., Fiedler, M., & Bijmolt, T. (2022). Determinants of consumers' attitudes towards digital advertising—A meta-analytic comparison across time and touchpoints. *Journal of Business Research, 153*, 445–466.
Meenaghan, T. (2001). Sponsorship and advertising: A comparison of consumer perceptions. *Psychology & Marketing, 18*(2), 191–215.
Moher, D., Liberati, A., Tetzlaff, J., Altman, D. G., & PRISMA Group. (2009). Preferred reporting items for systematic reviews and meta-analyses: The PRISMA statement. *Annals of Internal Medicine, 151*(4), 264–269.
Munn, Z., Peters, M. D., Stern, C., Tufanaru, C., McArthur, A., & Aromataris, E. (2018). Systematic review or scoping review? Guidance for authors when choosing between a systematic or scoping review approach. *BMC Medical Research Methodology, 18*, 1–7.
Oh, J., Kim, D. H., & Kim, D. (2022). Exploring experiential patterns depending on time lapses in virtual reality spectatorship (VRS): The role of interruption in reducing satiation. *Sustainability, 14*(24), 16678.
Otto, F., & Rumpf, C. (2018). Animation intensity of sponsorship signage: The impact on sport viewers' attention and viewer confusion. *Sport Business and Management: An International Journal, 8*(2), 177–194.
Pham, M. T., Rajić, A., Greig, J. D., Sargeant, J. M., Papadopoulos, A., & McEwen, S. A. (2014). A scoping review of scoping reviews: Advancing the approach and enhancing the consistency. *Research Synthesis Methods, 5*(4), 371–385.
Quach, S., Thaichon, P., Lee, J. Y., Weaven, S., & Palmatier, R. W. (2020). Toward a theory of outside-in marketing: Past, present, and future. *Industrial Marketing Management, 89*, 107–128.
Quach, S., Thaichon, P., Martin, K. D., Weaven, S., & Palmatier, R. W. (2022). Digital technologies: Tensions in privacy and data. *Journal of the Academy of Marketing Science, 50*(6), 1299–1323.
Regret Iyer, S., Pavlik, J., & Jin, S. V. (2022). Leveraging virtual reality (VR) for sports public relations and sports journalism: Qualitative analyses of VR content productions for 'Russia 2018' and 'Qatar 2022' FIFA world cups. *Journal of Sport & Tourism, 26*(4), 335–362.
Seo, Y. N., Kim, M., Lee, D., & Jung, Y. (2018). Attention to eSports advertisement: Effects of ad animation and in-game dynamics on viewers' visual attention. *Behaviour & Information Technology, 37*(12), 1194–1202.
Stalder, U. (2011). Digital out-of-home media: Means and effects of digital media in public space. In *Pervasive advertising* (pp. 31–56). Springer.
Stewart, K., Kammer-Kerwick, M., Auchter, A., Koh, H. E., Dunn, M. E., & Cunningham, I. (2019). Examining digital video advertising (DVA) effectiveness: The role of product category, product involvement, and device. *European Journal of Marketing, 53*(11), 2451–2479.
Sundar, S. S., Kim, J., & Gambino, A. (2017). Using theory of interactive media effects (TIME) to analysed digital advertising. In *Digital advertising* (pp. 86–109). Routledge.
Sung, J., & Park, S. B. (2017). The effects of consumer involvement and content types in virtual reality on attitude toward advertisement. *International Information Institute (Tokyo) Information, 20*(5B), 3521–3528.
Thaichon, P., & Quach, T. N. (2016). Integrated marketing communications and their effects on customer switching intention. *Journal of Relationship Marketing, 15*(1–2), 1–16.
Tsuji, Y. (2015). Sport sponsorship in the global marketplace. *Sports Management and Sports Humanities*, 75–88.

Tsuji, Y., Bennett, G., & Leigh, J. H. (2009). Investigating factors affecting brand awareness of virtual advertising. *Journal of Sport Management, 23*(4), 511–544.

Uhm, J. P., Lee, H. W., Kim, S., & Han, J. W. (2024). First-person experience in virtual reality sport advertisements: Transportation of embodied empathy. *PRESENCE: Virtual and Augmented Reality, 33*, 269–286

Violante, M. G., Vezzetti, E., & Piazzolla, P. (2019). Interactive virtual technologies in engineering education: Why not 360° videos? *International Journal on Interactive Design and Manufacturing (IJIDeM), 13*(2), 729–742.

Wang, X., Zhang, Z., & Jiang, Q. (2024). The effectiveness of human vs AI voice-over in short video advertisements: A cognitive load theory perspective. *Journal of Retailing and Consumer Services, 81*, 104005.

Wang, Y., & Yao, M. Z. (2020). Did you notice the ads? Examining the influence of telepresence and user control on the effectiveness of embedded billboard ads in a VR racing game. *Journal of Interactive Advertising, 20*(3), 258–272.

Wedel, M., Bigné, E., & Zhang, J. (2020). Virtual and augmented reality: Advancing research in consumer marketing. *International Journal of Research in Marketing, 37*(3), 443–465.

You, Y., Boyer, A., Jokela, T., & Piippo, P. (2017). *Selfie wall: A mixed reality advertising platform.* In 2017 IEEE International symposium on mixed and augmented reality (ISMAR-adjunct) (pp. 240–244). IEEE.

Digital Twins in the Metaverse: User Interface, Security, and Privacy Issues

Baljinder Kaur

Abstract

The application of digital twins within the metaverse represents a significant milestone toward integration of the virtual and real world. As an example, digital twins are sophisticated and highly functional virtual models of actual systems that enable real-time observation, simulation, and decision-making. Their integration, however, brings important problems such as user interface (UI) design, security, and privacy. This chapter tries to address these problems by focusing on the strategies of digital interaction design that goes far beyond the standard usability frameworks and strives for the effortless engagement with digital twins. The chapter also touches on security issues, highlighting the growing need for robust defenses against attacks, -usurped-sensitive-bow-data, and unauthorized access. Privacy issues are addressed in terms of data ownership, identity protection, and ethical custodianship in the metaverse. By doing so, the chapter aims to advance the discourse on digital twin systems by proposing comprehensive strategies that balance security, privacy, and user accessibility in the context of the metaverse.

1 Introduction

The combination of digital twins and the metaverse is changing the way humans interact with computers, as well as entire industries. Digital twins are virtual representations of physical objects, systems, or processes that can be monitored, simulated, and have decisions made in real-time. These models change automatically with the information provided by IoT devices, sensors, and other data

B. Kaur (✉)
Chandigarh Business School of Administration, Landran, Punjab, India
e-mail: baljinder.4006@cgc.edu.in

© The Author(s), under exclusive license to Springer Nature Singapore Pte Ltd. 2026
N. S. Jayawardena et al. (eds.), *Digital Advertising and Consumer Behavior*,
Management for Professionals, https://doi.org/10.1007/978-981-95-7809-2_15

sources. When placed in the metaverse which is a vast digital universe fueled by augmented reality (AR), virtual reality (VR), artificial intelligence (AI), and blockchain, digital twins allow for better interaction, immersion, and collaboration (Tao et al., 2019).

This integration benefits various industries including healthcare, manufacturing, smart cities and education. In healthcare, organs and bodies can be simulated which allows for precision medicine since doctors can test treatment plans virtually before applying them in the real world (Tobon et al., 2020). Other than these, manufacturing also benefits from optimized production, enhanced quality control, and even predictive maintenance (Leng et al., 2021). Digital twins are used in smart cities for traffic and energy consumption control as well as sustainability. They are also able to improve decision-making by using real-time simulations (Batty, 2018). In education, students have the opportunity to participate in practical, simulation-based learning that helps reinforce theoretical knowledge (Liu et al., 2022).

Even with the benefits of twin technology for digitally recreating physical objects, there are numerous issues, particularly in the user interface (UI) design, privacy, and security domains. Digital twins demand active participation through effortless and navigable systems in which users interface through touch, sight, and sound. UI frameworks generally do not support fully immersive experiences; new systems that use AR/VR as well as haptics are needed (Zhu et al., 2021). Also, it is important to note that different users have varying levels of competencies, therefore, any design framework that aims to focus on UI tend to cover a wide range of scopes.

A more developed approach to securing information shared through networks, and cyber space, in general, offers twin technology an added obstacle due to the use of sensitive data it collects, processes, and saves including personal health information, industrial metrics, and proprietary business data. Cyber threats including but not limited to data breaches, banned access, and identity theft are the greatest concerns (Fernandez & Nguyen, 2020). The application of strong protective measures needs to be in place; such as AI cybersecurity that predictably secures systems against attacks and blockchain that guarantees preserved data. Casino argues that Blockchain enhances the preservation of the blockage as well as the openness of its authority (2019). Alongside this, authentication with its multi-tier confirmation, end-to-end encryption becomes critical (Wang et al., 2021).

Security and privacy issues are closely related. Strict privacy laws are required due to the collection and processing of enormous volumes of industrial and personal data. Users might be at risk of data exploitation and surveillance in the absence of appropriate control mechanisms (Zuboff, 2019). Decentralized identity management, encryption technologies, and compliance with international data protection laws like the California Consumer Privacy Act (CCPA) and the General Data Protection Regulation (GDPR) are some solutions (Voigt & Von dem Bussche, 2017). To avoid data misuse, guarantee user consent, and get rid of biases in

AI-driven analytics, ethical considerations must be given top priority (Jobin et al., 2019).

Additionally, making sure that digital twins function equitably and do not reinforce prejudices in decision-making presents ethical difficulties. Digital twin frameworks must incorporate accountable AI models, transparent algorithms, and adherence to ethical AI principles (Floridi et al., 2020). Trust and acceptance of these technologies will increase if ethical conundrums like data ownership, algorithmic fairness, and user autonomy are resolved. To avoid unforeseen consequences, regulatory bodies must set clear guidelines for the ethical deployment of AI.

Usability, security, and privacy compliance are critical to the metaverse's successful incorporation of digital twins. To fully realize their potential in boosting innovation, cooperation, and productivity across industries, these issues must be resolved. In order to guarantee that digital twins develop into safe, approachable instruments that propel digital transformation, this chapter examines these problems and suggests solutions.

Key Takeaways

- For physical systems, digital twins offer real-time simulation, monitoring, and decision-making.
- By creating immersive and interactive environments, the metaverse improves applications for digital twins.
- Increased productivity, accuracy, and teamwork are advantageous for sectors like healthcare, manufacturing, and smart cities.
- Digital twins are used in education to create interactive simulations and immersive learning environments.
- UI design is essential for usability and accessibility, necessitating creative uses of haptic feedback, AR, and VR.
- Users with varying levels of technical expertise can access digital twins thanks to inclusive user interface design.
- Blockchain and AI-driven cybersecurity solutions are necessary to counter security threats like cyberattacks and data breaches.
- Privacy concerns demand ethical data management and adherence to international data protection standards.
- Blockchain improves digital twin transaction security and transparency.
- Predictive maintenance and real-time decision-making are enhanced by AI-driven analytics.
- Secure authentication, multi-factor authentication, and encryption protect digital twin data.
- To avoid prejudice and protect user rights, ethical considerations must be taken into account.
- It is important to highlight how regulatory frameworks define security and privacy standards for digital twins.

- Automation and real-time analytics can be improved by integrating AI and machine learning into digital twins.
- Innovation, security, and privacy must be balanced for digital twin integration to be successful.
- Scalable, safe, and intuitive digital twin frameworks should be the main focus of future advancements.
- By addressing UI, security, and privacy issues, digital twins in the metaverse will be able to become effective instruments for digital transformation and innovation.
- The future of digital twins in the metaverse will be shaped by ethical AI development and responsible data usage. UI design, security, and privacy continue to be important research and development areas as digital twins develop in the metaverse.

Industry and social interactions could be redefined by the convergence of these technologies. However, navigating the complexities of this transformation calls for careful planning, regulation, and innovation. In order to facilitate discussions on overcoming obstacles and optimizing advantages, this chapter offers a foundation for understanding digital twins in the metaverse.

Difficulties with Digital Twin User Interfaces

Real-time monitoring, simulation, and decision-making are made possible by the convergence of digital twins and the metaverse, which is revolutionizing how people engage with technology. Advanced virtual representations of real-world systems, processes, or objects, known as "digital twins," enable smooth transitions between the digital and real worlds (Tao et al., 2018). Digital twins can be deployed in the metaverse, a vast virtual space driven by blockchain, augmented reality, virtual reality, and artificial intelligence (Mystakidis, 2022). By providing immersive, data-driven experiences that improve operational efficiency and decision-making, this fusion has the potential to completely transform sectors like healthcare, manufacturing, smart cities, and education (Grieves & Vickers, 2017). But there are issues with privacy, security, and user interface (UI) design with this integration. In order to guarantee that digital twins in the metaverse are safe, secure, and compliant with privacy laws, this chapter explores these issues and suggests possible solutions.

Real-time data streams from sensors, IoT (Internet of Things) devices, and other data sources are used to continuously update digital twins, which act as dynamic representations of physical entities (Qi & Tao, 2018). By facilitating automation, predictive maintenance, and advanced analytics, these virtual models help businesses maximize their efficiency (Tao et al., 2019). Digital twins become more immersive and interactive when they are connected to the metaverse, enabling users to interact with digital copies in a manner that mimics interactions in the real world. For sectors where remote collaboration, real-time tracking, and simulation are essential, this integration has broad ramifications. Digital twins of human organs, for example, can be used in manufacturing to optimize production processes through real-time monitoring and predictive analytics, and in healthcare to enable remote surgeries and precision medicine (Liu et al., 2021).

By offering a persistent, interactive, and cooperative digital environment, the metaverse—which is based on decentralized and immersive technologies—improves the functionality of digital twins (Duan et al., 2021). Blockchain technology and data integrity are guaranteed, and AI-powered analytics allow for real-time decision-making using enormous datasets produced by digital twins (Zhou et al., 2023). In smart cities, where digital representations of utilities, traffic patterns, and infrastructure can be effectively managed to enhance urban planning and sustainability, the mutually beneficial relationship between digital twins and the metaverse is especially apparent (Shen et al., 2022). Digital twins can provide immersive learning experiences in the educational field by enabling students to interact with realistic models and simulations to improve comprehension and engagement (El Saddik, 2018).

UI Challenges in Digital Twins Within the Metaverse

Notwithstanding these benefits, integrating digital twins into the metaverse presents a number of difficulties, especially with regard to privacy, security, and user interface (UI) design. In order to guarantee usability and accessibility, user interface is essential (Gero et al., 2021). Creating responsive and user-friendly interfaces that enable smooth user interaction is still a major challenge as digital twins get more complicated. The creation of innovative interaction models that make use of AR, VR, and haptic feedback may be necessary because traditional UI paradigms might not be adequate for the immersive experiences that the metaverse requires (Skarbez et al., 2017). Another important component of UI development is making sure that interfaces continue to be accessible to people with different levels of technical expertise (Bowman et al., 2019).

Cognitive overload is a significant problem in UI design since users engage with enormous volumes of real-time data from digital twins. Information fatigue brought on by poorly designed interfaces can decrease decision-making effectiveness and increase user errors (Endsley, 2017). This problem can be lessened by creating adaptive interfaces that offer tailored user experiences based on AI-driven insights (Norman & Nielsen, 2020). Furthermore, maintaining cross-platform compatibility across various digital twin applications and metaverse environments continues to be a major concern (Sherman & Craig, 2018).

Security Challenges

Digital twins in the metaverse produce and handle enormous volumes of sensitive data, security is yet another significant worry (He & Yan, 2021). Strong security frameworks must be put in place because cyberthreats like identity theft, illegal access, and data breaches present serious risks (Yoo et al., 2022). Assuring the confidentiality and integrity of data shared in digital twin environments, blockchain technology and AI-driven cybersecurity measures can provide promising solutions to reduce these risks (Xu et al., 2021). To protect digital twins from malevolent actors, secure authentication protocols, multi-factor authentication, and end-to-end encryption must be implemented (Alaba et al., 2017).

Furthermore, adversarial attacks can manipulate AI models to generate inaccurate predictions or behaviors, making digital twins in the metaverse vulnerable (Biggio & Roli, 2018). Adopting strong machine learning algorithms and anomaly detection techniques is necessary to ensure resilience against such attacks (Papernot et al., 2016). Moreover, in order to guarantee data protection, the metaverse's decentralized structure calls for cooperative security governance across multiple stakeholders (Lesavre et al., 2020).

Privacy Issues

Since the deployment of digital twins entails gathering and processing both personal and industrial data, privacy and security are closely related (Zhou et al., 2022). Users might be vulnerable to data misuse, surveillance, and possible breaches in the absence of strict privacy laws and control systems (Acquisti et al., 2015).

Decentralized identity management, encryption, and adherence to international data protection regulations like the California Consumer Privacy Act and the General Data Protection Regulation (GDPR) are all necessary components of a comprehensive strategy to address these issues (Voigt & Von dem Bussche, 2017).

Making sure that digital twins in the metaverse don't violate people's rights or introduce unintended biases is another crucial ethical consideration (Floridi, 2021). According to Jobin et al. (2019), ethical AI principles must be followed when using AI and automation in digital twin applications to ensure accountability, transparency, and fairness. Risks related to data exposure can be reduced by putting privacy-preserving strategies like differential privacy and federated learning into practice (Abadi et al., 2016).

Key Takeaways

- Digital twins and the metaverse have the potential to revolutionize daily life and entire industries. But for these technologies to be widely used and succeed in the long run, they must continue to be safe, easy to use, and privacy-compliant (Wang et al., 2022).
- The main issues in UI design, security, and privacy are examined in this chapter, along with recent developments and solutions.
- Digital twins in the metaverse can be created as reliable and strong tools that improve productivity, creativity, and digital experiences across a variety of applications by tackling these important problems (Tao et al., 2022).

User Interface Challenges in Digital Twins

Effective interaction with digital twins in the metaverse requires a well-designed user interface (UI). The user interface (UI) serves as a conduit between users and the intricate data-driven features of digital twins, enabling smooth experiences in a range of applications, such as urban planning, manufacturing, and healthcare (Zhang et al., 2022). However, there are many obstacles to overcome when creating an effective user interface for digital twins, such as platform interoperability, real-time data visualization, and user experience.

Improving Usability and User Experience

For a realistic and easy-to-use experience when interacting with digital twins, highly immersive user interface elements are necessary (Johnson & Lee, 2021). The creation of 3D, haptic, and voice-based interfaces is often required because traditional 2D interfaces frequently fail to provide a completely interactive experience (Smith et al., 2020). It's still difficult to guarantee accessibility for a wide variety of users, including people with disabilities. To guarantee usability, even for those who are not familiar with digital twins, the user interface (UI) must have intuitive navigation and control mechanisms (Brown & Kim, 2021). Customizable and adaptive interfaces must be implemented in order to accommodate varying user preferences, tasks, and skill levels.

Visualization of Data in Real Time

Digital twins provide users with an up-to-date view of their virtual counterparts and thrive on real-time data representation (Wang et al., 2021). Complex datasets must be presented in an intuitive way by the user interface (UI) so that users can swiftly and efficiently make data-driven decisions. Overloading users with excessive information can reduce engagement, hinder decision-making, and increase cognitive load, necessitating an optimal balance between detail and clarity (Garcia et al., 2022). Real-time data can be better understood with the help of dynamic dashboards, interactive graphs, and augmented reality overlays. In order to help users concentrate on pertinent information while avoiding distractions from superfluous data streams, effective filtering and categorization mechanisms are crucial (Chen et al., 2020).

Platform Interoperability

According to Davis and White (2021), the metaverse is made up of a variety of platforms, each with unique hardware specifications, interaction paradigms, and capabilities. Ensuring that digital twins function across multiple environments, including VR headsets, mobile devices, and desktop applications, is a critical challenge. Developing standardized UI frameworks and cross-platform compatibility solutions can help bridge gaps between various platforms and ensure a seamless user experience (Singh et al., 2023). APIs and middleware solutions can facilitate interoperability, allowing digital twins to communicate efficiently across different ecosystems (Anderson, 2021). For users switching between devices, usability is improved and familiarity is ensured by maintaining consistent UI elements and user experience across platforms.

Optimization of Latency and Performance

Low-latency performance is necessary for responsive and seamless real-time interaction with digital twins in the metaverse (Thompson et al., 2022). Lag, delays, and decreased user engagement can result from poorly optimized user interface elements. Performance problems can be avoided and responsiveness increased by utilizing edge computing, AI-based predictive analytics, and effective rendering techniques (Martinez & Chang, 2023). The user experience can be improved by putting adaptive UI techniques into practice, which modify graphical fidelity according to network conditions.

Interactivity and User Engagement

For digital twins to be widely adopted in the metaverse, engagement is essential (Patel & Kumar, 2022). Gamification strategies, such as reward systems and interactive storytelling, can improve user retention and learning experiences. Incorporating social features, such as collaborative workspaces and multi-user environments, enhances the interactivity of digital twin interfaces (Lopez et al., 2023). AI-driven virtual assistants and chatbots can provide real-time guidance, helping users navigate complex UI elements and understand data insights (Wright, 2021).

The user interface is a critical component in ensuring the successful integration of digital twins within the metaverse. Addressing UI challenges requires a multidisciplinary approach that combines usability, accessibility, interoperability, and performance optimization. Digital twins can provide smooth and captivating user experiences through the use of creative solutions like immersive 3D interfaces, real-time data visualization methods, and standardized frameworks (Zhou & Li, 2023). Advances in AI, AR/VR, and adaptive computing will be crucial to the future of user interface design in digital twins, opening the door to a metaverse ecosystem that is more engaging and intuitive.

Key Takeaways

- Improving Usability and User Experience: To increase accessibility and usability, digital twins need immersive and user-friendly UI designs, such as 3D, haptic, and voice-based interfaces.
- Real-time data visualization: To avoid cognitive overload, user interfaces (UIs) must strike a balance between simplicity and intricacy by utilizing dashboards, augmented reality overlays, and dynamic data representations.
- Latency and Performance Optimization: Edge computing and AI-driven optimizations minimize delays, which are crucial for a seamless experience.
- User Interactivity and Engagement: AI-powered assistants, social collaboration, and gamification all improve user interaction and learning.

- Multidisciplinary Approach: Usability, accessibility, real-time data processing, and advanced computing must all be integrated for effective user interface design in digital twins.
- Prospects for the Future: More interactive and smooth digital twin experiences in the metaverse will be made possible by developments in AI, AR/VR, and adaptive computing.

Security Issues with Digital Twins

Digital twins' incorporation into the metaverse signifies a fundamental change in the way virtual and physical systems communicate. In order to provide real-time insights, predictive analytics, and improved operational efficiency, these digital counterparts of physical entities gather, process, and analyze enormous volumes of data. However, because digital twins handle sensitive data and communicate with intricate networks, they are vulnerable to a variety of cyberthreats, so security is still a top priority. To guarantee the availability, confidentiality, and integrity of digital twins in the metaverse, security threats must be addressed.

Unauthorized Access and Cyberthreats

Digital twins are extremely susceptible to phishing, hacking, and data breaches, among other cyberattacks. In order to alter data, obtain unauthorized control, or interfere with services, malicious actors may take advantage of system flaws. Important dangers consist of:

- Unauthorized Access: To enter digital twin networks without authorization, attackers may take advantage of lax authentication procedures or security flaws. System failures, reputational harm, and data theft may result from this.
- Hackers have the ability to manipulate data streams between digital and physical twins, which can result in compromised operations, inaccurate insights, and poorly informed decisions.
- Denial-of-Service (DoS) Attacks: These attacks involve sending a large number of requests to digital twin networks, which can lead to system slowdowns or outages.
- Insider Threats: Workers or others with authorized access may abuse their login information to change or steal data.
- Organizations must put strong cybersecurity measures in place to combat these threats, such as intrusion detection systems (IDS), multi-factor authentication (MFA), frequent security audits, and ongoing network monitoring.

Using Blockchain Technology to Boost Security

By offering a decentralized, unchangeable ledger that guarantees data integrity, authentication, and safe transactions, blockchain technology presents promising security solutions for digital twins. The following are some advantages of blockchain integration:

- **Data Integrity:** Blockchain creates an unchangeable record of all transactions and interactions, preventing unwanted data changes.
- **Decentralized Security:** Blockchain lowers the possibility of significant cyber-attacks by removing central points of failure.
- **Better Authentication:** By automating and enforcing security rules, smart contracts can guarantee that only authorized interactions take place.
- **Logs that cannot be tampered with:** Since every interaction is cryptographically recorded, tracking irregularities and spotting security breaches is made simpler.

Notwithstanding these benefits, there are drawbacks to blockchain deployment, including issues with scalability, high energy usage, and computational overhead. Blockchain protocol optimization, effective consensus techniques, and the integration of hybrid security solutions are necessary to meet these challenges.

Guaranteeing Safe Data Transfer

System integrity depends on digital twins and their physical counterparts having secure and dependable data communication. Important security precautions consist of:

- **End-to-end encryption makes sure that important information cannot be intercepted or changed by unauthorized parties.**
- **Zero-Trust Architecture**: This model requires constant authentication and verification of all users and devices because it assumes that threats may arise both inside and outside the network.
- **AI-Driven Threat Detection**: Real-time anomaly detection and mitigation are possible through the analysis of network traffic patterns by artificial intelligence (AI) and machine learning (ML).
- **Secure APIs and Protocols**: Data leaks and unwanted access are less likely when communication protocols are standardized and adequately secured.

By putting these tactics into practice, data flow security is improved, latency risks are decreased, and possible disruptions to digital twin operations are avoided.

Privacy Risks and Data Protection

Large volumes of data are gathered by digital twins, frequently including proprietary company data and personally identifiable information (PII). Financial fraud and identity theft are just two serious outcomes that can result from unauthorized access to or misuse of this data. The following are important privacy issues:

- **Data Ownership and Access Control**: It's crucial to ascertain who has access to digital twin data and make sure data protection regulations are followed.
- **Regulatory Compliance:** Digital twins have to abide by international privacy regulations like the California Consumer Privacy Act (CCPA) and the General Data Protection Regulation (GDPR).

- **Anonymization and Masking**: By protecting sensitive data with data anonymization, encryption, and masking techniques, privacy violations can be prevented.
- **Consent Management**: Users should have control over their data and understand how it is collected, stored, and shared.

Organizations must implement privacy-enhancing technologies, set up strict access controls, and make sure that all applicable legal frameworks are followed in order to reduce privacy risks.

Security of the Digital Twin Lifecycle

To ensure long-term integrity, digital twins must be secured at every stage of their lifecycle, from development and deployment to decommissioning. Important security factors include: • Secure Development Practices: Reducing security risks during development is achieved by implementing secure coding standards and carrying out vulnerability assessments.

Frequent Patch Management and Software Updates: Maintaining software components up to date helps stop known vulnerabilities from being exploited. Data Backup and Recovery: In the event of a system failure or cyber incident, regular backups of digital twin data guarantee speedy recovery. Decommissioning Procedures: Data leaks and unwanted access are avoided by properly retiring out-of-date digital twins.Organizations can decrease possible attack surfaces and improve resilience against changing threats by addressing security at every stage of the digital twin lifecycle.

Risks to Supply Chain Security

As digital twins frequently depend on outside suppliers and third-party integrations, supply chain security is a major worry. Among the risks are:

- **Third-Party Vulnerabilities**: Vendors' lax security procedures may leave digital twin ecosystems vulnerable to online attacks.
- **Compromised Hardware and Software**: Via compromised supply chain components, malicious actors may introduce malware or backdoors.
  - Lack of Transparency: Vulnerabilities are more likely when there is little insight into third-party security measures.
  - Organizations should implement stringent cybersecurity policies, carry out in-depth vendor security assessments, and set up real-time monitoring systems for third-party interactions in order to reduce supply chain risks.
  - Awareness of the Human Factor and Security Digital twins are still at serious risk from human error, including phishing attempts, weak passwords, and incorrectly configured security settings. The following are important tactics to raise security awareness:

    1. **Employee Awareness and Training Programs:** Social engineering attacks can be avoided with regular cybersecurity best practices training.

2. **Access Control Policies**: By putting the principle of least privilege (PoLP) into practice, users are guaranteed to have access to only the information and features that they require.
3. **Incident Response Planning:** Potential damages are reduced when staff members are equipped to react to security breaches in an efficient manner.

- Enforcing Multi-Factor Authentication (MFA) provides an additional layer of protection against unwanted access.
- Organizations can improve overall resilience against cyber threats and lessen human-related vulnerabilities by cultivating a strong security culture.
- Cyber threats, data privacy risks, and supply chain vulnerabilities are just a few of the many security issues surrounding digital twins in the metaverse. Advanced cybersecurity techniques, blockchain integration, secure communication protocols, and strong lifecycle management procedures are all necessary to meet these challenges. Protecting digital twin ecosystems also requires ensuring compliance with international regulations and cultivating a security-conscious workforce. Proactive security measures will be essential to maximizing the potential of digital twins as they develop further, protecting sensitive information, and preserving public confidence in the digital environment.

Key Takeaways

- Cyber Threats & Unauthorized Access: Because digital twins are vulnerable to phishing, DoS, and hacking attacks, strong cybersecurity measures like MFA, IDS, and ongoing monitoring are necessary.
- Blockchain for Security: Although it has scalability and energy issues, blockchain improves data integrity, authentication, and tamper-proof logging.
- Secure Data Transmission: End-to-end encryption, zero-trust architecture, and AI-driven threat detection help protect data exchanges.
- Privacy & Data Protection: Digital twins need to use anonymization methods, apply access controls, and abide by laws like GDPR.
- Lifecycle Security: Secure development, regular updates, data backup, and proper decommissioning ensure long-term security.
- Supply Chain Risks: Third-party vulnerabilities can compromise security, necessitating thorough vendor assessments and real-time monitoring.
- Human Factor & Security Awareness: Employee training, strong access controls, and MFA reduce risks associated with human error.

2 Conclusion

A revolutionary stage in the way people, companies, and entire ecosystems interact in virtual environments has begun with the incorporation of digital twins into the metaverse. Digital twins, which are virtual representations of real-world entities, have already shown promise in a number of industries, including supply chain management, manufacturing, healthcare, and smart cities. Digital twins present a previously unheard-of chance to produce lifelike simulations, improve decision-making, and create interactive experiences when paired with the metaverse's immersive and interactive features. But this convergence also presents a number of difficulties, especially in the areas of security, privacy, and user interface (UI) design. The degree to which digital twins can coexist in the metaverse in a secure and seamless manner will depend on how well these problems are resolved.

The design of digital twins' user interfaces in the metaverse is one of the main areas of concern. Existing interfaces, particularly those made for 2D screens, are insufficient for the metaverse's three-dimensional, intensely immersive environments. Digital twins must not only visually represent physical entities but also enable real-time interaction, customization, and data interpretation. Designing such interfaces requires balancing visual fidelity, performance optimization, and intuitive user experience. Furthermore, as digital twins in the metaverse will often involve complex data from IoT devices, sensors, and machine learning models, UI designers must simplify these data streams into comprehensible, user-friendly formats. If the interface design fails to bridge this complexity, users—especially those with limited technical expertise—will struggle to derive value from the digital twins.

In order to enhance the user's interaction with their digital counterparts, future user interface design should prioritize immersive navigation, spatial awareness, and multi-sensory feedback.

Security is another crucial factor that presents additional difficulties in a hyper-connected metaverse with digital twins. These twins often rely on real-time data streams sourced from physical assets, environments, and even human behavior. As a result, any breach compromising a digital twin could result in real-world disruptions, ranging from industrial sabotage to personal safety risks in healthcare applications. Current cybersecurity protocols struggle to address the complexity and dynamic nature of the metaverse, where interactions between digital twins, avatars, and virtual environments occur continuously. To secure this evolving landscape, the development of real-time threat detection systems that leverage artificial intelligence (AI) and machine learning will be critical. Such systems should monitor anomalous behavior, detect intrusions, and trigger automated containment measures before substantial harm occurs.

Because digital twins in the metaverse are interconnected, there is an increased chance of cascading cyberattacks, in which the compromise of one digital twin could lead to vulnerabilities in the entire network. Thus, it is imperative that multi-layered defenses like encryption, decentralized identity management, and secure communication protocols become commonplace. As blockchain technology develops, it can also be incorporated into digital twin security frameworks to improve data traceability and integrity by offering an unchangeable record of all interactions and modifications made within the metaverse.

Concerns about privacy are closely related to security, and they become more complicated when digital twins are linked to people, their personal preferences, behaviors, and even biometric data. In consumer-facing applications of digital twins in the metaverse, like healthcare, retail, and personal productivity, sensitive personal information is continuously processed, stored, and transmitted; in these situations, the risk of identity theft, unauthorized data mining, and profiling increases. To protect user privacy in the metaverse, transparent data policies, granular consent mechanisms, and user-centric privacy controls that enable people to specify what data their digital twins can access, share, and keep.

To ensure that every data collection point and processing step complies with privacy best practices, privacy-by-design principles must be incorporated into the digital twin development lifecycle. Clear rules on data ownership, cross-border data flows, and accountability should be established by future regulatory frameworks, which may be based on the GDPR but modified for the special characteristics of digital twins and the metaverse. In the absence of strong privacy protections, user confidence in metaverse digital twins may decline, impeding adoption and innovation.

Another important factor for the future development of digital twins in the metaverse is interoperability. Many digital twin platforms available today lack smooth integration with other digital environments and are proprietary.

Isolated digital twins will impede the coherent growth of larger ecosystems in the metaverse, where cross-platform mobility is crucial for fluid user experiences. The development of open standards and interoperable frameworks that enable digital twins to move between various metaverse platforms while maintaining their data, functionality, and identity should thus be the top priority of future research.

Future strategies should use artificial intelligence for security, anomaly detection, predictive maintenance, and automated digital twin optimization in order to successfully navigate these challenges. Digital twins can become more autonomous, able to identify inefficiencies, anticipate failures, and react proactively to changing circumstances by integrating AI-driven decision-making capabilities. The overall dependability of digital twins in the metaverse will be improved by this AI-powered autonomy, which will also decrease human oversight.

Furthermore, creating thorough governance frameworks will require encouraging cooperation between governments, tech firms, and academic institutions. These frameworks should address the ethical, legal, and technical dimensions of digital twins in the metaverse, ensuring that innovation progresses within responsible boundaries. Such collaboration should also focus on capacity building, equipping developers, businesses, and end-users with the necessary skills and knowledge to leverage digital twins safely and effectively.

In conclusion, the successful integration of digital twins into the metaverse depends on overcoming a triad of challenges: intuitive user interface design, robust cybersecurity, and privacy protection. Achieving this will require continuous innovation, cross-sector collaboration, and proactive regulation.

Digital twins in the metaverse have the potential to completely transform how people engage with digital environments if these obstacles are overcome. This could lead to everything from highly customized experiences to next-generation industrial automation. Although there are many potential advantages, they can only be achieved by responsible development that keeps user experience, security, and privacy at the forefront of the evolution of the digital twin metaverse.

References

Abadi, M., Chu, A., Goodfellow, I., McMahan, H. B., Mironov, I., Talwar, K., & Zhang, L. (2016). Deep learning with differential privacy. In *Proceedings of the 2016 ACM SIGSAC Conference on Computer and Communications Security (CCS '16)*, 308–318.

Acquisti, A., Brandimarte, L., & Loewenstein, G. (2015). Privacy and human behavior in the age of information. *Science, 347*(6221), 509–514.

Alaba, F. A., et al. (2017). Internet of things security: A survey. *Future Generation Computer Systems, 78*, 993–1017.

Anderson, J. (2021). Interoperability in digital twin platforms. *Journal of Virtual Systems, 8*(2), 45–60.

Batty, M. (2018). Digital twins. *Environment and Planning B: Urban Analytics and City Science, 45*(5), 817–820.

Biggio, B., & Roli, F. (2018). Wild patterns: Ten years after the rise of adversarial machine learning. *Pattern Recognition, 84*, 317–331.

Bowman, D. A., Hodges, L. F., McMahan, R. P., & Ragan, E. D. (2019). Questioning naturalism in 3D user interfaces. *Communications of the ACM, 62*(9), 78–88. https://doi.org/10.1145/3332165

Brown, T., & Kim, S. (2021). Accessibility in digital twin UI design. *Human-Computer Interaction Journal, 15*(4), 112–126.

Casino, F., Dasaklis, T. K., & Patsakis, C. (2019). A systematic literature review of blockchain-based applications: Current status, classification and open issues. *Telematics and Informatics, 36*, 55–81.

Chen, L., et al. (2020). Effective data filtering for digital twins. *International Journal of Smart Technologies, 12*(3), 78–92.

Davis, M., & White, P. (2021). Cross-platform compatibility in the Metaverse. *Virtual Reality & Applications, 9*(1), 33–47.

Duan, H., Li, Y., Fan, E., Lin, W., Wu, J., & Wang, T. (2021). Deep learning based intrusion detection for mobile networks. *IEEE Communications Surveys & Tutorials, 23*(3), 1680–1709. https://doi.org/10.1109/COMST.2021.3056593

El Saddik, A. (2018). Digital twins: The convergence of multimedia technologies. *IEEE MultiMedia, 25*(2), 87–92. https://doi.org/10.1109/MMUL.2018.023121167

Endsley, M. R. (2017). From here to autonomy: Lessons learned from human–automation research. *Human Factors, 59*(1), 5–27.

Fernandez, J. M., & Nguyen, T. (2020). Cybersecurity issues in digital twins. *Journal of Cyber Security Technology, 4*(2), 1–18.

Floridi, L. (2021). Artificial intelligence, deepfakes and a future of ectypes. *Philosophy & Technology, 34*(1), 1–5.

Floridi, L., Cowls, J., Beltrametti, M., et al. (2020). AI ethics: A systematic review of AI governance research. *Nature Machine Intelligence, 2*(6), 1–13.

Garcia, R., et al. (2022). Data visualization strategies for digital twins. *Advanced Computing Review, 17*(2), 90–105.

Gero, J. S., Kannengiesser, U., & Pourmohamadi, M. (2021). Commonalities in designing: Design cognition and computational models. *Design Studies, 75*, 101017. https://doi.org/10.1016/j.destud.2021.101017

Grieves, M., & Vickers, J. (2017). Digital twin: Mitigating unpredictable, undesirable emergent behavior in complex systems. In J. Kahlen, S. Flumerfelt, & A. Alves (Eds.), *Transdisciplinary Perspectives on Complex Systems*, 85–113. Springer, Cham.

He, Z., & Yan, Q. (2021). Cybersecurity in virtual reality: A review. *IEEE Access, 9*, 117086–117101.

Jobin, A., Ienca, M., & Vayena, E. (2019). The global landscape of AI ethics guidelines. *Nature Machine Intelligence, 1*(9), 389–399.

Johnson, R., & Lee, M. (2021). Immersive UI elements for digital twins. *Metaverse Studies Journal, 6*(2), 56–71.

Leng, J., et al. (2021). Digital twins-driven smart manufacturing: Connotation, reference model, applications and research issues. *Robotics and Computer-Integrated Manufacturing, 64*, Article 101924.

Lesavre, L., Varshney, K. R., & Slavin, R. (2020). Ethical AI: A systematic review of principles and challenges. In *Proceedings of the AAAI/ACM Conference on AI, Ethics, and Society*, 389–395.

Liu, Y., Chen, X., & Li, H. (2021). A survey of virtual reality technologies. *ACM Computing Surveys, 54*(4), 1–36. https://doi.org/10.1145/3459990

Liu, Y., et al. (2022). Digital twins in education: A comprehensive review. *Computers & Education, 181*, Article 104438.

Lopez, F., et al. (2023). Social features in digital twin interfaces. *Technology & Innovation, 19*(3), 58–74.

Martinez, D., & Chang, H. (2023). Optimizing digital twin performance with AI. *Computational Intelligence Review, 21*(1), 112–130.

Mystakidis, S. (2022). Metaverse. *Encyclopedia, 2*(1), 486–497. https://doi.org/10.3390/encyclopedia2010031

Patel, A., & Kumar, S. (2022). Gamification in digital twin UI. *Journal of Interactive Systems, 11*(4), 67–81.

Qi, Q., & Tao, F. (2018). Digital twin and big data towards smart manufacturing and industry 4.0: 360 degree comparison. *IEEE Access, 6*, 3585–3597. https://doi.org/10.1109/ACCESS.2017.2789765

Shen, C., Ho, J., & Lyytinen, K. (2022). Trust in artificial intelligence: A literature review and research agenda. *MIS Quarterly Executive, 21*(2), 1–23.

Sherman, W. R., & Craig, A. B. (2018). *Understanding virtual reality: Interface, application, and design* (2nd ed.). Morgan Kaufmann.

Singh, V., et al. (2023). Standardized frameworks for digital twin UI. *IEEE Transactions on Smart Systems, 29*(2), 89–102.

Skarbez, R., Brooks, F. P., Jr., & Whitton, M. C. (2017). A survey of presence and related concepts. *ACM Computing Surveys, 50*(6), Article 96. https://doi.org/10.1145/3134301

Smith, K., et al. (2020). Haptic and voice interfaces for digital twins. *Advanced Human-Machine Interfaces, 14*(1), 23–38.

Tao, F., et al. (2018). Digital twin and big data towards smart manufacturing and industry 4.0. *IEEE Transactions on Industrial Informatics, 14*(4), 1607–1616.

Tao, F., et al. (2019). Digital twin-driven product design, manufacturing and service with big data. *International Journal of Advanced Manufacturing Technology, 94*(9–12), 3563–3576.

Tao, F., Zhang, M., Liu, Y., & Nee, A. Y. C. (2022). *Digital twin driven smart manufacturing.* Academic Press.

Thompson, B., et al. (2022). Latency challenges in digital twin systems. *Computing Performance Journal, 30*(3), 50–65.

Tobon, C., et al. (2020). Digital twins in healthcare. *Health Informatics Journal, 26*(4), 2736–2750.

Voigt, P., & Von dem Bussche, H. (2017). *The EU general data protection regulation (GDPR).* Springer.

Wang, Q., et al. (2022). AI-powered cybersecurity solutions. *IEEE Transactions on Information Forensics and Security, 17*, 1254–1266.

Wang, Y., et al. (2021). Real-time data representation in digital twins. *Big Data Applications Journal, 18*(2), 34–49.

Wright, P. (2021). AI-driven virtual assistants in the Metaverse. *AI & Human Interaction, 13*(1), 15–29.

Xu, X., Lu, Y., Vogel-Heuser, B., & Wang, L. (2021). Industry 4.0 and digital twins in manufacturing: A review. *Engineering, 7*(4), 419–431.

Yoo, S., Guo, J., & Park, H. (2022). Secure data sharing in AI-driven systems. *IEEE Internet of Things Journal, 9*(12), 10123–10134.

Zhang, H., et al. (2022). UI Challenges in digital twin development. *Journal of Future Technologies, 22*(3), 99–115.

Zhou, J., et al. (2022). Digital twin security and privacy concerns: A systematic review. *IEEE Internet of Things Journal, 9*(1), 534–549.

Zhou, J., Zhang, L., & Xu, C. (2023). Advances in immersive virtual environments. *IEEE Transactions on Visualization and Computer Graphics, 29*(1), 345–356. https://doi.org/10.1109/TVCG.2022.3201234

Zhou, X., & Li, T. (2023). Innovative UI Solutions for the Metaverse. *Virtual Environments & UX Journal, 16*(2), 42–58.

Zhu, X., et al. (2021). UI design in immersive digital twins. *International Journal of Human-Computer Interaction, 37*(6), 505–521.

Zuboff, S. (2019). *The age of surveillance Capitalism: The fight for a human future at the new frontier of power*. PublicAffairs.

Implications of VR, AR, and XR in Marketing Practices: A Descriptive Literature Review

Jangyash Kumar Rout and Abhishek Kumar

Abstract

When technologies are undergoing rapid advancement in the present era it's evident that the corporate sector and the people around the globe would look for advanced technological features. Specifically, the increasing adoption of Augmented Reality (AR), Virtual Reality (VR), and Extended Reality (XR) help the corporate sector simplify organizational practices and allow people to experience more effective technology features. The focus of the research paper is to conduct a thorough descriptive review of the implications of AR, VR, and XR in the marketing area. To perform the descriptive review a total of 92 articles were located that are further classified and analyzed to find out the various implications of the technologies in improving the marketing performance in organizations. By conducting the descriptive review, it is found that most of the articles were published between 2000 and 2024. This shows the increasing interest of researchers in researching the implications of the marketing area. It was also found that AR, VR, and XR technologies are highly supportive of increasing customer experience and customer satisfaction by providing them with reality-based experiences about the products and services that help them make better purchase decisions.

J. K. Rout (✉)
Assistant Professor (Contractual), Odisha State Open University (OSOU), Sambalpur, Odisha, India
e-mail: jangyashkumarrout@gmail.com

Research Scholar, KIIT School of Management, KIIT Deemed to be University, Bhubaneswar, Odisha, India

A. Kumar
Professor, KIIT School of Management, KIIT Deemed to be University, Bhubaneswar, Odisha, India
e-mail: abhishekkr5@ksom.ac.in

© The Author(s), under exclusive license to Springer Nature Singapore Pte Ltd. 2026

N. S. Jayawardena et al. (eds.), *Digital Advertising and Consumer Behavior*, Management for Professionals, https://doi.org/10.1007/978-981-95-7809-2_16

1 Introduction

With the increasing popularity and adoption of Augmented Reality (AR), Virtual Reality (VR), and Extended Reality (XR) in the corporate sector around the world it is crucial to understand and study the implications of these technologies in optimizing the organizational performances (Vasarainen et al., 2021). The use of AR, VR, and XR is not limited to any specific sector industry or functional department but has wider application in handling various organizational activities smoothly including product design, streamlining operations & maintenance, customer engagement, improving employee training, improving operational efficiency in different industries, increase productivity, provide the customers with experiential purchase decision making, helping the managers take better realistic management decisions and improving the competitive edge of the organizations (Murala & Panda, 2023). AR, VR, and XR are applied in different industries & sectors including retail, marketing, logistics, healthcare, medicines, manufacturing, education, aviation, automobiles, real estate, architecture, and engineering. In the present research paper, the focus is plotted on studying the implications of VR, AR, and XR in supporting marketing practices by conducting a thorough descriptive literature review. By conducting the descriptive literature review it would be easier to find out the usefulness of these technologies in performing various marketing activities smoothly and accomplishing the marketing objectives.

2 Literature Review

The research paper is based on a descriptive literature review hence the major discussion and presentation of the literature review is done in the body of the paper. This section aims at simplifying the concepts, and understanding and provides a short introduction to the implications of VR, AR, and XR in marketing practices. To bring a good understanding of the topic of the research four sub-sections will be presented in this section including implications of virtual reality & its use in an organizational context, implications of augmented reality & its use in an organizational context, implications of extended reality & its use in an organizational context, and importance & need of using AR, VR & XR in performing marketing practices.

Implications of Virtual Reality (VR) and Its Use in Organizational Context

Saghafian et al. (2021) found various effective outcomes that could be derived by using VR as a supportive tool in solving crucial industrial operation challenges including multi-stakeholder management issues, support coordination issues, workload & communication issues, and technological maturity issues. According to Baceviciute et al. (2021), the implementation of VR is a very supportive tool to train working professionals in the corporate industries. The authors stated that the groups having VR software aligned could receive better training outcomes than those that didn't get associated with the VR software. Similar views are given by Rumsey and Dantec (2020) who stated that VR could bring manufacturing revolution and solve the issues of workforce shortage and unskilled labor effectively. Baniasadi et al. (2020) briefed about the usefulness of applying VR in medical treatment and education. VR optimizes the therapeutic as well as educational objectives providing the healthcare professionals improve the treatment quality and outcomes.

Implications of Augmented Reality (AI) and Its Use in Organizational Context

Masood and Egger (2020) stated the role of AI in supporting industrial digitalization through the Industrial Augmented Reality (IAR) application software. The IAR software is very easy to install and needs fewer updates which would increase the financial performance of the industrial organizations. Petruse et al. (2016) found various sustainability enhancement outcomes of using AI in organizational practices. As AR is highly supportive of product development, timely delivery, and shortening the manufacturing time it automatically promotes effective organizational and financial performance. Hall et al. (2015) detailed that the use of AR decreases the need for human power in designing, implementing, and monitoring new railway systems. By using the Human–Computer Interaction (HCI) that is aligned with AR technology it becomes easier to design & implement effective railway systems to improve the railway operational functions. According to Jaganathan (2023), the use of Web Augmented Reality (WebAR) could help organizations in navigating uncertainties and organizational crises. WebAR could be aligned with the systems as well as sub-systems of different organizational functions allowing the central database to identify if there is any gap between the targeted functional system and the actual organizational practices and would provide suggestions to rectify the gaps and solve the uncertainties.

Implications of Extended Reality (XR) and Its Use in Organizational Context

Berglund (2024) stated that XR is useful in redefining the existing systems that generate less or ineffective functional performances. XR is useful in terms of redesigning, executing & monitoring existing practices, deliberately examining the performance level of the employees and tallying with the targeted level, and redesigning the technological systems by implementing a forecasting-based decision-making process. Chuah (2019) detailed the implications of using XR in revitalizing the virtual experience of the stakeholders of an organization. With the increasing popularity of the 3D world without considering XR it is not possible to extend the realistic experience of the customers, employees, and other stakeholders in understanding the functions and quality patterns maintained by an organization. According to Zabel and O'Brien (2024), XR is a transformative tool that helps organizations optimize the transforming capabilities and replace the traditional technology use with reality-based technology platforms that provide a wide range of options to make realistic decisions, boost innovation, and create effective digital culture at the organization. Similar views are given by Vasarainen et al. (2021) who detailed that XR is supportive to employees in accomplishing work-life balance as the features and characteristics of XR allow them to reduce their work pressure. By using XR the employees could find a very supportive work environment where they need less support from the superiors in terms of guidance, coaching, and supervision to accomplish the challenging responsibilities.

3 Research Methodology

Research Approach

A literature review helps in conceptualizing the research topics and synthesizing prior research activities. Literature review promotes creating a cumulative culture through which a better understanding of the desired research field could be made (Snyder, 2019). Specifically in the Augmented Reality, Virtual Reality, and Extended Reality fields lack of review of articles not only hinders the progress of the field but keeps it hidden about the findings of the researchers on different areas of application & their beneficial outcomes in these topics. There are four methods of literature review followed by researchers including narrative review, descriptive review, vote counting, and Meta-analysis. The narrative review and descriptive review methods follow a qualitative approach whereas the vote counting and Meta-analysis methods follow a quantitative continuum to demonstrate their different emphases (Kim et al., 2016; Sukhera, 2022). In the present study, descriptive review is chosen as the research approach to conduct the research study.

In the descriptive review, the focus is on interpreting the patterns by considering selected and most relevant literature related to the research topic. Often, the researchers tried to quantify the classification of the literature in terms of the publication time, research outcomes, research methodology, and research topic & sub-topics. A descriptive review follows a systematic process including searching literature, locating literature, screening, filtering, classification, and analysis. The process of descriptive review begins with searching literature related to a specific topic or field as much as possible followed by categorizing them among different topics and subtopics (Kim et al., 2016). Before the categorization process irrelevant and inappropriate literature that match least to the topic of the research are removed. The topics and subtopics are then further classified into different areas including classification of literature by year, classification of literature by topics, classification of literature by types of literature, classification of literature by journals, and classification of literature by conference proceedings & book chapters (Fuertes et al., 2020). The outcomes of the descriptive review provide comprehensive summaries of the existing literature on a specific topic of research helping future researchers understand the topic more effectively to promote deep research.

Scope of the Research

While conducting a descriptive literature review the first step is to locate the most appropriate and relevant literature by conducting manual and online searches (Snyder, 2019). The AR, VR, and XR being the topics that got popular in the past 2 decades it is crucial to understand where and how to find relevant literature. With the easy availability of online databases including IEEE Xplore, ACM Digital Library, ProQuest, and Science Direct it becomes easier to spot the most suitable journals in relation to the application of AR, VR & XR in marketing & digital marketing contexts. Though the primary focus was based on locating literature related to the implications of VR, AR, and XR in digital marketing practices due to the availability of less literature the focus was widened and the overall marketing context is considered. Along with journal articles research papers in different international conference proceedings and book chapters related to the topic were also found. Overall, a total of 128 research papers were located.

Filtering Process

A systematic filtering process is followed to filter the irrelevant and unrelated research papers among the 128 research papers located. Firstly, research papers having duplications or available in multiple databases, panel talks, keynotes, and editorials were excluded by scanning the title of the research papers and abstracts of the articles. It helped to refine the quality of the research papers landed on a total of 109 articles. Secondly, each of the 109 articles was again reviewed thoroughly by going through the entire article to spot the focus of the research paper and its association with the research topic. This process excluded 17 articles and finally, a total of 92 articles were found to be most relevant to perform the descriptive review.

Classification Scheme

The 92 articles are classified into 4 broad topics and their subsequent sub-topics. All 92 articles were full-text reviewed and categorized into the most suitable topics and sub-topics to make it easier to understand and perform the descriptive review more perfectly. Though it is inevitable that an article categorized to a topic or sub-topic could relate to another topic and sub-topic it is tried to group the articles to the most appropriate groups. By allocating one article to a particular domain and sub-domain, it becomes easier to provide a simplified classification of the 92 articles. The four major topics include marketing strategy, retail marketing, digital marketing, and business transformation & development. A detailed brief of the articles along with their classified groups and sub-groups is presented in Table 1.

4 Research Analysis and Findings

The 92 articles are distributed to smoothen the analysis in terms of topics, year, types of literature, journal, conference proceedings, and book chapters. By distributing the articles, it becomes easier to map the outcomes of the authors of the articles in different fields of marketing by aligning AR, VR, and XR technologies.

Distribution of Articles by Topics

a. Marketing Strategy: This domain focuses on the impact of AR, VR & XR as strategic tools on the overall marketing practices except retail marketing and digital marketing domains. A total of 55 articles were located under this domain that were further sub-categorized into eight sub-domains. Under the improvement and customer experience highest number of articles (18) and under improvement of marketing & advertising practices second highest (17) articles among all the domains. These two sub-domains combined take more than 38% of the total 92 articles which shows that the role of AR, VR, and XR in improving the customer experience and optimizing the marketing & advertising practices is rapidly increasing.
   i. Reduction of customer perceived risks: Under this sub-domain, only one article was located that details the role of AR in redefining the reality concept and improving the perception of the customers towards the quality of the products (Rauschnabel et al., 2022).
   ii. Positive impact on consumer behavior: Under this sub-domain, four articles were located that detail the role of AR, VR, and XR in improving consumer behavior in the marketing practices of organizations. Luxury brands employ AR as a strategic marketing tool to improve brand equity (Javornik et al., 2021). AR media platforms are highly helpful in positively impacting the cognitive and emotional responses of consumers towards the purchase of premium products (Amorim et al., 2022). AR being used in

Table 1 Classification of literature

Sl. No.	Authors	Topic	Subtopic
1	Rauschnabel et al. (2022)	Marketing strategy	AR marketing
2	Kang et al. (2022)		Effective consumer purchase decisions
3	Sihi (2018)		
4	Ambika et al. (2024)		
5	Qin et al. (2021)		
6	Kazmi et al. (2021)		
7	Wang et al. (2022)		
8	Abrar (2018)		
9	Caboni and Hagberg (2019)	Marketing strategy	Effective marketing practices
10	Sung (2021)		
11	Subawa et al. (2021)		
12	Bae et al. (2020)		Improve branding practices
13	Prasad et al. (2022)		
14	Rauschnabel et al. (2019)		
15	Plotkina et al. (2022)		
16	Dadwal and Hassan (2016)	Marketing strategy	Improved marketing & advertising practices
17	Liao (2015)		
18	Lampropoulos et al. (2022)		
19	Sawan et al. (2021)		
20	Wu and Kim (2022)		
21	Horst and Dorner (2018)		
22	Barhorst et al. (2021)		
23	Jayawardena et al. (2023)		
24	Loureiro et al. (2019)		
25	Heller and Bar-Zeev (2021)		
26	Gasmi and Benlamri (2022)		
27	Goebert (2020)		

(continued)

Table 1 (continued)

Sl. No.	Authors	Topic	Subtopic
28	Cranmer et al. (2020)		
29	Barrera and Shah (2023)		
30	Yuce et al. (2021)		
31	Kim (2021)		
32	Ling et al. (2023)		
33	Flavian et al. (2019)	Marketing strategy	Improvement of customer experience
34	Wedel et al. (2020)		
35	Gaberli (2019)		
36	Yaoyuneyong et al. (2016)		
37	Alcaniz et al. (2019)		
38	Billewar et al. (2022)		
39	Chylinski et al. (2020)		
40	Gallardo et al. (2018)		
41	Du et al. (2022)		
42	Trunfio et al. (2021)		
43	Meegahapola and Perera (2017)		
44	Hammady et al. (2020)		
45	Kumar et al. (2023)		
46	Dehghani et al. (2020)		
47	Sung et al. (2021)		
48	Hoyer et al. (2022)		
49	Brengman et al. (2019)		
50	Rane et al. (2023)		
51	Javornik (2016)	Marketing strategy	Positive impact on consumer behavior
52	Do et al. (2020)		
53	Amorim et al. (2022)		

(continued)

Table 1 (continued)

Sl. No.	Authors	Topic	Subtopic
54	Javornik et al. (2021)		
55	Alimamy et al. (2017)		Reduction of customer-perceived risks
56	Park and Yoo (2020)	Retail marketing	Improved mobile shopping experience
57	Scholz and Duffy (2018)		
58	Ozturkcan (2020)		
59	Haile and Kang (2020)		
60	Morales et al. (2022)		Improved online shopping experience
61	Erdmann et al. (2023)		
62	Trivedi et al. (2022)		
63	Stoyanova et al. (2015)		
64	Fu'adi et al. (2021)		
65	Hilal (2023)		
66	Zhao et al. (2017)		
67	McLean and Wilson (2019)		
68	Pantano et al. (2017)		
69	Dogra et al. (2023)		
70	Alimamy and Gnoth (2022)		
71	Rajeb et al. (2023)	Retail marketing	Improved retail shopping experience
72	Lavoye et al. (2021)		
73	Tan et al. (2021)		
74	Yim et al. (2017)		Interactive customer experience
75	Moriuchi et al. (2020)		
76	Farah et al. (2019)		
77	Hilken et al. (2021)		Online experiential retailing
78	Kumar (2022)		
79	Bonetti et al. (2018)		
80	Luna-Nevarez and McGovern (2021)		Virtual Commerce

(continued)

Table 1 (continued)

Sl. No.	Authors	Topic	Subtopic
81	Li et al. (2022)	Digital marketing	Digital Content Marketing
82	Ibrahim and Evrim (2018)		E-business practices
83	Wang (2021)		Interactive Marketing
84	Krishen et al. (2021)		
85	Regt et al. (2021)		
86	Ekmail et al. (2021)		Tech Industry Transformation
87	Nalbant and Aydin (2023)	Digital marketing	Virtual customer experience with products and services
88	Neuburger et al. (2018)		
89	Zaki et al. (2023)		
90	Kim et al. (2023)		
91	Gatter et al. (2021)		
92	Farshid et al. (2018)	Business transformation and development	

Source Self Author Made

mobile AR apps attracts the attention of consumers easily in the tourism industry and provides them with a more realistic understanding of the tourist places before they make their purchase decisions (Do et al., 2020).

iii. Improvement of marketing & advertising practices: Under this sub-domain, 17 articles were located that briefs about the use of AR, VR, and XR as supportive tools in improving marketing & advertising practices. Most of the applications of AR, VR, and XR were located in improving the tourism marketing practices under this sub-domain (Cranmer et al., 2020; Dadwal & Hassan, 2016). In creating video advertisements, the role of AR is highly crucial and effective to attract the attention of the customers (Jayawardena et al., 2023). By using AR and VR technologies industrial players try to create momentum towards marketing and advertising practices (Liao, 2015; Loureiro et al., 2019). During the Covid-19 pandemic AR, VR, and XR technologies helped the organizations accelerate their marketing performance by creating sufficient audio-visual communication and virtual presence to keep the customers engaged (Gasmi & Benlamri, 2022). In the education sector, the use of AR and VR helps the students and their parents understand the courses more realistically and accurately followed by creating better career opportunities for the students (Lampropoulos et al., 2022). In the sports industry, the use of AR and VR helps in developing better marketing strategies and monitoring revenue diversification activities (Goebert, 2020; Sawan et al., 2021). In fashion retailing, user perceptions could be effectively improved by using AR and XR (Wu & Kim, 2022). In terms of increasing knowledge demonstration (Horst & Dorner, 2018) the role of AR, VR, and XR would become three crucial tools in marketing and the virtual world would help companies stick the customers and create potential customers with less effort (Barhorst et al., 2021; Heller & Bar-Zeev, 2021). Among marketers, the eagerness to adopt AR, VR, and XR is increasing (Barrera & Shah, 2023) not only to improve marketing performance but also to create a sustainable impact on marketing outcomes and generate more & more potential customers (Kim, 2021; Ling et al., 2023; Yuce et al., 2021).

iv. AR Marketing: Under this sub-domain, one article was located that detailed the future implications of the new AR marketing concept. The AR marketing concept is supported by the four BICK frameworks in which branding, inspiring, convincing & keeping marketing practices are closely aligned with all the marketing activities. AR marketing is considered to be the future of digital marketing and would assist future corporate professionals more effectively in reducing the dependency on human interaction with customers in keeping them attracted and engaged (Rauschnabel et al., 2022).

v. Effective consumer purchase decisions: Under this sub-domain, seven articles were located that briefed about the supportive role of AR, VR, and XR technologies in helping consumers simplify their purchase decisions. The 3D virtual reality stores through their informative features attract the attention of customers more effectively and help them make their purchase decisions easily (Kang et al., 2022). For new products when consumers find it difficult to understand the post-purchase benefits the AR and VR technologies help in increasing their understanding of the products (Ambika et al., 2024), (Qin et al., 2021; Sihi, 2018). In online shopping, the moderating role of AR helps organizations ensure deliberate consumer brand engagement (Abrar, 2018). AR and VR technology-aligned beauty brand apps find it easier to understand the expectations and needs of the customers for beauty and cosmetic products and monitor their purchase intentions (Wang et al., 2022).

vi. Improvement of branding practices: Under this sub-domain four articles were located that briefed about improving different branding and brand development practices. In the hospitality and tourism sector, the use of AR & XR helps organizations increase the brand loyalty of the customers (Bae et al., 2020). In the development of brand personality and brand equity AR and VR play a crucial role by providing customers with interactivity, modality, vividness, novelty, and media richness (Plotkina et al., 2022; Prasad et al., 2022). AR-aligned apps help customers improve their perception and evaluation of the products & services offered by different brands followed by indirectly improving brand awareness (Rauschnabel et al., 2019).

vii. Improvement of customer experience: Under this domain, 18 articles were located which is the highest among all the sub-domains in the research paper. AR, VR, and XR are found to be used as crucial tools in improving the virtual experience of the customers. In the AR, VR, and XR environment, the physical and virtual objects are integrated to provide the customers with a realistic experience of the products (Alcaniz et al., 2019; Flavian et al., 2019; Wedel et al., 2020). In tourism the use of AR and VR tools helps organizations improve the tourist experiences of the tourist places more realistically and create a positive impact on their perception and travel experiences (Gaberli, 2019; Hammady et al., 2020; Trunfio et al., 2021). AR is gradually shifting from being a tool to a marketing strategy forming different AR marketing practices and methods to improve the realistic experience of the customers (Brengman et al., 2019; Hoyer et al., 2022; Rane et al., 2023; Sung et al., 2021). In the retail sector AR and VR are revolutionizing marketing outcomes through 3D online shopping features, virtual in-store shopping experiences, and touching holograms with windows (Billewar et al., 2022; Dehghani et al., 2020; Meegahapola & Perera, 2017). In hypermedia print ads the use of AR increases consumer preferences and helps organizations create more sales revenue (Yaoyuneyong et al., 2016).

viii. Effective marketing practices: Under this sub-domain, 3 articles were located that detailed the effective marketing practices possible through the use of AR, VR, and XR technologies. In different marketing aspects, it is found that VR is transforming the Indonesian tourism sector (Subawa et al., 2021), AR is revolutionizing the mobile app advertising practices through shared social experience (Sung, 2021) and in retailing the application of AR assist the retailers to satisfy the customer needs by mapping their expectations through AR-based applications.

b. Retail Marketing: Under this domain a total of 25 articles were located that brief about various aspects of retail marketing. The 25 articles were further subcategorized by six sub-domains that include both physical as well as online & mobile retailing areas.

   i. Improved mobile shopping experience: Under this sub-domain four articles were located that brief about improved mobile shopping experience of the customers by using AR, VR, and XR in the mobile shopping apps. The perceived interactivity features of AR (Ozturkcan, 2020) allow consumers to increase their mental imagery in mobile shopping followed by creating positive behavioral intentions to purchase the products (Park & Yoo, 2020). The mobile AR features increase consumer brand relationships (Scholz & Duffy, 2018) and positively influence the purchase intentions of educated young adults to get engaged in mobile shopping more frequently (Haile & Kang, 2020).

   ii. Improved online shopping experience: Under this sub-domain, 11 articles were located that detail the positive outcomes of aligning AR, VR, and XR in online shopping. The application of AR and VR in e-commerce assists marketers in providing customization services to customers (Fu'adi et al., 2021; Morales et al., 2022), increases the online impulse purchase intention of customers (Erdmann et al., 2023; Trivedi et al., 2022) and provide better statistical analysis of the quality & other parameters related to a product (Stoyanova et al., 2015). Saudi customers are more attracted to AR-based online shops in which they prefer to buy clothes & accessories at home by taking the benefits of virtual experience-based shopping practices (Hilal, 2023). Personalization through AR and VR made it easier for organizations around the globe to create positive customer perceptions (Alimamy & Gnoth, 2022) and improve the interactiveness & innovation in online shopping services (Dogra et al., 2023).

iii. Improved retail shopping experience: Under this sub-domain, three articles were located that detailed the outcomes of using AR & VR in terms of improving the retail shopping experience of the customers. By using AR in retail settings, it becomes easier to align thousands of brands and provide customers with both physical as well as virtual realistic experiences to understand and feel the product features (Tan et al., 2021). From the consumer perspective there are various outcomes that could be derived by using AR, VR, and XR in retail and the better updates will be used the more realistic shopping experience could be provided to the consumers (Rajeb et al., 2023). AR is a very effective tool to increase consumer knowledge about the products and services at the physical stores not only by displaying the products but also by providing them with virtual personalization services (Lavoye et al., 2021).

iv. Interactive customer experience: Under this domain, three articles were located that detailed the generation of interactive customer experience by using AR, VR, and XR technologies. Rather than engaging chatbots the use of AR would be more effective in providing customers with an interactive experience with products (Moriuchi et al., 2020). In E-commerce, the interactive experience, enjoyment, immersion, and novelty help the customers make better and prompt purchase decisions followed by achieving positive marketing outcomes (Yim et al., 2017). The need for in-store product analysis and observation will gradually be replaced by the AR-based virtual shopping experience by providing customers with interactive sessions (Farah et al., 2019).

v. Online experiential retailing: Under this sub-domain, 3 articles were located that briefed about the online experiential retailing features of AR, VR, and XR technologies. The role of AR, VR, and XR is utmost crucial and highly supportive in providing customers with experiential retailing in online shopping sites that positively and effectively attract the attention of the customers to buy products (Hilken et al., 2021). The customer experience in terms of mental imagery, flow, immersion, and spatial presence becomes easier through experiential retailing by aligning AR & VR with online shopping platforms (Bonetti et al., 2018; Kumar, 2022).

vi. Virtual commerce: Under this subdomain, one article was located that details the increasing popularity of Virtual Commerce (V-commerce) in support of VR, AR & XR that would redefine and revolutionize retailing practices and would use less physical resources to satisfy the retail needs of the customers (Luna-Nevarez & McGovern, 2021).

c. Digital Marketing: Under this subdomain, 11 articles were located that were further sub-categorized into five sub-domains.

i. Digital content marketing: Under this domain, one article was located that details the effective usefulness of Mixed Reality Training Platforms in e-commerce platforms to evaluate and purchase intentions of the customers. The XR technology provides very realistic information about the products helping the customers decrease the doubts and lessen the risk of losing customers on the online shopping platforms (Li et al., 2022).

ii. E-business practices: Under this sub-domain, one article was located that details the usefulness of using AR in tourism to create customer leads by performing various digital marketing practices including multi-channel marketing, creating real-time consumer confidence, and promoting realistic information on various tourism products & services (Ibrahim & Evrim, 2018).

iii. Interactive marketing: Under this sub-domain, three articles were located that brief about the various interactive marketing practices in support of AR and VR tools. Through VR-based marketing, it becomes easier to convert storytelling to story doing and provide customers with interactive experiences on different digital platforms (Regt et al., 2021). In interactive marketing practices, the use of AR and VR helps in making the marketing activities more connected, empowered, and informed for the customers (Krishen et al., 2021; Wang, 2021).

iv. Tech industry transformation: Under this domain, one article is located that briefed about the usefulness of AR, VR, and XR technologies in transforming the marketing practices of various top technology corporations. By using AR and VR the tech industry found it easier to perform various digital marketing practices and keep the customers engaged (Ekmail et al., 2021).

v. Virtual customer experience with products & services: Under this sub-domain five articles were located that detailed the generation of virtual customer experience by using AR and VR technologies. The use of AR and VR helped the tourism industry add phygital tourist experiences and perform better digital marketing practices (Neuburger et al., 2018). With the increasing customer expectations and increasing adoption of digital marketing practices in the international market, it is becoming a challenge for organizations to understand customer expectations perfectly and provide them with relevant solutions. The AR and VR technologies in digital marketing increase virtual customer experiences with a wide range of products & services (Nalbant & Aydin, 2023). The generation alpha would get acquainted with the virtual experience of products and would seek more effective features in the future (Kim et al., 2023; Zaki et al., 2023). With the increasing need for a touch-based experience for customers before making their purchase decisions the use of AR, VR, and XR in digital marketing would help organizations handle the issue effectively (Gatter et al., 2021).

d. Business Transformation and Development: One article was located under this domain that details the transformative and sustainable development features an organization could derive by considering AR, VR, and XR-aligned marketing tools, technologies, software, and applications. In the near future, these three technologies will bring revolutionary support in terms of highly advanced technological applications to reduce the dependency on physical resources (Farshid et al., 2018) (Table 2).

Table 2 Distribution of articles by topics

Topic	Sub-topic	Number of articles	Percentage
Marketing strategy	AR Marketing	1	1.09
	Effective consumer purchase decisions	7	7.61
	Effective marketing practices	3	3.26
	Improvement of branding practices	4	4.35
	Improvement of marketing & advertising practices	17	18.5
	Improvement of customer experience	18	19.6
	Positive impact on consumer behavior	4	4.35
	Reduction of customer-perceived risks	1	1.09
Retail marketing	Improved mobile shopping experience	4	4.35
	Improved online shopping experience	11	12
	Improved retail shopping experience	3	3.26
	Interactive customer experience	3	3.26
	Online experiential retailing	3	3.26
	Virtual Commerce	1	1.09
Digital marketing	Digital Content Marketing	1	1.09
	E-business practices	1	1.09
	Interactive Marketing	3	3.26
	Tech Industry Transformation	1	1.09
	Virtual customer experience with products and services	5	5.43
Business transformation and development		1	1.09
Total		92	100

Source Self Author Made

Table 3 Distribution of articles by year

Year	Articles	Percentage
2015	2	2.17
2016	3	3.26
2017	5	5.43
2018	9	9.78
2019	9	9.78
2020	12	13
2021	22	23.9
2022	17	18.5
2023	12	13
2024	1	1.09
Total	92	100

Source Self Author Made

Distribution of Articles by Year

Among the total of 92 articles identified most (63) the articles were located between 2020 and 2023 which shows that the interest of the researchers was increased in the Covid-19 pandemic and post-pandemic period. With the deliberate development in the technology sector, the researchers also emphasized conducting their research more accurately and effectively by focusing on different new uses of AR, VR, and XR in performing various marketing practices. Specifically, the articles under sub-domains related to customer experience, virtual experience, experiential retailing and online shopping experience, and interactive marketing were located between 2020 and 2024. AR, VR, and XR are being used as a crucial tool to improve the customer experience through virtual interaction with products the researchers could narrow down their research areas in the future (Table 3).

Distribution of Articles by Types

Among 92 articles 82 (89.13%) articles were located as journal articles whereas rest 10 articles were located as conference papers (7.61%) and book chapters (3.26%) (Table 4).

Table 4 Distribution of articles by types

Distribution of literature by types		
Type	Number	Percentage
Journal article	82	89.13
Conference paper	7	7.609
Book chapter	3	3.261
Total	92	100

Source Self Author Made

Distribution of Articles by Journal Articles

Among the 92 articles published in different journals 10 (10.9%) were located in the Journal of Business, 7 (7.61%) were located in the Journal of Retailing & Consumer Services, 4 (4.35%) each were located in Frontiers in Psychology and Sustainability. The diversified distribution of literature in different reputed Scopus-indexed and ABDC-listed journals on the implications of VR, AR, and XR in marketing practices shows that researchers chose different journals to publish their research papers rather than considering specific or most popular journals. Most of the journals were based on marketing, business, management & technology, consumer studies, information technology, and technology marketing areas (Table 5).

Distribution of Articles by Conference Papers and Book Chapters

All the conference papers were found to be based on improving the customer experience and improvement of online shopping experience whereas the majority of the book chapters were based on improvement of marketing practices by using AR, VR, and XR technologies (Tables 6 and 7).

Table 5 Distribution of articles by journals

Distribution of literature by journal		
Journal name	Number	Percentage (total literature)
Asia Pacific Journal of Marketing and Logistics	1	1.09
Australasian Marketing Journal	1	1.09
Bahria University Journal of Management & Technology	1	1.09
Business Horizons	1	1.09
Change Management: An International Journal	1	1.09
Computers in Human Behavior	2	2.17
Current Issues in Tourism	1	1.09
Education Sciences	1	1.09
Frontiers in Psychology	4	4.35
Heliyon	1	1.09
Information, Communication & Society	1	1.09
International Journal of Consumer Studies	1	1.09
International Journal of Information Management	1	1.09
International Journal of Professional Business Review	1	1.09
International Journal of Research in Marketing	1	1.09
International Journal of Retail & Distribution Management	2	2.17
International Journal of Technology Marketing	1	1.09
Journal of Business Research	10	10.9
Journal of Consumer Behaviour	3	3.26
Journal of Heritage Tourism	1	1.09
Journal of Information Technology Teaching Cases	1	1.09
Journal of Interactive Advertising	2	2.17
Journal of Interactive Marketing	3	3.26
Journal of Internet Commerce	1	1.09
Journal of Marketing	1	1.09
Journal of Metaverse	1	1.09
Journal of Online Trust and Safety	1	1.09
Journal of Physics: Conference Series	1	1.09
Journal of Research in Interactive Marketing	2	2.17
Journal of Retailing and Consumer Services	7	7.61
Journal of Services Marketing	1	1.09
Journal of Strategic Marketing	2	2.17
Journal of Tourism Intelligence And Smartness	1	1.09
Jurnal The Messenger	1	1.09

(continued)

Table 5 (continued)

Distribution of literature by journal		
Journal name	Number	Percentage (total literature)
Leadership, Innovation, and Entrepreneurship as Driving Forces of the Global Economy	1	1.09
Management Decision	1	1.09
Marketing Intelligence & Planning	2	2.17
Mobile Information Systems	1	1.09
Psychology & Marketing	1	1.09
Psychology and Marketing	1	1.09
Scientific Works of The University of Food Technologies	1	1.09
Sports Innovation Journal	1	1.09
SSRN	1	1.09
Sustainability	4	4.35
Technology in Society	1	1.09
Telematics and Informatics	1	1.09
The International Review of Retail, Distribution, and Consumer Research	1	1.09
Tourism Management Perspectives	1	1.09
Tourism Planning and Destination Marketing	1	1.09
Virtual Reality	1	1.09
World Journal of Engineering	1	1.09
Total	82	89.1

Source Self Author Made

5 Conclusion

In future marketing practices AR, VR, and XR would revolutionize the marketing strategies as through the descriptive review it is found that AR, VR, and XR not only provide the customers with reality-based experiences to understand the products & services more perfectly but also strengthen their perceptual decisions. With the deliberate development in the AR, VR, and XR technologies the future marketing functions would avail wide features in performing the marketing and advertising practices. The improved interactive experiences to be provided to the customers would help organizations across the globe engage the customers, creating personalized interactions, performing virtual product demonstrations at virtual showrooms, and performing more effective interactive advertising practices. Presently AR, VR, and XR are widely used in tourism, retail, hospitality, museums, e-commerce, and education sectors in performing a wide range of marketing practices.

Table 6 Distribution of articles by conference proceedings

Distribution of literature by conference papers		
Conference papers	Number	Percentage (total literature)
Lecture Notes in Computer Science	1	1.09
EBEE '20: Proceedings of the 2020 2nd International Conference on E-Business and E-commerce Engineering	1	1.09
2018 IEEE International Symposium on Mixed and Augmented Reality Adjunct (ISMAR-Adjunct)	1	1.09
2017 Seventeenth International Conference on Advances in ICT for Emerging Regions (ICTer)	1	1.09
HCI-COLLAB 2022	1	1.09
2015 International Symposium on Innovations in Intelligent Systems and Applications (INISTA)	1	1.09
2021 13th International Conference on Information & Communication Technology and Systems (ICTS)	1	1.09
Total	7	7.61

Source Self Author Made

Table 7 Distribution of articles by book chapter

Distribution of literature by book chapters		
Book	Number	Percentage (total literature)
Mobile Computing and Wireless Networks: Concepts, Methodologies, Tools, and Applications	1	1.09
Augmented Reality and Virtual Reality	1	1.09
Novel AI and Data Science Advancements for Sustainability in the Era of COVID-19	1	1.09
Total	3	3.26

Source Self Author Made

With the increasing market competition, the adoption of AR, VR, and XR would help organizations reduce the resources needed and optimize the functional outputs. Through the descriptive review, it is also found that promoting AR, VR, and XR in marketing practices would be costly but in the long-term, the decision would create a sustainable impact on the overall organizational as well as financial performance. The user experience-design feature of AR, VR, and XR would improve in the future by providing more assistance in improving the experience of users virtually while making their purchase decisions. The present research would help future researchers in making their research focus narrow and define the individual use of AR, VR, and XR in assisting marketing and digital marketing practices. Future researchers could also focus on finding the significance of AR, VR, and XR in improving marketing practices from different aspects by conducting quantitative as well as qualitative research.

References

Abrar, K. (2018). Impact of augmented reality on consumer purchase intention with the mediating role of customer brand engagement: Moderating role of interactivity in online shopping. *Bahria University Journal of Management & Technology, 1*(2), 64–80.

Alcaniz, M., Bigne, E., & Guixeres, J. (2019, July 5). Virtual reality in marketing: A framework, review, and research agenda. *Frontiers in Psychology, 10*. https://doi.org/10.3389/fpsyg.2019.01530

Alimamy, S., & Gnoth, J. (2022, March). I want it my way! The effect of perceptions of personalization through augmented reality and online shopping on customer intentions to co-create value. *Computers in Human Behavior, 128*. https://doi.org/10.1016/j.chb.2021.107105

Alimamy, S., Deans, K., & Gnoth, J. (2017). Augmented reality: Uses and future considerations in marketing. *Leadership, Innovation and Entrepreneurship as Driving Forces of the Global Economy*,. https://doi.org/10.1007/978-3-319-43434-6_62

Ambika, A., Jain, V., Belk, R., Kasilingam, D., & Krishna, R. (2024). The role of augmented reality experiences in consumers' purchase intention toward new products. *Journal of Consumer Behaviour*. https://doi.org/10.1002/cb.2435

Amorim, I. P., Guerriero, J., Eloy, S., & Loureiro, S. M. (2022). How augmented reality media richness influences consumer behaviour. *International Journal of Consumer Studies, 46*(6), 2351–2366. https://doi.org/10.1111/ijcs.12790

Baceviciute, S., Cordoba, A. L., Wismer, P., Jensen, T. V., Klausen, M., & Makransky, G. (2021). Investigating the value of immersive virtual reality tools for organizational training: An applied international study in the biotech industry. *Journal of Computer Assisted Learning, 38*(2), 470–487. https://doi.org/10.1111/jcal.12630

Bae, S., Jung, T. H., Moorhouse, N., Suh, M., & Kwon, O. (2020). The Influence of Mixed Reality on Satisfaction and Brand Loyalty in Cultural Heritage Attractions: A Brand Equity Perspective. *Sustainability, 12*(7). https://doi.org/10.3390/su12072956

Baniasadi, T., Ayyoubzadeh, S. M., & Mohammadzadeh, N. (2020, May 18). Challenges and Practical Considerations in Applying Virtual Reality in Medical Education and Treatment. *Oman Medical Journal, 35*(3). https://doi.org/10.5001/omj.2020.43

Barhorst, J. B., McLean, G., Shah, E., & Mack, R. (2021). Blending the real world and the virtual world: Exploring the role of flow in augmented reality experiences. *Journal of Business Research, 122*, 423–436. https://doi.org/10.1016/j.jbusres.2020.08.041

Barrera, K. G., & Shah, D. (2023, January). Marketing in the Metaverse: Conceptual understanding, framework, and research agenda. *Journal of Business Research, 155*. https://doi.org/10.1016/j.jbusres.2022.113420

Berglund, A. (2024). Adopting extended reality: Navigating structures, processes and resources. *17th annual International Conference of Education, Research and Innovation*. 10312–10318. https://doi.org/10.21125/iceri.2024.2634

Billewar, S., Jadhav, K., Sriram, V. A., Mohd-Abdul, S., Gulati, K., & Bhasin, D. (2022). Retracted: The rise of 3D E-Commerce: The online shopping gets real with virtual reality and augmented reality during COVID-19. *World Journal of Engineering, 19*(2), 244–253. https://doi.org/10.1108/WJE-06-2021-0338

Bonetti, F., Warnaby, G., & Quinn, L. (2018). *Augmented reality and virtual reality in physical and online retailing: A review*. Springer.

Brengman, M., Willems, K., & Kerrybroeck, H. V. (2019). Can't touch this: The impact of augmented reality versus touch and non-touch interfaces on perceived ownership. *Virtual Reality, 23*, 269–280. https://doi.org/10.1007/s10055-018-0335-6

Caboni, F., & Hagberg, J. (2019). Augmented reality in retailing: A review of features, applications and value. *International Journal of Retail & Distribution Management, 47*(11), 1125–1140. https://doi.org/10.1108/IJRDM-12-2018-0263

Chuah, S. H. (2019, January 2). Why and who will adopt extended reality technology? *Literature Review, Synthesis, and Future Research Agenda.* SSRn. https://doi.org/10.2139/ssrn.3300469

Chylinski, M., Heller, J., Hilken, T., Keeling, D. I., Mahr, D., & de-Ruyter, K. (2020). Augmented reality marketing: A technology-enabled approach to situated customer experience. *Australasian Marketing Journal, 28*(4), 374–384. https://doi.org/10.1016/j.ausmj.2020.04.004

Cranmer, E. E., Dieck, M. C., & Fountoulaki, P. (2020, July). Exploring the value of augmented reality for tourism. *Tourism Management Perspectives, 35.* https://doi.org/10.1016/j.tmp.2020.100672

Dadwal, S. S., & Hassan, A. (2016). The augmented reality marketing: A merger of marketing and technology in tourism. *Mobile Computing and Wireless Networks: Concepts, Methodologies, Tools, and Applications.* https://doi.org/10.4018/978-1-4666-8751-6.ch004

Dehghani, M., Lee, S. H., & Mashatan, A. (2020, November). Touching holograms with windows mixed reality: Renovating the consumer retailing services. *Technology in Society, 63.* https://doi.org/10.1016/j.techsoc.2020.101394

Do, H. N., Shih, W., & Ha, Q. A. (2020). Effects of mobile augmented reality apps on impulse buying behavior: An investigation in the tourism field. *Heliyon, 6*(8), 1–9. https://doi.org/10.1016/j.heliyon.2020.e04667

Dogra, P., Kaushik, A. K., Kalia, P., & Kaushan, A. (2023). Influence of augmented reality on shopping behavior. *Management Decision, 61*(7), 2073–2098. https://doi.org/10.1108/MD-02-2022-0136

Du, Z., Liu, J., & Wang, T. (2022, June 16). Augmented reality marketing: A systematic literature review and an agenda for future inquiry. *Frontiers in Psychology, 13.* https://doi.org/10.3389/fpsyg.2022.925963

Ekmail, F. A., Abumandil, M. S., Alkwaja, M. I., & Alaklouk, S. A. (2021). Augmented reality and virtual reality revolutionize rusiness transformation in digital marketing tech industry analysts and visionaries during Coronavirus (COVID 19). *Journal of Physics: Conference Series, 1860.* https://doi.org/10.1088/1742-6596/1860/1/012012

Erdmann, A., Mas, J. M., & Arilla, R. (2023). Value-based adoption of augmented reality: A study on the influence on online purchase intention in retail. *Journal of Consumer Behaviour, 22*(4), 912–932. https://doi.org/10.1002/cb.1993

Farah, M. F., Ramadan, Z. R., & Harb, D. H. (2019). The examination of virtual reality at the intersection of consumer experience, shopping journey and physical retailing. *Journal of Retailing and Consumer Services, 48*, 136–143. https://doi.org/10.1016/j.jretconser.2019.02.016

Farshid, M., Paschen, J., Eriksson, T., & Kietzmann, J. (2018). Go boldly!: Explore augmented reality (AR), virtual reality (VR), and mixed reality (MR) for business. *Business Horizons, 61*(5), 657–663. https://doi.org/10.1016/j.bushor.2018.05.009

Flavian, C., Ibanez-Sanchez, S., & Orus, C. (2019). The impact of virtual, augmented and mixed reality technologies on the customer experience. *Journal of Business Research, 100*, 547–560. https://doi.org/10.1016/j.jbusres.2018.10.050

Fu'adi, D. K., Hidayanto, A. N., Inan, D. I., & Phusavat, K. (2021). The implementation of augmented reality in e-commerce customization: A systematic literature review. *2021 13th international conference on information & communication technology and system (ICTS)* (pp. 12–17). Surabaya, Indonesia. https://doi.org/10.1109/ICTS52701.2021.9608322

Fuertes, G., Alfaro, M., Vargas, M., Gutierrez, S., Ternero, R., & Sabattin, J. (2020, January 30). Conceptual framework for the strategic management: A literature review—Descriptive. *Journal of Engineering.* https://doi.org/10.1155/2020/6253013

Gaberli, U. (2019). Tourism in digital age: An explanation for the impacts Oo virtual, augmented and mixed reality technologies on tourist experiences. *Journal of Tourism Intelligence and Smartness, 2*, 61–69.

Gallardo, C., Rodriguez, S. P., Chango, I. E., Quecedo, W. X., Santana, J., Acosta, A. G., Andaluz, V. H., et al. (2018, July 14). Augmented reality as a new marketing strategy. *Lecture Notes in Computer Science*, 351–362. https://doi.org/10.1007/978-3-319-95270-3_29

Gasmi, A., & Benlamri, R. (2022). Augmented reality, virtual reality and new age technologies demand escalates amid COVID-19. *Novel AI and Data science advancements for sustainability in the Era of COVID-19* (Chapter 4).

Gatter, S., Maack, V. H., & Rauschnabel, P. A. (2021, December 20). Can augmented reality satisfy consumers' need for touch? *Psychology & Marketing, 39*(3), 508–523. https://doi.org/10.1002/mar.21618

Goebert, C. (2020, September). Augmented reality in sport marketing. *Sports Innovation Journal*. https://doi.org/10.18060/24227

Haile, T. T., & Kang, M. (2020). Mobile Augmented Reality in Electronic Commerce: Investigating User Perception and Purchase Intent Amongst Educated Young Adults. *Sustainability, 12*(21). https://doi.org/10.3390/su12219185

Hall, N., Lowe, C., & Hirsch, R. (2015). Human factors considerations for the application of augmented reality in an operational railway environment. *Procedia Manufacturing, 3*, 799–806. https://doi.org/10.1016/j.promfg.2015.07.333

Hammady, R., Ma, M., & Strathearn, C. (2020, January 20). User experience design for mixed reality: A case study of HoloLens in museum. *International Journal of Technology Marketing, 13*(3–4), 354–375. https://doi.org/10.1504/IJTMKT.2019.104600

Heller, B., & Bar-Zeev, A. (2021). The Problems with immersive advertising: In AR/VR, nobody knows you are an Ad. *Journal of Online Trust and Safety*, 1–14. https://doi.org/10.54501/jots.v1i1.21

Hilal, N. S. (2023). The Impact of the Use of Augmented Reality on Online Purchasing Behavior Sustainability: The Saudi Consumer as a Model. *Sustainability, 15*(6), https://doi.org/10.3390/su15065448

Hilken, T., Chilinski, M., Keeling, D. I., Heller, J., Ruyter, K., & Mahr, D. (2021, Oct 4). How to strategically choose or combine augmented and virtual reality for improved online experiential retailing. *Psychology and Marketing, 39*(3), 495–507. https://doi.org/10.1002/mar.21600

Horst, R., & Dorner, R. (2018). Opportunities for virtual and mixed reality knowledge demonstration. *2018 IEEE International Symposium on Mixed and Augmented Reality Adjunct (ISMAR-Adjunct)* (pp. 381–385). Munich, Germany. https://doi.org/10.1109/ISMAR-Adjunct.2018.00110

Hoyer, W. D., Kroschke, M., & Shankar, V. (2022, Jan 31). Transforming the customer experience through new technologies. *Journal of Interactive Marketing, 51*(1). https://doi.org/10.1016/j.intmar.2020.04.001

Ibrahim, I., & Evrim, C. (2018). Mobile marketing: Usage of augmented reality in tourism. *Scientific Works of University of Food Technologies, 65*(1), 205–210.

Jaganathan, K. (2023). Navigating organizational crises and uncertainties through web augmented reality (WebAR). *The Central European Journal of Social Sciences and Humanities, 61*(134), 45–54. https://doi.org/10.34739/zn.2023.61.05

Javornik, A. (2016). Augmented reality: Research agenda for studying the impact of its media characteristics on consumer behaviour. *Journal of Retailing and Consumer Services, 30*, 252–261. https://doi.org/10.1016/j.jretconser.2016.02.004

Javornik, A., Duffy, K., Rokka, J., Scholz, J., Nobbs, K., Motala, A., & Goldenberg, A. (2021). Strategic approaches to augmented reality deployment by luxury brands. *Journal of Business Research, 136*, 284–292. https://doi.org/10.1016/j.jbusres.2021.07.040

Jayawardena, N. S., Thaichan, P., Quach, S., Razzaq, A., & Behl, A. (2023, May). The persuasion effects of virtual reality (VR) and augmented reality (AR) video advertisements: A conceptual review. *Journal of Business Research, 160*. https://doi.org/10.1016/j.jbusres.2023.113739

Kang, H. J., Shin, J. H., & Ponto, K. (2022, February 15). How 3D Virtual Reality Stores Can Shape Consumer Purchase Decisions: The Roles of Informativeness and Playfulness. *Journal of Interactive Marketing, 49*(1). https://doi.org/10.1016/j.intmar.2019.07.002

Kazmi, S. H., Ahmed, R. R., Soomro, K. A., Hashem, A. R., Akhtar, H., & Parmar, V. (2021). Role of Augmented Reality in Changing Consumer Behavior and Decision Making: Case of Pakistan. *Sustainability, 13*(24). https://doi.org/10.3390/su132414064

Kim, H., Sefcik, J. S., & Bradway, C. (2016). Characteristics of qualitative descriptive studies: A systematic review. *Research in Nursing Health, 40*(1), 23–42. https://doi.org/10.1002/nur.21768

Kim, J. (2021). Advertising in the Metaverse: Research agenda. *Journal of Interactive Advertising, 21*(3), 141–144. https://doi.org/10.1080/15252019.2021.2001273

Kim, J. H., Kim, M., Park, M., & Yoo, J. (2023, February). Immersive interactive technologies and virtual shopping experiences: Differences in consumer perceptions between augmented reality (AR) and virtual reality (VR). *Telematics and Informatics, 77*. https://doi.org/10.1016/j.tele.2022.101936

Krishen, A. S., Dwivedi, Y. K., Bindu, N., & Kumar, K. S. (2021). A broad overview of interactive digital marketing: A bibliometric network analysis. *Journal of Business Research, 131*, 183–195. https://doi.org/10.1016/j.jbusres.2021.03.061

Kumar, H. (2022). Augmented reality in online retailing: A systematic review and research agenda. *International Journal of Retail & Distribution Management, 50*(4), 537–559. https://doi.org/10.1108/IJRDM-06-2021-0287

Kumar, H., Gupta, P., & Chauhan, S. (2023, January 20). Meta-analysis of augmented reality marketing. *Marketing Intelligence & Planning, 41*(1), 110–123. https://doi.org/10.1108/MIP-06-2022-0221

Lampropoulos, G., Keramopoulos, E., Diamantaras, K., & Evangelidis, G. (2022). Augmented Reality and Virtual Reality in Education: Public Perspectives, Sentiments, Attitudes, and Discourses. *Education Sciences, 12*(11). https://doi.org/10.3390/educsci12110798

Lavoye, V., Mero, J., & Tarkiainen, A. (2021). Consumer behavior with augmented reality in retail: A review and research agenda. *The International Review of Retail, Distribution and Consumer Research, 31*(3), 299–329. https://doi.org/10.1080/09593969.2021.1901765

Li, C. H., Chan, O. L., Chow, Y. T., Zhang, X., Tong, P. S., Li, S. P., Keung, K. L., et al. (2022, June 30). Evaluating the effectiveness of digital content marketing under mixed reality training platform on the online purchase intention. *Frontiers in Psychology, 13*. https://doi.org/10.3389/fpsyg.2022.881019

Liao, T. (2015). Augmented or admented reality? The influence of marketing on augmented reality technologies. *Information, Communication & Society, 18*(3), 310–326. https://doi.org/10.1080/1369118X.2014.989252

Ling, G. S., Senathirajah, A. R., & Haque, R. (2023). Changes in marketing: Key factors influencing adoption of virtual reality amongst marketers. *Change Management: An International Journal, 23*(1), 14–29.

Loureiro, S. M., Gurreiro, J., Eloy, S., Langaro, D., & Panchapakesan, P. (2019). Understanding the use of virtual reality in marketing: A text mining-based review. *Journal of Business Research, 100*, 514–530. https://doi.org/10.1016/j.jbusres.2018.10.055

Luna-Nevarez, C., & McGovern, E. (2021). The rise of the virtual reality (VR) Marketplace: Exploring the antecedents and consequences of consumer attitudes toward V-commerce. *Journal of Internet Commerce, 20*(2), 167–194. https://doi.org/10.1080/15332861.2021.1875766

Masood, T., & Egger, J. (2020, February). Adopting augmented reality in the age of industrial digitalisation. *Computers in Industry, 115*. https://doi.org/10.1016/j.compind.2019.07.002

McLean, G., & Wilson, A. (2019). Shopping in the digital world: Examining customer engagement through augmented reality mobile applications. *Computers in Human Behavior, 101*, 210–224. https://doi.org/10.1016/j.chb.2019.07.002

Meegahapola, L., & Perera, I. (2017). Enhanced in-store shopping experience through smart phone based mixed reality application. *2017 Seventeenth International Conference on Advances in ICT for Emerging Regions (ICTer)* (pp. 1–8). Colombo, Sri Lanka. https://doi.org/10.1109/ICTER.2017.8257810

Morales, J., Silva-Aravena, F., Valdés, Y., & Baltierra, S. (2022). Virtual reality and augmented reality applied to e-commerce: A literature review. *HCI-COLLAB 2022, 1707*. https://doi.org/10.1007/978-3-031-24709-5_15

Moriuchi, E., Landers, V. M., Colton, D., & Hair, N. (2020). Engagement with chatbots versus augmented reality interactive technology in e-commerce. *Journal of Strategic Marketing, 29*(5), 375–389. https://doi.org/10.1080/0965254X.2020.1740766

Murala, D. K., & Panda, S. K. (2023). The role of immersive reality (AR/VR/MR/XR) in Metaverse. In *Metaverse and immersive technologies: An introduction to industrial, business and social applications*. Wiley.

Nalbant, K. G., & Aydin, S. (2023, June 30). Development and transformation in digital marketing and branding with artificial intelligence and digital technologies dynamics in the metaverse universe. *Journal of Metaverse*. https://doi.org/10.57019/jmv.1148015

Neuburger, L., Beck, J., & Egger, R. (2018). The 'Phygital' tourist experience: The use of augmented and virtual reality in destination marketing. *Tourism Planning and Destination Marketing*, 183–202. https://doi.org/10.1108/978-1-78756-291-220181009

Ozturkcan, S. (2020, August 13). Service innovation: Using augmented reality in the IKEA place app. *Journal of Information Technology Teaching Cases, 11*(1). https://doi.org/10.1177/2043886920947110

Pantano, E., Rese, A., & Baier, D. (2017). Enhancing the online decision-making process by using augmented reality: A two country comparison of youth markets. *Journal of Retailing and Consumer Services, 38*, 81–95. https://doi.org/10.1016/j.jretconser.2017.05.011

Park, M., & Yoo, J. (2020, January). Effects of perceived interactivity of augmented reality on consumer responses: A mental imagery perspective. *Journal of Retailing and Consumer Services, 52*. https://doi.org/10.1016/j.jretconser.2019.101912

Petruse, R. E., Grecu, V., & Chiliban, B. M. (2016). Augmented reality applications in the transition towards the sustainable organization. *Computational Science and Its Applications -- ICCSA 2016*. https://doi.org/10.1007/978-3-319-42111-7_33

Plotkina, D., Dinsmore, J., & Racat, M. (2022). Improving service brand personality with augmented reality marketing. *Journal of Services Marketing, 36*(6), 781–799. https://doi.org/10.1108/JSM-12-2020-0519

Prasad, K., Tomar, A. S., & Soni, H. (2022). A conceptual model for building the relationship between augmented reality, experiential marketing & brand equity. *International Journal of Professional Business Review, 7*(6). https://doi.org/10.26668/businessreview/2022.v7i6.1030

Qin, H., Peak, D. A., & Prybutock, V. (2021, January). A virtual market in your pocket: How does mobile augmented reality (MAR) influence consumer decision making? *Journal of Retailing and Consumer Services, 58*. https://doi.org/10.1016/j.jretconser.2020.102337

Rajeb, A., Rajeb, K., & Treiblmaier, H. (2023). How augmented reality impacts retail marketing: A state-of-the-art review from a consumer perspective. *Journal of Strategic Marketing, 31*(3), 718–748. https://doi.org/10.1080/0965254X.2021.1972439

Rane, N., Choudhary, S., & Rane, J. (2023). Metaverse marketing strategies: Enhancing customer experience and analysing consumer behaviour through leading-edge metaverse technologies, platforms, and models. *SSRN*. https://doi.org/10.2139/ssrn.4624199

Rauschnabel, P. A., Babin, B. J., Dieck, M. C., Krey, N., & Jung, T. (2022). What is augmented reality marketing? Its definition, complexity, and future. *Journal of Business Research, 142*, 1140–1150. https://doi.org/10.1016/j.jbusres.2021.12.084

Rauschnabel, P. A., Felix, R., & Hinsch, C. (2019). Augmented reality marketing: How mobile AR-apps can improve brands through inspiration. *Journal of Retailing and Consumer Services, 49*, 43–53. https://doi.org/10.1016/j.jretconser.2019.03.004

Regt, A., Plangger, K., & Barnes, S. J. (2021). Virtual reality marketing and customer advocacy: Transforming experiences from story-telling to story-doing. *Journal of Business Research, 136*, 513–522. https://doi.org/10.1016/j.jbusres.2021.08.004

Rumsey, A., & Dantec, C. A. (2020, March). Manufacturing change: The impact of virtual environments on real organizations. *CHI '20: Proceedings of the 2020 CHI Conference on Human Factors in Computing Systems*. https://doi.org/10.1145/3313831.3376535

Saghafian, M., Laumann, K., & Stogstad, M. R. (2021, Sep 22). Organizational challenges of development and implementation of virtual reality solution for industrial operation. *Frontiers in Psychology, 12*. https://doi.org/10.3389/fpsyg.2021.704723

Sawan, N., Eltweri, A., Lucia, C. D., Cavaliere, L. P., Faccia, A., & Mosteanu, N. R. (2021). Mixed and Augmented Reality Applications in the Sport Industry. *EBEE '20: Proceedings of the 2020 2nd International Conference on E-business and E-commerce Engineering* (pp. 55–59). https://doi.org/10.1145/3446922.3446932

Scholz, J., & Duffy, K. (2018). We ARe at home: How augmented reality reshapes mobile marketing and consumer-brand relationships. *Journal of Retailing and Consumer Services, 44*, 11–23. https://doi.org/10.1016/j.jretconser.2018.05.004

Sihi, D. (2018). Home sweet virtual home: The use of virtual and augmented reality technologies in high involvement purchase decisions. *Journal of Research in Interactive Marketing, 12*(4), 398–417. https://doi.org/10.1108/JRIM-01-2018-0019

Snyder, H. (2019). Nov). Literature review as a research methodology: An overview and guidelines. *Journal of Business Research, 104*, 333–339. https://doi.org/10.1016/j.jbusres.2019.07.039

Stoyanova, J., Brito, P. Q., Georgieva, P., & Milanova, M. (2015). Comparison of consumer purchase intention between interactive and augmented reality shopping platforms through statistical analyses. *2015 International Symposium on Innovations in Intelligent SysTems and Applications (INISTA)* (pp. 1–8). Madrid, Spain. https://doi.org/10.1109/INISTA.2015.7276727

Subawa, N. S., Widhiasthini, N. W., Astawa, I. P., Dwiatmadja, C., & Permatasari, N. P. (2021). The practices of virtual reality marketing in the tourism sector, a case study of Bali, Indonesia. *Current Issues in Tourism, 24*(23), 3284–3295. https://doi.org/10.1080/13683500.2020.1870940

Sukhera, J. (2022). Narrative reviews: Flexible, rigorous, and practical. *Journal of Graduate Medical Education, 14*(4), 414–417. https://doi.org/10.4300/JGME-D-22-00480.1

Sung, E. C. (2021). The effects of augmented reality mobile app advertising: Viral marketing via shared social experience. *Journal of Business Research, 122*, 75–87. https://doi.org/10.1016/j.jbusres.2020.08.034

Sung, E., Bae, S., Han, D. I., & Kwan, O. (2021, Oct). Consumer engagement via interactive artificial intelligence and mixed reality. *International Journal of Information Management, 60*. https://doi.org/10.1016/j.ijinfomgt.2021.102382

Tan, Y. C., Chandukala, S. R., & Reddy, S. K. (2021, Feb 1). Augmented Reality in Retail and Its Impact on Sales. *Journal of Marketing, 86*(1). https://doi.org/10.1177/0022242921995449

Trivedi, J., Kasilingam, D., Arora, P., & Soni, S. (2022). The effect of augmented reality in mobile applications on consumers' online impulse purchase intention: The mediating role of perceived value. *Journal of Consumer Behaviour, 21*(4), 896–908. https://doi.org/10.1002/cb.2047

Trunfio, M., Lucia, M. D., Campana, S., & Magnelli, A. (2021). Innovating the cultural heritage museum service model through virtual reality and augmented reality: The effects on the overall visitor experience and satisfaction. *Journal of Heritage Tourism, 17*(1), 1–19. https://doi.org/10.1080/1743873X.2020.1850742

Vasarainen, M., Paavola, S., & Vetoshkina, L. (2021). A systematic literature review on extended reality: Virtual, augmented and mixed reality in collaborative working life setting. *International Journal of Virtual Reality, 21*(2), 1–28. https://doi.org/10.20870/IJVR.2021.21.2.4620

Wang, C. (2021). New frontiers and future directions in interactive marketing: Inaugural Editorial. *Journal of Research in Interactive Marketing, 15*(1), 1–9. https://doi.org/10.1108/JRIM-03-2021-270

Wang, Y., Ko, E., & Wang, H. (2022). Augmented reality (AR) app use in the beauty product industry and consumer purchase intention. *Asia Pacific Journal of Marketing and Logistics, 34*(1), 110–131. https://doi.org/10.1108/APJML-11-2019-0684

Wedel, M., Bigne, E., & Zhang, Z. (2020). Virtual and augmented reality: Advancing research in consumer marketing. *International Journal of Research in Marketing, 37*(3), 443–465. https://doi.org/10.1016/j.ijresmar.2020.04.004

Wu, Y. F., & Kim, E. Y. (2022, Aug 4). Users' perceptions of technological features in augmented reality (AR) and virtual reality (VR) in fashion retailing: A qualitative content analysis. *Mobile Information Systems*. https://doi.org/10.1155/2022/3080280

Yaoyuneyong, G., Foster, J., Johnson, E., & Johnson, D. (2016). Augmented reality marketing: Consumer preferences and attitudes toward hypermedia print ads. *Journal of Interactive Advertising, 16*(1), 16–30. https://doi.org/10.1080/15252019.2015.1125316

Yim, M. Y., Chu, S. C., & Sauer, P. L. (2017). Is augmented reality technology an effective tool for e-commerce? An interactivity and vividness perspective. *Journal of Interactive Marketing, 39*(1), 89–103. https://doi.org/10.1016/j.intmar.2017.04.001

Yuce, A., Aydogdu, V., Yuce, S. G., & Katirci, H. (2021). Phygitally yours: Examination of virtual reality experiences in digital sports and recreational games. *Jurnal the Messenger, 13*(1), 1–18. https://doi.org/10.26623/themessenger.v13i1.2481

Zabel, C., & O'Brien, D. (2024). Understanding dynamic capabilities in emerging technology markets: Antecedents, sequential nature, and impact on innovation performance in the extended reality industry. *European Journal of Innovation Management, 27*(9), 305–336. https://doi.org/10.1108/EJIM-07-2023-0574

Zaki, H., Fernandez, D., Dastane, O., Aman, A., & Sanusi, S. (2023). Virtual reality in digital marketing: Research agenda based on bibliometric reflection. *Marketing Intelligence & Planning, 41*(4), 505–524. https://doi.org/10.1108/MIP-12-2022-0568

Zhao, X., Shi, C., You, X., & Zong, C. (2017, January 26). Analysis of Mental Workload in Online Shopping: Are Augmented and Virtual Reality Consistent? *Frontiers in Psychology, 8*. https://doi.org/10.3389/fpsyg.2017.00071

MIX
Papier aus verantwortungsvollen Quellen
Paper from responsible sources
FSC® C105338

If you have any concerns about our products,
you can contact us on
ProductSafety@springernature.com

In case Publisher is established outside the EU,
the EU authorized representative is:
Springer Nature Customer Service Center GmbH
Europaplatz 3, 69115 Heidelberg, Germany

Printed by Libri Plureos GmbH
in Hamburg, Germany